Legal Aspects of Marine Protected Areas in the Mediterranean Sea

This book provides a comprehensive overview of the legal basis for the establishment and further development of area-based conservation tools in the Mediterranean Sea, with a particular emphasis placed on the transboundary area-based conservation instruments available for the Adriatic and Ionian Seas.

Identifying and analysing both marine protected areas (MPAs) as traditional area-based tools enabling marine habitat and species conservation, the book discusses other effective area-based conservation measures (OECMs) with a transboundary perspective. Providing responses to the complex set of challenges raised by the variety of tools and levels of intervention involved, the book provides solutions which identify practical ways in which marine spaces can be protected in the macro-region. Through exploring the trend towards exclusive economic zones, the book discusses the adoption of a coherent and co-ordinated Mediterranean network of transboundary area-based conservation tools.

The book will be of interest to policy makers, practitioners and academics with an interest in public international law, law of the sea and sustainable ocean governance.

Mitja Grbec is Attorney-at-Law in Koper (Slovenia); Visiting Lecturer at the International Maritime Law Institute of the International Maritime Organization (IMO IMLI, Msida, Malta); Assistant Professor at University of Primorska, Faculty of Management (Koper, Slovenia); Secretary-General of the Maritime Law Association of Slovenia; and Titulary Member of the Comité Maritime International.

Tullio Scovazzi was Professor of International Law in the Universities of Parma, Genoa, Milan, and Milano-Bicocca (Italy); and is an Associate Member of the Institut de Droit International.

Ilaria Tani is Attorney-at-Law in Milan (Italy); Adjunct Professor of International Law of the Sea and Maritime Law at University of Milano-Bicocca (Italy); and Former Associate Legal Officer at the Division for Ocean Affairs and the Law of the Sea, Office of Legal Affairs, United Nations (UNDOALOS, New York, United States).

IMLI Studies in International Maritime Law

Series Editor: Professor Norman A. Martínez Gutiérrez

Director of the IMO International Maritime Law Institute

The IMO International Maritime Law Institute (IMLI) was established under the auspices of the International Maritime Organization, a specialised agency of the United Nations.

The Institute is an international centre for the training of specialists in international maritime law. It contributes to the development and dissemination of knowledge and expertise in the international regime of merchant shipping and related areas of maritime law and the general law of the sea, with special reference to the international regulations and procedures for safety and efficiency of shipping and the prevention of marine pollution. For further information on the Institute please visit its website at: www.imli.org.

The series is dedicated to publishing original, scholarly contributions which analyse key issues in international maritime law. The works published in the series will be of interest to an audience of students and scholars in maritime law, maritime lawyers and barristers, and professionals in the shipping industry.

Available Titles:

European Sustainable Carriage of Goods
The Role of Contract Law
Ellen Eftestøl-Wilhelmsson

Shipbreaking in Developing Countries
A Requiem for Environmental Justice from the Perspective of Bangladesh
Saiful Karim

Autonomous Ships and the Law
Edited by Henrik Ringbom, Erik Røsæg, Trond Solvang

Transport Law on Passenger Rights
Edited by Marko Pavliha

Legal Aspects of Marine Protected Areas in the Mediterranean Sea
Edited by Mitja Grbec, Tullio Scovazzi and Ilaria Tani

For more information about this series, please visit: www.routledge.com/

Legal Aspects of Marine Protected Areas in the Mediterranean Sea

An Adriatic and Ionian Perspective

Edited by Mitja Grbec, Tullio Scovazzi and Ilaria Tani

Routledge
Taylor & Francis Group
LONDON AND NEW YORK

First published 2023
by Routledge
4 Park Square, Milton Park, Abingdon, Oxon OX14 4RN

and by Routledge
605 Third Avenue, New York, NY 10158

Routledge is an imprint of the Taylor & Francis Group, an informa business

British Library Cataloguing-in-Publication Data
A catalogue record for this book is available from the British Library

ISBN: 978-1-032-43564-0 (hbk)
ISBN: 978-1-032-43569-5 (pbk)
ISBN: 978-1-003-36796-3 (ebk)

DOI: 10.4324/9781003367963

Typeset in Times New Roman
by Apex CoVantage, LLC

Contents

Foreword

It is my great pleasure to be invited to introduce this important, learned book dealing with the complex, intricate, legal regimes and processes regulating area-based conservation mechanisms, including the traditional marine protected areas, with a focus on the Adriatic and Ionian Seas. These semi-enclosed seas, with a great maritime history and tradition, are surrounded by many littoral States protecting their own maritime interests.

The notion of enclosed and semi-enclosed seas has a long-standing recognition in the history of international law. Publicists recognized it and held the importance of cooperation to deal with the peculiarities of such seas. Despite this recognition, in 1958 the first United Nations Conference on the Law of the Sea did not include the notion in any of the four conventions it adopted. The 1982 United Nations Convention on the Law of the Sea has a short, but significant, Part IX dedicated to enclosed and semi-enclosed seas. This recognition was mainly the result of efforts by Italy, which in 1968 presented a memorandum to the UN Seabed Committee aimed at ensuring that such seas, which have their own characteristics, received specific consideration in the future law of the sea. Article 123 of the 1982 Convention holds that the States bordering an enclosed or semi-enclosed sea should cooperate with each other in the exercise of their rights and in the performance of their duties under this Convention; to this end, States shall endeavour, directly or through an appropriate regional organization, to coordinate *inter alia* the implementation of their rights and duties with respect to the protection and preservation of the marine environment. As all States surrounding the Adriatic and Ionian Seas are parties to the 1982 Convention, it is expected that they undertake regional cooperation to protect the marine environment.

With this background the authors have undertaken a compelling and comprehensive examination of area-based conservation in one of the most complex, at times turbulent, restricted maritime areas in the Mediterranean. It commences by considering the Adriatic and Ionian Seas as areas of the wider Mediterranean. This is important due to the interdependency of the said seas.

Transboundary area-based conservation approaches have an important role, especially in the relatively confined areas of semi-enclosed seas, as due regard is paid to the ecosystem approach and the goal of marine spatial planning. This work provides an excellent, in-depth examination of the international and regional legal mechanisms for area-based conservation, particularly marine protected areas.

The 1982 Convention does not specifically mention marine protected areas; nevertheless, there is considerable support for the view that the setting up of such areas is now included in the obligation arising out of customary international law to preserve and protect the marine environment. Indeed, one of the merits of this study is the review of the relevant general State practice which has developed. The authors examine the establishment of marine protected areas or area-based conservation measures under international conventions including the Convention on Biological Diversity, the International Convention for the Regulation of Whaling, the International Convention for the Prevention of Pollution from Ships, and the Convention for the Protection of Underwater Cultural Heritage. Significantly the study also analyzes the numerous relevant regional agreements including the Protocol concerning Specially Protected Areas and Biological Diversity in the Mediterranean; the Convention on the Conservation of European Wildlife and Natural Habitats; the Agreement on the Conservation of Cetaceans of the Black Sea, Mediterranean Sea and Contiguous Atlantic Area; and the Agreement establishing the General Fisheries Commission for the Mediterranean.

Noteworthy is the analysis of the complex and sophisticated area-based marine conservation prescriptions under European Union law. This aspect of the study is of immense importance given that the littoral States of the Adriatic and Ionian Seas are either members of the European Union or aspiring for membership. Consequently, an extension of the European legal order throughout the maritime areas of both seas can be envisaged. Also significant is the book's consideration of the ramifications once all Adriatic and Ionian States establish an exclusive economic zone thereby eliminating the high seas and increasing the focus on area-based environmental protection.

The plethora of legal agreements and instruments reviewed illustrates the complex degrees of interaction among a variety of levels of cooperation from national, sub-regional, regional to international levels – all of which are important in securing the full effectiveness of marine protected areas and other area-based conservation processes.

Almost all littoral States have enacted legislation relating to protected areas, even though they differ with regard to comprehensiveness and sophistication. An interesting chapter offers a review of national laws as they affect the establishment of national marine protected areas. While the analysis is necessarily concise, it is certainly interesting to see the various national legal positions surrounding the Adriatic and Ionian Seas together with the level of implementation.

Legal frameworks in the Adriatic and Ionian Seas exist, and the study concludes that the littoral States have demonstrated an impressive capacity to engage in an effective manner. The present challenge these States face is to develop further the said frameworks to improve the environmental well-being of their seas and peoples.

This learned book provides original and innovative approaches to deal with the challenge of protecting the marine environment in semi-enclosed seas. It also identifies several unresolved problems and provides interesting and plausible response strategies.

The authors have made an excellent contribution to the well-being of the Adriatic and Ionian Seas by providing a most valuable tool that will greatly assist the efforts to protect the marine areas of the littoral States. Indeed, it is submitted that this study is of relevance to other seas, for many of its findings and proposals have a universal interest.

I fully recommend this impressive book. I feel it is of great interest and utility not only to officials who have to bear the burden of implementing maritime environmental obligations but also to diplomats, scholars, academics, and students.

David Joseph Attard
Judge. Former Vice-President of the International Tribunal for the Law of the Sea (ITLOS, Hamburg, Germany). Former Director of the International Maritime Law Institute of the International Maritime Organization (IMO IMLI, Msida, Malta).

Preface

The objective of this book is to provide a comprehensive overview of the legal basis, under international law and the relevant regional legal frameworks, for the establishment and further development of area-based conservation tools in the Mediterranean Sea, with a particular emphasis placed on the transboundary area-based conservation instruments available for the Adriatic and Ionian Seas. Specifically, the aim is to identify and analyze the concepts and functioning of both marine protected areas (MPAs), as traditional area-based tools enabling marine habitat and species conservation, and other effective area-based conservation measures (OECMs), as a more recent addition to the picture. The regional focus considers the means of transboundary cooperation in marine conservation that are currently in place among the States bordering the Adriatic and Ionian Seas: these include States that are already members to the European Union (Croatia, Greece, Italy, and Slovenia) as well as States that have been granted the candidate status by the organization and, as such, are in the process of transposing the regional legislation into their national laws, including the *acquis* concerning nature protection (Albania, Bosnia and Herzegovina, and Montenegro). Once a State is a member to the European Union, any extension of its jurisdiction – typically, through the declaration of an exclusive economic zone – would automatically entail the extension of the European Union legal order and policies on that part of the sea (as it happened with the declaration of the exclusive economic zone of Croatia). Such order includes, *inter alia*, the European Union's Integrated Maritime Policy (EU-IMP), having the Marine Strategy Framework Directive (MSFD) as its environmental pillar, as well as marine spatial planning as one of the most important cross-sectoral policies.

In the wait to formally act as a united group pursuing common environmental goals after accession to the European Union by the four candidate countries, all the previously mentioned States already cooperate – also together with North Macedonia, San Marino, and Serbia – in the context of the European Union Strategy for the Adriatic and Ionian Region (EUSAIR), one of the four macro-regional strategies adopted by the European Commission and endorsed by the European Council (the other three covering the Baltic Sea, the Danube Region, and the Alpine Region). Specifically, the third thematic pillar of EUSAIR – focusing on environmental quality – identifies as pivotal the marine environment and is coordinated by representatives of one European Union member State (Slovenia) and a candidate country

(Bosnia and Herzegovina). In this context, transboundary cooperation through area-based conservation tools can play an important role, paying due regard to the ecosystem approach and the goals of marine spatial planning. For instance, within the latter, the concept of blue corridors certainly represents a measure that could substantially improve the functional connectivity of ecological networks and ensure – among other goals and besides the strict protection of key biodiversity areas – also sustainable fishing and shipping activities in the macro-region.

The analysis pursued in the book seemed necessary in light of the key European Union's commitments in the field of nature protection provided by the so-called 2030 Biodiversity Strategy, which, *inter alia*, sets targets to legally protect at least 30 per cent of the European Union's marine waters and integrate ecological corridors as part of a trans-European nature network; to strictly protect at least one-third of the already existing European Union's protected areas, including marine and coastal sites; and to effectively manage all protected areas, including in the marine and coastal environment, by defining clear conservation objectives and measures as well as by monitoring them appropriately.

Based on the 2030 Biodiversity Strategy, the European Union's member States – and soon-to-be fellow countries – will be responsible for designating further protected and strictly protected areas in their coastal and marine environments and may do so through the application of different strategies.

A first strategy includes the expansion of the NATURA 2000 Network, or of the so-called Emerald Network, as well as the establishment of MPAs under national schemes. This book, therefore, explores the opportunity to expand these networks in the macro-region, with particular emphasis on the Northern or Central Adriatic, the Channel of Otranto area (South Adriatic) and the Ionian Sea. In the context of this strategy, the transboundary cooperation between Bosnia and Herzegovina and Croatia is considered a case of special interest.

A second strategy involves the establishment of transboundary MPAs and OECMs in accordance with the provisions of international, regional, and subregional legal and policy frameworks. To this purpose, after providing an overview of the juridical status of the Adriatic and Ionian marine waters as parts of a wider semi-enclosed sea and defining the global legal basis for marine area-based conservation, this book explores the opportunities offered by regional and subregional legal and policy instruments focusing on different subjects though united by common environmental goals. The analysis, therefore, ranges from considerations such as the opportunity of the eventual ratification by Greece and Bosnia and Herzegovina of the Protocol concerning Specially Protected Areas and Biological Diversity in the Mediterranean (Barcelona, 1995) to the acknowledgment of the management shortcomings of the *Pelagos Sanctuary*; from a review of the criteria defining parts of the Adriatic and Ionian Seas as Ecologically or Biologically Significant Marine Areas within the framework of the Convention on Biological Diversity (Rio de Janeiro, 1992) to the proposal of a network of species-related conservation tools, such as MPAs for cetaceans, or non-nature-related instruments, such as underwater cultural heritage protected sites; from the assessment of current and upcoming OECMs under the mandate of the General Fisheries Commission for the Mediterranean (the so-called fishery restricted areas) to the potential strength of transboundary cooperation in the Adriatic and Ionian context through specific initiatives, intergovernmental bodies, and strategies put in place by the bordering States at a sub-regional level; from the challenges and opportunities related to the establishment of an international marine park through the means of a European Grouping of Territorial Cooperation in the Adriatic and Ionian Seas to the feasibility of the creation of one or more Particularly Sensitive Sea Areas within the mandate of the International Maritime Organization (IMO), both in the macro-region and beyond. Thus, under this perspective, the book also expects to shed some light on the complex degrees of interaction among a variety of levels of cooperation: national, sub-regional, regional, and international.

Two critical perspectives eventually complement the legal analysis contained in this book. The first, provided by the Co-coordinator of the third thematic pillar of EUSAIR, Mitja Bricelj, embraces an environmental policy methodology in identifying the key elements for the successful achievement of sustainable development objectives in the wider Mediterranean region, namely: the establishment of multi-stakeholder settings for transboundary cooperation, a coherent and continued application of the ecosystem approach, and the implementation of marine spatial planning as a crucial cross-cutting policy tool enabling transboundary cooperation. The second perspective, offered by Iztok Škerlič, Director of the EUSAIR Facility Point Project Partner (Slovenia), illustrates the EUSAIR Action Plan and its contribution to the goals of an efficiently integrated management of the coastal zone as well as the interactions between the goals of the blue economy and environmental quality within the macro-regional strategy.

With a view to providing responses to the complex set of challenges raised by the variety of tools and levels of intervention, conclusions and ways forward are provided that identify practical implementation instruments through which a truly transboundary perspective may guide the further development of protected marine spaces in the macro-region. An essential consideration in defining the ways forward lies in that once all remaining coastal States that have not yet done so decide to proclaim an exclusive economic zone – namely Albania, Italy (which has adopted in 2021 a framework law that needs to be implemented through presidential decree), Greece, and Montenegro – the high seas will disappear from the Adriatic and Ionian Seas. Such trend toward the establishment of exclusive economic zones could soon become an incentive toward the adoption of a coherent and coordinated Mediterranean – and Adriatic and Ionian – network of transboundary area-based conservation tools.

Mitja Grbec
Tullio Scovazzi
Ilaria Tani

Acknowledgments

This book is partially based on, and represents an upgraded and updated version of, the issue paper *The Legal Basis for the Establishment and Further Development of Marine Protected Areas in the European Union Strategy for the Adriatic and Ionian Region (EUSAIR) with Particular Emphasis on Transboundary Marine Protected Areas*, prepared at the end of 2021 within the Interreg ADRION strategic project EUSAIR Facility Point: WP T1.2 – Administrative and operational support to Thematic Steering Groups.

The authors gratefully acknowledge the generous support provided in that regard by the Municipality of Izola/Isola and by the EUSAIR Facility Point Project Partner at the Municipality of Izola (Slovenia). Of particular relevance were the sound comments and constant inputs – received both during the process of preparation as well as following the review of the draft issue paper – by Mitja Bricelj, PhD, EUSAIR Pillar 3 Co-coordinator at the Ministry of Environment and Spatial Planning of Republic of Slovenia, and Iztok Škerlič, MSc., Director of the EUSAIR Facility Point Project Partner at the Municipality of Izola. Both experts were eventually invited to contribute to this book. Moreover, the Institute of Water of the Republic of Slovenia (*Inštitut za vode Republike Slovenije*) granted its permission to use two charts (Figures 10.2 and 10.3) from the publication edited by Mitja Bricelj, *Handbook for Recognizing and Planning Green Infrastructure* (Ljubljana, 2021). The overall result would have not been possible without the support and guidance of the previously mentioned professionals and institutions.

In addition, the authors wish to extend their sincere thanks to *Istituto Idrografico della Marina* (the Italian Hydrographic Institute of the Navy) for its permission to use five charts representing existing maritime limits and boundaries in the Adriatic and Ionian Sea (Figures 1.5, 1.6, 1.7, 1.8, and 1.9). These charts are the result of joint researches undertaken by jurists and cartographers and are included in the book edited by Ilaria Tani, Nicola Marco Pizzeghello, and Stefano Ferrero, *Atlas of Maritime Limits and Boundaries in Central Mediterranean: Legal Texts and Illustrative Maps* (Genoa, 2020).

The authors, furthermore, acknowledge with gratitude the permission by Routledge to reproduce in this book some texts, as well as illustrations (Figures 1.1, 1.2, 1.4, and 6.1), that were included in a previous work of one of the authors, Mitja Grbec, *Extension of Coastal State Jurisdiction in Enclosed and Semi-Enclosed*

Seas. A Mediterranean and Adriatic Perspective (London and New York, 2014). Moreover, the authors thank the Specially Protected Areas Regional Activity Centre, the Mediterranean Biodiversity Centre of the UN Environment – Mediterranean Action Plan, for the permission to include in this book a map representing the distribution of Specially Protected Areas of Mediterranean Importance (Figure 7.1).

Recognizing the crucial contribution provided by non-governmental organizations in the progress toward an improved protection of marine habitats and related biodiversity, the authors ultimately wish to thank *Global Fishing Watch* for the permission to use three maps (Figures 6.6, 6.7, and 6.8) showing human activities around a submarine protected site off Capo Santa Maria di Leuca (Italy).

Mitja Grbec
Tullio Scovazzi
Ilaria Tani

Abbreviations and Acronyms

ACCOBAMS	Agreement on the Conservation of Cetaceans of the Black Sea, Mediterranean Sea and Contiguous Atlantic Area (Monaco, 1966)
ADRIAMED	Scientific Cooperation to Support Responsible Fisheries in the Adriatic Sea
ADRIPLAN	ADRiatic Ionian Maritime Spatial PLANning
ADRIREP	Adriatic Traffic Reporting System
AII	Adriatic-Ionian Initiative
AIS	Automated identification system
APM	Associated protective measure
Areas Protocol	Protocol concerning Specially Protected Areas and Biological Diversity in the Mediterranean (Barcelona, 1995)
ATBA	Area to be avoided
Ballast Water Convention	International Convention for the Control and Management of Ships' Ballast Water and Sediments (London, 2004)
BALMAS	Ballast Water Management System for Adriatic Sea Protection Project
Barcelona Convention	Convention for the Protection of the Marine Environment and the Coastal Region of the Mediterranean (Barcelona, 1976, amended in 1995)
BARCO OFOG	Barcelona Convention Offshore Oil and Gas Group
Belgrade Agreement	Agreement on Cooperation and Prevention of Pollution of the Adriatic Waters and its Coastal Zones (Belgrade, 1974)
Bern Convention	Convention on the Conservation of European Wildlife and Natural Habitats (Bern, 1979)
CAMP	Coastal Area Management Program
CBD	Convention on Biological Diversity (Rio de Janeiro, 1992)
CCH	Cetacean Critical Habitat

CIESM	International Commission for the Scientific Exploration of the Mediterranean Sea
CISE	Common Information Sharing Environment
CMS	Convention on the Conservation of Migratory Species of Wild Animals (Bonn, 1979)
Coastal Zone Protocol	Protocol on Integrated Coastal Zone Management in the Mediterranean (Madrid, 2008)
CRF	Common Regional Framework
DST	Decision support tool
EBSA	Ecologically or Biologically Significant Marine Areas in Need of Protection in Open Waters and Deep-sea Habitats
ECOAST	New methodologies for an ecosystem approach to spatial and temporal management of fisheries and aquaculture in coastal areas
EFH	Essential fish habitat
EGTC	European Grouping of Territorial Cooperation
EO	Ecological objective
EPPA	European Union Environment Partnership Programme for Accession
ETC	European Territorial Cooperation
EU	European Union
EU-BS 2030	European Union's Biodiversity Strategy for 2030
EU-IMP	European Union Integrated Marine Policy
EUSAIR	European Union Strategy for the Adriatic and Ionian Region
FAO	Food and Agriculture Organization of the United Nations
FRA	Fisheries Restricted Area
GEF	Global Environment Facility
GFCM	General Fisheries Commission for the Mediterranean
GWP-Med	Global Water Partnership – Mediterranean
ICZM	Integrated Coastal Zone Management
IHO	International Hydrographic Organization
IMAP	Integrated Monitoring Assessment Programme of the Mediterranean Sea and Coast and Related Assessment Criteria
IMMA	Important Marine Mammal Area
IMO	International Maritime Organization
IMS	Integrated Maritime Surveillance
ISA	International Seabed Authority
IUCN	International Union for the Conservation of Nature
IUCN-WCPA	IUCN World Commission on Protected Areas
IWC	International Whaling Commission
Jakarta Mandate	Jakarta Mandate on Marine and Coastal Biological Diversity

Land-Based Protocol	Protocol for the Protection of the Mediterranean Sea against Pollution from Land-Based Sources (Athens, 1980, as amended in 1996)
m	meter
MAP	Mediterranean Action Plan
MARPOL	International Convention for the Prevention of Pollution from Ships (London, 1973, amended in 1978)
MEPC	Marine Environment Protection Committee
MESMA	Monitoring and Evaluation of Spatially Managed Areas
MPA	Marine protected area
MSFD	Marine Strategy Framework Directive
MSP	Marine Spatial Planning
MUSES	Multi-Use in European Seas
NAMIRS	North Adriatic Maritime Incident Response System
NECA	NO_x Tier III Emission Control Area
n.m.	nautical mile
NOAA	National Oceanic and Atmospheric Administration of the United States
OECM	Other effective area-based conservation measure
Offshore Protocol	Protocol concerning Pollution resulting from Exploration and Exploitation of the Continental Shelf, the Seabed and its Subsoil (Madrid, 1994)
OSPAR Convention	Convention for the Protection of the Marine Environment of the North East Atlantic (Paris, 1992)
PAP/RAC	Priority Actions Programme Regional Activity Centre
PORTODIMARE	GeoPORtal of Tools & Data for sustainable Management of coAstal and maRine Environment
Post-2020 SAP BIO	Post-2020 Advisory Committee of the Strategic Action Programme for the Conservation of Biological Diversity and Sustainable Management of Natural Resources
PMIB	*Parc Marin International des Bouches de Bonifacio*
PSSA	Particularly Sensitive Sea Area
RAMOGE	Agreement on the Protection of the Waters of the Mediterranean Shore (Monaco, 1976, amended in 2003)
REMPEC	Regional Marine Pollution Emergency Response Centre for the Mediterranean Sea
SAC	Special Area of Conservation
SBS	Sea Basin Strategy
SBSTTA	Subsidiary Body on Scientific, Technical and Technological Advice
SCI	Site of Community Importance
SDG	Sustainable Development Goal
SECA	Sulphur Emission Control Area

SHAPe	Shaping an Holistic Approach to Protect the Adriatic Environment between coast and sea
Ships Protocol	Protocol concerning Cooperation in Preventing Pollution from Ships and, in Cases of Emergency, Combating Pollution of the Mediterranean Sea (Valletta, 2002)
SOLAS	International Convention for the Safety of Life at Sea (London, 1974, as amended)
SPA	Special Protection Area
SPA/RAC	Specially Protected Areas Regional Activity Centre
SPAMI	Specially Protected Areas of Mediterranean Importance
SUPREME	Supporting Maritime Spatial Planning in the Eastern Mediterranean
TAP	Trans Adriatic Pipeline
TEC	Treaty Establishing the European Community
TFEU	Treaty on the Functioning of the European Union
Trilateral Commission	Joint Commission for the Protection of the Adriatic Sea
TSG	Thematic Steering Group
UNCED	United Nations Conference on Environment and Development (Rio de Janeiro, 1992)
UNCLOS	United Nations Convention on the Law of the Sea (Montego Bay, 1982)
UNEP	United Nations Environment Programme
UNESCO	United Nations Organization for Education, Science and Culture
UNESCO-IHP	International Hydrological Programme of UNESCO
VME	Vulnerable marine ecosystem
VMS	Vessel monitoring system
VTS	Vessel traffic service
WP	Work package

Figures

Contributors

Mitja Bricelj, Co-coordinator of Pillar 3 of the European Union Strategy for the Adriatic and Ionian Region (EUSAIR) at the Ministry of Environment and Spatial Planning of the Republic of Slovenia.

Mitja Grbec, Attorney-at-Law in Koper (Slovenia). Visiting Lecturer at the International Maritime Law Institute of the International Maritime Organization (IMO IMLI, Msida, Malta), and Assistant Professor at University of Primorska, Faculty of Management (Koper, Slovenia). Secretary-General of the Maritime Law Association of Slovenia and Titulary Member of the *Comité Maritime International*.

Tullio Scovazzi, Professor of international law (now retired) in the Universities of Parma, Genoa, Milan, and Milano-Bicocca (Italy). Associate Member of the *Institut de droit international*.

Iztok Škerlič, Director of the European Union Strategy for the Adriatic and Ionian Region (EUSAIR) Facility Point Project Partner based in the Municipality of Izola (Slovenia).

Ilaria Tani, Attorney-at-Law in Milan (Italy). Adjunct Professor of International Law of the Sea and Maritime Law at University of Milano-Bicocca (Italy). Former Associate Legal Officer at the Division for Ocean Affairs and the Law of the Sea, Office of Legal Affairs, United Nations (UNDOALOS, New York, United States).

1 The Adriatic and Ionian Seas as Part of the Wider Mediterranean Sea[1]

Mitja Grbec and Tullio Scovazzi

1.1. Geographical and Political Considerations

Throughout history, the Mediterranean Sea has been known by a number of alternative names. During Roman times, it was commonly referred to as the *Mare Nostrum*, and from this expression it may be implied that it was, to a certain extent, also a *Mare Clausum*. Noteworthy is the fact that its current name is derived from the Latin word *mediterraneous*, meaning "in the middle of the earth" or "between lands". The name Mediterranean, therefore, clearly emphasizes the enclosed position of this sea between not less than three continents – Africa, Asia, and Europe.

Nowadays, quite contrary from ancient times, the Mediterranean coastline, which extends to approximately 22,500 km, is shared by 23 States.[2] The overall surface of the Mediterranean Sea amounts to about 2,500,000 km^2, while its average depth is approximately 1,500 m. The Mediterranean Sea stretches over a distance of 3,500 km (from Gibraltar to the east).[3] As recalled in a recent document,

> The Mediterranean Sea is the world largest semi-enclosed sea. It is considered a biodiversity hotspot, representing just 0.3% of the global ocean volume while hosting 4 to 18% of identified global marine species. In addition

1 Chapter 1 of this book is partially based and represents an upgraded version of Chapter 1 of Grbec, *Extension of Coastal State Jurisdiction in Enclosed and Semi-Enclosed Seas. A Mediterranean and Adriatic Perspective*, London and New York, 2014. For the purposes of this book, the Mediterranean Sea is defined as per Art. 1, para. 1, of the Convention for the Protection of the Marine Environment and the Coastal Region of the Mediterranean (Barcelona, 1976, as amended in 1995; Barcelona Convention), the Black Sea being excluded from the definition.

2 Albania, Algeria, Bosnia and Herzegovina, Croatia, Cyprus, Egypt, France, Greece, Israel, Italy, Lebanon, Libya, Malta, Monaco, Montenegro, Morocco, Palestine, Slovenia, Spain, Syria, Tunisia, Turkey, and the United Kingdom (as regards Gibraltar and the two Sovereign Base Areas of Akrotiri and Dhekelia on the island of Cyprus). Eight among the Mediterranean bordering States are members of the European Union, an international organization that exercises, *inter alia*, an exclusive competence for fisheries management and conservation and shared competences with its member States in the field of protection of the marine environment.

3 For more details, see Leanza, *Il regime giuridico internazionale del mare Mediterraneo*, Napoli, 2008.

DOI: 10.4324/9781003367963-1

to its biodiversity value, the Mediterranean has significant historical, cultural and socio-economic value.[4]

The Mediterranean Sea is an international waterway linking the Atlantic and Indian Oceans through the Suez Canal, and both of them with the Black Sea, through the Turkish straits of Bosporus and Dardanelles. Some major islands (Sicily, Sardinia, Corsica, Cyprus, and Crete) and a great number of smaller islands and islets are situated in the Mediterranean.

Also due to the slow exchange of waters through the Strait of Gibraltar, the Mediterranean Sea is at great risk of pollution.[5] Marine living resources are under pressure from overfishing. Liquid and gaseous hydrocarbons have been found in the continental shelf along the southern and eastern Mediterranean shores.

Another important characteristic of the Mediterranean Sea is that it comprises a number of sub-seas (Figure 1.1) which are either indented inside the continent (e.g., the Adriatic Sea) or situated between a continent and islands (e.g., the Tyrrhenian Sea). The main sub-seas in the Western Basin include the Alboran Sea (bordered by Spain, the British Overseas Territory of Gibraltar, Morocco, and Algeria), the Balearic Sea (between the Spanish coast and the Balearic Islands), and the Ligurian and Tyrrhenian Seas, lying between mainland Italy and the islands of Corsica, Sardinia, and Sicily. The sub-seas in the Central and Eastern Mediterranean include the Aegean, Ionian, and Adriatic Seas. At least geographically speaking, the Adriatic and Ionian are, therefore, two distinct sub-seas of the wider Mediterranean Sea. The common denominator of the mentioned sub-seas, both in the Western and Eastern Basins, is a restricted space, coupled in the majority of cases with narrow connections to other sub-seas. A clear example in this regard is represented by the Channel of Otranto, linking the Adriatic to the Ionian Sea and wider (Central) Mediterranean.

The Mediterranean countries differ as far as their internal political systems and levels of economic development are concerned. Highly populated cities, ports of worldwide significance, important industrial areas, and renowned seaside resorts are located along the Mediterranean shores. The difficulties in the Mediterranean are accentuated by some longstanding political problems as, for example, the presence of the United Kingdom enclave of Gibraltar on the Iberian Peninsula and the presence of the Spanish enclaves and small islands along the Moroccan coast, coupled with the still difficult relationship of Israel with its Arab neighbours (e.g., Lebanon). The delimitation of maritime boundaries in the Eastern Mediterranean is complicated furthermore by the still divided condition of Cyprus and by the tense relations between Greece and Turkey in the Aegean Sea.

4 Post-2020 regional strategy for marine and coastal protected areas and other effective area-based conservation measures in the Mediterranean, annexed to Decision IG.25/12, adopted by the parties to Barcelona Convention at their 2021 Antalya meeting (doc. UNEP/MED IG 25/27, p. 444).

5 More than 80 years is the period needed for the exchange of Mediterranean waters through the Strait of Gibraltar. See Leanza, *op. cit.*, p. 8.

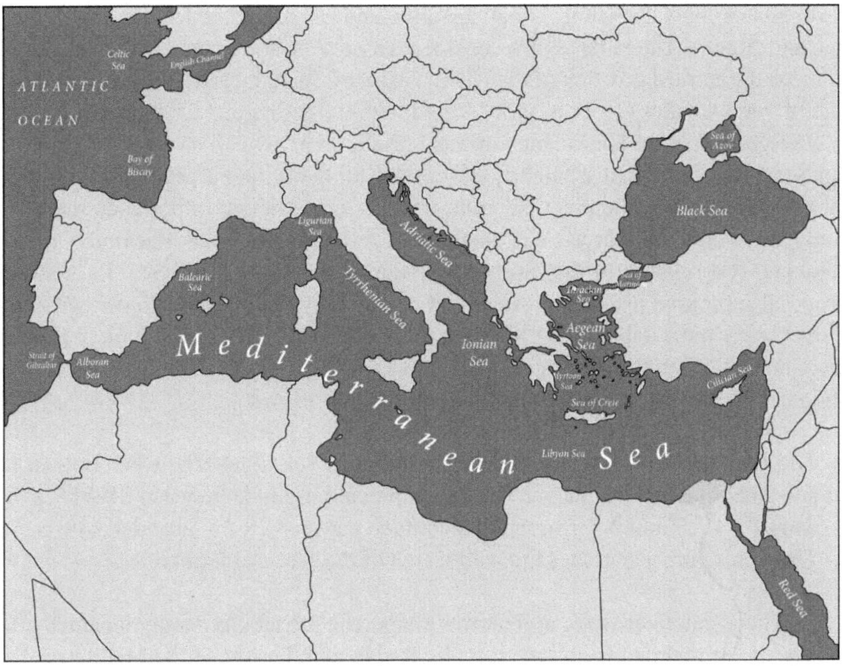

Figure 1.1 The Mediterranean Sea and its sub-seas

Source: Copyright (Routledge©2014) From *Extension of Coastal State Jurisdiction in Enclosed or Semi-Enclosed Seas: A Mediterranean and Adriatic Perspective* by Mitja Grbec. Reproduced by permission of Taylor and Francis Group, LLC, an informa business

Navies of bordering and non-bordering States cruise the Mediterranean, which is a region of major strategic importance. These factors complicate, among others, the delimitation of maritime zones and the process of extension of coastal State jurisdiction in the Mediterranean Sea and its sub-seas[6] and have, as such, represented an important obstacle to regional and sub-regional cooperation. It is, nonetheless, important to note that, despite the fact that not all Mediterranean States are parties to the United Nations Convention on the Law of the Sea (Montego Bay, 1982; UNCLOS),[7] all States bordering the Adriatic and Ionian Seas are parties to it.

The Adriatic Sea, as a sub-sea of the Mediterranean, may be defined as a narrow, shallow, and temperature warm semi-enclosed sea, forming a distinct sub-region within the Mediterranean Sea region.[8] The Adriatic is nowadays surrounded by

6 Grbec, Extension of Coastal State Jurisdiction in the Mediterranean: Quasi EEZs or Real sui-generis Zones? in Martínez Gutiérrez (ed.), *Serving the Rule of International Maritime Law: Essays in Honour of Professor David Joseph Attard*, London and New York, 2010, p. 181.

7 Israel, Libya, Syria, and Turkey are not parties to the UNCLOS.

8 Vidas, Particularly Sensitive Sea Areas: The Need for Regional Cooperation in the Adriatic Sea, in Ott (ed.), *Croatian Accession to the European Union: Institutional Challenges*, Zagreb, 2006, p. 359.

seven States: Italy, Slovenia, Croatia, Bosnia and Herzegovina, Montenegro, Albania, and Greece. The latter is also considered as an Adriatic State, mostly as a result of the geographical position of the Greek island of Corfu located at its entrance and due to some smaller Greek islands located within the Channel of Otranto.

The geographical coordinates of the Adriatic Sea, as well as those of the Ionian Sea as explained later, slightly differ depending on the purpose of the specific measurement. From the practical point of view, of particular importance seem the coordinates contained in various documents of the International Maritime Organization (IMO) relating to the safety of navigation in the Adriatic Sea. In the joint proposal submitted in 2003 by Albania, Croatia, Italy, Serbia and Montenegro, and Slovenia on the establishment of new recommended traffic separation schemes/recommended routes system and other new routeing measures in the Adriatic Sea, endorsed by the IMO, the Adriatic is described as follows:

> The Adriatic Sea is the part of the Mediterranean Sea situated between Balkan and Apennine peninsulas, on the geographical longitude between 012°15' E and 019°45' E and the geographical latitude between 39°45' N and 45°45' N. The south border includes the whole area of the Strait of Otranto.

Due to its relatively long and narrow shape, the Adriatic is deeply indented into the European mainland and linked to the Ionian and the rest of the Mediterranean Sea only through the Channel of Otranto. The surface of the Adriatic Sea amounts to 138,595 km^2, while the total length of the Adriatic coastline is around 7,912 km, more than half of which is composed of the coastline of the numerous islands fringing particularly the Eastern Adriatic coasts. The length of the Adriatic Sea from Venice and the mouth of the River Butrinit in Albania amount to almost 475 n.m. It is noteworthy that the average width of the Adriatic is only 85 n.m.

The Adriatic Sea is also an important route of international navigation. The main navigation route in the Adriatic Sea goes from the "wider" Mediterranean Sea (Ionian) through the approximately 45 n.m. wide Channel of Otranto and towards one of the Northern Adriatic ports: Trieste (Italy), Koper (Slovenia), and Rijeka (Croatia).

The Adriatic marine environment is extremely sensitive and represents an almost unique ecosystem.[9] It has been alleged that its environmental conditions are mostly a result of the specific exchange of waters with the Ionian Sea and the wider Mediterranean through the Otranto Channel and the Palagruža threshold separating the shallower Northern Adriatic from the deeper Southern Adriatic and, furthermore, by the inputs of freshwater from the mountains in the Eastern and the rivers in the Western part.[10] Its living resources can be generally qualified as highly diversified, with numerous species, but low abundance, which in turn makes the Adriatic's ecosystem particularly vulnerable.

9 Joint Expert Group of the Adriatic States on the PSSA, *Designation of the Adriatic Sea as a Particularly Sensitive Area*, Draft Proposal (Second Draft), 2007, p. 2. Copy on file with the authors.

10 *Ibid.*, p. 2.

Figure 1.2 The Adriatic Sea

Source: Copyright (Routledge©2014) From *Extension of Coastal State Jurisdiction in Enclosed or Semi-Enclosed Seas: A Mediterranean and Adriatic Perspective* by Mitja Grbec. Reproduced by permission of Taylor and Francis Group, LLC, an informa business

The ecosystem of the Ionian Sea,[11] which is bordered only by two States (Greece and Italy), seems to be in comparison with the Adriatic's ecosystem less vulnerable,

11 The limits of the Ionian Sea, as defined by the International Hydrographic Organization, are the following: *On the North*. A line running from the mouth of the Butrinto River (39° 44' N) in Albania, to Cape Karagol in Corfu (39° 45' N), along the North Coast of Corfu to Cape Kephali (39° 45' N) and from thence to Cape Santa Maria di Leuca in Italy. *On the East*. From the mouth of the Butrinto River in Albania down the coast of the mainland to Cape Matapan. *On the South*. A line from Cape Matapan to Cape Passero, the Southern point of Sicily. *On the West*. The East coast of Sicily and the Southeast coast of Italy to Cape Santa Maria di Leuca: International Hydrographic Organization, *Limits of Oceans and Seas*, 3rd ed., *IHO Special Publication*, No. 23, Monaco, 1953, p. 17.

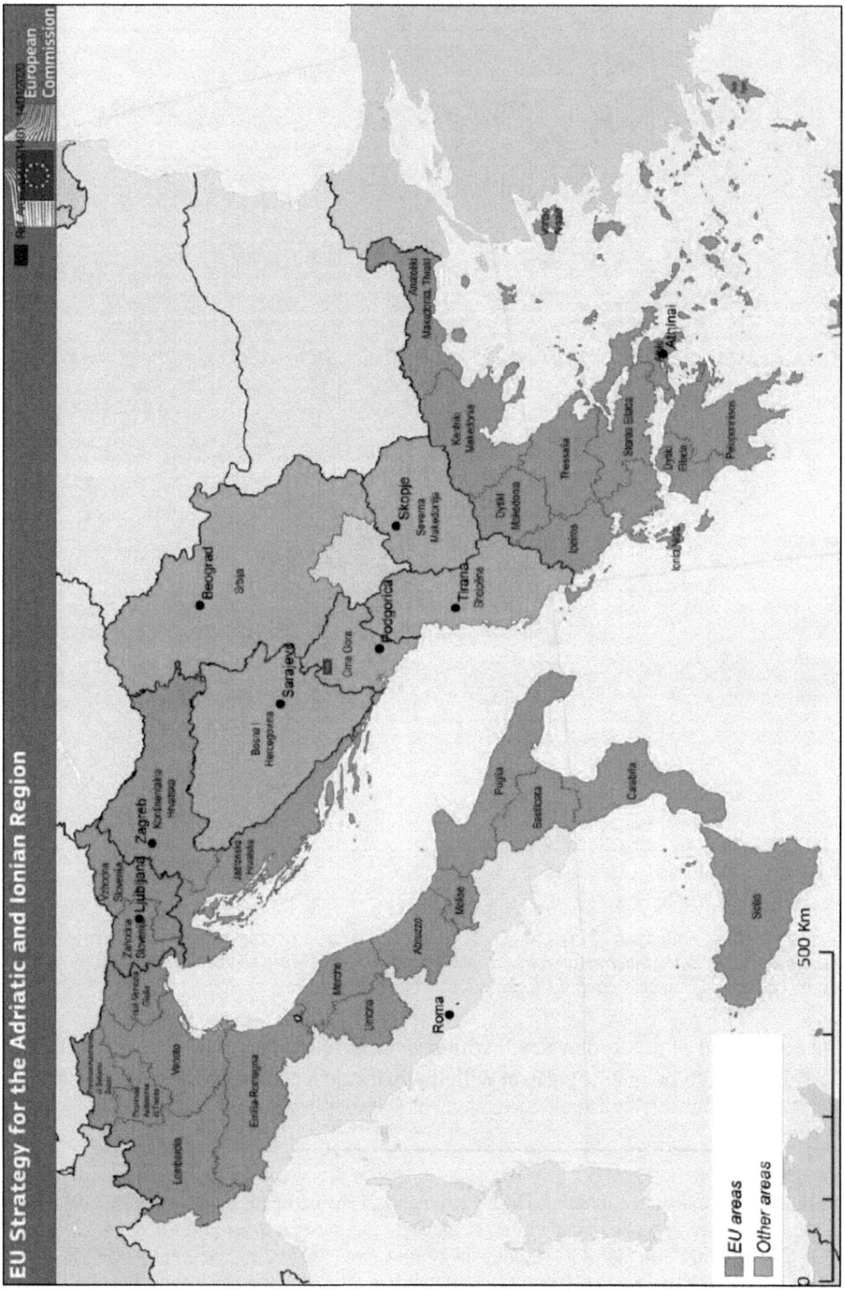

Figure 1.3 The EUSAIR area

Source: doc. COM (2020) 132 final

due to the fact that the Ionian Sea is not so narrow and has – differently from the Adriatic Sea – a wide opening towards the wider (Central) Mediterranean. The Ionian Sea differs from the Adriatic Sea also with regard to its depth. While the depth of the Adriatic Sea generally does not reach more than 40 m, the Ionian Sea is deeper and even includes the deepest point in the Mediterranean Sea (5,269 m at the southwest of the Peloponnese). As a result, it has been argued that the Ionian Sea is, in comparison with the Adriatic Sea, better oxygenated with a higher abundance of species. Taking however into account that the Adriatic Sea is connected to the wider Mediterranean Sea exclusively through the narrow Otranto Channel and the Ionian Sea, the activities within, and the environmental status of, the Adriatic Sea have a profound impact on the environment and the ecosystem of the Ionian Sea. It may be asserted, accordingly, that the Adriatic and Ionian ecosystems are closely interconnected.

The political map of the Adriatic and Ionian region still shows a division between States that are members of the European Union (Croatia, Greece, Italy, and Slovenia) and other States (Albania, Bosnia and Herzegovina, and Montenegro), although it is important to note that all the other States aspire to join the European Union in a not-too-distant future. This organization, also through its policies and macro-regional strategy (i.e., through the EUSAIR),[12] has become an important actor and catalyst in the context of Adriatic-Ionian cooperation.[13]

The Adriatic and Ionian region is a functional area, primarily defined by the Adriatic and Ionian Seas basin. It is home to more than 70 million people and paramount for Europe's geographical continuity.[14]

1.2. The Present Juridical Picture of the Mediterranean Waters

From the standpoint of contemporary law of the sea, there are at least four important implications of the previously explained size and configuration on the juridical status of the Mediterranean Sea, also in the context of the Adriatic and Ionian Seas, as sub-seas or sub-regions of the wider Mediterranean Sea.

The first implication is that there is no point in the Mediterranean, including within the Adriatic and Ionian Seas, which is located at a distance of more than 200 n.m. from the nearest land or island. In practical terms, this means that Mediterranean coastal States, including those bordering the Adriatic and Ionian Seas, are not in a position to extend their jurisdiction up to the maximum extent permitted by international law (200-mile external limit of the exclusive economic zone). Similarly, the limited maritime space available also means that almost every extension of jurisdiction creates new neighbours and triggers the need for delimitation of

12 Discussed further in this book (Chapter 3.D and Chapter 11).

13 Slim and Scovazzi, *Study of the Current Status of Ratification, Implementation and Compliance with Maritime Agreements and Conventions Applicable to the Mediterranean Sea Basin*, Part 2, 2009, pp. 67–68.

14 European Commission, *For a Prosperous and Integrated Adriatic and Ionian Region*, 2014.

actual or potential zones of sovereign rights or jurisdiction between adjacent and opposite States.

Secondly, due the proximity between Mediterranean States, including between States bordering the Adriatic and Ionian Seas, the extension of jurisdiction by one coastal State, in most cases, affects the interests of more than just another neighbouring State. An excellent example is the complicated geographical situation in the Ionian Sea and generally Central Mediterranean, where the extension of jurisdiction by one State up to the maximum extent permitted by international law, would affect the interest of up to four neighbouring States, namely Greece, Italy, Libya, and Malta (see Figure 1.4).

Thirdly, since the continental shelf exists *ipso facto* and *ab initio*, there is no space in the Mediterranean Sea, including within the Adriatic and Ionian Seas, for an outer continental shelf on the basis of Art. 76 UNCLOS, nor obviously for the Area, that is the seabed beyond the limits of national jurisdiction, in accordance with Part XI UNCLOS.

In fact, Mediterranean States are still far from taking a uniform attitude as regards the extent and nature of their coastal zones. Looking at the map, a patchwork of different kinds of coastal zones mixed with holes of high seas is immediately visible.[15] However, the situation is likely to change in the future because of the growing trend towards the establishment of exclusive economic zones. The present picture of coastal zones in the Mediterranean is the following.

Maritime internal waters. Several Mediterranean States (Albania, Algeria, Croatia, Cyprus, Egypt, France, Greece, Italy, Libya, Malta, Morocco, Montenegro, Spain, Tunisia, and Turkey) have enacted legislation measuring the breadth of the territorial sea not from the low-water mark, but from straight baselines joining points located on the mainland or islands. Historical bays are claimed by Italy (Gulf of Taranto) and Libya (Gulf of Sidra).

Territorial sea. Most Mediterranean States have established a 12-n.m. territorial sea. The exceptions are the United Kingdom (3 n.m. for Gibraltar and the Sovereign Base Areas of Akrotiri and Dhekelia), Greece (6 n.m., but 12 n.m. in the Ionian Sea up to Cape Tenaron),[16] and Turkey (6 n.m. in the Aegean Sea, but 12 n.m. elsewhere).

Contiguous zone. Some states (Algeria, Cyprus, Egypt, France, Malta, Morocco, Spain, Syria, and Tunisia) have established 24-n.m. contiguous zones for customs, fiscal, immigration, or sanitary purposes. Algeria, Cyprus, France, Italy, and Tunisia exercise rights in the field of archaeological and historical objects found at sea within the 24-n.m. limit (so-called archaeological contiguous zone).

Sui generis zones (fishing zone, ecological protection zone). Some coastal States have proclaimed a *sui generis* zone beyond the territorial sea, namely a fishing

15 See Scovazzi, Harlequin and the Mediterranean, in Wolfrum, Seršić and Šošić (eds.), *Contemporary Developments in International Law – Essays in Honour of Budislav Vukas*, Leiden, 2016, p. 291.

16 The Greek territorial sea in the Ionian Sea has recently been extended from 6 to 12 n.m. by Law No. 4767 of 21 January 2021.

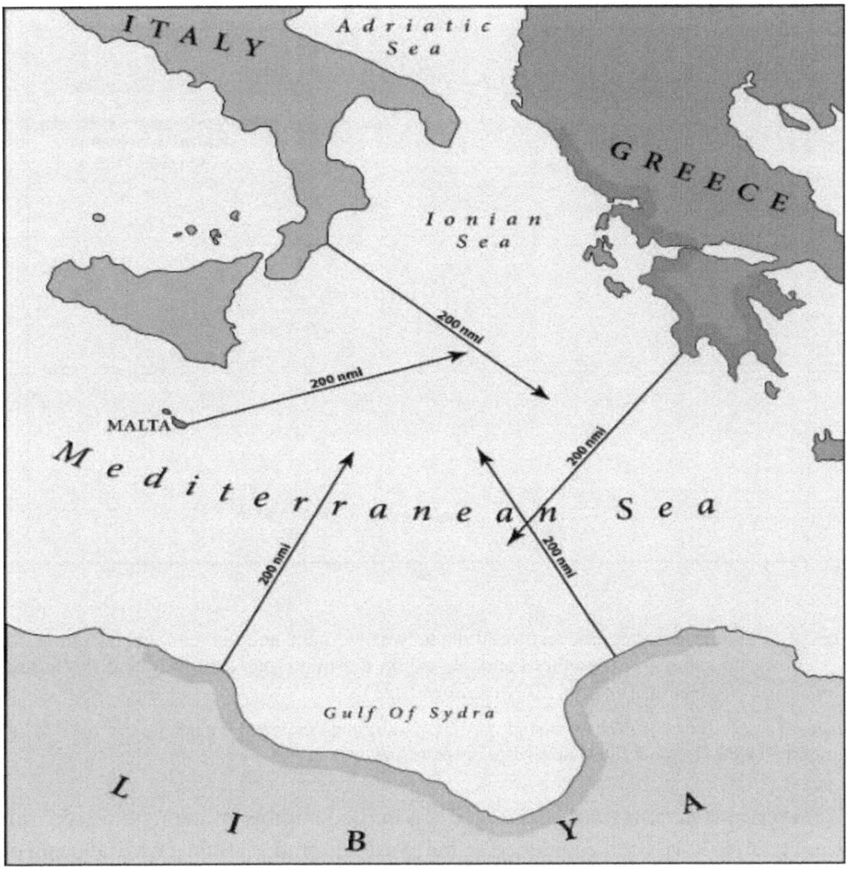

Figure 1.4 Overlapping claims in the Ionian Sea and Central Mediterranean

Source: Copyright (Routledge©2014) From *Extension of Coastal State Jurisdiction in Enclosed or Semi-Enclosed Seas: A Mediterranean and Adriatic Perspective* by Mitja Grbec. Reproduced by permission of Taylor and Francis Group, LLC, an informa business

zone or an ecological protection zone. While neither of them is mentioned in the UNCLOS, they are not prohibited either. They encompass only some of the rights that can be exercised within the exclusive economic zone. Such a fragmentation of rights does not seem incompatible with the UNCLOS, considering that the right to do less is implied in the right to do more.

Fishing zones of different width have been proclaimed by Libya (62 n.m.), Malta (25 n.m.) and Tunisia (depth of 50 m). An ecological protection zone has been proclaimed by Italy but only as regards the waters of the Ligurian and Tyrrhenian Seas.

Exclusive economic zone. A number of Mediterranean States have established an exclusive economic zone (Algeria, Croatia, Cyprus, Egypt, Israel, Lebanon, Morocco, France, Spain, and Syria) or have adopted legislation enabling the future establishment of such a zone (Italy, Libya, Montenegro, and Tunisia).

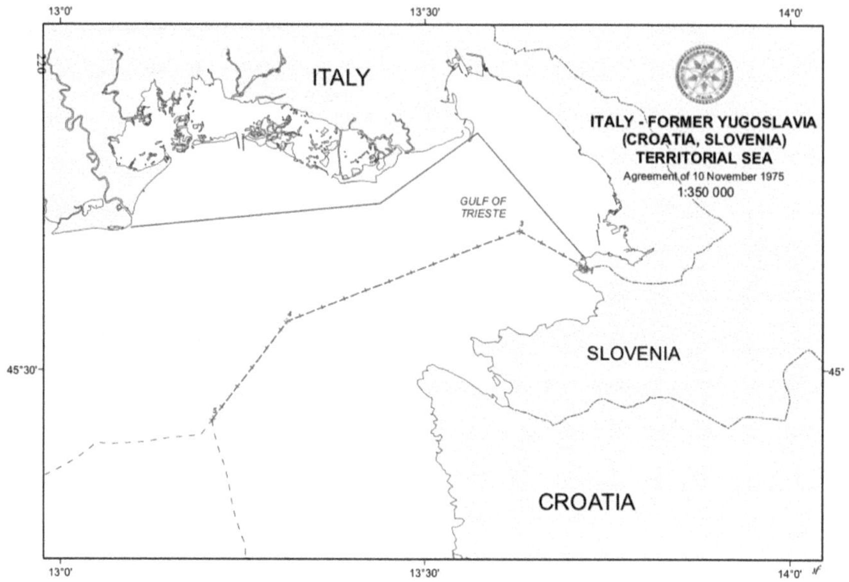

Figure 1.5 Delimitation of the territorial sea between Croatia and Slovenia, on the one hand, and Italy, on the other hand. Based on the treaty between Italy and the former Yugoslavia (Osimo, 10 November 1975)

Source: Tani, Ferrero, and Pizzeghello (eds.), Atlas of Maritime Limits and Boundaries in Central Mediterranean: Legal Texts and Illustrative Maps, Genoa, 2020, p. 220

As regards *maritime boundaries*, only a limited number of the required delimitation treaties have been concluded so far by Mediterranean States with adjacent or opposite coasts, and not all of them have entered into force.[17] Several instances of maritime boundaries are still unsettled, including some that are quite complex to handle due to the peculiar geographical configuration of the coastlines of the States concerned (concave or convex coastlines, islands located on the so-called wrong side of the median line, coastal enclaves, etc.).

In particular, as regards the Adriatic and Ionian Seas, the boundary of the territorial sea between Italy, on the one hand, and Croatia and Slovenia, on the other, has been determined in 1975 by the treaty concluded in Osimo by Italy and the former Yugoslavia (Figure 1.5).

The territorial sea boundary between Croatia and Slovenia has been settled by the arbitral award of 29 June 2017 (Figure 1.6). However, the two States concerned have taken different positions about the validity of the award.[18]

17 See Scovazzi, Maritime Delimitations in the Mediterranean Sea, in *Cursos Euromediterraneos Bancaja de Derecho Internacional*, 2004–2005, p. 349; Oanta, Maritime Delimitations in the Mediterranean: Current Challenges, in *Italian Yearbook of International Law*, 2021, p. 5.

18 According to Slovenia, the award is binding. According to Croatia, the 2009 arbitration agreement was terminated before the date of the award. Award available at pca-cpa.org/en/cases/3/. The question of the validity of the arbitral award was however addressed and solved by the Arbitral Tribunal with a partial award dated 30 June 2016 (available at pcacases.com/web/sendAttach/1787).

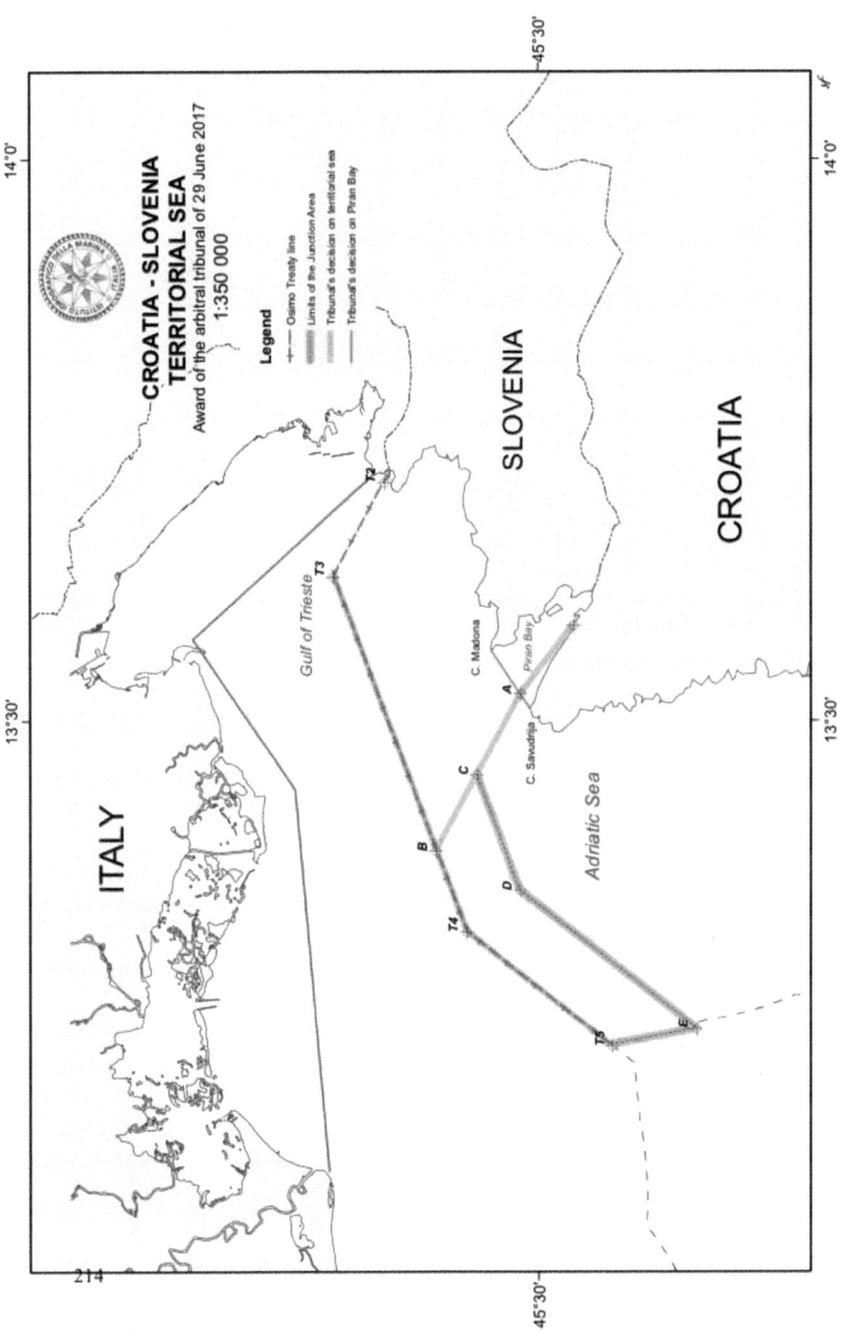

Figure 1.6 Delimitation of the internal waters, territorial sea, and "junction area" between Croatia and Slovenia, settled by the arbitral award of 29 June 2017

Source: Tani, Ferrero, and Pizzeghello (eds.)(*op. cit.* in Figure 1.5), p. 214

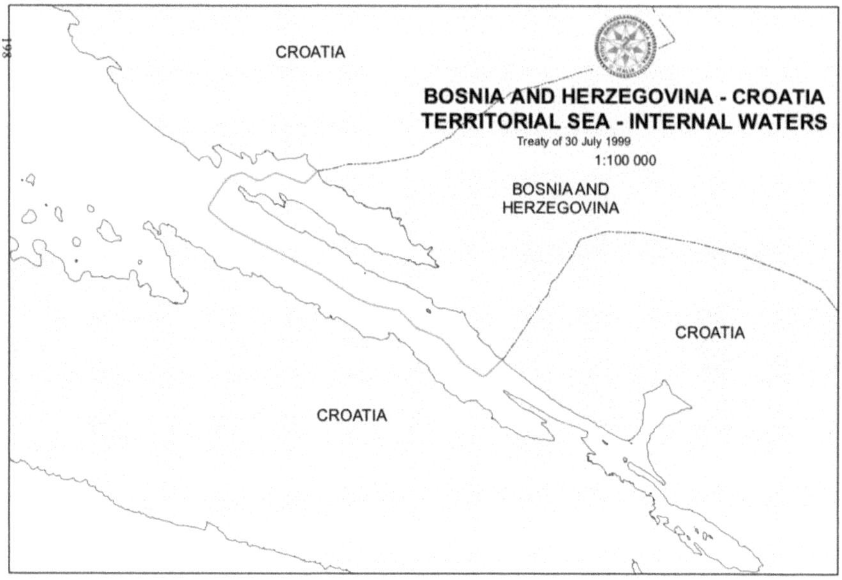

Figure 1.7 Delimitation of the internal waters and territorial sea between Bosnia and Herzegovina and Croatia, based on the treaty on the State border between the two States (Sarajevo, 30 July 1999)

Source: Tani, Ferrero and Pizzeghello (eds.) (*op. cit.* in Figure 1.5), p. 198

The boundary between the marine internal waters of Croatia and the territorial sea of Bosnia and Herzegovina has been provisionally established by the 1999 Treaty on the State border between the two countries (Figure 1.7).

The territorial sea boundary between Croatia and Montenegro was provisionally delimited by the 2002 protocol between Croatia and the former Yugoslavia.[19] There is no agreement of maritime delimitation between Albania and Montenegro. A delimitation of the territorial sea and other maritime zones between Albania and Greece was effected under an agreement signed in Tirana in 2009. However, it is unlikely that it will ever enter into force because, in 2010, the Albanian constitutional court found that the agreement was vitiated by procedural and substantive violations of the constitution and the UNCLOS.

As far as the other maritime zones are concerned, the agreement between Italy and the former Yugoslavia on the delimitation of the continental shelf (Rome,

19 Map in Grbec, *op. cit.*, Figure 4.3, p. 164.

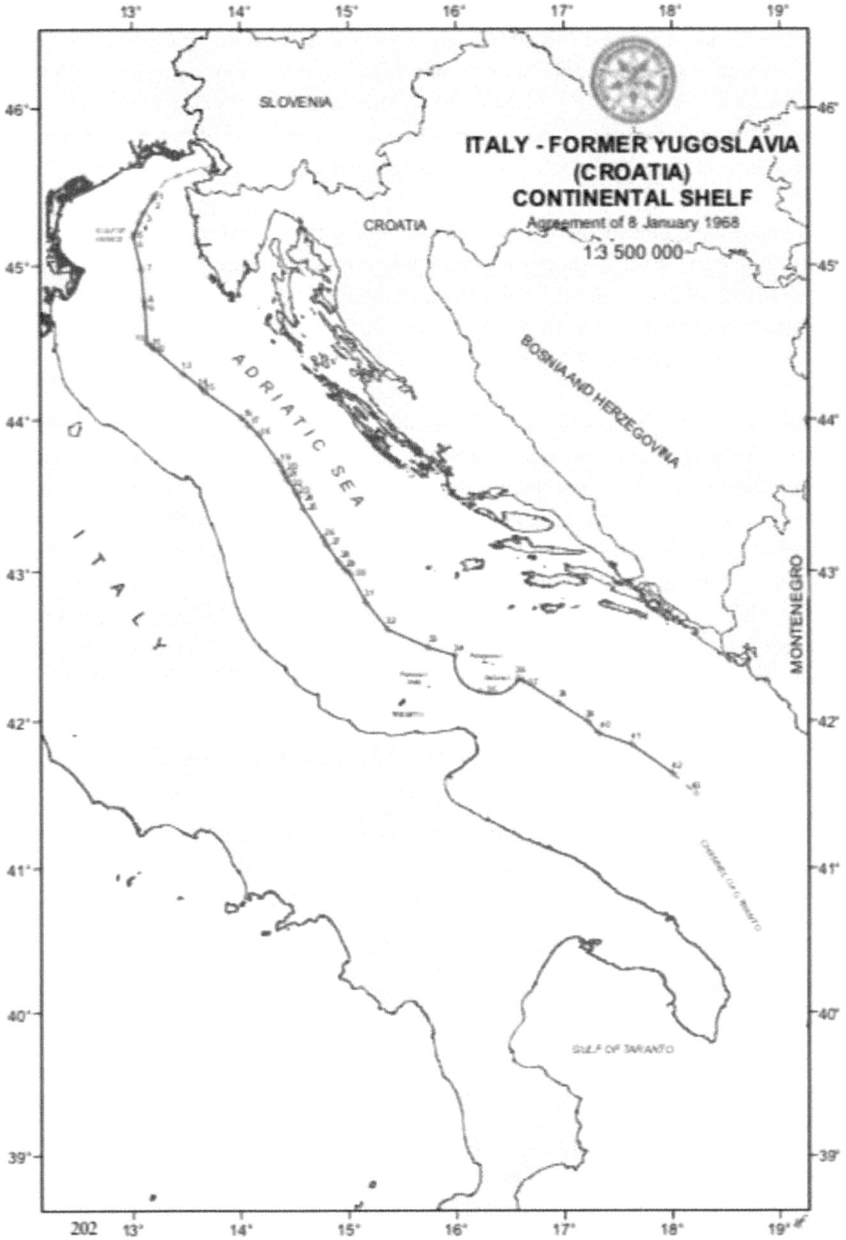

Figure 1.8 Delimitation of the continental shelf between Croatia and Italy, based on the Treaty between Italy and the former Yugoslavia on the delimitation of the continental shelf (Rome, 8 January 1968)

Source: Tani, Ferrero, and Pizzeghello (eds.) (*op. cit.* in Figure 1.5), p. 202

1968) (Figure 1.8)[20] applies today in the relationship between Italy and the successor State Croatia.[21] The 1968 agreement does not delimit the exclusive economic zones, which at that time did not exist, nor does it apply anymore between Italy and Montenegro.[22] However, on 24 May 2022, Italy and Croatia concluded an Agreement on the delimitation of the exclusive economic zones that has not yet entered into force. Based on Article 1(1) of the said Agreement:

> the boundary line of the exclusive economic zones to which the Parties are entitled to exercise, respectively, their sovereign rights and jurisdiction under international law coincides with the continental shelf boundary between the Parties in accordance with the Agreement of 1986 and the technical adjustment Agreement of 2005.

It follows that the 2022 agreement is intended, upon its entry into force, to represent a "single purpose boundary", applicable both to the continental shelf and to the delimitation of the Croatian and the (future) Italian exclusive economic zone.[23]

In the Ionian Sea, the continental shelf has been delimited by the agreement between Greece and Italy (Athens, 1977). Recently, the two States have concluded another agreement on the delimitation of their respective maritime zones (Athens, 2020), which will apply to the respective exclusive economic zones if and when they are established by them.[24] The 2020 agreement follows, for the superjacent waters, the same boundary line that was agreed upon in 1977 for the seabed.

1.3. Implications of the Recent Process of Extension of Coastal State Jurisdiction in the Adriatic and Ionian Seas

As already remarked, once all Mediterranean States, including those bordering the Adriatic and Ionian Seas, will proclaim their exclusive economic zones, the high seas itself, as well as the high seas regime based on Part VII UNCLOS, will

20 This is the first treaty concluded for the delimitation of a maritime boundary in the Mediterranean Sea.

21 According to Art. 43, para. 2, of the Croatian Maritime Code of 27 January 1994 (not in force anymore), "the boundary line of the continental shelf between the Republic of Croatia and the Republic of Italy has been established by the agreement between Italy and the former Federative Socialist Republic of Yugoslavia in 1968".

22 The memorandum between Italy and Montenegro on the succession of Montenegro to the bilateral treaties (Podgorica, 2012) does not list the 1968 agreement among the treaties that remain in force between Italy and Montenegro. It follows that, for the time being, the last two segments of the 1968 agreement (from point 41 to point 42 and from point 42 to 43) do not represent anymore a maritime boundary.

23 Article 4 provides that the 2022 shall enter into force on the date of the receipt of the last written notification by which the Parties have notified each other, through diplomatic channels, of the completion of their internal procedures necessary for its entry into force. Text of the 2022 Agreement available at www.unimc.it/maremap/it/EEZagreementItalyCroatia.pdf

24 Concluded on 9 June 2020, entry into force on 8 November 2021 (*Law of the Sea Bulletin* No. 108, p. 16).

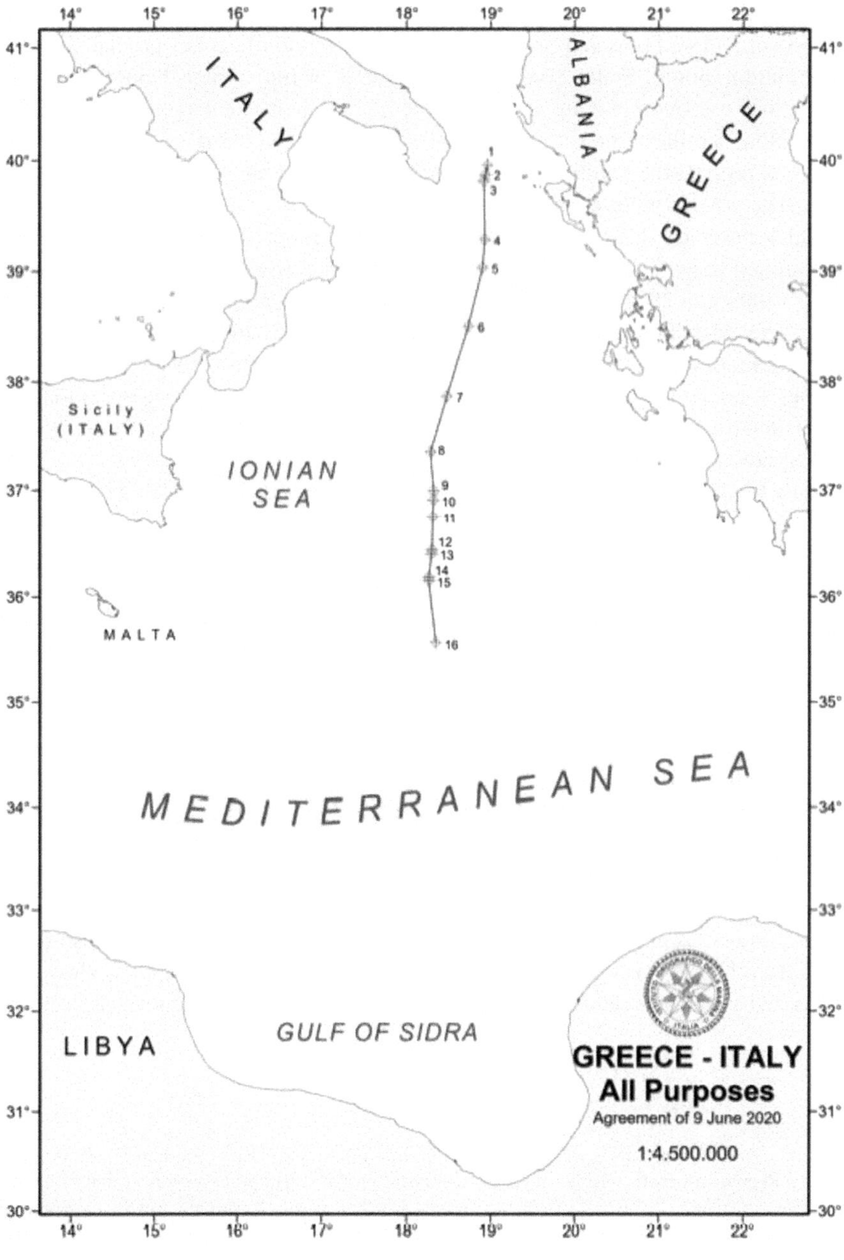

Figure 1.9 Delimitation between Greece and Italy of their respective maritime zones (Athens, 9 June 2020)

Source: Tani, Ferrero, and Pizzeghello (eds.) (*op. cit.* in Figure 1.5), p. 244, as amended in the forthcoming update of the book

disappear from the Mediterranean, including the Adriatic and Ionian Seas. Despite the recent and still ongoing process of exclusive economic zones proclamation or delimitation, not all States bordering the Adriatic or Ionian Seas have proclaimed an exclusive economic zone or have implemented their exclusive economic zone legislation, similarly as within the wider Mediterranean. An evolving situation exists as regards the nature and extent of coastal zones in the Adriatic and Ionian Seas. The present picture is the following.

On 5 February 2021, the Croatian Parliament adopted a Decision whereby it proclaimed an exclusive economic zone in the Adriatic Sea.[25] This replaces the previous (2003 and 2004) decisions establishing an ecological and fishery protection zone. The outer limit of the Croatian exclusive economic zone temporarily follows the delimitation line established under the 1968 Agreement between Italy and the former Yugoslavia[26] as well as the continuation of the provisional delimitation line provisionally defined by the 2002 Protocol between Croatia and the former Yugoslavia (now Montenegro).

Italy has adopted Law 14 June 2021, No. 91, on the creation of an exclusive economic zone.[27] However, such law provides that the Italian exclusive economic zone will, in fact, be established by a subsequent decree to be adopted by the government. The outer limits of the zone will be determined by agreements between Italy and the adjacent or opposite States concerned. Pending the conclusion of such agreements, the outer limits "are established with a view to not jeopardizing or hampering the final agreements" (Art. 1, para. 3). As the implementing decree has not yet been adopted, the legal condition of the waters located on the Italian side of the Adriatic and Ionian Seas still consists of a 12-n.m. territorial sea followed by an area of high seas.[28]

According to the legislation of Montenegro (Law of 26 December 2007), the regime of the exclusive economic zone shall apply from the date of the decision of the Assembly to declare such zone (Art. 45). Such a decision has not yet been taken.

It does not seem that Albania has claimed an exclusive economic zone so far.

Greece has not proclaimed an exclusive economic zone yet either. However, it has many times declared that it reserves the right to do so whenever it deems it

25 Text available at www.un.org/depts/los/LEGISLATIONANDTREATIES/PDFFILES/DecisionEEZRepublicofCroatia.pdf. For a general comment on the recent process of extension of coastal States jurisdiction, see Bickl, EEZ in the Adriatic. Challenges and Opportunities in a Semi-Enclosed Sea, *The NCLOS Blog*, Posted on 22 December 2020, available at site.uit.no/nclos/2020/12/22/eezs-in-the-adriatic-challenges-and-opportunities-in-a-semi-enclosed-sea/.

26 See Figure 1.8.

27 See Cataldi, The Italian Law Authorizing the Creation of an Exclusive Economic Zone, in *Italian Yearbook of International Law*, 2021, p. 29; Scovazzi, The Italian Exclusive Economic Zone, in *Questions of International Law*, 2022, p. 39.

28 An ecological protection zone has been established by Italy under Law 8 February 2006, No. 61, and Decree 27 October 2011, No. 209, only as regards the Ligurian and Tyrrhenian Seas.

appropriate. The already mentioned Agreement of delimitation of future maritime zones, concluded in 2020 by Greece and Italy, goes in this direction.

It, thus, appears that several Adriatic or Ionian coastal States that are in a position to do so[29] are moving towards the establishment of an exclusive economic zone. Despite the many unsettled boundaries, there is no doubt that Mediterranean States are entitled to establish exclusive economic zones whenever they wish.[30] International law allows any coastal State to establish an exclusive economic zone, including those States that border an enclosed or semi-enclosed sea, provided that maritime boundaries are not unilaterally imposed by one State on its adjacent or opposite neighbours.[31]

The legal implications of such a situation are noteworthy. On one hand, there are still substantial areas beyond limits of national jurisdiction in the Adriatic and Ionian Seas, whereby the high seas regime is, therefore, still applicable. On the other hand, such high seas area are potential or future exclusive economic zones awaiting proclamation or delimitation.[32] It is likely that such transitional situation will change in the near future.[33]

A question that has arisen in the past in relation to the process of extension of coastal State jurisdiction in the Mediterranean Sea, including the Adriatic and Ionian Seas, has been whether, taking into account that the so-called Barcelona System in principle applies also to the high seas and having in mind its evolving character,

29 For geographical and legal reasons, Bosnia and Herzegovina and Slovenia are not in a position to establish an exclusive economic zone. Slovenia proclaimed in 2005 a zone of ecological protection (whose provisional limits completely overlapped with part of the Croatian ecological and fishery protection zone) but has repealed the said proclamation in 2018, following the award of the arbitral tribunal in 2017, according to which Slovenia is not entitled to a continental shelf or zones of jurisdiction. See Permanent Court of Arbitration, Case No. 2012–04 in the Matter of An Arbitration under the Arbitration Agreement between the Government of the Republic of Croatia and the Government of the Republic of Slovenia, signed on 4 November 2009, Final Award, 29 June 2017, available at pcacases.com/web/sendAttach/2172.

30 In fact, exclusive economic zones have been established in other enclosed or semi-enclosed seas, such as the Baltic Sea, the Caribbean Sea, and the Black Sea.

31 As remarked by the International Court of Justice in the judgment of 18 December 1951 on the *Fisheries* case (United Kingdom v. Norway), "the delimitation of sea areas has always an international aspect; it cannot be dependent merely upon the will of the coastal State as expressed in its municipal law. Although it is true that the act of delimitation is necessarily a unilateral act, because only the coastal State is competent to undertake it, the validity of the delimitation with regard to other States depends upon international law" (International Court of Justice, *Reports of Judgments, Advisory Opinions and Orders,* 1951, p. 20).

32 See Grbec, *op. cit.*, Chapter 3.1, and Treves, *Potential Exclusive Economic Zones in the Mediterranean,* Paper Delivered at the 11th Mediterranean Research Meeting, Florence and Montecatini Terme, 24–27 March 2010, p. 4.

33 With regard to the present legal status of the waters beyond the limits of the territorial sea in the Mediterranean Sea, including the Adriatic and Ionian Seas, reference should be made to the fact that, despite the current process of extension of jurisdiction in the mentioned seas, the jurisdictional status of the Mediterranean Sea still differs from others enclosed or semi-enclosed seas. A significant percentage of the Mediterranean waters are still high seas and are, therefore, beyond the jurisdiction of coastal States. See discussion in Grbec, *op. cit.*, Chapter 3, and Bickl, *op. cit.*

how much would the extension of jurisdiction by coastal States actually increase their prescriptive and enforcement powers in the field of the protection and preservation of the marine environment. This question has been particularly interesting in light of the already existing continental shelf regime and of the limitations provided by the UNCLOS on the regulation of navigation by a coastal State in its exclusive economic zone.

This was due to the fact that certain sources of pollution would not be affected for purely geographical reasons (e.g., land-based pollution), while, as stated, with regard to pollution from sea-bed activities, the prescriptive and enforcement powers of Mediterranean coastal States are already available under the continental shelf regime.[34] Some authors interestingly argued that the added value of establishing exclusive economic zones or ecological zones in the Mediterranean would mainly relate to the protection and preservation of wildlife and biodiversity – a matter not so extensively regulated by UNCLOS.[35] It seems, however, necessary not to underestimate the limited, but nonetheless important, "functional jurisdiction", including both prescriptive and enforcement rights, that the coastal State can exercise in its exclusive economic zone in the field of protection and preservation of the marine environment, particularly with regard to the prevention of ship-source pollution and preservation of biodiversity.[36]

An important power given to the coastal State in its exclusive economic zone is to be found in Art. 211, para. 6, UNCLOS, which provides that a coastal State may, where existing international rules are inadequate and subject to the approval by the IMO, establish an area within its exclusive economic zone for which it may prescribe laws for the prevention of pollution from vessels "implementing such international rules and standards or navigational practices as are made applicable, through the [IMO] for special areas", or in certain cases even other national measures approved by the IMO.[37] It should be noted, however, that there seem to be no cases of "specially protected areas" established solely under the complicated provisions of Art. 211, para. 6, UNCLOS. A better option in the Adriatic and Ionian Seas seems to include, as discussed further in this study, the designation of Particularly Sensitive Sea Areas (PSSAs) or Specially Protected Areas of Mediterranean Importance (SPAMIs), based on the relevant IMO guidelines or the provisions of

34 Arts. 208, para. 1, and 214 UNCLOS.

35 Art. 194, para. 5, UNCLOS provides that "[t]he measures taken in accordance with this Part [Part XII] shall include those necessary to protect and preserve rare or fragile ecosystems as well as the habitat of depleted, threatened or endangered species and other forms of marine life". Regarding the protection of biodiversity, see also Art. 61, para. 4, UNCLOS.

36 Worthy of mention are also the enforcement powers provided to the coastal State by Art. 220 UNCLOS in cases where there is a "serious damage or threat of serious damage" to the marine environment by a vessel navigating in the coastal States' exclusive economic zone (or, alternatively, ecological protection zone). Such powers may include measures such as "physical inspection" and ultimately the "institution of proceedings" and "detention" of the violating vessel. See Art. 220, paras. 3–6, UNCLOS.

37 See Churchill and Lowe, *The Law of the Sea*, Manchester, 1999, p. 395.

the relevant protocol to the Barcelona Convention.[38] However, neither the designation nor the implementation of the regime of a potential PSSA or that of a SPAMI depends upon the extension of coastal State jurisdiction, that is, upon the proclamation of an exclusive economic zone or *sui generis* zone of jurisdiction.

Reference should also be made to the fact that the extension of jurisdiction by a European Union member State automatically entails the extension of the European Union legal order in that part of the sea,[39] which seems to be particularly relevant for current and future European Union member States in the Adriatic and Ionian Seas.[40]

In conclusion, far from being the manifestation of excessive unilateralism, the establishment of a consistent jurisdictional framework in the form of exclusive economic zones and the disappearance of the high seas could lead to the strengthening of regional cooperation in the Mediterranean Sea, with special regard to the aim of managing living resources and addressing environmental concerns. It is difficult to see how the future Mediterranean governance could be built on the vacuum determined by the persistence of high seas areas or on the confusion created by different kinds of coastal zones.[41] The extension of coastal States' jurisdiction will entail the responsibility of such States to apply to a broader extent of waters their legislation for the protection of the marine environment and the sustainable development of marine living resources, including, in the case of European Union member States, the European Union legislation.

In particular, the present trend towards the establishment of exclusive economic zones could become an incentive towards the adoption of a coherent and coordinated Mediterranean network of marine protected areas and other effective area-based conservation measures. The UNCLOS and the other treaties applicable at the world or regional level promote the establishment of protected areas and other effective area-based conservation measures in any kind of marine spaces, irrespective of their legal condition. In doing so, there is a need to comply with the UNCLOS and customary international law and to take into account that the regime applicable in coastal areas and, in particular, the rights that are granted to the coastal States vary in accordance with the legal condition of the waters where

38 Both types of area-based protection tools are analyzed further in this book.

39 See Churchill, The European Union and the Challenges of Marine Governance: From Sectoral Response to Integrated Policy? in Vidas and Schei (eds.), *The World Ocean in Globalisation: Climate Change, Sustainable Fisheries, Biodiversity, Shipping, Regional Issues*, Leiden and Boston, 2011, p. 412. The precise extent of such powers depends, however, on the nature of the proclaimed zone (e.g., exclusive economic zone, fisheries protection zone, ecological protection zone).

40 For further discussion see Chapter 4 of this book. Adriatic States may, in this regard, be conveniently divided between European Union members States (Croatia, Italy, Slovenia, and Greece) and candidate States (Albania, Bosnia and Herzegovina, Montenegro, and, within the EUSAIR, also Serbia and North Macedonia).

41 See Scovazzi, International Cooperation as regards Protection of the Environment and Fisheries in the Mediterranean Sea, in *Anuario de Derecho Internacional*, 2018, p. 304.

the protected area is established (marine internal waters, territorial sea, exclusive economic zone, continental shelf).[42]

1.4. The Mediterranean, Adriatic, and Ionian Seas as Juridically Enclosed or Semi-enclosed Seas

A final consideration when discussing the juridical status and the relation between the Mediterranean and its sub-seas may be on whether the Adriatic and Ionian Seas, as sub-seas of the wider Mediterranean Sea, form also separate juridical enclosed or semi-enclosed sea on the basis of the provisions of Part IX UNCLOS ("Enclosed or semi-enclosed seas").[43]

It has been argued that States bordering enclosed and semi-enclosed seas are under at least a *bona fide* obligation to exercise their rights and perform their duties under UNCLOS in the light of the general duty of cooperation embodied in Part IX UNCLOS.[44] Such assertion is, *inter alia*, based on the introductory element of Art. 123 UNCLOS, which seems to provide a general good faith obligation for States bordering enclosed or semi-enclosed seas to endeavour to cooperate in the exercise of all their rights and in the performance of all their duties under UNCLOS. It is suggested that although such general obligation is not enforceable *per se*, it affects the way in which other provisions of the UNCLOS should be interpreted and applied by States bordering enclosed or semi-enclosed seas.[45]

In accordance with the opinion discussed by various authors,[46] it is clear that at least both the Mediterranean and the Adriatic Seas are classified, on the basis of Part IX UNCLOS (Art. 122),[47] as legal enclosed or semi-enclosed seas. Both seas are, in fact, surrounded by more than one State; both are linked to another sea or ocean through a narrow outlet (or outlets)[48]; and, should proclamations of exclusive economic zones or other zones of jurisdiction occur, in both cases their surface would not just primarily, but entirely, be made up of exclusive economic zones or other jurisdictional zones of the surrounding States.

42 See Caffio, La cooperazione marittima tra i paesi adriatici, in *Rivista Marittima*, October 2021, p. 2.

43 See Sersic, The Adriatic Sea: Semi-enclosed Sea in a Semi-Enclosed Sea, in Cataldi (ed.), *The Mediterranean and the Law of the Sea at the Dawn of the 21st Century*, Bruxelles, 2002, p. 329.

44 See discussion in Grbec, *op. cit.*, Chapter 2.

45 *Ibid.*

46 See Leanza, *op. cit.*, p. 1. See also Škrk, Exclusive Economic Zones in Enclosed or Semi-Enclosed Sea, in Vukas (ed.), *The Legal Regime of Enclosed or Semi-Enclosed Seas: The Particular Case of the Mediterranean, in Contributions to the Study of Comparative and International Law*, Zagreb, 1988, p. 164.

47 "For the purposes of this Convention [UNCLOS], enclosed or semi-enclosed sea means a gulf, basin or sea surrounded by two or more States and connected to another sea or the ocean by a narrow outlet or consisting entirely or primarily of the territorial seas and exclusive economic zones of two or more coastal States".

48 Even if one adopts the position that the approximately 40-n.m. wide Channel of Otranto does not qualify as a "narrow outlet", the Adriatic Sea still fulfils the second alternative requirement of Art. 122 of UNCLOS.

Although the separate juridical status of the Ionian Sea in relation with Part IX UNCLOS may not have been discussed to such extent as has been the case with the Mediterranean and Adriatic Seas, it is possible to put forward the argument that also the Ionian Sea, similarly as the Adriatic Sea (or together with the Adriatic Sea), can be qualified as a separate juridical enclosed or semi-enclosed sea. In fact, also the Ionian Sea fulfils the broad legal and geographical criteria provided by Art. 122 UNCLOS. It is beyond any doubt also a "gulf, basin or sea surrounded by two or more States and consisting entirely or primarily of the territorial seas and exclusive economic zones of two or more coastal States".

The classification of the Mediterranean and the Adriatic Seas (and Ionian Sea) as juridical enclosed or semi-enclosed seas based on Part IX UNCLOS does not stem exclusively from the fulfilment of the prevalently geographical criteria embodied in Art. 122 UNCLOS. This fact may also be implied by the already established or envisaged cooperation amongst States bordering the Mediterranean and the Adriatic Seas (and Ionian Sea), which in certain cases even predated the adoption of the UNCLOS.[49]

Furthermore, it seems reasonable that in the case of a sub-sea forming part of a wider juridical enclosed or semi-enclosed sea, an important factor in its classification, in addition to the requirements embodied in Art. 122 UNCLOS, is also the level of autonomy that a certain sub-sea shows in relation to the principal sea.[50]

Having established that the Mediterranean, Adriatic, and Ionian Seas are juridical enclosed or semi-enclosed seas, it is worth reiterating that Art. 123 UNCLOS, titled "Cooperation of States bordering enclosed or semi-enclosed seas" provides as follows:

> States bordering an enclosed or semi-enclosed sea should cooperate with each other in the exercise of their rights and in the performance of their duties under this Convention. To this end they shall endeavour, directly or through an appropriate regional organization:
>
> (a) to coordinate the management, conservation, exploration and exploitation of the living resources of the sea;
> (b) to coordinate the implementation of their rights and duties with respect to the protection and preservation of the marine environment;
> (c) to coordinate their scientific research policies and undertake where appropriate joint programmes of scientific research in the area;
> (d) to invite, as appropriate, other interested States or international organizations to cooperate with them in furtherance of the provisions of this article.

49 See, for example, the adoption of the MAP in 1975 and the conclusion of the 1974 Belgrade Agreement between Italy and the former Yugoslavia.

50 See Leanza, *op. cit.*, p. 13. It is not completely clear what is the appropriate test to determine whether a certain sub-sea shows the necessary level of autonomy. It is suggested that a useful consideration, in addition to the already established level of cooperation among the bordering States, is whether a sub-sea is forming a separate management (functional) sub-region within the wider marine region.

It can thus be concluded that States bordering the same enclosed or semi-enclosed sea are under a good faith obligation to establish among themselves closer means of cooperation than those applying in other seas.

Noteworthy is the fact that the Joint Declaration on the Trilateral Cooperation in the North Adriatic, signed in Ljubljana on 21 April 2021 by the Ministers of Foreign Affairs of Croatia, Italy, and Slovenia stresses in this regard that

> the Adriatic Sea is a semi-enclosed sea with a unique coastal landscape and an ecosystem of marine biodiversity that the coastal states have a shared responsibility to protect and promote. Bearing in mind the cooperation of states bordering semi-enclosed seas as enshrined in the [UNCLOS], they [Ministers] agreed on the importance of joint addressing the present and future challenges to the protection of the Adriatic Sea and the sustainability of its resources, such as long-term impacts of pollution, climate change and sea level rise, and loss of biodiversity.[51]

1.5. Conclusive Summary

An important consideration with regard to the juridical status of the Adriatic and Ionian Seas is that once all coastal States will proclaim an exclusive economic zone – namely Albania, Italy, Greece, and Montenegro, in addition to Croatia, which has already proclaimed a full exclusive economic zone in 2021 – the high seas will disappear from the Adriatic and Ionian Seas. The present trend towards the establishment of exclusive economic zones could become an incentive towards the adoption of a coherent and coordinated Mediterranean – and Adriatic and Ionian – network of marine protected areas and other effective area-based conservation measures. The UNCLOS and other treaties applicable at the world or regional level promote the establishment of marine protected areas and other effective area-based conservation measures in any kind of marine spaces, irrespective of their legal condition. In doing so, there is a need to comply with the UNCLOS and customary international law and to take into account that the regime applicable in coastal areas and, in particular, the rights that are granted to coastal States vary in accordance with the legal condition of the waters where the marine protected area is established (internal waters, territorial sea, exclusive economic zone, continental shelf). The extension of jurisdiction by a European Union member State (e.g., Croatia) automatically entails the extension of the European Union legal order and policies on that part of the sea (as it happened with the Croatian exclusive economic zone). Such order includes, as further discussed in other chapters of this work, *inter alia*, the European Union Integrated Maritime Policy (IMP), having the European Union Marine Strategy Framework Directive (MSFD) as its environmental pillar,

51 Text available at www.mvep.hr/files/file/2021/Joint-Declaration-on-the-Trilateral-Cooperation-in-the-North-Adriatic.pdf.

the Birds and Habitats Directives with their NATURA 2000 Network of protected areas and Marine Spatial Planning (MSP) as one of the most important cross-sectoral policies. The MSFD clearly identifies the Adriatic Sea as a separate management sub-region (eco-region) within the wider Mediterranean region, while the Ionian Sea forms a separate sub-region, together with the Central Mediterranean. Both the Adriatic and Ionian Seas also qualify as juridical 'enclosed or semi-enclosed seas' based on the provisions of Part IX UNCLOS. Accordingly, coastal States are under a good faith obligation to establish among themselves closer means of cooperation than those applying in other marine spaces. Currently, all States bordering the Adriatic and Ionian Seas are parties to the UNCLOS.

2 The Global Legal Basis for Marine Area-based Conservation

Tullio Scovazzi

2.1. The Domestic and International Dimension of Marine Protected Areas

This chapter elaborates on the main policy and legal instruments that have been adopted at the global level and are specifically relevant for the subject of marine protected areas (MPAs) and other effective area-based conservation measures (OECMs).

If a protected area is located, totally or partially, in marine waters or sea-bed, it is considered an MPA.[1] Depending on the situation, MPAs could include lagoons, estuaries, subtidal aquatic beds (kelp beds, seagrass beds, tropical marine meadows), coral reefs, intertidal muds, sand or salt flats and marshes, deep-water coral reefs, deep-water vents, open ocean habitats, as well as different kinds of sea-bed (continental shelf, continental slope, continental rise, deep ocean floor, oceanic ridges).

While the UNCLOS does not specifically mention MPAs, only implicitly referring to them in Art. 194, para. 5,[2] there is solid support for the proposition that the establishment of such areas is included in the obligation arising from customary international law to preserve and protect the marine environment. In this regard, it is easy to find that a general practice has developed and is accepted as law by States, as this chapter is intended to show.

MPAs are usually established at the national level on the basis of the domestic legislation of the State concerned and according to a heterogeneous and not always consistent terminology (park, reserve, sanctuary, monument, no-take zone, closed area, seascape, etc.). Different authorities can be in charge of their institution and

1 For more elaboration on the concept of marine protected area, see para. 2.3.C.a.

2 On marine protected areas, see Scovazzi (ed.), *Marine Specially Protected Areas – The General Aspects and the Mediterranean Regional System*, The Hague, 1999; Scovazzi, Marine Protected Areas in Waters beyond National Jurisdiction, in Ribeiro (ed.), *30 Years after the Signature of the United Nations Convention on the Law of the Sea*, Coimbra, 2014, p. 209; Scovazzi and Tani, Problems Posed by Marine Protected Areas Having a Transboundary Character, in Mackelworth (ed.), *Marine Transboundary Conservation and Protected Areas*, London, 2016, p. 17; Duan, *The International Legal Regime relating to Marine Protected Areas in Areas beyond National Jurisdiction: Identifying and Addressing Gaps*, Leiden, 2022.

DOI: 10.4324/9781003367963-2

management (e.g., national or regional authorities) and different kinds of protection measures can be envisaged within them (e.g., interdictions or restrictions relating to discharge or dumping of waste, passage or anchoring of ships, exploitation of biological or mineral resources, scientific research). In this regard, States are entitled to exercise a broad margin of discretion that is the manifestation of their sovereignty.

However, MPAs also have an international dimension, especially where they have a transboundary character or are intended to be included in networks that occur in semi-enclosed seas bordered by several countries. This is why the subject of MPAs is also regulated by customary international law as well as by a number of international treaties that set forth rights and obligations for the States parties and have been concluded at different levels: global, regional, and sub-regional. An additional level is given by the legislation (regulations and directives) enacted by the European Union, applying to the 27 States that are members of this international organization.

While relatively recent, the notion of OECMs goes in the same direction, being it is understood as an additional opportunity, different from the establishment of an MPA, to achieve the objective of long-term conservation.[3]

2.2. The Main Global Policy Instruments

A number of international policy instruments call for action towards the establishment of MPAs and the adoption of OECMs.

According to Agenda 21, the action programme for the 21st century adopted in 1992 in Rio de Janeiro by the United Nations Conference on Environment and Development, States, acting individually, bilaterally, regionally or multilaterally and within the framework of the International Maritime Organization (IMO) and other relevant international organizations, should assess the need for additional measures to address degradation of the marine environment. Agenda 21 stresses the importance of protecting and restoring endangered marine species as well as preserving habitats and other ecologically sensitive areas, both on the high seas and in the zones under national jurisdiction. In particular:

> States commit themselves to the conservation and the sustainable use of marine living resources on the high seas. To this end, it is necessary to: . . .
>
> e) Protect and restore marine species;
> f) Preserve habitats and other ecologically sensitive areas.
>
> (para. 17.46)

> States should identify marine ecosystems exhibiting high levels of biodiversity and productivity and other critical habitat areas and provide necessary limitations on use in these areas, through, *inter alia*, designation of protected areas
>
> (para. 17.86)

3 See more elaboration on this concept in para. 2.3.C.e.

The Plan of Implementation of the World Summit on Sustainable Development (Johannesburg, 2002) confirms the need to promote the conservation and management of the oceans and "maintain the productivity and biodiversity of important and vulnerable marine and coastal areas, including in areas within and beyond national jurisdiction" (para. 32, a). To achieve this aim, the Plan puts forward the objective of a representative network of marine protected areas and the deadline of 2012 for its achievement. States are invited to

> develop and facilitate the use of diverse approaches and tools, including . . . the establishment of marine protected areas consistent with international law and based on scientific information, including representative networks by 2012 and time/area closures for the protection of nursery grounds and periods.
>
> (para. 32, c)

In Johannesburg, the concept of a "network" of MPAs gained further acknowledgement as an important objective. It was recognized that, wherever appropriate, MPAs should not be established in isolation but within a logical and integrated frame. Networks offer advantages in comparison to individual MPAs because they can encompass representative examples of regional biodiversity as well as an adequate number and spread of critical habitats. This is especially useful for migratory species, such as cetaceans, and for straddling stocks moving between waters subject to the jurisdiction of neighboring countries as well as beyond national jurisdiction. Moreover, networks can contribute to protection, conservation or sustainable development goals in at least other two ways, fostering an integrated management of marine and coastal areas: from a social perspective, they can help resolve and manage conflicts in the use of natural resources; and, from an economic perspective, they can facilitate the efficient use of human and financial resources within a given region.[4]

However, as States realized that the objective to establish a representative network of MPAs by the year 2012 could not be achieved, they shifted the envisaged deadline to 2020 and set forth the ratio of 10 per cent of marine and coastal areas to be included in systems of protected areas. According to *The Future We Want*, which is the outcome document of the United Nations Conference on Sustainable Development, held in Rio de Janeiro in 2012 (Rio+20 Conference),[5] States

> reaffirm the importance of area-based conservation measures, including marine protected areas, consistent with international law and based on best available scientific information, as a tool for conservation of biological diversity and sustainable use of its components . . . [and] note decision X/2 of the tenth meeting of the Conference of the Parties to the Convention on

4 See IUCN World Commission on Protected Areas (IUCN-WCPA), *Establishing Marine Protected Area Networks – Making it Happen*, Washington, 2008.

5 Doc. A/RES/66/288 of 11 September 2012.

Biological Diversity, held in Nagoya, Japan, from 18 to 29 October 2010, that, by 2020, 10 per cent of coastal and marine areas, especially areas of particular importance for biodiversity and ecosystem services, are to be conserved through effectively and equitably managed, ecologically representative and well-connected systems of protected areas and other effective area-based conservation measures.

(para. 177)[6]

On 25 September 2015, at the outcome of the United Nations summit for the post-2015 development agenda, the United Nations General Assembly adopted Resolution 70/1, *Transforming Our World: The 2030 Agenda for Sustainable Development*, which defines 17 Sustainable Development Goals (SDGs). Within SDG 14 ("Conserve and sustainably use the oceans, seas and marine resources for sustainable development"), Goal 14.5 provides for an invitation specifically directed at the establishment of MPAs and the adoption of OECMs:

By 2020, conserve at least 10 per cent of coastal and marine areas, consistent with national and international law and based on the best available scientific information.

The last United Nations General Assembly Resolution on Oceans and the Law of the Sea (Resolution 77/248 of 30 December 2022) reaffirms the invitation to make use of area-based management tools, including MPAs, and recalls the 10 per cent commitment. In particular, the General Assembly

Calls upon States to strengthen, in a manner consistent with international law, in particular the Convention, the conservation and management of marine biodiversity and ecosystems, and national policies in relation to area-based management tools, including marine protected areas (para. 282); Recalls that, in "The future we want", States reaffirmed the importance of area-based conservation measures, including marine protected areas, consistent with international law and based on best available scientific information, as a tool for conservation of biological diversity and sustainable use of its components, and noted decision X/2 of the tenth meeting of the Conference of the Parties to the Convention on Biological Diversity, that by 2020, 10 per cent of coastal and marine areas, especially areas of particular importance for biodiversity and ecosystem services, are to be conserved through effectively and equitably managed, ecologically representative and well-connected systems of protected areas and other effective area-based conservation measures;

(para. 283)

6 Reference is made to Target 11 of the Annex to Decision X/2 adopted in 2010 by the Conference of the parties to the CBD (Strategic Plan for Biodiversity 2011–2020 and the Aichi Biodiversity Targets).

> Encourages States, in this regard, to further progress towards the establishment of marine protected areas, including representative networks, and calls upon States to further consider options to identify and protect ecologically or biologically significant areas, consistent with international law and on the basis of the best available scientific information.
>
> (para. 284)

2.3. The Main Global Legal Instruments

A review of the main treaties of global scope of application that are relevant for the subject of MPAs in the Mediterranean Sea will be made hereunder. Other instruments could be added, such as the Convention on Wetlands of International Importance Especially as Waterfowl Habitat (Ramsar, 1971)[7] and the Man and the Biosphere Programme, established in 1971 by the United Nations Organization for Education, Science and Culture (UNESCO).[8] However, they seem of limited importance for the purposes of this study.

A. The United Nations Convention on the Law of the Sea

Many rules of customary international law are reflected in the provisions of the UNCLOS, the treaty of codification that today regulates all aspects of international law of the sea. It entered into force on 16 November 1994 and is today binding for 168 parties. Most Mediterranean States are parties to the UNCLOS, with the exception of Israel, Libya, Syria and Turkey. The European Union is also a party to it.

The UNCLOS, moving from the assumption that "the problems of the ocean space are closely interrelated", includes among its objectives the equitable and efficient utilization of the resources of oceans and seas, the conservation of their living resources and "the study, protection and preservation of the marine environment" (Preamble). According to Art. 192:

> States have the obligation to protect and preserve the marine environment.

This general provision also corresponds to a customary rule of international law. Part XII of the UNCLOS ("Protection and preservation of the marine

7 Wetlands are defined by the convention as

> areas of marsh, fen, peatland or water, whether natural or artificial, permanent or temporary, with water that is static of flowing, fresh, brackish or salt, including areas of marine water the depth of which at low tide does not exceed six metres.
>
> (Art. 1, para. 1)

8 The world network of biosphere reserves includes "areas of terrestrial and coastal-marine ecosystems which are internationally recognized for promoting and demonstrating a balanced relationship between people and nature". They are used for testing interdisciplinary approaches to understanding and managing changes and interactions between social and ecological systems, including conflict prevention and management of biodiversity.

environment") specifies the obligations that bind States at both the global and the regional level with respect to different sources of marine pollution (from land-based sources, from seabed activities, from dumping, from vessels, from the atmosphere).[9]

MPAs are implicitly referred to in Art. 194, para. 5, UNCLOS, which includes among the measures for the protection and preservation of the marine environment "those necessary to protect and preserve rare or fragile ecosystems as well as the habitat of depleted, threatened or endangered species and other forms of marine life".[10] This provision has a general scope of application. It covers any kind of rare or fragile marine ecosystems, including their living and non-living components, as well as any kind of depleted, threatened or endangered species, irrespective of the legal condition of the waters or seabed where they are located (marine internal waters, territorial sea, exclusive economic zone, continental shelf, high seas, seabed beyond national jurisdiction). It goes without saying that the typical, even if not the only, measure to protect such ecosystems and species is the establishment of an MPA.

Although for geographical reasons the matter may be of limited relevance for the Mediterranean Sea,[11] an intergovernmental conference is today taking place, as convened by United Nations General Assembly Resolution 72/249 of 24 December 2017, to address the question of conservation and sustainable use of marine biological diversity in areas beyond national jurisdiction. "Measures such as area-based management tools, including marine protected areas" are among the main topics being discussed by the conference, with a view to developing an international legally binding instrument under the UNCLOS, probably a third UNCLOS implementation agreement.[12]

Rules of international law of the sea on the legal regime of different marine spaces and the activities that are carried out therein must be taken into consideration in the process for the establishment of MPAs and the determination of the measures applicable therein. In this regard, the UNCLOS provisions also reflect customary international law. The rules applying to marine waters subject to different regimes are the following.

9 Notably, pollution from noise is missing.

10 Rare or fragile marine ecosystems present various characteristics and are found in areas which have different legal conditions. While wetlands, lagoons or estuaries are located along the coastal belt, other kinds of ecosystems, such as seamounts, hydrothermal vents or submarine canyons, are frequently found at a certain distance from the coast, including in areas located beyond the limits of national jurisdiction.

11 As already remarked in Chapter 1, when all the Mediterranean coastal States establish their exclusive economic zones, no area in the Mediterranean Sea will be located beyond national jurisdiction.

12 For the revised draft text of an agreement see doc. A/CONF.232/2020/3 of 18 November 2019 and for the present developments in the negotiations see the statement by the President of the conference in doc. A/CONF.232/2022/9 of 14 September 2022.

a. Internal Maritime Waters

The internal marine waters are located on the land-ward side of the low-water line, which is the normal baseline of the territorial sea, or on the land-ward side of the straight baselines from which, in certain cases (such as bays, deep indentations or fringes of islands in the immediate vicinity of the coast), the territorial sea can be measured.

In the internal maritime waters, the coastal State exercises full sovereignty and is accordingly entitled also to establish marine protected areas.

b. Territorial Sea

Within the 12-n.m. territorial sea, which includes the seabed and its subsoil, the coastal State is granted sovereignty and is entitled to establish MPAs. However, the coastal State may not hamper the innocent passage through its territorial sea of ships flying the flag of other States.[13] It follows that the measures associated with the establishment of a marine protected area in the territorial sea cannot be applied by the coastal State in a manner that would prevent the innocent passage of foreign ships.

The rule that foreign ships have the right to pass through the territorial sea does not necessarily mean that any such ship has the right to pass in any portion of the territorial sea without any regulation. Art. 22 UNCLOS provides that the coastal State, where necessary having regard to the safety of navigation and without discrimination, may require ships, in particular tankers, nuclear-powered ships and ships carrying nuclear or hazardous substances, to use certain designated lanes or traffic separation schemes.

c. Exclusive Economic Zone

Within the 200-n.m. exclusive economic zone, the coastal State has sovereign rights for the purpose of exploring and exploiting the natural resources of the water column, the seabed and subsoil, whether living or nonliving, and producing energy from the water, currents and winds. In addition, it has jurisdiction, with regard to the establishment of artificial islands, installations and structures, to marine scientific research as well as to the protection and preservation of the marine environment. All the other States enjoy some specified high seas freedoms related to maritime communications, namely the freedoms of navigation, overflight and laying of submarine cables and pipelines, as well as of other international lawful uses of the seas related to these freedoms.

As far as the living resources of the exclusive economic zone are concerned, the coastal State has two primary responsibilities: first, it is required to ensure, through proper conservation and management measures, that the resources are not endangered by overexploitation (Art. 61 UNCLOS); second, it is under the duty to promote the objective of their optimum utilization (Art. 62 UNCLOS), granting

13 Art. 19 UNCLOS explains the meaning of innocent passage and lists the activities that are incompatible with it.

to other interested States access to the surplus of resources where its capacity to harvest does not reach the total allowable catch.

It follows that the coastal State may well declare marine protected areas in its exclusive economic zone, as long as the measures enacted do not hamper the exercise by other States of their freedom of navigation and other freedoms and rights stated in the UNCLOS. Moreover, in view of the coastal State's duty to promote the optimum utilization of the living resources, the establishment of marine protected areas where fishing activities are prohibited could be subject to objection by other States, where not supported by sufficient scientific evidence.

Certain living resources are subject to specific rules. For example, Art. 65 UNCLOS provides that the coastal State or the competent international organization may prohibit, limit or regulate the exploitation of marine mammals more strictly than stated in the provisions of the UNCLOS relating to the exclusive economic zone. This means that MPAs for marine mammals may be established in the exclusive economic zone with a view to prohibiting on a permanent basis the hunting of these species, without any consideration of optimum utilization objectives.

The UNCLOS does not grant the coastal State the right to unilaterally adopt measures, such as the establishment of an MPA, which could interfere with freedom of navigation within its exclusive economic zone. However, under Art. 211, para. 6, the coastal State may request the competent international organization, that is the IMO, to ascertain the presence of the conditions for the establishment of a "clearly defined area" where special measures apply, due to oceanographical and ecological conditions, the need to protect its resources and the particular character of the traffic.[14]

d. Continental Shelf

Under the definition given by Art. 76 UNCLOS, the continental shelf of a coastal State comprises the seabed and subsoil of the submarine areas that extend beyond its territorial sea throughout the natural prolongation of its land territory to the outer edge of the continental margin, or to a distance of 200 n.m. from the baselines of the territorial sea, where the outer edge of the continental margin does not extend up to that distance. Due to the fact that in the Mediterranean Sea no point is located at a distance of more than 200 n.m. from the nearest land or island, all Mediterranean seabed beyond coastal States' territorial seas falls under the regime of the continental shelf and needs to be delimited by the States concerned.

The regime of MPAs on the continental shelf is equivalent, in principle, to the regime applicable to such areas within the waters of the exclusive economic zone. However, there is a need of a careful *mutatis mutandis* exercise, due to the different kinds of marine activities involved.[15]

14 So far, no coastal State has made use of Art. 211, para. 6, UNCLOS, probably because of the complexity of the procedure envisaged in this provision.

15 The laying of cables and pipelines is relevant for the continental shelf. Fishing is relevant in the case of sedentary species, as defined in Art. 77, para. 4, UNCLOS. However, the obligation of the coastal State to promote the optimum utilization does not apply to such resources.

e. High Seas

All parts of the sea that are not included in the exclusive economic zone, the territorial sea or the internal marine waters of a State constitute the high seas. On the high seas there is no coastal State by definition and no State may validly purport to subject any part of the high seas to its sovereignty.

The high seas are subject to a regime of freedom that encompasses different activities, such as navigation, overflight, laying of submarine cables and pipelines, construction of artificial islands and other installations, fishing or scientific research. According to customary international law, as reflected in the UNCLOS, these activities are to be exercised by all States with due regard for the interests of other States in their exercise of the freedom of the high seas (Art. 87, para. 2).

The high seas regime is based on the exclusive jurisdiction of any State over vessels to which it has granted its nationality and, consequently, fly its flag. Except in exceptional cases (piracy, hot pursuit), no State can impose its own jurisdiction over vessels flying the flag of other States. It follows that no State can unilaterally establish a marine protected area on the high seas and claim that ships flying a foreign flag abide by the relevant provisions. Regrettably, as not all the flag States exercise the due control on the activities carried out by the ships flying their flag, instances of so-called flags of convenience occur.

It would seem that the adoption of measures of environmental protection on the high seas are doomed to remain highly ineffective if such measures may only apply to the ships flying the flag of the enacting States while all other ships remain exempted from complying with them. However, it would be a mistake to think that the freedom of the high seas is always an insurmountable obstacle against the adoption of environmental measures therein, including the establishment of MPAs.

The interested States are free to establish an MPA on the high seas under a treaty that they conclude. It is true that a treaty does not create either obligations or rights for a third State without its consent and that a State which is not a party to a treaty establishing a marine protected area on the high seas is not bound by the provisions of such a treaty; nor are the ships flying its flag. In this connection, the main question is how to prevent conservation measures agreed upon by certain States from being frustrated by non-party States which enjoy the benefits of such measures without burdening themselves with the corresponding duties (so-called free-rider States).

However, it is also true that, as already outlined, the freedom of the high seas is not unlimited. It may be exercised only under the conditions laid down in the UNCLOS and in other rules of customary international law. States are under the general obligation to protect and preserve the marine environment everywhere in the sea, including by adopting measures to preserve and protect rare or fragile ecosystems as well as the habitat of depleted, threatened or endangered species and other forms of marine life (Art. 194, para. 5, UNCLOS). The freedom to fish on the high seas is qualified by the obligation to adopt measures for the conservation of living resources (Arts. 117 and 119 UNCLOS) as well as by the duty to cooperate in their management in order to maintain and restore both harvested and associated species (Art. 118 UNCLOS).

In connection with the principle of exclusive jurisdiction of the flag State over its vessels on the high seas, international law creates a corresponding obligation requiring the flag State to ensure a genuine link between it and the ship (Art. 91, para. 1, UNCLOS) and to "effectively" exercise such jurisdiction and control in administrative, technical and social matters (Art. 94, para. 1, UNCLOS). Every State is legally bound to ensure that its vessels on the high seas observe all applicable international rules concerning, *inter alia*, the prevention, reduction and control of marine pollution or the sustainable exploitation of marine resources.

Many multilateral agreements have been concluded to regulate fishing in high seas areas. There are instances of treaties that, in addressing the problem of free-rider States, put emphasis on the customary international law obligations that their behavior infringes.[16] The same could occur also in the field of protection of the marine environment. Where no other option is left, it could be justified to adopt lawful countermeasures to deter activities by third parties that undermine the conservation and management measures agreed upon by the States that have established an MPA on the high seas. For example, according to Art. 28, para. 2, of the Protocol concerning Specially Protected Areas and Biological Diversity in the Mediterranean,[17] the parties undertake to adopt appropriate measures, consistent with international law, to ensure that no one engages in any activity contrary to the principles or purposes of the protocol.

f. Seabed Beyond National Jurisdiction

The seabed beyond national jurisdiction (so-called Area) and its mineral resources are subject to the innovative regime of the common heritage of mankind (Part XI UNCLOS). For geographical reasons, this regime is not relevant for the Mediterranean Sea, a semi-enclosed sea of limited dimension.

In any case, MPAs also occur in the Area. Art. 145 of the UNCLOS requires that necessary measures be taken with respect to mining activities in the Area to ensure effective protection for the marine environment from harmful effects which may arise from such activities. In this regard, by a Decision of 26 July 2012, the Council of the International Seabed Authority (ISA) approved the environmental management plan for the *Clarion-Clipperton Zone*, including the designation, on a provisional basis, of a network of areas of particular environmental interest, as defined in an annex to the decision.[18] Moreover, according to Regulation 31, para. 6, of the 2013 Regulations on Prospecting and Exploration for Polymetallic

16 See Art. 8, paras. 3 and 4, of the Agreement for the Implementation of the Provisions of the United Nations Convention on the Law of the Sea of 10 December 1982 Relating to the Conservation and Management of Straddling Fish Stocks and Highly Migratory Fish Stocks (New York, 1995) and Recommendation 06–13 concerning trade measures, adopted in 2006 by the International Commission for the Conservation of Atlantic Tunas (ICCAT), established by the International Convention on the Conservation of Atlantic Tunas (Rio de Janeiro, 1966).

17 See Chapter 3.

18 Doc. ISBA/18/C/22 of 22 July 2012.

Nodules in the Area and Related Matters,[19] the ISA Council may establish "preservation reference zones", where "no mining shall occur to ensure representative and stable biota of the seabed in order to assess any changes in the biodiversity of the marine environment".

B. The International Convention for the Regulation of Whaling

The International Convention for the Regulation of Whaling (Washington, 1946) was adopted "recognizing the interest of the nations of the world in safeguarding for future generations the great natural resources represented by the whale stocks" (Preamble). Eighty-eight States are parties to it, including nine Mediterranean States.[20]

Under the Convention, the International Whaling Commission (IWC) may adopt regulations with respect to the conservation and utilization of whale resources, fixing, *inter alia*, "open and closed waters, including the designation of sanctuary areas" (Art. V, para. 1). Sanctuaries where commercial whaling is prohibited were established by the IWC in the Indian Ocean (1979) and the Southern Ocean (1994). They cover extremely large extents of high seas waters, where whaling for commercial purposes is prohibited.[21]

C. The UN Convention on Biological Diversity

The United Nations Convention on Biological Diversity (Rio de Janeiro, 1992; CBD) entered into force on 29 December 1993 and is now binding on 196 parties, including all the 23 Mediterranean States and the European Union. The parties affirm "that the conservation of biological diversity is a common concern of humankind" and declare themselves "concerned that biological diversity is being significantly reduced by certain human activities" (Preamble).

The CBD sets out a series of measures for *in-situ* conservation of biological diversity, defined as

> all variability among living organisms from all sources including, *inter alia*, terrestrial, marine and other aquatic ecosystems and the ecological complexes of which they are part; this includes diversity within species, between species and of ecosystems.
>
> (Art. 2)

Parties are required, as far as possible and as appropriate, to "establish a system of protected areas or areas where special measures need to be taken to conserve biological diversity" (Art. 8, *a*), to "develop, where necessary, guidelines for the selection, establishment and management of protected areas where special measures need to be taken to conserve biological diversity" (Art. 8, *b*) and to "regulate or

19 Doc. ISBA/19/C/17 of 22 July 2013.

20 Croatia, Cyprus, France, Israel, Italy, Monaco, Morocco, Slovenia, and the United Kingdom.

21 For the protection of cetaceans in the Mediterranean see also Chapters 3 and 6 of this book.

manage biological resources important for the conservation of biological diversity whether within or outside protected areas, with a view to ensuring their conservation and sustainable use" (Art. 8, *c*). The parties are bound to apply the convention "with respect to the marine environment consistently with the rights and obligations of States under the law of the sea" (Art. 22, para. 2).

a. The Notion of Marine Protected Area

The notion of MPA has today a solid conceptual background. Already in the late '80s, the International Union for the Conservation of Nature (IUCN) put forward a general definition of MPA, to be understood as

> any area of intertidal or subtidal terrain, together with its overlying water and associated flora, fauna, historical and cultural features, which has been reserved by law or other effective means to protect part or all of the enclosed environment.[22]

In 2008, the IUCN elaborated a revised definition of "protected area", as

> A clearly defined geographical space, recognized, dedicated and managed, through legal or other effective means, to achieve the long term conservation of nature with associated ecosystem services and cultural values.[23]

The CBD, that is a binding instrument today in force for many countries, provides for the following definition:

> "Protected area" means a geographically defined area which is designated or regulated and managed to achieve specific conservation objectives.
>
> (Art. 2)

22 IUCN General Assembly Resolution 17.38, 1988, para. 2, lett. b. According to the guidelines elaborated by IUCN in 1999, to be called a marine protected area, the total area of sea encompassed by it has to exceed the area of land within its boundaries, or the marine part of a large protected area has to be sufficient in size to be classified as a marine protected area in its own right. Moreover, the marine protected area (and accordingly the provisions for its management) should cover not only the seabed but also at least part of the water column above with its flora and fauna (see Kelleher, *Guidelines for Marine Protected Areas*, Gland-Cambridge, 1999).

23 See Dudley, *Guidelines for Applying Protected Areas Management Categories*, Gland, 2008; Day, Dudley, Hockings, Holmes, Laffoley, Stolton, Wells and Wenzel, *Guidelines for Applying Protected Areas Management Categories to Marine Protected Areas*, 2nd ed., Gland, 2019. The IUCN categories of protected areas are: "strict nature reserve" (protected area managed mainly for science); "wilderness area" (protected area managed mainly for wilderness protection); "national park" (protected area managed mainly for ecosystem protection and recreation); "natural monument" (protected area managed mainly for conservation of specific natural features); "habitat/species management area" (protected area managed mainly for conservation through active management); "protected landscape/seascape" (protected area managed mainly for landscape/seascape conservation and recreation); and "managed resource protected area" (protected area managed mainly for the sustainable use of natural ecosystems).

In 2002, the Subsidiary Body on Scientific, Technical and Technological Advice (SBSTTA) of the CBD recommended to the Conference of the parties the following definition, specifically applicable to marine and coastal areas:

> "Marine and coastal protected area" means any defined area within or adjacent to the marine environment, together with its overlying waters and associated flora, fauna, and historical and cultural features, which has been reserved by legislation or other effective means, including custom, with the effect that its marine and/or coastal biodiversity enjoys a higher level of protection than its surroundings.[24]

It thus appears that the notion of MPA, depending on the context, may relate to sites that are completely offshore, entirely coastal or a combination of the two. Three cumulative conditions are required to qualify a marine area as protected. It is any area of marine waters or seabed that (1) is delimited within precise boundaries, including, if appropriate, buffer zones; and (2) is afforded a stricter protection (3) for ensuring specific nature conservation objectives. Other characteristics that should preferably be met, also in order to avoid that marine protected area are established only on paper, are (4) a suitable size, location and design that deliver the conservation values; (5) a management plan or equivalent that addresses the need for conservation and achieves social and economic goals; and (6) the provision of financial resources and staff capacity to effectively implement the protection measures.[25]

In the case of a "network" of MPAs, the IUCN has put forward the following definition:

> An MPA network can be defined as a collection of individual MPAs or reserves operating cooperatively and synergistically, at various spatial scales, and with a range of protection levels designed to meet objectives that a single reserve cannot achieve.[26]

b. The Jakarta Mandate

Particularly relevant in the field of MPAs is the programme of action to implement the CBD in marine and coastal ecosystems (Jakarta Mandate on Marine and Coastal Biological Diversity) agreed in 1995 and reviewed and updated in 2004 by the Conference of the Parties (Decision VII/5).

The Jakarta Mandate provides guidance on integrated marine and coastal area management, the sustainable use of living resources and marine and coastal

24 Doc. UNEP/CBD/SBSTTA/8/9/Add.1, 27 November 2002.

25 IUCN-WCPA, *Applying IUCN's Global Conservation Standards to Marine Protected Areas (MPA)*, Gland, 2018, p. 2.

26 *Ibid.*, p. 12.

protected areas. Annex II ("Guidance for the Development of a National Marine and Coastal Biodiversity Management Framework") to Decision VII/5 recommends that the legal or customary frameworks of marine and coastal protected areas clearly identify prohibited activities contrary to the objectives of such areas as well as activities that are allowed, with clear restrictions or conditions to ensure that they will not be contrary to the objectives of the marine protected area, and a decision-making process for all other activities (para. 6). Under Appendix 3 ("Elements of a Marine and Coastal Biodiversity Management Framework") to the same decision, integrated networks of marine and coastal protected areas should consist of marine and coastal protected areas, where threats are managed for the purpose of biodiversity conservation or sustainable use and where extractive uses may be allowed, as well as of representative marine and coastal protected areas, where extractive uses are excluded and other significant human pressures are removed or minimized, to enable the integrity, structure and functioning of ecosystems to be maintained or recovered (para. 5).

In 2006, the Conference of the Parties (Decision VIII/24 on protected areas) recognized that

> marine protected areas are one of the essential tools to help achieve conservation and sustainable use of biodiversity in marine areas beyond the limits of national jurisdiction, and that they should be considered as part of a wider management framework consisting of a range of appropriate tools, consistent with international law and in the context of best available scientific information, the precautionary approach and ecosystem approach; and that application of tools beyond and within national jurisdiction need to be coherent, compatible and complementary and without prejudice to the rights and obligations of coastal States under international law.
>
> (para. 38)

c. The Ecologically or Biologically Significant Marine Areas

In 2008, the Conference of the parties adopted a set of "Scientific criteria for identifying ecologically or biologically significant marine areas in need of protection in open waters and deep-sea habitats" (Annex I to Decision IX/20; so-called CBD EBSA criteria), namely "uniqueness or rarity",[27] "special importance for life history stages of species",[28] "importance for threatened, endangered or declining

27 "Area contains either (i) unique ('the only one of its kind'), rare (occurs only in few locations) or endemic species, populations or communities, and/or (ii) unique, rare or distinct habitats or ecosystems, and/or (iii) unique or unusual geomorphological or oceanographic features".

28 "Areas that are required for a population to survive and thrive".

species and/or habitats",[29] "vulnerability, fragility, sensitivity, or slow recovery",[30] "biological productivity",[31] "biological diversity",[32] and "naturalness".[33]

The Conference also adopted the "Scientific guidance for selecting areas to establish a representative network of marine protected areas, including in open-ocean waters and deep-sea habitats" (Annex II). It lists the required network properties and components, namely "ecologically and biologically significant areas", "representativity", "connectivity", "replicated ecological features", and "adequate and viable sites". The Conference of the parties proposed "four initial steps to be considered in the development of representative networks of marine protected areas" (Annex III), namely "scientific identification of an initial set of ecologically or biologically significant areas", "develop/chose a biogeographic habitat and/or community classification scheme", "drawing upon steps 1 and 2 . . ., iteratively use qualitative and/or quantitative techniques to identify sites to include in a network" and "assess the adequacy and viability of the selected sites".

The Conference of CBD parties held in 2012 adopted Decision XI/17 which identifies in an Annex several areas meeting the EBSA criteria in the Western South Pacific region, in the Wider Caribbean and Western Mid-Atlantic region and in the Mediterranean region. For instance, in the Mediterranean region, 80 EBSAs are identified, including four in the Adriatic Sea, namely *Northern and central Adriatic*, *Polygon 1*, *Polygon 2*, and *Central western Adriatic*, and five in the Ionian Sea, namely *Ionian*, *Polygon 6*, *Eastern Ionian Sea*, *Lophelia and Madrepora in Gulf of Taranto*, and *Lophelia reefs*.

The Annex to Decision XII/22, adopted by the Conference of the parties held in 2014, provides the results of seven regional workshops on the description of areas meeting the scientific criteria for EBSAs. The workshop for the Mediterranean, held in Malaga in 2014, describes 15 EBSAs, including three located in the Adriatic and Ionian Seas (*Northern Adriatic*,[34] *Jabuka/Pomo Pit*[35] and *South Adriatic Ionian Strait*).[36]

29 "Area containing habitat for the survival of and recovery of endangered, threatened, declining species or area with significant assemblages of such species".

30 "Areas that contain a relatively high proportion of sensitive habitats, biotopes or species that are functionally fragile (highly susceptible to degradation or depletion by human activity or by natural events) or with slow recovery".

31 "Area containing species, populations or communities with comparatively higher natural biological productivity".

32 "Area contains comparatively higher diversity of ecosystems, habitats, communities, or species, or has higher genetic diversity".

33 "Area with a comparatively higher degree of naturalness as a result of the lack of or low level of human-induced disturbance or degradation".

34 "Part of the Northern Adriatic Basin, off the coasts of Italy, Slovenia and Croatia. The area is roughly delimited by the 9 m isobaths, encompassing the area above the straight line linking Ancona (Conero) and the island of Ilovik. The area is located in the northern part of the North Adriatic Sea Basin, with an average depth of 35 m and is strongly influenced by the Po river plume".

35 "The area encompassing three distinct, adjacent depressions, with maximum depths of ca. 270, respectively. The area extends 4.5 nautical miles from the 200 m isobath. The area encompassing the adjacent depressions, the Jabuka (or Pomo) Pit is situated in the Middle Adriatic Sea and has a maximum depth of 200–260 m".

36 "The area is located in the centre of the southern part of the Southern Adriatic basin and in the northern part of the Ionian Sea. It includes the deepest part of the Adriatic Sea on the western side and it encompasses a coastal area in Albania (Sazani Island and Karaburuni peninsula). It also covers the

The EBSAs criteria can provide to the interested States useful information on where marine protected areas could be established according to scientific evidence. They do not enter into the political and legal questions that are linked to creation of MPAs. As recalled by Decision X/29, adopted by the Conference of the parties held in 2012,

> the application of the ecologically or biologically significant areas (EBSAs) criteria is a scientific and technical exercise, that areas found to meet the criteria may require enhanced conservation and management measures, and that this can be achieved through a variety of means, including marine protected areas and impact assessments, and . . . the identification of ecologically or biologically significant areas and the selection of conservation and management measures is a matter for States and competent intergovernmental organizations, in accordance with international law, including the United Nations Convention on the Law of the Sea.[37]

As stressed by the representative of the European Union at the 15th Conference of the CBD parties,

> the identification of ecologically or biologically significant marine areas was a geographical, not a legal, process whose outcomes should continue to result from a scientific and technical exercise and should not be used to prejudge any issues of the sovereignty, sovereign rights or jurisdiction of coastal States or the rights of other States.[38]

d. The Aichi Targets and the Kunming-Montreal 2030 Global Targets

In 2010, the 10th Conference of the parties to the CBD held in Nagoya (Aichi prefecture) adopted the Strategic Plan for Biodiversity 2011–2020 (Decision X/2), with its 20 Aichi Biodiversity Targets. According to Target 11,

> By 2020, at least 17 per cent of terrestrial and inland water areas, and 10 per cent of coastal and marine areas, especially areas of particular importance for biodiversity and ecosystem services, are conserved through effectively and equitably managed, ecologically representative and well connected systems of protected areas and other effective area-based conservation measures, and integrated into the wider landscapes and seascapes.

As it can be noticed, also the new notion of OECMs contributes towards the achieving of the 10 per cent objective.

---

slopes in near Santa Maria di Leuca. The area is located in the centre of the southern part of the Southern Adriatic basin and the northern Ionian Sea".

37 Para. 26.

38 CBD/COP/15/L.1/Add.2 of 17 December 2022, para. 63.

Important developments have recently occurred as regards targets. In December 2022, taking into account the varying levels of progress towards the achievement of the Aichi Biodiversity Targets, the 15th Conference of the parties, held in Kunming (2021) and Montreal (2022), adopted the Kunming-Montreal Global Biodiversity Framework, which should be used as a strategic plan for the implementation of the CBD. Building on the Strategic Plan for Biodiversity 2011–2020, its achievements, gaps, and lessons learned, and on the experience and achievements of other relevant multilateral environmental agreements, the Kunming-Montreal Global Biodiversity Framework sets out an ambitious plan to implement broad-based action to bring about a transformation in societies' relationship with biodiversity by 2030, in line with the 2030 Agenda for Sustainable Development and its SDGs, and to ensure that, by 2050, the shared vision of living in harmony with nature is fulfilled.[39] The Framework sets forth four long-term goals for 2050 related to the 2050 Vision for Biodiversity and 23 action-oriented global targets for urgent action over the decade to 2030 that should be implemented consistently and in harmony with the CBD and its Protocols and other relevant international obligations, taking into account national circumstances, priorities and socio-economic conditions. Some of the targets are particularly important for the purposes of marine spatial planning and MPAs:

Target 1. Ensure that all areas are under participatory integrated biodiversity inclusive spatial planning and/or effective management processes addressing land and sea use change, to bring the loss of areas of high biodiversity importance, including ecosystems of high ecological integrity, close to zero by 2030, while respecting the rights of indigenous peoples and local communities.

Target 3. Ensure and enable that by 2030 at least 30 per cent of terrestrial, inland water, and of coastal and marine areas, especially areas of particular importance for biodiversity and ecosystem functions and services, are effectively conserved and managed through ecologically representative, well-connected and equitably governed systems of protected areas and other effective area-based conservation measures, recognizing indigenous and traditional territories, where applicable, and integrated into wider landscapes, seascapes and the ocean, while ensuring that any sustainable use, where appropriate in such areas, is fully consistent with conservation outcomes, recognizing and respecting the rights of indigenous peoples and local communities, including over their traditional territories.[40]

As it can be noticed, the area conservation objective is upgraded to 30 per cent, but postponed to 2030 (so-called 30–30 objective).[41]

39 CBD/COP/15/L.25 of 18 December 2022, p. 4.

40 Target 3 calls for action to "ensure that by 2030 at least 30 per cent of areas of degraded terrestrial, inland water, and coastal and marine ecosystems are under effective restoration, in order to enhance biodiversity and ecosystem functions and services, ecological integrity and connectivity".

41 Will the area conservation objective in 2030 be upgraded and postponed again? Time will tell.

e. The Notion of Other Effective Area-based Conservation Measures

Aichi Target 11 and Kunming-Montreal Target 3 distinguish between "protected areas", including MPAs, and "other effective area-based conservation measures". The distinction between the two different, but concurring, concepts is becoming a fundamental aspect of current trends in environmental policy and law and deserves particular attention.

In 2018, the parties to the CBD agreed on the definition, guiding principles, common characteristics and criteria for identification of other effective area-based conservation measures (Decision XIV/8). The definition is the following:

> "Other effective area-based conservation measure" means a geographically defined area other than a Protected Area, which is governed and managed in ways that achieve positive and sustained long-term outcomes for the *in situ* conservation of biodiversity, with associated ecosystem functions and services and, where applicable, cultural, spiritual, socio-economic, and other locally relevant values.

It can be inferred that "other effective area-based conservation measures" is a broad-ranging and multipurpose concept.[42] While MPAs are established exclusively for conservation purposes, OECMs, while indirectly contributing to conservation objectives, may be adopted also for other purposes, such as fishing, safety of navigation or preservation of the cultural heritage.

Annex III to Decision XIV/8 provides technical advice on OECMs as well as criteria for their identification. It explains, *inter alia*, that OECMs apply to areas that are not currently recognized or reported as a protected area or parts of a protected area and may be adopted also for protecting cultural, spiritual, socio-economic, and other relevant values.

Annex IV to Decision XIV/8 puts forward considerations in achieving Aichi Biodiversity Target 11 in marine and coastal areas and generally categorizes OECMs different from MPAs, as "territories and areas governed and managed by indigenous peoples and local communities",[43] "area-based fisheries management measures",[44] and "other sectoral area-based management approaches".[45]

42 It seems implied in the expression "marine protected areas and other effective area-based conservation measures" that marine protected areas are a kind of area-based conservation measure; however, the latter notion is broader and not limited to marine protected areas.

43 In these types of approaches, some or all of the governance and/or management authority is often ceded to the indigenous peoples and local communities, and conservation objectives are often tied to food security, and access to resources for indigenous peoples and local communities.

44 These are formally established, spatially defined fishery management and/or conservation measures, implemented to achieve one or more intended fishery outcomes. The outcomes of these measures are commonly related to sustainable use of the fishery. However, they can also often include protection of, or reduction of impact on, biodiversity, habitats, or ecosystem structure and function.

45 There are a range of area-based measures applied in other sectors at different scales and for different purposes. These include, for example, Particularly Sensitive Sea Areas (areas designated by the

The designation of corridors inside networks of MPAs can also be considered as OECMs. In short, while established for other purposes (for example, fishing, shipping, underwater archaeology, security, etc.), OECMs are nonetheless relevant, because they also indirectly achieve conservation purposes.

The adoption of the definition and criteria for OECMs opens new opportunities for States to assess the potential of such measures for nature conservation purposes and to recognize and report them also for the objective of achieving Aichi Biodiversity Target 11 and its successor target under the post-2020 Global Biodiversity Framework.[46]

D. The Convention Concerning the Protection of the World Cultural and Natural Heritage

The Convention concerning the Protection of the World Cultural and Natural Heritage (Paris, 1972), which binds 194 States today, applies to immovable properties having an "outstanding universal value" (Art. 11, para. 2). States parties are bound to ensure their "identification, protection, conservation, presentation and transmission to future generations" (Art. 4). Cultural, natural or mixed properties may be included in the World Heritage List established by the Convention.

Properties nominated for the List should have adequately delineated boundaries. However, only properties located in the territory of a State party can be nominated for inclusion on the List (Art. 4). The high seas seem consequently excluded from the geographical scope of application of the convention.[47] So far, a number of properties located in waters subject to national jurisdiction – marine internal waters, territorial sea or exclusive economic zone – appear on the List, such as *Papahānaumokuākea* (United States), *Phoenix Islands Protected Area* (Kiribati) and *French Austral Lands and Seas* (France).

E. The Convention for the Prevention of Pollution From Ships

The International Convention for the Prevention of Pollution from Ships, called MARPOL (London, 1973, amended in 1978), aims at preventing and minimizing pollution from ships, both accidental and operational. Six technical annexes are

---

International Maritime Organization for protection from damage by international maritime activities because of ecological, socioeconomic or scientific significance), Areas of Particular Environmental Interest (areas of the seafloor designated by the International Seabed Authority for protection from damage by deep-seabed mining because of biodiversity and ecosystem structure and function), approaches within national work on marine spatial planning, as well as conservation measures in other sectors.

46 This is what is being envisaged by the post-2020 regional strategy for marine and coastal protected areas and other effective area-based conservation measures in the Mediterranean Sea (doc. UNEP/MED WG.502/12 of 22 May 2021).

47 For the attempts to enlarge the application of the World Heritage Convention to the high seas see Freestone, Laffoley, Douvere and Badman, *World Heritage in the High Seas: An Idea Whose Time Has Come*, World Heritage Reports No. 44, Paris, 2016.

attached to it. The MARPOL entered into force on 2 October 1983 and 160 States are parties to it, including 20 Mediterranean States.[48]

The MARPOL, which was adopted within the framework of the IMO, provides for the establishment of Special Areas, which may also include the high seas, where particularly strict standards are applied to discharges from ships. Special Areas provisions are contained in Annexes I (Regulations for the Prevention of Pollution by Oil), II (Regulations for the Control of Pollution by Noxious Substances in Bulk) and V (Regulations for the Prevention of Pollution by Garbage from Ships).[49] The whole Mediterranean Sea area is a Special Area for the purposes of Annexes I (prevention of pollution by oil) and V (prevention of pollution by garbage from ships). In 2022 it was designated an emission control area for sulphur oxides for the purposes of Annex VI (air pollution from ships).

a. The Particularly Sensitive Sea Areas

Particularly relevant in the field of OECMs is the decision by the IMO Assembly to adopt, under Resolution A.720(17) of 6 November 1991, revised by Resolutions A.927(22) of 29 November 2001 and A.982(24) of 1 December 2005, a set of Guidelines for the identification of Particularly Sensitive Sea Areas (PSSAs), where special measures can be established to prevent pollution from ships. A PSSA is defined as

> an area that needs special protection through action by IMO because of its significance for recognized ecological or socio-economic or scientific reasons and which may be vulnerable to damage by international maritime activities.

It is intended to function as:

> a comprehensive management tool at the international level that provides a mechanism for reviewing an area that is vulnerable to damage by international shipping and determining the most appropriate way to address that vulnerability.[50]

To be identified as a PSSA, an area should meet at least one among a number of ecological criteria (uniqueness or rarity; critical habitat; dependency; representativity; diversity; productivity; spawning or breeding grounds; naturalness; integrity; vulnerability; biogeographic importance), social, cultural and economic

48 Albania, Algeria, Croatia, Cyprus, Egypt, France, Greece, Israel, Italy, Lebanon, Libya, Malta, Montenegro, Morocco, Slovenia, Spain, Syria, Tunisia, Turkey, and the United Kingdom.

49 For example, under Regulation 1, para. 10, of Annex I, "special area means a sea area where for recognized technical reasons in relation to its oceanographical and ecological condition and to the particular character of its traffic the adoption of special mandatory methods for the prevention of sea pollution by oil is required".

50 Guidance Document for Submitting PSSA Proposals to IMO (MEPC Cir/398).

criteria (economic benefit; recreation; human dependency) or scientific and educational criteria (research; baseline and monitoring studies; education). In addition, the area should be at risk from international shipping activities, taking into consideration vessel traffic (operational factors; vessel types; traffic characteristics; harmful substances carried) and natural factors of hydrographical, meteorological and oceanographic character. The 2005 revised PSSAs guidelines specify that at least one of the relevant criteria should be present in the entire proposed PSSA, though this does not have to be the same criterion throughout the area. Cultural heritage has been reinstated as a criterion under the label of "social, cultural and economic criteria".

PSSAs may be located within or beyond the limits of the territorial sea. They are identified by the Marine Environment Protection Committee of the IMO on proposals by one or more member States and under a procedure which takes place at the multilateral level.

PSSA proposals should be accompanied by proposals for "associated protective measures" (APMs), identifying the legal basis for each measure. APMs that may be taken in PSSAs include those available under IMO instruments and cannot be extended to fields different from shipping. They encompass the following four options: designation of an area as a Special Area under MARPOL Annexes I, II, V and VI; adoption of ships' routeing systems under the 1974 International Convention for the Safety of Life at Sea, including areas to be avoided, that is, areas within defined limits in which either navigation is particularly hazardous or it is exceptionally important to avoid casualties and which should be avoided by all ships or by certain classes of ships; reporting systems near or in the area; other measures, such as compulsory pilotage schemes or vessel traffic management systems.

The IMO has established 17 PSSAs so far, including one located in the Mediterranean Sea (the Strait of Bonifacio).[51] In 2022 the IMO Marine Environment Protection Committee agreed in principle on the proposal for the designation of a PSSA in the northwestern Mediterranean Sea to protect cetaceans from international shipping, submitted by France, Italy, Monaco, and Spain, inviting the proponents to further develop the associated measures.[52]

F. The Convention on the Protection of the Underwater Cultural Heritage

The Convention for the Protection of the Underwater Cultural Heritage (Paris, 2001) was concluded within the framework of UNESCO. It aims at protecting the underwater cultural heritage, which is recognized as part of the cultural heritage of mankind. Seventy-two States, including fifteen Mediterranean States,[53] are parties

51 See Chapter 6 of this book.

52 MEPC 79/10 of 9 September 2022.

53 Albania, Algeria, Bosnia and Herzegovina, Croatia, Egypt, France, Italy, Lebanon, Libya, Montenegro, Morocco, Palestine, Slovenia, Spain, and Tunisia. On the application of the Convention to the Mediterranean Sea, see Scovazzi, The Protection of Underwater Cultural Heritage in the Mediterranean Sea, in *Italian Yearbook of International Law*, 2021, p. 73.

to this Convention, which entered into force on 2 January 2009. The Convention defines underwater cultural heritage as

> a) . . . all traces of human existence having a cultural, historical or archaeological character which have been partially or totally under water, periodically or continuously, for at least 100 years such as:
>
> (i) sites, structures, buildings, artefacts and human remains, together with their archaeological and natural context;
> (ii) vessels, aircraft, other vehicles or any part thereof, their cargo or other contents, together with their archaeological and natural context; and
> (iii) objects of prehistoric character.
>
> b) Pipelines and cables placed on the seabed shall not be considered as underwater cultural heritage.
> c) Installations other than pipelines and cables, placed on the seabed and still in use, shall not be considered as underwater cultural heritage.
>
> (Art. 1, para. 1)

According to the Convention, "the preservation in situ of underwater cultural heritage shall be considered as the first option" (Art. 2, para. 5). Some States have established MPAs around underwater cultural properties (for example, Italy by two decrees of 7 August 2002 has created the submarine parks of *Gaiola*, in the Gulf of Naples, and of *Baia*, in the Gulf of Pozzuoli). From the point of view of the protection of the environment, this kind of measure could be considered among the other effective area-based conservation measures.

Art. 6 of the Convention encourages States parties to enter into bilateral, regional or other multilateral agreements that would ensure better protection of underwater cultural heritage. The possibility to negotiate regional agreements should be carefully considered by the States bordering enclosed or semi-enclosed seas where the underwater cultural heritage is particularly rich, such as the Mediterranean Sea. In 2003, an intergovernmental Conference on Cooperation in the Mediterranean for the Protection of the Underwater Cultural Heritage was held in Syracuse and discussed the possibility of an agreement on the protection of the underwater cultural heritage in the Mediterranean Sea that would include the establishment of specially protected areas of Mediterranean cultural importance. However, no further steps towards the finalization of this project have so far been taken.

2.4. Conclusive Summary

All the main policy instruments approved at the international level in the last three decades, such as Agenda 21 (1992), the Plan of Implementation of the World Summit on Sustainable Development (2002), *The Future We Want* (2012), the 2030 Agenda for Sustainable Development (2015), as well and the United Nations General Assembly Resolutions on Oceans and the Law of the Sea, call for action towards the establishment of MPAs and the adoption of OECMs. This action can be considered as a corollary of the customary international law obligation to protect the marine environment and as applicable to any kind of marine waters, irrespective of their legal condition (internal waters, territorial sea, exclusive economic zone, continental shelf, high seas, seabed beyond national jurisdiction).

Rules of international law of the sea on the legal regime of different marine spaces and the activities that are carried out therein must be taken into consideration in the process for the establishment of MPAs and the implementation of the measures provided therein. However, it would be a mistake to think that the freedom of the high seas is an insurmountable obstacle against the adoption of environmental measures, including the establishment of MPAs. Even if treaties do not apply to third parties, also non-party States are bound to abide by general provisions of international law and not to undermine the reasonable measures for the protection of the environment and the sustainable development of marine resources that have been agreed upon by other States. MPAs are implicitly referred to in Art. 194, para. 5, UNCLOS, which includes among the measures for the protection and preservation of the marine environment those necessary to protect and preserve rare or fragile ecosystems as well as the habitat of depleted, threatened or endangered species, and other forms of marine life.

The establishment of MPAs is also envisaged, as a special measure to conserve biological diversity, by the CBD. Sectoral treaties provide for the establishment of effective area-based conservation measures as a means to achieve their objective: this is the case of the International Convention for the Regulation of Whaling, as regards sanctuary areas, the MARPOL, as regards special areas, or the Convention for the Protection of Underwater Cultural Heritage, as regards the preservation *in situ* of this heritage.

The general trend to protect the marine environment by establishing MPAs or adopting OECMs is confirmed by the practice developed within the CBD, where EBSAs have been identified and the objective to protect by 2030 at least 30 per cent of sea areas has been put forward, as well as within the IMO, where PSSAs have been identified and navigation therein has been subjected to restrictions. The new concept of OECM has been elaborated to identify measures that, while being adopted for other purposes (fishing, shipping, underwater archaeology, security, etc.), indirectly contribute to the achievement of conservation objectives.

3 The Regional and Sub-regional Legal Basis for Marine Area-based Conservation

Mitja Grbec and Tullio Scovazzi[1]

3.1. Regional Instruments and Their Coordination With Global Instruments

Treaties having a regional or sub-regional scope of application are relevant for the protection of the environment in several seas, including the establishment of marine protected areas (MPAs). The presence of different levels of international regulation – global, regional, sub-regional, and bilateral[2] – may raise the question of their coordination and of possible conflicts between them. Normally, substantive conflicts do not occur between different environmental treaties, as these instruments are inspired by similar general principles and protection objectives. The regional or sub-regional treaties usually provide for a more specific and enhanced protection than that achieved through global treaties (criterion of the added value), as it would be useless to merely reproduce at the regional or sub-regional level the same regime that can be found in global treaties.

However, the multiplication and stratification of provisions contained in different treaties may in principle create very complex legal problems, where successive treaties relating to the same subject-matter are in principle applicable. Under Art. 30 of the Vienna Convention on the Law of Treaties,

> 1. . . . the rights and obligations of States parties to successive treaties relating to the same subject-matter shall be determined in accordance with the following paragraphs.
> 2. When a treaty specifies that it is subject to, or that it is not to be considered as incompatible with, an earlier or later treaty, the provisions of that other treaty prevail.

1 In this chapter, paras. 3.1 and 3.2 are to be attributed to Tullio Scovazzi; paras. 3.3 and 3.4 to Mitja Grbec.

2 An instance of bilateral treaty containing, *inter alia*, a provision on marine protected areas is the recent treaty between France and Italy on strengthened bilateral cooperation (Rome, 21 November 2021). According to Art. 6, para 9,

> les Parties s'engagent à promouvoir et soutenir la coopération entre leurs aires protégées et entre leurs parcs terrestres ou marins, y compris dans le cadre des accords régionaux et mondiaux sur la préservation de la biodiversité.

DOI: 10.4324/9781003367963-3

3. When all the parties to the earlier treaty are parties also to the later treaty but the earlier treaty is not terminated or suspended in operation under article 59, the earlier treaty applies only to the extent that its provisions are compatible with those of the later treaty.
4. When the parties to the later treaty do not include all the parties to the earlier one:

   a) as between States parties to both treaties the same rule applies as in paragraph 3;
   b) as between a State party to both treaties and a State party to only one of the treaties, the treaty to which both States are parties governs their mutual rights and obligations.

Accordingly, from a logical point of view, the questions to be addressed in order to determine the rights and obligations of States in cases of successive treaties are the following:

a) whether the States concerned are parties to both the earlier and the later treaty (a *ratione personae* question);
b) if they are parties to both treaties, whether a provision of the earlier treaty and a provision of the later one relate to the same subject-matter and have the same scope of territorial application (a *ratione materiae* and a *ratione loci* question);
c) if so, whether one of the two treaties specifies that it is subject to the other;
d) if not, whether and to what extent the two provisions in question are incompatible; in this respect and whenever possible, the provisions should be interpreted according to a meaning that leads to their reconciliation; for instance, a specific provision contained in a treaty may be compatible with a more general provision contained in another treaty (*lex specialis derogat legi generali*);
e) finally, if reconciliation between the two provisions is not possible, it must be determined which one is the later treaty[3] and, consequently, which is the prevailing provision according to Art. 30, para. 3, of the Vienna Convention.[4]

Luckily, the UNCLOS, the only global treaty on the law of the sea from the point of view of both its general subject matter and its world application, states that its provisions on the protection of the environment are without prejudice to the specific obligations assumed by States under special conventions and agreements concluded previously which relate to the protection and preservation of the marine environment and to agreements which may be concluded in the furtherance of the general principles set forth in the UNCLOS itself (Art. 237, para. 1). However,

3 Incidentally, this is a problematic question. It may be asked whether the concepts of "earlier" and "later" are to be determined according to the dates of signature of the two treaties or to the dates of their entry into force at the international level or to the dates on which the treaties have become binding in the relationship between the States concerned. The answer is far from being clear.

4 Under Art. 44, para. 3, of the 1969 Vienna Convention on the Law of Treaties, the provisions of a treaty are separable, as far as termination is concerned.

"specific obligations assumed by States under special conventions, with respect to the protection and preservation of the marine environment, should be carried out in a manner consistent with the general principles and objectives" of the UNCLOS (Art. 237, para. 2).[5]

Coming to the specific case of the Mediterranean Sea, all the instruments of the Barcelona System,[6] while presenting a number of innovative aspects, seem fully consistent with the general principles and objectives of the UNCLOS, bringing an added value at the regional level to the global regime for the protection of the marine environment.

In the case of the Agreement on the Conservation of Cetaceans of the Black Sea, Mediterranean Sea and Contiguous Atlantic Area (Monaco, 1996; ACCOBAMS),[7] Art. XI, para. 1, provides that

> the provisions of this Agreement shall not affect . . . the rights or obligations of any Party deriving from any existing treaty, convention or agreement to which it is a party, except where the exercise of those rights and obligations would threaten the conservation of cetaceans.

Also the ACCOBAMS seems fully consistent with the general principles and objectives of UNCLOS. It can, thus, be concluded that no significant substantive conflicts may be noticed between the provisions of the main treaties applicable in the field of MPAs.

From the point of view of international law, the European Union legislative instruments, such as regulations and directives, can be compared to national legislation in force for the States that are members of the European Union. For these States, the European Union instruments replace national legislation, where they are enacted in a subject-matter for which the European Union is entitled to exercise its competence, either exclusive (i.e., fisheries) or shared (i.e., the protection of the environment). Thorny legal questions would arise for European Union member States in the hypothetical case in which an international treaty to which they are parties is found in conflict with a European Union instrument. However, no specific instances can be envisaged in the case of MPAs.

Forms of cooperation relevant for the establishment of MPAs have been established in some regions.

For example, in 2016, the parties to the Convention on the Conservation of Antarctic Marine Living Resources (Canberra, 1980)[8] adopted Conservation Measure

5 The conditional mood ("should be carried out") does not contribute to the clarity of this provision.

6 See Chapter 3.1.A of this book.

7 See Chapter 3.1.B of this book.

8 See Cordonnery, Hemmings and Kriwoken, Nexus and Imbroglio: CCAMLR, the Madrid Protocol and Designating Antarctic Marine Protected Areas in the Southern Ocean, in *International Journal of Marine and Coastal Law*, 2015, p. 727.

91–05 (2016), establishing the Ross Sea region MPA.[9] It extends for over 1.5 million km² of sea and is the world's largest MPA. It includes a no-take general protection zone, where no commercial fishing is allowed; a special research zone, where limited research fishing for krill and toothfish is permitted; and a krill research zone, where controlled research fishing for krill is permitted.

In 2003, the parties to the Convention for the Protection of the Marine Environment of the North East Atlantic (Paris, 1992; OSPAR Convention) adopted Recommendation 2003/3 on a network of MPAs, subsequently amended by Recommendation 2010/2, based on the purpose to make further efforts "to ensure the ecological coherence of the network of marine protected areas in the North-East Atlantic, in particular through inclusion of areas in deeper water". This enabled the parties to establish in 2010 six MPAs that regard waters or seabed located beyond national jurisdiction.[10] All 12 OSPAR parties have contributed to the OSPAR network of MPAs, both in their national waters as well as collectively in areas beyond national jurisdiction. The network today comprises 583 areas with a total surface of about 1.5 million km², corresponding to 11 per cent of the North East Atlantic.

Another relevant instance is the Mediterranean Sea, where a number of instruments aiming at the protection of the marine environment and at the sustainable exploitation of living resources have been concluded and will be examined hereunder.[11]

A. The Convention for the Protection of the Marine Environment and the Coastal Region of the Mediterranean and Its Protocols

Twenty-one Mediterranean States and the European Union are parties to the Convention for the Protection of the Marine Environment and the Coastal Region of the Mediterranean (Barcelona, 1976, amended in 1995; Barcelona Convention) and its Protocols, including all the Adriatic and Ionian States.[12] The Barcelona Convention is a framework treaty, adopted under the auspices of the UNEP Mediterranean

9 The measure was adopted

> desiring to implement Articles IX.1(f) and 2(g) of the CAMLR Convention, which provide that conservation measures, formulated on the basis of the best scientific evidence available, may designate the opening and closing of areas, regions or subregions for purposes of scientific study or conservation, including special areas for protection and scientific study.

10 Namely *Milne Seamount Complex*, *Charlie-Gibbs South*, *Altair Seamount*, *Antialtair Seamount*, *Josephine Seamount* and *Mar North of the Azores*. See Rodríguez, OSPAR Regulatory Regime for Establishing Marine Protected Areas in Areas beyond National Jurisdiction of the OSPAR Maritime Area, in Juste Ruiz and Bou Franch (dir.), *Derecho del mar y sostenibilidad ambiental en el Mediterráneo*, Valencia, 2014, p. 443.

11 As regards marine scientific research, the only regional organization having a specific competence is the International Commission for the Scientific Exploration of the Mediterranean Sea (CIESM), whose constitutive assembly was held in Madrid in 1919. It is engaged in promoting fundamental research activities.

12 The Convention entered into force on 12 February 1978 and the amendments on 9 July 2004.

Action Plan (UNEP-MAP),[13] which has been concluded "to prevent, abate, combat and to the fullest possible extent eliminate pollution of the Mediterranean Sea Area and to protect and enhance the marine environment in that area so as to contribute towards its sustainable development" (Art. 4, para. 1). It is complemented by seven Protocols,[14] which together with the Convention and the related policy instruments, compose the so-called Barcelona System. This is a flexible tool which has been constantly updated and allows for adequate and relatively prompt normative and policy responses to new threats to the Mediterranean environment.[15]

The Barcelona Convention is open to the participation by States, as well as the European Union and similar regional economic groupings at least one member of which is a coastal State of the Mediterranean Sea and which exercise competence in fields covered by the Barcelona Convention (Art. 30). The European Union is a party to the Barcelona Convention and some of its Protocols, together with the Mediterranean member States.

In 1995, the geographical coverage of the Convention was extended to include all maritime waters of the Mediterranean Sea, irrespective of their legal condition.[16] The scope of territorial application of the Protocols is flexible, in the sense that any of them may extend the area to which it applies, to include also some terrestrial areas, such as coastal lands.

The amended text of the Barcelona Convention recalls and applies at the regional level the main principles embodied in the instruments adopted by the 1992 Rio Conference (the Declaration on Environment and Development and the Programme of action Agenda 21), such as sustainable development, the precautionary principle, the integrated management of the coastal zones, the use of best available techniques and best environmental practices, as well as the promotion of environmentally sound technology, including clean production technologies.

Compliance with the Barcelona Convention and its Protocols, as well as with the decisions and recommendations adopted during the meetings of the parties, is assessed on the basis of the periodical reports that the parties are bound to transmit at regular intervals to the United Nations Environment Programme. Such reports, which are examined at the biannual meetings of the parties, relate to the legal, administrative, or other measures taken by the parties; their effectiveness; and the problems encountered in their implementation. The meeting of the parties can recommend, when appropriate, the necessary steps to bring about full compliance

13 For a general discussion, see Raftopoulos, The Mediterranean Response to Global Challenges: Environmental Governance and the Barcelona Convention System, in Vidas and Schei (eds.), *op. cit.*, p. 507; Raftopoulos, Sustainability Governance, Public Trust and the Conventional Protection of the Mediterranean Environment, in Juste Ruiz and Bou Franch (dir.), *op. cit.*, p. 35.

14 No one may become a party to the Convention, unless it is a party to at least one of the Protocols. No one may become a party to a Protocol, unless it is a party to the Convention (Art. 29).

15 See Scovazzi, The Protection of the Marine Environment in the Mediterranean: Ideas behind the Updating of the "Barcelona System", in Cataldi (ed.), *op. cit.*, p. 269.

16 The original text of the Barcelona Convention did not apply to internal waters. See Art. 1, para. 2.

with the Convention and the Protocols and to promote the implementation of decisions and recommendations (Arts. 26 and 27).

In 2008, the meeting of the parties adopted the procedures and mechanisms on compliance and established a compliance committee. Its objective is "to facilitate and promote compliance with the obligations under the Barcelona Convention and its Protocols, taking into account the specific situation of each Contracting Party, in particular those which are developing countries".

Seven Protocols have been adopted within the framework of the Barcelona Convention, namely:

- the Protocol for the Prevention of the Pollution of the Mediterranean Sea by Dumping from Ships and Aircraft (Barcelona, 1976), which, as amended in Barcelona in 1995, has been called Protocol for the Prevention and Elimination of Pollution of the Mediterranean Sea by Dumping from Ships and Aircraft or Incineration at Sea[17]; the amended Protocol has not yet entered into force and the original Protocol binds today 20 States and the European Union, including 6 Adriatic or Ionian States (the exception is Montenegro);
- the Protocol concerning Cooperation in Preventing Pollution from Ships and, in Cases of Emergency, Combating Pollution of the Mediterranean Sea (Valletta, 2002; in force from 17 March 2004; Ships Protocol),[18] which is intended to replace the previous Protocol concerning Co-operation in Combating Pollution of the Mediterranean Sea by Oil and Other Harmful Substances in Cases of Emergency (Barcelona, 1976)[19]; the 2002 Protocol is in force for 16 States and the European Union, including 5 Adriatic or Ionian States (the exceptions are Albania and Bosnia and Herzegovina);
- the Protocol for the Protection of the Mediterranean Sea against Pollution from Land-Based Sources (Athens, 1980; Land-Based Protocol), which, as amended in Syracuse in 1996, has been called Protocol for the Protection of the Mediterranean Sea against Pollution from Land-Based Sources and Activities[20]; the Protocol is in force for 21 States and the European Union, including all the Adriatic and Ionian States[21];
- the Protocol concerning Specially Protected Areas and Biological Diversity in the Mediterranean (Barcelona, 1995; Areas Protocol),[22] which is intended to replace the previous Protocol concerning Mediterranean Specially Protected Areas (Geneva, 1982)[23]; the Areas Protocol is today in force for 16 States and the European Union, including 5 Adriatic or Ionian States (the exceptions are Bosnia and Herzegovina and Greece);[24]

17 The Protocol entered into force on 12 February 1978.
18 The Protocol entered into force on 17 March 2004.
19 The Protocol entered into force on 12 February 1978.
20 The Protocol entered into force on 17 June 1983 and the amendments on 11 May 2008.
21 However, Bosnia and Herzegovina is not a party to the amended Protocol.
22 The Protocol entered into force on 12 December 1999.
23 The Protocol entered into force on 23 March 1986.
24 Bosnia and Herzegovina and Greece are parties to the previous 1982 Protocol.

- the Protocol concerning Pollution resulting from Exploration and Exploitation of the Continental Shelf, the Seabed and its Subsoil (Madrid, 1994: Offshore Protocol)[25]; the Protocol is in force for seven States and the European Union, including two Adriatic or Ionian States (Albania and Croatia);
- the Protocol on the Prevention of Pollution of the Mediterranean Sea by Transboundary Movements of Hazardous Wastes and their Disposal (Izmir, 1996)[26]; the Protocol is in force for seven States, including two Adriatic or Ionian States (Albania and Montenegro);
- the Protocol on Integrated Coastal Zone Management in the Mediterranean (Madrid, 2008; Coastal Zone Protocol)[27]; the Protocol is in force for 11 States and the European Union, including 4 Adriatic or Ionian States (Albania, Croatia, Montenegro, and Slovenia).

Three Protocols to the Barcelona Convention are of particular relevance for this study, as they envisage explicit provisions for the establishment or management of marine or coastal areas to which a special protection regime applies. Such areas may be extended beyond national jurisdictions and given a transboundary character, if the parties to the relevant Protocols wish to do so. This is done by including in the relevant marine protected areas waters that encompass portions of maritime zones (i.e., internal waters, territorial sea, exclusive economic zone, continental shelf) pertaining to different States or even portions of the high seas.

a. The Areas Protocol

The Areas Protocol[28] is applicable to all the marine waters of the Mediterranean, irrespective of their legal condition, as well as to the seabed, its subsoil, and to the terrestrial coastal areas designated by each party, including wetlands.[29] The extension of the geographical coverage of the instrument was felt necessary to protect also those highly migratory marine species (such as marine mammals), which cross the artificial boundaries drawn by man in the sea.

In order to overcome the difficulties due to different types of Mediterranean coastal zones and unsettled maritime boundaries,[30] the Areas Protocol includes two disclaimer provisions (Art. 2, paras. 2 and 3).[31]

25 The Protocol entered into force on 24 March 2011.

26 The Protocol entered into force on 18 March 2008.

27 The Protocol entered into force on 24 March 2011 and is today in force for 12 parties.

28 See Scovazzi, Marine Protected Areas in the Mediterranean, in Juste Ruiz and Bou Franch (dir.), *op. cit.*, p. 425; Vezzani, The Conservation of Biodiversity in the Mediterranean Sea through Marine Protected Areas: The Barcelona System Faced with the Expansion of Coastal State Jurisdiction, in *Italian Yearbook of International Law*, 2021, p. 141.

29 On the contrary, the application of the previous instrument was limited to the territorial sea of the parties and did not cover the high seas.

30 On the legal condition of marine waters in the Adriatic and Ionian region, see Chapter 1 of this book.

31 The model of the disclaimer provisions was Art. IV of the Antarctic Treaty (Washington, 1959).

Under the Areas Protocol, parties are called to protect areas of particular natural or cultural value through the establishment of specially protected areas. A particular case is given by the Specially Protected Areas of Mediterranean Importance (SPAMIs), which are included in a list (so-called SPAMI List) established by the Areas Protocol. This list may include sites which "are of importance for conserving the components of biological diversity in the Mediterranean; contain ecosystems specific to the Mediterranean area or the habitats of endangered species; are of special interest at the scientific, aesthetic, cultural or educational levels". The procedures for the establishment and listing of SPAMIs are specified in detail in the Protocol. For instance, as regards an area located partly or wholly on the high seas, the proposal must be made "by two or more neighbouring parties concerned" and the decision to include the area in the SPAMI List is taken by consensus by the parties during their periodical meetings.

Once the areas are included in the SPAMI List, all the parties agree "to recognize the particular importance of these areas for the Mediterranean", "to comply with the measures applicable to the SPAMIs and not to authorize nor undertake any activities that might be contrary to the objectives for which the SPAMIs were established". This gives to the SPAMIs and to the measures adopted for their protection an *erga omnes partes* effect. As regards the relationship with third countries, the parties are called to "invite States that are not Parties to the Protocol and international organizations to cooperate in the implementation" of the Protocol. They also "undertake to adopt appropriate measures, consistent with international law, to ensure that no one engages in any activity contrary to the principles and purposes" of the Protocol. This provision aims at facing the problems arising from the fact that any treaty, including the Areas Protocol, can create rights and obligations only for the parties.

The Areas Protocol is completed by three Annexes, which were adopted in 1996 in Monaco, namely the "Common criteria for the choice of protected marine and coastal areas that could be included in the SPAMI List" (Annex I), the "List of endangered or threatened species" (Annex II) and the "List of species whose exploitation is regulated" (Annex III).

According to Annex I, the sites included in the SPAMI List must be "provided with adequate legal status, protection measures and management methods and means" (para. A, e) and must fulfill at least one of six general criteria ("uniqueness", "natural representativeness", "diversity", "naturalness", "presence of habitats that are critical to endangered, threatened or endemic species", "cultural representativeness"). The SPAMIs must be awarded a legal status that guarantees their effective long-term protection (para. C.1) and must have a management body, a management plan, and a monitoring programme (paras. from D.6 to D.8).

So far, 39 SPAMIs have been listed, as proposed by 11 States parties to the Areas Protocol (Albania, Algeria, Cyprus, France, Italy, Lebanon, Monaco, Morocco, Slovenia, Spain, and Tunisia). Among them, the *Pelagos Sanctuary for the conservation of marine mammals*, jointly proposed by France, Italy, and Monaco, and the *Cetacean Migration Corridor* off the coasts of Spain cover also waters located beyond the territorial sea.

With specific reference to the Adriatic and Ionian Seas, six areas have been included in the SPAMI List so far: *Miramare* Marine Protected Area (Italy); *Plemmirio* Marine Protected Area (Italy); *Torre Guaceto* Marine Protected Area and Natural Reserve (Italy); *Porto Cesareo* Marine Protected Area (Italy); *Karaburun Sazan* National Marine Park (Albania); and Landscape Park *Strunjan* (Slovenia), in their respective order of listing.

A number of decisions adopted by the meetings of the parties are particularly relevant for the application of the Areas Protocol. In 2008, by Decision IG 17/12, the meeting of the parties adopted the Procedure for the revision of the areas included in the SPAMI List, establishing an ordinary and an extraordinary review procedure and providing for a period of provisional nature, if so recommended by a review. In 2019, by Decision IG.24/6, the meeting of the parties requested the Secretariat to elaborate an ambitious and transformational post-2020 roadmap on MPAs and OECMs in the Mediterranean, in line with the Post-2020 Global Biodiversity Framework of the Convention on Biological Diversity and other regional and global processes, and in consultation with relevant global and regional organizations. In 2021, by Decision IG.25/12,[32] the meeting of the parties adopted the Post-2020 Regional Strategy for marine and coastal protected areas and OECMs in the Mediterranean. It identified two post-2020 targets as follows:

1. By 2030, at least 30 per cent of the Mediterranean Sea is protected and conserved through well connected, ecologically representative and effective systems of marine and coastal protected areas and other effective area-based conservation measures, ensuring adequate geographical balance, with the focus on areas particularly important for biodiversity.
2. By 2030, the number and coverage of marine and coastal protected areas with enhanced protection levels is increased, contributing to the recovery of marine ecosystems.

According to the Post-2020 Regional Strategy, there is a clear need to expand the marine and coastal protected areas network and to establish a greater balance across countries, sub-regions and habitats coverage to achieve a greater ecological representation. The tool of OECM is critical to help advance towards the 30 per cent target coverage for the Mediterranean.

b. The Offshore Protocol

The Offshore Protocol sets forth obligations incumbent on the parties with respect to activities carried out by operators who can also be private persons, either natural or juridical. This kind of obligations are to be understood in the sense that each party is bound to exercise the appropriate legislative, executive, or judicial activities in order to ensure that the operators comply with the provisions of the Offshore

32 UNEP/MED IG.25/27 of 10 December 2021.

Protocol. The parties are also bound to ensure that liability for damage – caused by activities to which the Offshore Protocol applies – is imposed on operators, who are required to pay prompt and adequate compensation, and that operators have and maintain insurance cover or other financial security in order to pay compensation for damages caused by the activities covered by the instrument.

The definition of "operator" is broad, as it includes not only persons authorized to carry out activities (for example, the holder of a license) or who carry out activities (for example, a subcontractor) but also any person who does not hold an authorization, being *de facto* in control of activities. The parties are under an obligation to exercise due diligence in order to make sure, within the seabed under their jurisdiction, that no one engages in activities which have not previously been authorized or which are exercised illegally.

The geographical coverage of the Offshore Protocol – which encompasses the whole "Mediterranean Sea Area" as defined in the Barcelona Convention (Art. 1) – may be extended by any of the parties to include wetlands or coastal areas of their national territory. The Offshore Protocol provides for the Regional Marine Pollution Emergency Response Centre for the Mediterranean Sea (REMPEC) to play an important role in support of the implementation of the instrument. The Offshore Protocol is complemented by the 2016 Mediterranean Offshore Action Plan. In this context, the Barcelona Convention Offshore Oil and Gas Group (BARCO OFOG), through its Sub-Group on environmental impact, deals, *inter alia*, with "precautions for specially protected areas".

All activities in the Offshore Protocol area, including the erection of installations on site, are subject to the prior written authorization by the competent authority of a party. Before granting the authorization, the authority must be satisfied that the installation has been constructed according to international standards and practice and that the operator has the technical competence and the financial capacity to carry out the activities. Authorization must be refused if there are indications that the proposed activities are likely to cause significant adverse effects on the environment that could not be avoided by compliance with specific technical conditions.[33] In particular, special restrictions or conditions may be established for the granting of authorizations for activities in specially protected areas.

In the context of the Offshore Protocol, "precautions" are envisaged, in particular for specially protected areas that have been identified under the Areas Protocol or established by a party. Measures of protection may be taken by the parties either individually or through multilateral or bilateral cooperation, with a view to preventing, abating, combating, and controlling pollution arising from activities in these areas. In addition to those measures referred to in the Areas Protocol, for the granting of authorization the measures of the Offshore Protocol may encompass, *inter alia*: special restrictions or conditions when granting authorizations for such areas, including the preparation and evaluation of environmental impact assessments and the elaboration of special provisions concerning monitoring, removal of

33 This obligation can be seen as an application of the precautionary principle.

installations, and prohibition of any discharge, as well as an intensified exchange of information among operators, the competent authorities, parties, and UNEP regarding matters which may affect such areas (Art. 21).

It was recently reported that, as regards special measures to prevent, abate, combat, and control pollution, two parties mentioned the complete prohibition of offshore activities in specially protected areas or in areas considered as strict reserves.[34]

c. The Coastal Zone Protocol

The third instrument of the Barcelona System that proves particularly relevant for this study is the Coastal Zone Protocol, which addresses the increase in anthropic pressure on the Mediterranean coastal zones.[35] This instrument provides Mediterranean States with a legal and technical tool to ensure the sustainable development throughout the shores of this regional sea. The importance of this Protocol lies also in the fact that it represents the first treaty ever adopted specifically devoted to the coastal zone.

The Coastal Zone Protocol defines "integrated coastal management" as:

> a dynamic process for the sustainable management and use of coastal zones, taking into the account at the same time the fragility of coastal ecosystems and landscapes, the diversity of activities and uses, their interactions, the maritime orientation of certain activities and uses and their impact on both the marine and land parts.
>
> (Art. 2, g)

The precise delimitation of the geographical coverage of the Coastal Zone Protocol gave rise to lengthy discussion during the negotiations. It was finally agreed (Art. 3) that the seaward limit of the coastal zone is the external limit of the territorial sea and its landward limit is the limit of the competent coastal units as defined by parties. However, parties may establish different limits, insofar as certain conditions occur. This instrument certainly opens up to the opportunity of building transboundary integrated coastal management, also through the recourse to transboundary area-based management tools.

Art. 6 of the Coastal Zone Protocol lists a number of general principles of integrated coastal zone management. For instance, parties are bound to formulate "land use strategies, plans and programmes covering urban development and socio-economic activities, as well as other relevant sectoral polices". They must take into account in an integrated manner "all elements relating to hydrological, geomorphological, climatic, ecological, socio-economic and cultural systems", so

34 UNEP/MED WG.515/Inf.12 of 11 August 2021, para. 330.

35 See Prieur, Le protocole de Madrid à la convention de Barcelone relatif à la gestion intégrée des zones côtières de la Méditerranée, in Juste Ruiz and Bou Franch (dir.), *op. cit.*, p. 462.

as "not to exceed the carrying capacity of the coastal zone and to prevent the negative effects of natural disasters and of development".

Parties are also required to take into account the diversity of activities in the coastal zone and to give priority "where necessary, to public services and activities requiring, in terms of use and location, the immediate proximity of the sea".

Art. 8 provides for the establishment of a 100-m zone where construction is not allowed. However, "adaptations" are allowed "for projects of public interest" and "in areas having particular geographical or other local constraints, especially related to population density or social needs, where individual housing, urbanization or development are provided for by national legal instruments". Other important obligations of the parties relate to "limiting the linear extension of urban development and the creation of new transport infrastructure along the coast", "providing for freedom of access by the public to the sea and along the shore", and "restricting or, where necessary, prohibiting the movement and parking of land vehicles, as well as the movement and anchoring of marine vessels in fragile natural areas on land or at sea, including beaches and dunes".

Besides the need for protection of marine habitats, attention should also be paid to the terrestrial configuration of the Adriatic coast, which includes several features of this kind. Sand dune habitat types are still in good condition in Albania, while in Croatia sand dune plant communities are fragmentarily developed and in Montenegro under strong human impact.[36] Touristic facilities, for example along the Italian region of Emilia Romagna, have taken over the protection of coastal ecosystems. However, coastal sand dunes along the Adriatic coasts host high levels of biodiversity and provide a substantial ecosystem services supply. The latter includes climate regulation, protection from wind and aerosol, erosion regulation, recreation and tourism, and existence value of biodiversity.[37] Transboundary coastal ecosystems along the Eastern Adriatic coast would benefit from cooperation by adjacent States in the implementation of the Coastal Zone Protocol.

Some provisions of the Coastal Zone Protocol deal with specific activities, such as "agriculture and industry", "fishing", "aquaculture", "tourism, sporting and recreational activities", "utilization of specific natural resources and infrastructure", "energy facilities, ports and maritime works and structure" (Art. 9, para. 2), as well as with certain specific coastal ecosystems, such as "wetlands and estuaries", "marine habitats", "coastal forests and woods", and "dunes" (Art. 10). Due emphasis is granted to risks affecting the coastal zone, in particular climate change (Art. 22) and coastal erosion (Art. 23). The Priority Actions Programme Regional Activity Centre (PAP/RAC) assists the parties to the Coastal Zone Protocol in meeting their obligations.

36 Šilc et al., Sand Dune Vegetation along the Eastern Adriatic Coast, in *Phytocoenologia*, 2016, pp. 339–355.

37 Drius et al., Not Just a Sandy Beach. The Multi-Service Value of Mediterranean Coastal Dunes, in *Science of the Total Environment*, 2019, pp. 1139–1155.

In the Mid-Term Evaluation of the Action Plan for the implementation of the Coastal Zone Protocol (2012–2019),[38] an example can be found of transboundary cooperation by two States bordering the marine basin of concern. The "'Buna/Bojana Integrated Management Plan" has been jointly prepared by Albania and Montenegro in the framework of the MedPartnership project by PAP/RAC, the Global Water Partnership – Mediterranean (GWP-Med), and the International Hydrological Programme of UNESCO (UNESCO-IHP), in cooperation with a team of experts of the two countries, under the guidance of the Albanian Ministry of Environment, Forestry and Water Management and the Montenegrin Ministry of Sustainable Development and Tourism. It is the first pilot case testing the implementation of the Water Framework Directive and the Coastal Zone Protocol. With reference to the transboundary initiative, the parties acknowledged the complexity of the task. In particular, they reported that

> a number of difficulties were encountered since the beginning of the plan preparation. These were related in the first place to the significant difference in availability and type of data, insufficient local expertise, different legal systems, etc. In spite of all that, the Plan has been drafted and it is undergoing the consultation and harmonization process with national administrations and key stakeholders. Hopefully, it will represent a bundle full of lessons learned, ready to be replicated in other areas in the Mediterranean.[39]

A Common Regional Framework (CRF) for integrated coastal zone management was adopted by the meeting of the parties in 2019.[40] Tools to implement the CRF include monitoring activities; environmental assessments; coordination of planning processes and governance mechanisms; marine spatial planning; land policy; economic, financial, and fiscal instruments; training; communication and information; and international cooperation.

B. The Agreement on the Conservation of Cetaceans of the Black Sea, Mediterranean Sea and Contiguous Atlantic Area

The Agreement on the Conservation of Cetaceans of the Black Sea, Mediterranean Sea and Contiguous Atlantic Area (Monaco, 1996; ACCOBAMS) is one of the agreements concluded within the framework of the Convention on the Conservation of Migratory Species of Wild Animals (Bonn, 1979; CMS).[41]

In the preamble of the CMS, the parties recognize "that wild animals in their innumerable forms are an irreplaceable part of the earth's natural system which

38 Decision IG.22/11 (Annex), UNEP(DEPI)/MED IG.22/28.

39 *Ibid.*, para. 40.

40 Decision IG.24/5 (Annex), UNEP/MED IG.24/22.

41 See Scovazzi, The Agreement on the Conservation of Cetaceans of the Black Sea, the Mediterranean Sea and the Contiguous Atlantic Area, in Mekouar and Prieur (coord.), *Droit, humanité et environnement – Mélanges en l'honneur de Stéphane Doumbé-Billé*, Bruxelles, 2020, p. 589.

must be conserved for the good of mankind" and declare themselves aware "that each generation of man holds the resources of the earth for future generations and has an obligation to ensure that this legacy is conserved and, where utilized, is used wisely". Migratory animals face several threats, especially during their movements, such as pollution of habitats, deterioration of natural stop-over places, and direct hazards from hunting or fishing. The parties to the CMS acknowledge "the need to take action to avoid any migratory species becoming endangered" (Art. II, paras. 1 and 2).[42] Fifteen cetacean species are listed in Appendix I ("Endangered migratory species") and many others in Appendix II ("Migratory species having an unfavourable conservation status").

The CMS calls for the conclusion of specific agreements for the protection of certain species worldwide or in particular regions. Art. IV, para. 4, encourages the parties "to take action with a view to concluding agreements for any population or any geographically separate part of the population of any species or lower taxon of wild animals, numbers of which periodically cross one or more national jurisdictional boundaries".

ACCOBAMS, which is one of the agreements concluded under Art. IV, para. 4, CMS, was opened for signature in Monaco on 24 November 1996 and entered into force on 1 June 2001. It is now binding on 24 out of the 29 States that border the marine waters to which it applies. The only State in the region of concern for this study that is not a party to ACCOBAMS is Bosnia and Herzegovina. The European Union has not yet ratified the instrument, even though it has the right to do so.

As regards its main principles and objectives, ACCOBAMS is one of the products of the trend towards international cooperation for the protection of the environment that has taken place after the United Nations Conference on Environment and Development (Rio de Janeiro, 1992; UNCED). The major environmental principles embodied in the Rio Declaration on Environment and Development are found in the ACCOBAMS text. In the preamble, the parties recognize that cetaceans must be conserved for the benefit of present and future generations (so-called principle of intergenerational equity) and that their conservation is a common concern. They acknowledge the importance of integrating actions to conserve cetaceans with activities related to socio-economic development, including fishing and free circulation of vessels (principle of sustainable development). They stress the need to ensure cooperation among all the stakeholders, namely States, regional economic integration organizations, intergovernmental organizations, and the non-governmental sector. They call for the provision of assistance, in a spirit of solidarity, to developing range States for research, training, monitoring, and the establishment or improvement of scientific and administrative institutions.

42 "Migratory species" means the entire population or any geographical separate part of the population of any species or lower taxon of wild animals, a significant proportion of whose members cyclically and predictably cross one or more jurisdictional boundaries (Art. I, para. 1, a). "Habitat" means any area in the range of a migratory species which contains suitable living conditions for that species (Art. I, para. 1, g).

Art. II, para. 4, binds the parties to apply the precautionary principle in implementing the measures prescribed under the Agreement. According to para. 1, c, of Annex 2, environmental impact assessment is required for allowing activities that may affect cetaceans or their habitat, including fisheries, offshore exploration and exploitation, nautical sports, tourism and cetacean watching, as well as for establishing the conditions under which such activities may be conducted.

The ACCOBAMS parties declare in the preamble that cetaceans "are an integral part of the marine ecosystem which must be conserved for the benefit of present and future generations, and that their conservation is a common concern". Several threats adversely affect the conservation status of cetaceans in the waters where ACCOBAMS applies, such as degradation and disturbance of their habitats, pollution, reduction of food resources, use and abandonment of non-selective fishing gear, as well as deliberate and incidental catches, as stated in the ACCOBAMS preamble.[43]

ACCOBAMS binds the parties to achieve and maintain a favourable conservation status for cetaceans.[44] The main obligations of the parties are to prohibit any deliberate taking of cetaceans, to create and maintain a network of specially protected areas to conserve cetaceans (Art. II, para. 1) and to take the measures specified in the conservation plan (Annex 2).

According to Art. I, para. 2, ACCOBAMS applies to all cetaceans that have a range which lies entirely or partly within the Agreement area or that accidentally or occasionally frequent the Agreement area. In order to avoid ambiguity, a list of cetaceans covered by the Agreement is drawn up in Annex 1. It includes three species of the Black Sea and eighteen species of the Mediterranean Sea and contiguous Atlantic waters. The list is only indicative (Art. I, para. 2) and, consequently, also other species of cetaceans can be covered by ACCOBAMS.

It is worth mentioning that ACCOBAMS does not contain any provisions that exclude its application to military ships or State-owned ships in general. It follows that military activities fall under the scope of ACCOBAMS.

43 A more detailed list of threats affecting cetaceans is found in an introductory note on *ACCOBAMS – A Biodiversity Conservation Tool for the Mediterranean and Black Seas*, published in the booklet containing the official text of ACCOBAMS.

44 Under Art. I, para. 3, ACCOBAMS, the expression favourable conservation status has to be defined as it is in Art. I, para. 1, c, CMS:

> Conservation status will be taken as "favourable" when: (1) population dynamics data indicate that the migratory species is maintaining itself on a long-term basis as a viable component of its ecosystems; (2) the range of the migratory species is neither currently being reduced, nor is likely to be reduced, on a long-term basis; (3) there is, and will be in the foreseeable future sufficient habitat to maintain the population of the migratory species on a long-term basis; and (4) the distribution and abundance of the migratory species approach historic coverage and levels to the extent that potentially suitable ecosystems exist and to the extent consistent with wise wildlife management.

ACCOBAMS applies in general to all "maritime waters" within the "Agreement area", irrespective of their legal condition, be they maritime internal waters,[45] territorial seas, exclusive economic zones, fishing zones, ecological protection zones, or high seas. An important element from the legal point of view is represented by the disclaimer provisions contained in ACCOBAMS (Art. I, para. 1, b and c):

> Nothing in this Agreement nor any act adopted on the basis of this Agreement shall prejudice the rights and obligations, the present and future claims or legal views of any State relating to the law of the sea . . ., in particular the nature and the extent of marine areas, the delimitation of marine areas between States with opposite or adjacent coasts, freedom of navigation on the high seas, the right and the modalities of passage through straits used for international navigation and the right of innocent passage in territorial seas, as well as the nature and extent of the jurisdiction of the coastal State, the flag State and the port State.
>
> No act or activity undertaken on the basis of this Agreement shall constitute grounds for claiming, contending or disputing any claim to national sovereignty or jurisdiction.

In fact, while all the States bordering the Black Sea and the contiguous Atlantic area have established an exclusive economic zone beyond a 12-n.m. territorial sea, there is at present in the Mediterranean Sea a great variety of coastal zones subject to national jurisdiction beyond the territorial sea.[46]

As provided for in Art. XIII, ACCOBAMS is open for signature and ratification "by any range State, whether or not areas under its jurisdiction lie within the Agreement area". "Range State" is defined as "any State that exercises sovereignty and/or jurisdiction over any part of the range of a cetacean population covered by this Agreement, or a State, flag vessels of which are engaged in activities in the Agreement area which may affect the conservation of cetaceans" (Art. I, para. 3, g). In turn, "range" is defined as "all areas of water that a cetacean inhabits, stays in temporarily, or crosses at any time on its normal migration route within the Agreement area" (Art. I, para. 3, f).

From these two definitions, it may be inferred that also States which do not border the waters of the Agreement area can become parties to ACCOBAMS, provided that they exercise sovereignty or jurisdiction over waters falling within the range of cetaceans that stay temporarily or cross the waters falling under the Agreement area. Moreover, also other States are entitled to become parties to ACCOBAMS, provided that ships flying their flag are engaged in activities which may affect the conservation of cetaceans (for example, shipping, as it entails the risk of collisions with cetaceans, or naval exercises, as they produce underwater noise). Participation

45 However, under Art. XV, a reservation may be entered in respect of a specifically delimited part of internal waters.

46 See Chapter 1 of this book.

by the non-regional States concerned could only strengthen the cooperation established under ACCOBAMS.

As mentioned previously, ACCOBAMS is also open to the participation by regional economic integration organizations at least one member of which is a range State, such as the European Union. According to its rules, this international organization is entitled to exercise an exclusive competence in the field of fisheries and a competence shared with its member States in the field of the protection of the environment. The European Union (at that time European Community) did participate to the negotiations for ACCOBAMS and pointed out that it is:

> fully committed to the conservation of these species. As a matter of fact, all cetaceans are fully protected under the EU Directive for the conservation of natural habitats, and of wild flora and fauna.
>
> Furthermore, this draft agreement has some important aspects in relation with fisheries regulations, a matter of full Community competence. This implies that any disposition dealing specifically with the regulation of fisheries will have to be agreed upon within the framework of the Common Fisheries Policy, by all the Member States of the European Union, before it can be agreed upon by those Member States who will become Parties to the proposed agreement.

Reference is made in the statement to Directive 92/43 of 21 May 1992 on the conservation of natural habitats and of wild fauna and flora. The legislation adopted by the European Union in the field of fisheries includes numerous enactments that are frequently revised and updated. Instruments of special relevance for ACCOBAMS include Regulation No. 1005/2008 of 29 September 2008, establishing a Community system to prevent, deter, and eliminate illegal, unreported, and unregulated fishing, and Regulation No. 1224/2009 of 20 November 2009, establishing a Community control system for ensuring compliance with the rules of the common fisheries policy as well as the legislation prohibiting the use of drift nets.

One of the main obligations of the Parties to ACCOBAMS is to "prohibit and take all necessary measures to eliminate, where this is not already done, any deliberate taking of cetaceans" (Art. II, para. 1). Under Art. I, para. 3, the term "taking" is to be intended in the very broad meaning as it is defined in Art. I, para. 1, i, CMS, that is, "taking, hunting, fishing, capturing, harassing, deliberate killing or attempting to engage in any such conduct".

Not only whaling in any of its forms, but also all activities which may harass cetaceans are consequently banned in the Agreement area. This kind of ban is in full conformity with the UNCLOS: in fact, according to Art. 65, nothing in Part V (that is, the UNCLOS part dealing with the exclusive economic zone) "restricts the right of a coastal State or the competence of an international organization, as appropriate, to prohibit, limit or regulate the exploitation of marine mammals more strictly than provided for" in Part V itself.

Two exceptions to the interdiction of "taking" are envisaged by Art. II, para. 2, namely in emergency situations and for research purposes. The exceptions are defined in very strict terms. The emergency situations are only those "where exceptionally unfavourable or endangering conditions" for the conservation status of cetaceans occur, as indicated in Annex 2, para. 6. Research activities which may entail the "taking" of cetaceans are only those aimed at maintaining their favourable conservation status. They must be "non-lethal", that is, not resulting in the killing of these animals, and "*in situ*", that is carried out in their natural habitat and not in other places (laboratories, dolphinaria, etc.).

Coming to the specific purpose of this study, it is to be considered that cetaceans use vast spaces and require specific environments for their natural needs and behaviors. This is why another main obligation of Parties to ACCOBAMS is to establish a network of marine protected areas that would contribute to achieve and maintain a favourable conservation status for cetaceans. Under Art. II, para. 1,

> Parties . . . shall co-operate to create and maintain a network of specially protected areas to conserve cetaceans.

In this regard, para. 3 of Annex 2 to ACCOBAMS makes a specific reference to the Barcelona Convention and its Areas Protocol as the appropriate framework within which specially protected areas can be established that serve as habitats for cetaceans or provide important food resources for them. In addition to this explicit reference, para. 3 of Annex 2 to ACCOBAMS leaves open the possibility to use for this purpose "other appropriate instruments".

a. The Proposed Marine Protected Areas for Cetaceans

The ACCOBAMS parties still have to achieve the objective of creating and maintaining a network of specially protected areas to conserve cetaceans. Such areas should coincide with those sites recognized as Cetaceans Critical Habitats (CCHs). Their identification is based on the overlapping of Important Marine Mammal Areas (IMMAs) and the mapping of anthropogenic threats.

Resolution 3.22, adopted in 2007 by the meeting of the parties and titled "Marine Protected Areas for Cetaceans", includes the first list of MPAs recommended by the Scientific Committee of ACCOBAMS. The list comprises 18 sites. The instrument contains a number of criteria for the selection of protected areas, together with a format for the related proposal (Annex 1), as well as a set of guidelines for the establishment and management of MPAs for cetaceans (Annex 2).

Resolution 4.15, adopted in 2010 and entitled "Marine Protected Areas of Importance for Cetaceans Conservation", added new sites to the previous list (which reaches now 22 sites) and encouraged the States concerned to promote the institution of the areas of special importance for cetaceans to ensure their effective management. It is worth mentioning that the ACCOBAMS parties noted with satisfaction, *inter alia*, the progress towards the inclusion in the NATURA 2000 Network of the *Cres-Lošinj* MPA in Croatia for the protection of some small cetacean species.

Resolution 6.24, adopted in 2016 and titled "New Areas of Conservation of Cetaceans Habitats", took note, *inter alia*, of the revised guidelines for the establishment and management of MPAs for cetaceans; encouraged MPA managers of areas within CCHs to implement relevant management actions; encouraged the parties to update regularly the list of areas containing CCHs in collaboration with the Scientific Committee; and requested the Task Manager on CCH, the regional representatives, and the coordinators of conservation plans to revise the existing CCHs, taking into account the proposed IMMAs and the threat-based management approach, evaluate the effectiveness of management within CCHs, and revise and update the relevant tools.

The ACCOBAMS parties are still working on the revised identification of CCHs in the ACCOBAMS area, with the view of proposing spatial management measures. Prospects do not seem promising, as the last Meeting of ACCOBAMS Parties, held in 2022, failed to adopt a draft resolution that encouraged parties to implement relevant measures in identified CCHs.[47]

A detailed identification of the proposed CCHs within the framework of ACCOBAMS is available in Figure 3.1. The map is currently being updated through a threat management approach that combines both the inventory of human activities and the distribution of the populations of cetaceans. In the Adriatic and Ionian region, four CCHs are proposed. The "Waters along east coast of the Cres-Lošinj archipelago" (No. 15 on the map) is identified as an area of special importance for the bottlenose dolphin; the "Sazani Island–Karaburuni Peninsula (Adriatic and Ionian Sea, Albania)" (No. 6 on the map) and the "Eastern Ionian Sea and the Gulf of Corinth (Greece)" (No. 5 on the map) are identified as areas of special importance for the common dolphin and other cetaceans; the "Southwest Crete and the Hellenic Trench (Greece)" (No. 19 on the map) is identified as an area of special importance for the sperm whale. The map pictures the *Pelagos Sanctuary* and the proposed CCHs.

In addition to the identification and establishment of specially protected areas for cetaceans, at least two other issues relating to cetacean conservation are worth mentioning, as they prove particularly relevant to the Adriatic region. New research in the area of interest for this study – in particular, the northern Adriatic – shows that local dolphins contain high levels of polychlorinated biphenyls (PCBs), highly toxic chemicals, and that females pass on their pollutant burden to their young.[48]

47 The representative of Italy expressed concerns on the legal framework and the scientific robustness of the mechanism proposed in this resolution and emphasized the position of Italy that it is not the moment to accept the proposed draft resolution.
(Report of the Eighth Meeting of the Parties to ACCOBAMS, doc. ACCOBAMS-MOP8/2022/Doc. 31 of December 2022, para. 212)

48 The study was led by Morigenos – Slovenian Marine Mammal Society from Piran (Slovenia): Genov et al., Linking Organochlorine Contaminants with Demographic Parameters in Free-ranging Common Bottlenose Dolphins from the Northern Adriatic Sea, in *Science of the Total Environment*, 2019, pp. 200–212.

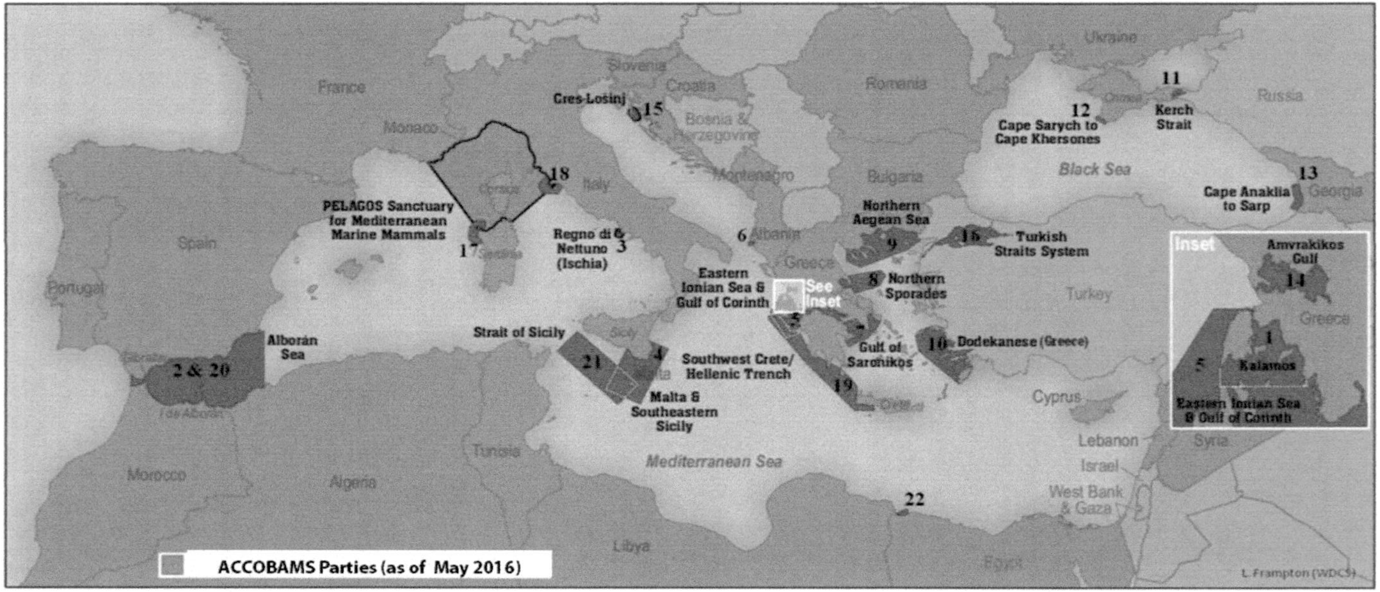

Figure 3.1 Proposed Cetacean Critical Habitats (CCHs)

Source: Map available on the official website of ACCOBAMS, updating "Map of proposed Marine Protected Areas" attached to ACCOBAMS Resolution 4.15 (doc. ACCOBAMS-MOP4/2010/Res.4.15)

The study is noted by the Secretariat of ACCOBAMS, which publicized extensively the results on its website. Another issue of concern for the area of this study relates to the noise produced by offshore exploration activities in the Adriatic Sea and their impact on cetaceans.[49]

C. The Agreement for the Establishment of the General Fisheries Commission for the Mediterranean

The General Fisheries Commission for the Mediterranean (GFCM) was established by an agreement concluded in 1949 as an institution within the framework of the Food and Agriculture Organization of the United Nations (FAO).[50] Twenty-two States and the European Union are today parties to the GFCM Agreement, including six Adriatic or Ionian States (the exception being Bosnia and Herzegovina).

According to the 2014 amendments, the objective of the GFCM Agreement is to ensure the conservation and sustainable use, at biological, social, economic, and environmental level, of living marine resources as well as the sustainable development of aquaculture in an area of application that includes "all marine waters of the Mediterranean Sea and the Black Sea" (Art. 3, para. 1).

The GFCM is entitled to adopt "recommendations" on conservation and management measures aimed at ensuring long-term sustainability of fishing activities, in order to preserve the marine living resources, as well as the economic and social viability of fisheries and aquaculture. In adopting such recommendations, the GFCM must give particular attention to measures to prevent overfishing and minimize discards, paying particular attention to the potential impact on small-scale fisheries and local communities (Art. 5, a). The GFCM is also called to formulate appropriate measures based on the best scientific advice available, taking into account relevant environmental, economic, and social factors (Art. 5, b), and to take the appropriate measures to ensure compliance with its recommendations to deter and eradicate illegal, unreported, and unregulated fishing activities (Art. 5, f).

The GFCM can formulate and recommend appropriate measures in various fields, namely the conservation and management of living marine resources; the minimization of impacts for fishing activities on living marine resources and their ecosystems; the adoption of multiannual management plans based on an ecosystem approach to fisheries to guarantee the maintenance of stocks above levels which can produce maximum sustainable yield and consistent with actions already taken at national level; the establishment of fisheries restricted areas (FRAs) for

49 The issue of anthropogenic noise as a threat to cetaceans and marine life in general is attentively followed within the framework of ACCOBAMS, and several initiatives are led in order to gather more accurate information, which is more abundant for the Northern Adriatic and still poor as regards the waters of Albania and Montenegro.

50 The GFCM Agreement entered into force on 20 February 1952. See Ferri, The Legal Regime Governing Mediterranean Fisheries: The General Fisheries Commission for the Mediterranean of the FAO and the Added-value of Article XIV Bodies, in *Italian Yearbook of International Law*, 2021, p. 189.

the protection of vulnerable marine ecosystems, including but not limited to, nursery and spawning areas; the collection, submission, verification, storing, and dissemination of data and information, consistent with relevant data confidentiality requirements; actions to prevent, deter, and eliminate illegal, unreported, and unregulated fishing, including mechanisms for effective monitoring, control, and surveillance; and the solution of situations of non-compliance (Art. 8, b).

The recommendations referred to in Art. 8, b, are adopted by a two-thirds majority of the parties present and voting (Art. 13, para. 1). Despite their name, the "recommendations" adopted under Art. 8, b, have a binding nature. Parties are under an obligation to give effect to such recommendations (Art. 14, para. 1), unless they cast an objection to them within 120 days from the date of notification (Art. 13, para. 3). The GFCM recommendations so far adopted relate to a broad range of matters, including driftnets; closed seasons; FRAs; mesh size; management of demersal fisheries; plans of actions; red coral; incidental bycatch of seabirds or turtles; conservation of monk seal; records of vessels; port State control; lists of vessels engaged in illegal, unreported, and unregulated fishing; logbooks; and vessel monitoring systems.

a. The Fisheries Restricted Areas

Particularly notable for the purposes of this study are the measures on the establishment of FRAs in order to protect the deep-sea sensitive habitats. According to the definition given by the GFCM:

> fisheries restricted area (FRA) means a geographically-defined area in which some specific fishing activities are temporarily banned or restricted in order to improve the exploitation and conservation of demersal stocks.

FRAs, which can be considered as an example of OECMs, have been established by Recommendation 30/2006/3, which prohibits fishing with towed dredges and bottom trawl nets within *Lophelia Reef off Capo Santa Maria di Leuca*, the *Nile Delta Area Cold Hydrocarbon Seeps* and the *Eratosthenes Seamount*; Recommendation 33/2009/1, repealed by Recommendation 44/2021/5 on the establishment of a FRA in the *Gulf of Lion* to protect spawning aggregations and deep-sea sensitive habitats; Recommendation 41/2017/3 on the FRA in the *Jabuka/Pomo Pit* in the Adriatic Sea, amended by Recommendation 44/2021/2; and Recommendation 44/2021/3 on the establishment of a FRA in the *Bari Canyon* in the southern Adriatic Sea. By Resolution 44/2021/3, the parties adopted a roadmap for the establishment of an FRA in the southern Adriatic Sea.[51]

Among the other measures adopted within the GFCM framework, also Recommendation 2005/1 on the management of certain fisheries exploiting demersal and

51 The specific FRAs that are relevant to the Ionian and Adriatic Seas are addressed in Chapter 6 of this book.

deep-water species can be recalled, insofar as it prohibits the use of towed dredges and trawl nets fisheries at depths beyond 1000 m in all the GFCM area.

GFCM members are under the duty to notify, each year, the Executive Secretary of the GFCM with a report on the implementation of the management measures adopted. The GFCM Scientific Advisory Committee on Fisheries evaluates the impact of the implementation of such management measures and recommends, if necessary, to the GFCM either possible adjustments or new additional measures.

It is worth noting that at the first meeting of the Post-2020 Advisory Committee of the Strategic Action Programme for the Conservation of Biological Diversity and Sustainable Management of Natural Resources (Post-2020 SAP BIO) in the Mediterranean Region, the representative of the GFCM emphasized that the conservation of biodiversity is an important topic for GFCM and that GFCM and UNEP-MAP are in a position to go hand in hand to help Mediterranean countries to ensure a balance between conservation and food production. The Memorandum of Understanding between UNEP-MAP and GFCM is an example of institutional framework for cooperation between the parties of a regional sea convention and a regional fisheries management organization. To enhance this cooperation, the representative of GFCM put emphasis on the monitoring of fishery restricted areas as an opportunity to highlight how special protection measures can serve both fisheries and biodiversity conservation.[52]

D. The Convention on the Conservation of European Wildlife and Natural Habitats

The Convention on the Conservation of European Wildlife and Natural Habitats (Bern, 1979; Bern Convention) was adopted within the framework of the Council of Europe. Fifty States and the European Union are parties to the Bern Convention, including all the Adriatic or Ionian States.

The Bern Convention requires parties to take the appropriate and necessary legislative and administrative measures to ensure the conservation of the habitats of wild flora and fauna species, especially those specified in Appendices I ("Strictly Protected Flora Species") and II ("Strictly Protected Fauna Species"), and of endangered natural habitats (Art. 4.1). The parties also undertake to give special attention to the protection of areas that are of importance for the migratory species specified in Appendices II and III ("Protected Fauna Species") and which are appropriately situated in relation to migration routes, as wintering, staging, feeding, breeding. or moulting areas (Art. 4.3). Several marine animals are listed in Appendices II and III.

Under the Bern Convention, the Emerald Network was developed. It is made up of "areas of special conservation interest" and is based on the same principles as the

52 Process for the Elaboration of the Post-2020 Strategic Action Programme for the Conservation of Biodiversity and Sustainable Management of Natural Resources in the Mediterranean Region (Post-2020 SAP BIO), Online Advisory Committee Meeting, 2 April 2020, Meeting Report, paras. 61–64.

European Union NATURA 2000 Network,[53] being a *de facto* extension of the network to non-European Union States. It is relevant for the whole Mediterranean basin.

According to Recommendation 16 (1989) of the Standing Committee on Areas of Special Conservation Interest, areas of special conservation interest should meet one or more of the following conditions:

- contribute substantially to the survival of threatened species, endemic species, or any species listed in Appendices I and II;
- support significant numbers of species in an area of high species diversity or important populations of one or more species;
- contain an important and/or representative sample of endangered habitat types;
- contain an outstanding example of a particular habitat type or a mosaic of different habitat types;
- represent an important area for one or more migratory species; or
- otherwise contribute substantially to the achievement of the objectives of the Convention.

The same Committee, by Resolution No. 4 (1996) listed endangered natural habitats requiring specific conservation measures, by Resolution No. 5 (1998) adopted the rules for the Network of Areas of Special Conservation Interest (Emerald Network) and by Resolution No. 8 (2012) provided for the national designation of adopted Emerald sites and the implementation of management, monitoring, and reporting measures.

A "revised calendar for the implementation of the Emerald network of areas of special conservation interest 2011–2020" was adopted in 2015. It includes the assessment of proposed Emerald sites in six West-Balkan countries, namely Albania, Bosnia and Herzegovina, Croatia, Montenegro, North Macedonia, and Serbia.

3.2. Sub-regional Instruments Outside the Adriatic and Ionian Seas

A. The RAMOGE Agreement

France, Italy, and Monaco concluded an Agreement on the Protection of the Waters of the Mediterranean Shore (Monaco, 1976, amended in 2003; RAMOGE).[54] It applies to the territorial sea and coastal zone in an area located within two parallels of longitude that includes the French Region Provence–Alpes-Côte d'Azur, the Principality of Monaco, and the Italian Region Liguria. The Agreement aims at preventing and combating pollution and degradation of the marine and coastal environment, preserving biodiversity, and setting up a pilot zone to achieve these aims. It establishes a Commission, entrusted with several tasks, including the updating of a plan of prompt intervention in cases of pollution (Ramogeplan).

53 See Chapter 4 of this book.

54 The Agreement entered into force on 1st March 1981. On the Agreement, see Scovazzi, La révision de l'Accord RAMOGE, in *Annuaire de Droit Maritime et Océanique*, 2004, p. 107.

B. The Pelagos Sanctuary *Agreement*

France, Italy, and Monaco also concluded an Agreement on the Creation in the Mediterranean Sea of a Sanctuary for Marine Mammals (Rome, 1999; *Pelagos Sanctuary*).[55] This is the first treaty ever concluded at the international level with the specific objective to establish a sanctuary for marine mammals. Having a trans-boundary character, it will be subsequently examined.[56]

3.3. Sub-regional Instruments Within the Adriatic and Ionian Seas[57]

Adriatic sub-regional cooperation has been, in the past, particularly accentuated in the field of protection and preservation of the marine environment, even outside the Barcelona Convention institutional framework.

Prior to 1990, due to the isolationist policy of Albania, this had been understood as a *de facto* cooperation between Italy and the former Yugoslavia.[58] The two States took active part in the existing Mediterranean cooperative arrangements, which included, beside the Barcelona System, also the GFCM,[59] in the field of fisheries, and the International Commission for the Scientific Exploration of the Mediterranean Sea (CIESM),[60] in the field of marine scientific research, while specific sub-regional forms of cooperation were primarily aimed at supplementing those already existing at the regional Mediterranean level.

The four main existing forums for sub-regional cooperation within the Adriatic and Ionian may be accordingly summarized as follows:

1. additional sub-regional cooperation within the institutional framework of the Barcelona Convention and its protocols;
2. cooperation within the Joint Commission for the Protection of the Adriatic Sea and its Coastal Zones (Quadrilateral Commission), based on the 1974 Belgrade Agreement between Italy and former Yugoslavia;
3. cooperation within the framework of the intergovernmental Adriatic-Ionian Initiative (AII); and
4. cooperation within the framework of the European Union Strategy for the Adriatic and Ionian region (EUSAIR).

55 The Agreement entered into force on 21 February 2002. See Le Hardy, La protection des mammifères marins en Méditerranée – L'accord créant le sanctuaire corso-liguro-provençal, in Cataldi (ed.), *op. cit.*, p. 241; Notarbartolo di Sciara and Agardy, Building on the Pelagos Sanctuary for Mediterranean Marine Mammals, in Mackelworth (ed.), *Marine Transboundary Conservation and Protected Areas*, Abingdon, 2016, p. 162.

56 See Chapter 6 of this book.

57 This paragraph is partially based on Grbec, *op. cit.*, Chapter 5.4.

58 Albania acceded to the Barcelona Convention in 1990. There was also substantial cooperation between Greece and Italy, which was however focused on the Ionian Sea.

59 See discussion in Grbec, *op. cit.*, Chapter 5.2.

60 *Ibid.*, Chapter 5.3.

Reference should be made to the fact that enhanced sub-regional partnership requires also cooperation among various cooperative networks, as, for example, the Quadrilateral Commission and AII[61] or – nowadays, an even more outstanding example – cooperation and coordinated action between the AII, EUSAIR, and the Quadrilateral Commission.[62]

A. Sub-regional Cooperation Within the Institutional Framework of the Barcelona Convention and Its Protocols

It is beyond doubt that the main instrument for environmental protection in the Mediterranean is the already-mentioned Barcelona Convention with its Protocols. As it has been remarked, "international environmental governance cannot be fully understood if it is not approached simultaneously as a multiplicity of conventional regimes governance and as a process of continuous and structured negotiation".[63]

This is a consideration entirely valid also for the Adriatic-Ionian sub-region. It is accordingly suggested that the Barcelona System has to be read and applied together with different conventional regimes managing the protection of the environment and sustainable development, both at the regional and global level.[64] The relation between the legal instruments of the Barcelona System and the various IMO Conventions related to ship-source pollution represents a prime example in this regard.[65] However, reference should be made to the fact that not all Mediterranean and Adriatic or Ionian States are parties to the Protocols to the Barcelona Convention. Reference should be also made to the potential problems related with the enforcement of the provisions of certain Protocols against non-parties, particularly on the Adriatic and Mediterranean high seas.[66]

The evolving Barcelona System is a prime example of proper application of Part IX of the UNCLOS in enclosed or semi-enclosed seas. An appropriate functioning of the system in the Adriatic and Ionian requires, however, specific sub-regional cooperation in the implementation of the Protocols that are already in force and applicable to all States bordering the Adriatic and Ionian and even more accentuated in areas covered by Protocols that have not been widely ratified on the wider Mediterranean level and within the Adriatic and Ionian region. It is important to point

61 See discussion further in this chapter.

62 See discussion further in this chapter.

63 Raftopoulos, *op. cit.*, p. 509.

64 *Ibid.*, p. 508.

65 See, as an example, the Regional Strategy for Prevention of and Response to Marine Pollution from Ships prepared by the Regional Marine Pollution Emergency Response Centre for the Mediterranean Sea (REMPEC) in 2005. The first specific objective of the regional strategy relates to the ratification of relevant IMO Conventions (vessel source pollution) by Mediterranean States. See UNEP(DEC)/MED IG. 16/10, 30 September 2005, Annex 1, p. 1. See also Mediterranean Strategy for Prevention of and Response to Marine Pollution from Ships (2022–2031) and its Action Plan, Note by the Secretariat, REMPEC/WG.51/5, 8 April 2021.

66 See also Juste Ruiz, *Mediterranean Cooperation and Third States*, Paper Delivered at the 11th Mediterranean Research Meeting, Florence and Montecatini Terme, 24–27 March 2010, pp. 9–13.

out that all Adriatic and Ionian States are now parties to the framework Barcelona Convention, following the accession of Bosnia and Herzegovina to the latter on 19 October 2020. It is, furthermore, important to note that the amended Barcelona Convention and the Protocols that have been so far acceded to by the European Union are forming part of the European Union legal order. This, however, does not necessarily eliminate the need for additional sub-regional cooperation in the Adriatic Sea and Adriatic-Ionian region, although such cooperation may have different forms and extents and considering that it can be undertaken in the Adriatic-Ionian region primarily in the context, or at least by taking into account, relevant European Union policies and regulations. Reference should be finally made to the fact that practically all Protocols to the Barcelona Convention include provisions which directly or impliedly call or at least allow additional sub-regional cooperation.[67]

A prime example of a sub-regional Adriatic cooperation in the implementation of a Protocol to the Barcelona Convention is represented by the 2005 Agreement on the Sub-Regional Contingency Plan for Prevention of, Preparedness for, and Response to Major Marine Pollution Incidents in the Adriatic Sea, concluded by Croatia, Italy, and Slovenia.[68] This Sub-Regional Contingency Plan was adopted within the institutional framework of the Barcelona Convention and in conformity with Art. 17 of the Ships Protocol.

The reasoning for the adoption of an Adriatic contingency plan is clearly explained in the Preamble to the 2005 Agreement, which provides that:

> The Mediterranean Sea in general and the Adriatic Sea in particular, is the major route for transporting of oil and that there is a permanent risk of pollution, which imposes on the Mediterranean coastal States in the Adriatic sub-region an obligation to constantly develop measures for preventing pollution from ships and to organize and prepare response to marine pollution incidents, and that such permanent efforts have to be made at national, sub-regional and regional levels.[69]

The approach adopted by the 2005 Agreement is indeed noteworthy. This sub-regional Agreement was initially concluded only by the three Adriatic European Union member States (Croatia, Italy, and Slovenia), which were, at the time, already parties to the Ships Protocol and, supposedly, capable of implementing it. The Agreement, however, left the door open and envisaged the successive accession by the remaining Adriatic States.[70] Such a geographical "build-up" approach

67 See, for example, Art. 5 of the Land-Based Protocol, and Arts. 17 and 18 of the Coastal Zone Protocol. See more extensive discussion of the various and possibilities for additional sub-regional cooperation within a Protocol to the Barcelona Convention in Grbec, *op. cit.*, Chapters 5.1.3.1–5.1.3.5.

68 Agreement of 9 November 2005 concluded in Portorož, Slovenia.

69 *Ibid.*

70 Art. 4 provides: "Other parties to the Barcelona Convention and its Prevention and Emergency Protocol, in the Adriatic sub-region, may join this Agreement subject to the consent of the Signatories of the Agreement".

may represent a useful precedent also for the Adriatic and Ionian implementation of some other Protocols to the Barcelona Convention and cooperation in other fields. It is, to a certain extent, unfortunate that the said sub-regional agreement, although being ratified by Croatia and Slovenia, has not been so far ratified by Italy.

There are some perspectives, nonetheless, that the 2005 Agreement will be, in the near future, upgraded and extended to other States in the Adriatic and Ionian region.[71] Noteworthy is the fact that a Joint Declaration on the Trilateral Cooperation in the North Adriatic, signed by the Ministers of Foreign Affairs of Italy, Slovenia, and Croatia on April 2021 in Ljubljana, provides that "bearing in mind the need for integrated and coordinated action in cases of pollution accidents and their prevention, the sides will consider the need to review the Agreement on the Sub-Regional Contingency Plan" (for prevention of, preparedness for, and response to major marine pollution accidents in the Adriatic Sea).[72] Furthermore, the Development and Implementation of the Adriatic-Ionian sub-regional oil spill contingency plan has been included in June 2021 as one of the main objectives (flagships) within Pillar 3 (Environmental Quality) of the EUSAIR for the period 2021–2027.

It would derive that, at least traditionally or outside the framework of European Union law and macro-regional policies, the two main forms of Adriatic-Ionian sub-regional cooperation have been, on the one hand, a sub-regional cooperation in the implementation of a certain Protocol to the Barcelona Convention within its institutional framework and, on the other hand, a cooperation in a field not directly addressed by the Barcelona Convention (i.e., safety of navigation), outside the institutional framework of the Barcelona Convention (i.e., Quadrilateral Commission, AII).

B. Cooperation Within the Joint Commission for the Protection of the Adriatic Sea Established by the 1974 Belgrade Agreement

An important milestone in the sub-regional environmental protection of the Adriatic, which even preceded the adoption the Barcelona Convention and its Mediterranean Action Plan, was the conclusion in 1974 of the Agreement on Cooperation and Prevention of Pollution of the Adriatic Waters and its Coastal Zones (Belgrade Agreement), concluded between Italy and the former Yugoslavia.[73] Notably, in the

71 In the Ancona Declaration, adopted at the 12th Adriatic and Ionian Council of 5 May 2010, the members of the Adriatic and Ionian Council "encourage the application of the criteria foreseen by the 'Sub-Regional Contingency Plan for Prevention of, Preparedness for, and Response to Major Marine Pollution Incidents in the Adriatic Sea' by all AII Participating States" (para. 17).

72 See discussion *infra* in this chapter, sub-para. A.

73 The Agreement entered into force on 20 April 1977 and seems still in force for Italy and some of the successor States of the former Yugoslavia, namely Slovenia and Croatia. In the Joint Declaration on the Trilateral Cooperation in the North Adriatic, signed in Ljubljana on 21 April 2021, Croatia, Italy, and Slovenia "discussed the continuation of the Joint Commission for the Protection of the Adriatic Sea's work, which produced significant results in the past".

same period Greece and Italy also concluded an Agreement on the Protection of the Marine Environment of the Ionian Sea and its Coastal Zones (Rome, 1979).[74]

The Belgrade Agreement did not contain specific provisions regarding the protection of the Adriatic marine environment and was more intended as a framework for the identification of various problems and a forum for the conclusion of additional agreements in this field.[75] Its main achievement was the establishment of a Joint Commission for the Protection of the Adriatic Sea against pollution. The latter, however, did not have decision-making powers and its goals were primarily to carry out research activities and to advise the two governments on any question relating to marine pollution. It is noteworthy that the scope of application of the Belgrade Agreement extended to all Adriatic waters, including, therefore, the high seas.[76]

Although the raging war on the territories of the former Yugoslavia stopped for almost ten years a comprehensive Adriatic multilateral (sub-regional) cooperation, trilateral cooperation continued during the 1990s between Croatia, Italy, and Slovenia within the already-mentioned framework of the Commission for the protection of the Adriatic Sea, although in a form and under the name of a "Commission for the Protection of the Adriatic Sea and Coastal Area from Pollution", many times referred to also as a "Trilateral Commission". The latter replaced the Italo-Yugoslav Commission established on the basis of the Belgrade Agreement and achieved substantial results, also due to the work of its sub-commissions, first among which the Working Group for environmentally safe-sea traffic.[77] The latter has been at the origin of the preparation of important agreements between the three States particularly in the field of safety of navigation and prevention of ship-source pollution, therefore in areas not directly addressed by existing regional cooperative arrangements.

Noteworthy is the fact that the Trilateral Commission, which was joined by Montenegro in 2010 and is nowadays accordingly referred as the "Quadrilateral Commission", has undertaken (or should have undertaken) its work in four subcommissions, each covering "priority areas" of Adriatic cooperation. In addition to the sub-commission for ballast water management and the sub-commission for the preparation of amendments to the sub-regional (Adriatic) contingency plan, reference should be made to the sub-commission for the unification of methods of assessment and development of indicators to assess the state of the marine environment. The latter was established with the specific aim of coordinating activities and

74 The Agreement entered into force on 3 February 1983. The Agreement provides for the establishment of a joint commission. The parties undertake to adopt all possible measures to ensure that exploration and exploitation of the continental shelf will not prejudice the ecological balance or other legitimate uses of the Ionian Sea.

75 Gestri, I rapporti di vicinato marittimo tra l'Italia e gli Stati nati dalla dissoluzione della Iugoslavia, in Ronzitti (ed.), *I rapporti di vicinato dell'Italia con Croazia, Serbia-Montenegro e Slovenia*, Rome, 2005, pp. 207–208.

76 See Art. 1.

77 See Gestri, *op. cit.*, p. 208.

exchanging information regarding the implementation of the Maritime Strategy Framework Directive (MSFD) among Adriatic States.[78] These sub-commissions were joined in 2010 by the sub-commission on integrated coastal zone management in the Adriatic. Noteworthy is the fact that at the 12th ordinary meeting of the Commission for the Protection of the Adriatic Sea Waters and Coastal Areas, held in Portorož on 27–28 October 2011, the member States decided to rename the existing three sub-commissions as follows: (1) sub-commission for implementing the MSFD; (2) sub-commission for the integrated coastal zone management and sustainable development; and (3) sub-commission for ballast-water management and contingency plan.[79]

It is, nonetheless, regrettable that the activities of the Quadrilateral Commission, and particularly its sub-commissions, have substantially diminished in the period 2011–2022, particularly as they were supposed to cover some of the most important recognized areas of needed sub-regional cooperation. Reference should be, nonetheless, made to the 2021 Joint Declaration on the Trilateral Cooperation in the North Adriatic, signed in Ljubljana on 21 April 2021. The Ministers of Foreign Affairs of Croatia, Italy, and Slovenia recalled in the introduction to the Joint Declaration "the IMO Traffic Separation Schemes in the North Adriatic and the arrangements reached within the framework of the Joint Commission for the Protection of the Adriatic Sea and coastal areas against pollution", while in the part related to environmental protection, they reconfirmed their commitment to the protection of the Adriatic Sea and to intensifying their cooperation in this regard. Reference was also made to the fact that the three sides "discussed the continuation of the Joint Commission for the Protection of the Adriatic Sea's work, which produced significant results in the past".[80]

It is suggested, accordingly, that the Quadrilateral Commission may nowadays be regarded as one of the most important institutional frameworks for the cooperation of Adriatic States, particularly in the context of Northern Adriatic. Its activities, in fact, have not just covered the field of marine environmental protection but have also related to the holistic governance of the Adriatic Sea and its coastal zones. Its potential, however, still has to be fully exploited, through an enhanced coordination with other regional (Mediterranean) and sub-regional (Adriatic and Ionian) cooperative frameworks, particularly the EUSAIR. A weakness of the Quadrilateral Commission, at least in comparison with the AII and EUSAIR, is represented by the fact that, having the former its legal base in the Belgrade Agreement between Italy and the former Yugoslavia, as well as in subsequent arrangements concluded – after the dissolution of the Yugoslav federation – between Croatia, Italy, and Slovenia, it does not include all coastal States bordering the Adriatic and Ionian (i.e., Albania and Greece) nor all States members to the AII and EUSAIR

78 See Chapter 4 of this book.

79 See Grbec, *op. cit.*, section 5.1.3.5. Minutes of the 2011 Meeting on file with the authors.

80 Text available at www.mvep.hr/files/file/2021/Joint-Declaration-on-the-Trilateral-Cooperationin-the-North-Adriatic.pdf.

(i.e., Serbia and North Macedonia). Noteworthy is the fact that, on occasion of the 12th Ordinary Meeting held in Portorož, Slovenia, on 27 and 28 October 2011, the Commission for the Protection of the Adriatic Sea Waters and Coastal Areas tasked the then Croatian presidency to officially invite Albania and Bosnia and Herzegovina to join the Commission.[81]

C. Cooperation Within the Framework of the Intergovernmental Adriatic-Ionian Initiative

It is noteworthy that one of the important documents for the Adriatic and Adriatic-Ionian sub-regional cooperation, which eventually paved the way to the AII some ten years later and, among others, started the era of the active involvement of the European Union (through the European Commission) in the process of the sub-regional Adriatic-Ionian Cooperation, was signed less than three weeks after the proclamation of independence of Croatia and Slovenia (25 June 1991) and the breaking up of the war on the territories of the former Yugoslavia. Reference is made here to the Declaration on the Adriatic Sea, signed in Ancona (Italy) on 13 July 1991.[82] The importance of the 1991 Declaration derives from the fact that it was the first multilateral document aimed at the protection of the Adriatic Sea, signed not just by Italy and by two successor States of the former Yugoslavia but also by Albania, Greece, and the European Commission. The adopted document was, therefore, a political declaration, drafted, however, with strong wording and clear commitments. The signatories declared their firm intention to cooperate in the environmental protection of the Adriatic Sea and the preservation of its ecological balance and to undertake joint comprehensive regional programmes in this regard.

81 Another example of good practice which may be taken into account, both with regard to the management of marine protected areas in particular and the holistic governance of the Adriatic eco-region in general, is represented – although in a different ecological context – by the work of the International Sava River Basin Commission. The latter was established on the basis of, and with the aim to, implement the Framework Agreement on the Sava River Basin, concluded in 2004 by the riparian States: Bosnia and Herzegovina Croatia, Serbia, and Slovenia. The key objective of the Framework Agreement (and of the Commission) is to achieve the sustainable development of the region through transboundary cooperation. Particular emphasis is paid on the following goals: (1) to set up an international regime of navigation on the Sava River; (2) to establish sustainable water management; (3) to prevent or limit hazards (i.e., floods) and eliminate or at list reduce their negative consequences. Four protocols to the Framework Convention have been already concluded in the fields of Regime of Navigation (2004), Flood Protection (2015), Prevention of Water Pollution Caused by Navigation and Sediment Management (both in 2017). See in that regard Željko, *Sava Commission: Good Practice of River Basin Management*, Presentation Delivered at the Workshop: What can EUSAIR do to Enable the Blue and Green Sustainable Growth in EUSAIR: MSP in EUSAIR State of the Art, 9 November 2021, ppt available at www.adriatic-ionian.eu/wp-content/uploads/2021/11/Item-5_ISBRC-River-basing-management_Dragan-Zeljko.pdf. See also available at www.savacommission.org/.

82 At that time, it was disputed whether Yugoslavia still represented also the Republic of Slovenia and the Republic of Croatia, which both formally proclaimed independence on 25 June 1991.

The next important milestone in the Adriatic sub-regional cooperation was the launching of the AII and the signature of the Ancona Declaration in 2000. The roots of the AII are related to the Stability Pact for South Eastern Europe, which was promoted during the 1990s by the European Union as a result of the Balkan crisis and primarily addressed to all States existing in the region and aspiring to join the European Union. Within that instrument, the Italian government presented – on the occasion of the European Union Summit, held in October 1999 in Tampere (Finland) – the proposal of the AII. The latter got immediate support from the European Commission and from Greece, at that time the second European Union member State in the region.

The AII was accordingly established, and the Ancona Declaration adopted at the Conference on Development and Security in the Adriatic and Ionian, held on 19 and 20 May 2000, and signed by almost all Adriatic States (with the exclusion at that time of Serbia-Montenegro)[83] and the European Union. The AII is, therefore, an intergovernmental organization, which today includes among its membership ten States: Albania, Bosnia and Herzegovina, Croatia, Greece, Italy, Montenegro, North Macedonia, Serbia, Slovenia, and San Marino.

Although the Ancona Declaration, at least in its maritime part, seems to build on the structure and content of the already discussed (1991) Adriatic Sea Declaration, reference should be made to the fact that it is broader in its scope of application. The aim of the Ancona Declaration (and of AII in general) is, in fact, not only to achieve the protection and preservation of the Adriatic Sea and its ecological balance but also to foster peace and security in the Adriatic and Ionian Region by promoting sustainable economic growth and environmental protection and by exploiting cultural heritage that the countries in this region share.[84] The second important difference between the two documents is represented by the geographical scope of application. The Ancona Declaration is not focused on the Adriatic Sea only but on the Adriatic and Ionian region.

An interesting question has been whether the Ancona Declaration treats the Adriatic and Ionian as a separate marine region or sub-region of the wider Mediterranean Sea. It would seem, however, that the expression "Adriatic and Ionian region" refers to the overall territories of all the signatories and not specifically to the Adriatic and Ionian seas. This can be implied from Art. 1 of the Declaration, where emphasis is placed on the Adriatic and Ionian as an "area of peace, stability and increasing prosperity", while the ultimate answer seems to be provided by the preamble to the Ancona Declaration, according to which the aim of the Declaration is to foster "synergies, coordination and complementarities between the Adriatic and the Ionian cooperation network launched at the Conference". The original aim of the so-called Ancona Process seems to have been to better coordinate and to foster synergies between two – at that time, distinct – cooperation networks, that

83 Serbia and Montenegro joined the AII in 2002. After the dissolution of the union in 2006, both Serbia and Montenegro retained their membership.

84 Preamble, para. 4.

is, the Adriatic and Ionian Seas. Such interpretation seems to find its confirmation also in the MSFD, which defines the Adriatic and Ionian Seas as two separate sub-regions of the Mediterranean Sea[85] and seems to be ultimately confirmed by the concluded agreements within the framework of the AII at the time of the launching of the Initiative.

The AII was, therefore, originally launched with the aim of providing common and concerted solutions to shared problems, from fighting against organized criminality to the need to protect the natural environment of the Adriatic-Ionian Sea.[86] Areas of cooperation, more specifically, included economics; transport and tourism cooperation; sustainable development and protection of the environment; cooperation in the fields of culture, science, and education; and cooperation in the fight against illegal activities.[87] However, particularly after the accession of Slovenia and Croatia to the European Union, in 2004 and 2013 respectively, and also following a somehow increased support and involvement of the European Union (Commission) within the process of Adriatic and Ionian sub-regional cooperation, cooperation within the AII has gradually assumed different forms, which include the establishment of partnerships involving Adriatic and Ionian networks, such as the Forum of the Adriatic and Ionian Chambers of Commerce, the Forum of Adriatic and Ionian Cities and Towns, and UniAdrion (the Adriatic and Ionian network of Universities).[88]

The AII is, therefore, an intergovernmental organization with member States (four European Union members and six non-members), with a permanent Secretariat and permanent bodies, the most important being the Adriatic and Ionian Council. The latter is the decision-making political body of the AII, which meets once a year at the level of Ministers of Foreign Affairs. The Committee of Senior Officials acts as the executive body of the AII, where each member State has one representative.[89] The AII, as a regional intergovernmental organization, is accordingly a broader and obviously a distinct cooperative arrangement from that of the Quadrilateral Commission that founds its legal basis in the Belgrade Agreement.

When it comes to the relation of AII with other cooperative arrangements in the Adriatic and Ionian Seas, noteworthy is the fact that the Ancona Declaration provides an express link to the Barcelona Convention. Art. 5 of the Declaration, in fact, stresses "the need to take into account the Adriatic and Ionian dimension within the Convention for the Protection of the Mediterranean Sea against pollution". This reinforces the assertion that cooperation undertaken within the framework of AII is not intended to conflict with that directly undertaken within the framework of the Barcelona Convention, nor, as it will be seen later in our discussion, with the EUSAIR and the Quadrilateral Commission.

85 See Art. 4, para. 2, of the European Union Marine Strategy Framework Directive.

86 See available at www.aii-ps.org/about/who-we-are.

87 *Ibid.*

88 *Ibid.*

89 See available at www.aii-ps.org/about/working-structures/committee-of-senior-officials-cso.

In this regard, it is important to point out that the majority of the agreements in the maritime field concluded within the framework of the AII at the time of the launching of the AII in 2000, and particularly those in the field of safety of navigation in the Adriatic Sea, were prepared by the then Trilateral Commission (subcommission on safety of navigation), and formally adopted on the occasion of the launching of the AII in Ancona in 2000.

The common characteristic of the agreements adopted at that time, particularly those in the field of safety at sea concluded on the occasion or in the month following the launching of the AII Initiative in May 2000, is that they relate either to the Adriatic (i.e., Northern Adriatic) or to the Ionian, and not to the Adriatic *and* Ionian basin. The goals of the Ancona Declaration have been in the past prevalently achieved through a coordinated network of bilateral or trilateral binding agreements on a certain topic and not, generally speaking, through a single multilateral convention involving all Adriatic States and the European Union.[90] Such agreements may be broadly divided in four groups.

The first group relates to cooperation in the field of search and rescue operations in the Adriatic and Ionian Seas, where four (separate) bilateral agreements were concluded between Italy and its maritime neighbours (Slovenia, Croatia, Albania, and Greece).[91]

A second group of agreements, based obviously on the successful conclusion of the first group of agreements, related to the establishment of a mandatory vessel reporting system in the Adriatic (ADRIATIC TRAFFIC/ADRIREP).[92] A trilateral Memorandum of Understanding was concluded between Italy, Slovenia, and Croatia,[93] supplemented by two bilateral agreements concluded between Italy and Albania and between Italy and (Serbia) Montenegro.[94] In 2002, the IMO, upon

90 Such build up approach can be implied also from para. 7 of the Preamble, which provides that States

> build upon a multifaceted network of bilateral relations that they intend to further strengthen by promoting new bilateral agreements, such as those signed in the framework of the present Conference, which can create a homogeneous, multilateral pattern of cooperation through shared content and objectives.

91 Memorandum of Understanding between the Government of the Republic of Slovenia and the Government of the Italian Republic on Cooperation in Search and Rescue Operations at the North Adriatic Sea (Ancona, 19 May 2000), in force since 11 July 2007; Memorandum of Understanding between the Government of the Republic of Croatia and the Government of the Italian Republic on Cooperation in Search and Rescue Operations in the Adriatic Sea (Ancona, 19 May 2000), in force since 16 May 2001; Memorandum of Understanding between Albania and Italy on Co-operation in SAR Operations in the Adriatic Sea (Ancona, 19 May 2000) in force since 27 December 2001; Memorandum of Understanding between Greece and Italy on Co-Operation in SAR Operations at the Adriatic Sea (Ancona, 19 May 2000), in force since 11 February 2002.

92 See Gestri, *op. cit.*, p. 209, footnotes 117–119.

93 See Memorandum of Understanding between the Government of the Republic of Slovenia, the Government of the Republic of Croatia and the Government of the Italian Republic on Mandatory Ship Reporting System in the Adriatic Sea (Ancona 19 May 2000) in force since 1 July 2003.

94 Agreement between Italy and Yugoslavia on Mandatory Ship Reporting System in the Adriatic Sea (Adriatic Traffic) (Rome, 11 December 2000) in force since 28 April 2002; Memorandum of Understanding between Albania and Italy on Mandatory Ship Reporting System in the Adriatic Sea

a joint proposal by all Adriatic States, also formally confirmed the ADRIATIC TRAFFIC/ADRIREP with its entry into force as of 1 July 2003.[95] Since then, all oil tankers of 150 gross tonnage and above and all ships exceeding 300 gross tonnage and carrying dangerous or polluting goods as cargo, need to report to the designated Adriatic coastal authorities their entry into the Adriatic, their position at certain points, and their departure from the Adriatic Sea. In the elaboration of a comprehensive Adriatic System, the Adriatic States opted, therefore, for a two-tier approach. The first step was a conclusion of a series of bilateral and trilateral binding agreements between themselves, while the second was the submission of a joint proposal to the IMO.

The same approach has been followed with the third group of agreements, which relate to the establishment of a common routeing system and traffic separation schemes in the Adriatic. A Memorandum of Understanding has been concluded between Italy, Croatia, and Slovenia relating to the Northern Adriatic,[96] coupled with bilateral agreements between Italy and (Serbia) Montenegro and Albania regarding routeing measures in parts of the central and southern Adriatic.[97] Although the agreed traffic separation schemes did not cover the entire Adriatic, in 2003, the Adriatic States concerned jointly proposed to the IMO the confirmation of the agreed measures.[98] These measures were then confirmed on 28 May 2004[99] and are still in force. This is an important consideration also for the purposes of the present analysis, as the established traffic separation (routeing) measures schemes are a measure which should be taken into account when considering, for example, the setting of new marine (transboundary) protected areas and in the process of marine spatial planning.

(Adriatic Traffic) (Ancona, 19 May 2000) in force since 19 May 2000. See also Gestri, *op. cit.*, pp. 210–211, footnotes 120–123.

95 Resolution MSC.139(76), Mandatory Ship Reporting Systems, 5 December 2002. See also the establishment of a mandatory ship reporting system in the Adriatic Sea known as ADRIATIC TRAFFIC submitted by Albania, Croatia, Italy, Slovenia, and Yugoslavia, NAV 47/3/4, 30 March 2001.

96 Memorandum of Understanding between the Government of the Republic of Slovenia, the Government of the Republic of Croatia and the Government of the Italian Republic on the Establishment of a Common Routeing System and Traffic Separation Scheme in the Northern Part of the Northern Adriatic (Ancona, 19 May 2000) in force since 31 December 2004.

97 Memorandum of Understanding between Croatia and Italy on the Establishment of a Common Routing System and Traffic Separation Scheme in North and Central part of the Adriatic Sea (Ancona, 19 May 2000) in force since 16 May 2001; Agreement between Italy and Yugoslavia on the Establishment of a Common Routing System and Traffic Separation Scheme in the Adriatic Sea (Rome, 11 December 2000) in force since 28 April 2002; Memorandum of Understanding between Albania and Italy on the Establishment of a Common Routing System and Traffic Separation Scheme in Southern Adriatic Sea (Ancona, 19 May 2000) in force since 19 May 2000.
See Gestri, *op. cit.*, p. 210, footnotes 123–126.

98 See *Establishment of new recommended Traffic Separations Schemes and other new Routeing Measures in the Adriatic Sea*, IMO Doc. NAV 49/3/07, 23 March 2003.

99 See IMO, Report of the Maritime Safety Committee on its Seventy-Eight Session, MSC 78/26 of 28 May 2004, p. 86, and Annex 21 and New and Amended Traffic Separation Schemes, COLREG.2/Circ. 54 of 28 May 2004.

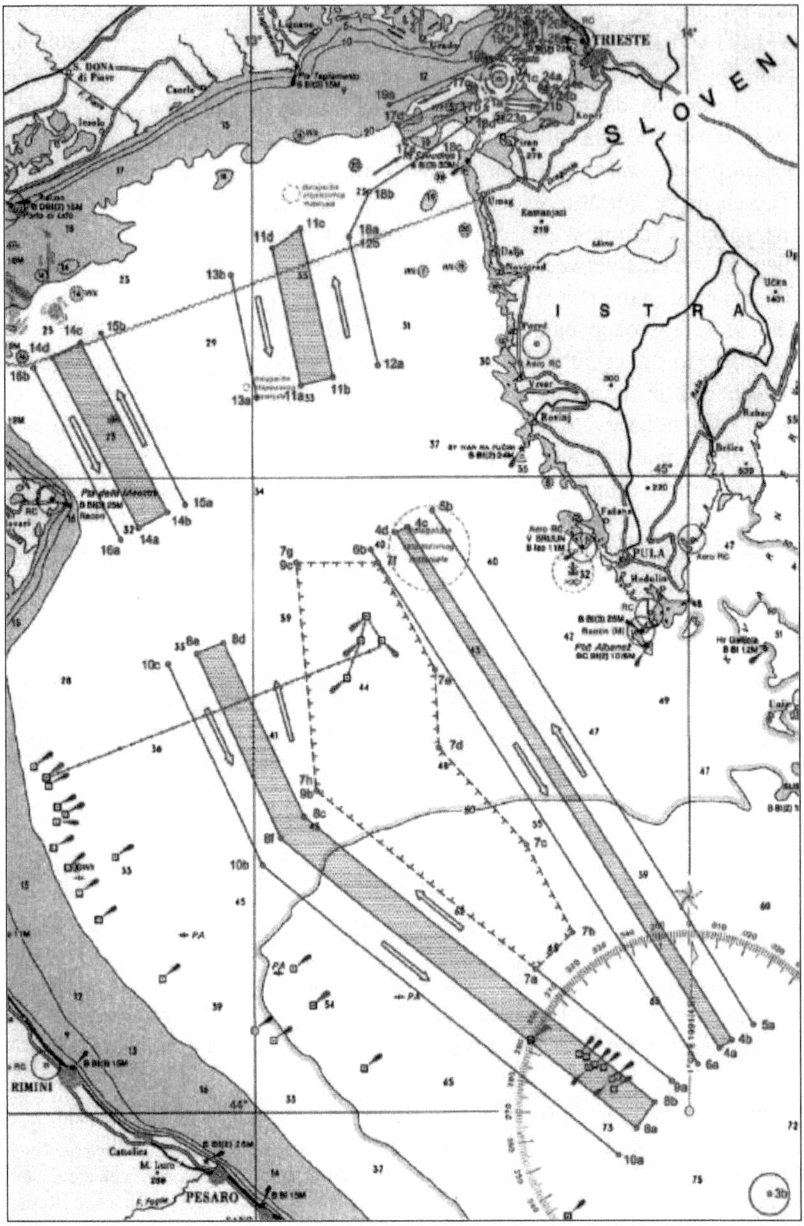

Figure 3.2 Proposed traffic separations schemes in the Northern Adriatic Sea[100]

Source: IMO Doc. NAV 49/3/07 of 23 March 2003

100 *Establishment of new recommended Traffic Separations Schemes and other new Routeing Measures in the Adriatic Sea*, IMO Doc. NAV 49/3/07, 23 March 2003, Appendix 2. The approved version did not include the roundabout within the Gulf of Trieste. See also map available at www.gov.si/teme/pomorske-karte-in-publikacije/#group-37899-1.

Finally, the fourth group of agreements relates to the establishment of a joint system of Vessel Traffic Services (VTS) in the Adriatic Sea. A network of bilateral agreements was concluded in 2000 between Italy, on the one side, and Slovenia, Croatia, Albania, and (Serbia) Montenegro, on the other side, for the Adriatic Sea; as well as between Italy and Greece, regarding the Ionian Sea.[101]

The *modus* used with regard to the preparation and adoption of the discussed agreements in the field of safety at sea represented an interesting precedent and shed some light also on the future possible relation between the AII and other cooperative arrangements (i.e., the Quadrilateral Commission and EUSAIR). As a regional (political) intergovernmental body including both European Union member and non-member States, the AII may represent also in the future an appropriate political forum where sub-regional agreements are finally adopted at the intergovernmental level, after having been previously prepared and agreed upon at expert levels, at times within the framework of other sub-regional cooperative arrangements (i.e., within one of the sub-commissions of the Quadrilateral Commission, EUSAIR thematic groups, etc.).[102]

An important change in the functioning and orientation of the AII occurred in 2010 after the European Union support for multilateral sub-regional cooperation became clear and following the successful adoption of the European Union Strategy for the Baltic Sea in 2009. Since 2010, the AII has been one of the main advocates of the idea of a macro-region for the Adriatic and the Ionian Seas, based, *inter alia,* on a common historical and cultural heritage, the concept of a shared sea, the need to protect the marine environment from pollution, the opportunity of sustainable development and growth, and the common goal to make the Adriatic and Ionian basin an internal sea of the European Union, once the integration

101 Memorandum of Understanding between Italy and Slovenia for the Establishment of a Common VTS in the Adriatic Sea (Ancona, 19 May 2000); Memorandum of Understanding between Croatia and Italy for the Establishment of a Common VTS in the Adriatic Sea (Ancona, 19 May 2000); Agreement between Italy and Yugoslavia for the Establishment of a Common VTS in the Adriatic Sea (Rome, 11 December 2000); Memorandum of Understanding between Albania and Italy for the Establishment of a Common VTS in the Adriatic Sea (Ancona, 19 May 2000); and Memorandum of Understanding between Greece and Italy for the Establishment of VTS Systems in the Ionian Sea (Ancona, 19 May 2000).

102 An important development, which will represent an additional forum for cooperation within the Adriatic and Ionian Seas in the field of safety at sea, is represented by the signature, by the bodies in charge of the control of the maritime transport (i.e., the maritime authorities), of a Memorandum of Cooperation on Establishing of the Maritime Safety Permanent Transnational Network. Despite the fact that the said Memorandum will not constitute an international agreement giving rise to rights and obligations under international law, and, accordingly, will not create any legally binding or financial rights or obligations for its signatories, the instrument will nonetheless provide for an additional framework of cooperation and coordination among its Parties. Based on the provisions of Art. 1, paras. 2 and 3, of the draft Memorandum of Cooperation, the main objectives of the Network will be to promote systematic coordination and cooperation in the field of maritime safety in the Adriatic and Ionian Region, as well as to harmonize, standardize, develop, and improve technical, technological, and operational activities for raising the efficiency, quality, and availability of public maritime safety services. The Network will be supported by several Thematic Working Groups ensuring expert, technical, and operational support and assistance to the Network activities. Copy of the Memorandum on file with the authors.

process in the region is concluded. Based on that, the Ministries of Foreign Affairs of the eight countries of the AII approved, under Italian chairmanship, a Declaration on the Support of the European Union Strategy for the Adriatic Ionian Basin (5 May 2010, Ancona, Italy).[103]

Also as a result of said activities, the European Council gave mandate to the European Union Commission in December 2012 to present a new strategy,[104] which became the EUSAIR and was finally endorsed by the European Council on 24 October 2014.[105]

D. Cooperation Within the Framework of the European Union Strategy for the Adriatic and Ionian Region (EUSAIR)

As already emphasized, an important driver of the Adriatic-Ionian sub-regional cooperation, particularly in the field of protection and preservation of the marine environment of the Adriatic and Ionian Seas, has been played by the European Union, particularly through its Commission. This is, of course, straightforward, taking into account the full European Union membership of Croatia, Italy, Greece, and Slovenia; the European perspective of other States in the region; and the exclusive or shared competences of the European Union in maritime affairs (i.e., fisheries and environment, respectively).

An important landmark occurred with the adoption of the 2007 Communication of the Commission regarding an Integrated Maritime Policy for the European Union (the Blue Book),[106] which advocates the exploitation of the potential of the sea in order to achieve growth in an environmentally sustainable manner. Furthermore, in 2008, the MSFD was adopted, with the objective of providing "a framework within which Member States shall take the necessary measures to achieve or maintain good environmental status in the marine environment by the year 2020 at latest".[107] Of particular importance in the Mediterranean and Adriatic context have been the adopted Communication by the Commission and the efforts by the European Union to promote an Integrated Maritime Policy (EU-IMP) for a better Governance of the Mediterranean.[108] The latter were subsequently reflected in the

103 Declaration of the Adriatic Ionian Council on the support to the EUSAIR. Text available at www.esteri.it/mae/resource/doc/2019/03/12_declaration_of_the_aic_on_the_support_to_the_eu_strategy_final.pdf.

104 Communication from the Commission to the European Parliament, the Council, the European Economic and Social Committee on the Regions concerning the European Union Strategy for the Adriatic and Ionian Region, Brussels, 17 June 2014, COM (2014) 357 final.

105 Council conclusions on the European Union Strategy for the Adriatic and Ionian Region (EUSAIR), General Affairs Council Meeting, Brussels, 29 September 2014.

106 COM (2007) 575 final, Brussels, 10 October 2007.

107 Art. 1, para. 1. See also Communication from the Commission to the Council and the European Parliament Establishing an Environmental Strategy for the Mediterranean, 5 September 2006, COM (2006) 475 final.

108 Communication from the Commission to the Council and the European Parliament of 11 November 2009, *Towards an Integrated Maritime Policy for better governance in the Mediterranean*, COM (2009)/0466 final.

adopted Communication by the Commission on "Maritime Strategy for the Adriatic and Ionian Seas" in 2012,[109] which sets out the framework for the elaboration of a "coherent maritime strategy and corresponding Action Plan by the end of 2013". The Communication aimed to provide a framework for the adaptation of the EU-IMP to the needs and potential of the Adriatic and Ionian Seas and coastal areas and reflected the established European Union's position that "sea-basin cooperation is a milestone in the development and implementation of the EU's Integrated Maritime Policy".

A further important development in the sub-regional Adriatic-Ionian cooperation occurred during the same year (2012), when, as already mentioned, the European Council requested the European Commission to prepare the EUSAIR, finally adopted by a Council Decision in 2014. Noteworthy is the fact that the said strategy was jointly developed by the Commission and the Adriatic-Ionian region countries and stakeholders in order to address areas of common interest.[110] The strategy and accompanying Action Plan[111] built upon (and upgraded) the Maritime Strategy for the Adriatic-Ionian Seas, adopted by the Commission on 30 November 2012, which, *inter alia*, addressed blue growth opportunities for the sea basin. Moreover, it based itself on the lessons from other, at that time, existing macro-regional strategies (i.e., the European Union Strategy for the Baltic Sea Region and the European Union Strategy for the Danube region) also with regard to cooperation with States non-member of the European Union.[112] Reference should be made in this regard to the fact that the EUSAIR is one of the currently four macro-regional strategies, including also the European Union Strategy for the Baltic Sea Region (2009), the European Union Strategy for the Danube Region (2011), and the European Union Strategy for the Alpine Region (2016). Equivalently to the AII intergovernmental initiative, the EUSAIR currently includes ten countries: four European Union member States (Croatia, Greece, Italy, and Slovenia) and six non-member States (Albania, Bosnia and Herzegovina, Montenegro, Serbia, North Macedonia, and San Marino).[113] However, differently from the intergovernmental AII, the EUSAIR is a result of, and is based on, the relevant European Union policies (i.e., those related to macro-regions in general) and, as such, forms an integral part of the European Union legal order (*acquis*).

The declared general objectives of the EUSAIR is "to promote sustainable economic and social prosperity in the region through growth and jobs creation

109 *A Maritime Strategy for the Adriatic and Ionian Seas*, 30 November 2012, COM (2012) 713 final.

110 See available at www.adriatic-ionian.eu/about-eusair/.

111 See Commission Staff Working Document, *Action Plan, Accompanying the Communication from the Commission to the European Parliament, the Council, the European Economic and Social Committee and the Committee of the Regions Concerning the European Union Strategy for the Adriatic and Union Region*, 2 April 2020, COM (2020) 132 final.

112 Communication from the Commission to the European Parliament, the Council, the European Economic and Social Committee and the Committee of the Regions concerning the EUSAIR, 17 June 2014, COM (2014) 357 final.

113 San Marino was the last State to join EUSAIR (and AII) on 14 February 2022. See in that regard available at www.adriatic-ionian.eu/2022/02/14/san-marino-has-officially-been-included-into-eusair/.

and by improving its attractiveness, competitiveness and connectivity, while preserving the environment and ensuring healthy and balances marine and coastal ecosystems".[114] The Council conclusions on the EUSAIR, adopted in Brussels on 29 September 2014, recognize in this regard the potential of macro-regional strategies also

> as an integrated framework relating to Member States and non-EU countries in the same geographical area in order to address common challenges and to benefit from strengthen cooperation, to contribute to the economic, social and territorial cohesion of the EU, therefore supporting the achievements of EU objectives and in particular the promotion of growth and job.[115]

Macro-regional strategies, including the EUSAIR, are based on the principle of no new funds, no additional European Union formal structures, and no new legislation. Accordingly, macro-regional strategies are based on the idea that each one should contribute to an improved (optimal) use of existing financial resources, better use of (already) existing institutions, and better implementation of existing legislation.[116] It is asserted that the application of the said (restrictive) principles leaves, as already discussed, ample room for coexistence with other already formalized regional cooperative arrangements (i.e., AII).

The participating countries of the EUSAIR agreed in this regard on areas of mutual interest (thematic pillars) with relevance for the entire Adriatic and Ionian sub-region. The EUSAIR is actually built on four priority areas (thematic pillars): (1) blue growth; (2) connecting the region; (3) environmental quality; and (4) sustainable tourism. There are two cross-cutting issues: (1) research, innovation, and small and medium enterprises (SMEs); and (2) capacity building, including communication. Each pillar addresses, in turn, some specific topics. The first pillar includes the topics of blue technologies, fisheries and aquaculture, and maritime and marine governance and services. The second pillar includes the topics of maritime transport, intermodal connections to the hinterland, and energy networks. The third pillar includes the topics of marine environment and transnational terrestrial habitats and biodiversity. The fourth pillar includes the topics of diversified tourism offerings (products and services) and sustainable and responsible tourism management (innovation and quality).

For the purposes of this analysis, it is important to point out that the objective of Pillar 3, coordinated by Slovenia and Bosnia and Herzegovina, is supposed to address environmental quality through cooperation at the level of the Adriatic and Ionian region. Such cooperation should contribute to a good environmental status for marine and coastal ecosystems, reducing pollution of the sea; limiting,

114 *Ibid.*, para. 1.

115 Council conclusions on the EUSAIR, General Affairs Council meeting, 29 September 2014, section 8.

116 *Ibid.*, section 10.

mitigating, and compensating soil sealing; reducing air pollution; and halting loss of biodiversity and degradation of ecosystems.

According to the 2012 Commission communication, pressure on marine and coastal ecosystems is reduced through better knowledge of biodiversity and coordinated implementation of legislation on marine spatial planning and integrated coastal management (i.e., the MSFD and the Common Fisheries Policy). Furthermore, improving transboundary and high seas networks of marine protected areas and exchanging best practices among their managing authorities further preserves biodiversity. Examples of targets set at that time included (among others):

1. Enhancement of the NATURA 2000 and Emerald networks and establishment of a coherent network of Marine Protected Areas under the Marine Strategy Framework Directive by 2020; and
2. Ten per cent surface coverage by 2020 of the Adriatic and Ionian Seas by marine protected areas, in line with international commitments.[117]

Noteworthy is the fact that, according to the EUSAIR flagships 2021–2027 adopted at the extraordinary EUSAIR Governing Board meeting of 10 June 2020, the flagships related to Pillar 3 on environmental quality are: (1) development and implementation of the Adriatic-Ionian sub-regional oil spill contingency plan; (2) protection and enhancement of natural terrestrial habitats and ecosystems; (3) promotion of sustainable growth in the Adriatic and Ionian region by implementing integrated coastal zone management (ICZM) and marine spatial planning (MSP) also to contribute to a common regional framework (CRF) on ICZM of the Barcelona Convention and the monitoring and management of marine protected areas.[118]

The first flagship addressed the need of examination and extension of the already discussed contingency plan for the Northern Adriatic to other Adriatic and Ionian countries, as well as possible risks and future events or circumstances that could damage the Adriatic and Ionian macro-region environment, taking also into account the provisions of the Seabed Protocol and of the European Union Directive 2013/30 of 12 June 2013 on safety of offshore oil and gas operations.[119]

The aim of the second flagship is to try to establish protection and enhancement of natural terrestrial habitats and ecosystems, with particular attention to the ecological connectivity of blue and green corridors and infrastructures.

The third flagship has as its main rationale the assumption that the extension of MSP and ICZM to the whole Adriatic and Ionian region would help

117 Communication from the Commission to the European Parliament, the Council, the European Economic and Social Committee on the Regions concerning the European Union Strategy for the Adriatic and Ionian Region, 17 June 2014, COM (2014) 357 final. See in this regard also OECD, *OECD EUSAIR Synthesis Report: Multi-level Governance and Cross-Sector Practices Supporting EUSAIR*, 24 July 2019, p. 18 (Slovenia's green and blue corridors initiative).

118 See available at www.adriatic-ionian.eu/wp-content/uploads/2020/07/EUSAIR-flagships-GB_F.pdf.

119 See also Grbec, *op. cit.*, Chapter 5.1.3.4.

strengthen and develop sustainable growth (economic and touristic), decrease pollution, protect unique biodiversity, and increase quality of life. Apart from promoting sustainable development, one of the main goals is to facilitate the adoption of coastal and maritime spatial plans (under the relevant European Union instruments and the Barcelona System) by defining gaps in marine and coastal knowledge.[120]

When it comes to the governance structure of the EUSAIR, reference should be made to the fact that also in accordance with the Commission Report on Governance of macro-regional strategies of 10 May 2014 and the related Council Conclusions of 21 October 2014, three interrelated levels of governance are applicable, namely: (i) political leadership and ownership; (ii) coordination; and (iii) implementation. Apart from the highest political level, consisting of Ministers for European Union Funds and Ministers of Foreign Affairs of the nine participating countries, the EUSAIR governance is composed of the Governing Board, which has a coordination role,[121] while the implementation of the EUSAIR and its Action plan is prevalently in the hands of four Thematic Steering Groups (TSG), each group being linked to a specific pillar.[122] It is interesting that TSGs are chaired as a general rule by two States, one European Union member States and one non-member State. Greece and Montenegro are in charge of pillar 1. Italy, Serbia, and North Macedonia govern pillar 2. Slovenia and Bosnia and Herzegovina chair pillar 3. Croatia and Albania are in charge of pillar 4.

When it comes to the relation with other cooperative arrangements, the EUSAIR was, in fact, intended to be an upgrade of, and to benefit from, the experience of more than a decade of intergovernmental cooperation within the AII, which had already at that time created strong links among the participating countries. As mentioned, the AII was one of the main promoters of the adoption of the Adriatic and Ionian macro-regional strategy. The current coexistence and complementarity between the AII and the EUSAIR are, indeed, remarkable.

Following the adoption of the EUSAIR in 2014, the AII had to redefine its role in the new macro-regional context. The two institutions count, in fact, the same participating States and share a similar mission. Accordingly, there was a clear risk of duplication of activities. It was found that an alignment of the two institutions (and their priorities) was necessary in order to make them both more effective and

120 See available at www.adriatic-ionian.eu/wp-content/uploads/2020/07/EUSAIR-flagships-GB_F.pdf.

121 See available at www.adriatic-ionian.eu/about-eusair/governance/.

122 See Joint Statement of the Representatives of the Countries Participating in the EU Strategy for the Adriatic and Ionian Region on a Governance and Management System, Set up in Partnership with the European Commission for the Implementation of the Strategy, 18 November 2014. Text available at ec.europa.eu/regional_policy/sources/cooperate/adriat_ionian/pdf/joint_statement_governance_en.pdf.

complementary. Three types of activities were – successfully – undertaken in this regard, in order to achieve the said goal:

1. the merging of the EUSAIR and AII highest political levels. The Adriatic Ionian Council and the EUSAIR Ministerial Meeting act as the highest political level for both the AII and the EUSAIR in a coordinated way. In fact, already at the first EUSAIR Annual Forum, held in Dubrovnik in May 2016, the political levels of the AII and EUSAIR, represented by the Ministers of Foreign Affairs and the authorities for European Union Funds of the participating countries, were merged into a so-called Adriatic and Ionian Council/EUSAIR Ministerial Meeting;
2. the round tables organized within the AII framework were aligned with the EUSAIR priorities, thus transforming them into a tool at the disposal of the EUSAIR governance, to be used particularly by the EUSAIR TSGs; and
3. a change in the type of participants within the activities of the AII, from governmental representatives to other stakeholders (local authorities, commercial sector, universities, etc.). Emphasis is, therefore, placed on those who will have to implement the Action Plan.

Despite being legally two separate cooperative arrangements, the AII and the EUSAIR are nowadays complementary: they have the same priorities with intertwined governance structure and, in particular, are both involved in the EUSAIR implementation. It is accordingly asserted that sub-regional cooperation, particularly that of relevance for the whole Adriatic and Ionian region and, in particular, that falling under one of the four EUSAIR pillars, should be nowadays better undertaken within the auspices of the EUSAIR, in close cooperation with the AII and the previously mentioned Quadrilateral Commission.

3.4. Conclusive Summary

No significant substantive conflicts may be noticed between the provisions of the main treaties applicable in the field of marine protected areas, as all these instruments are inspired by similar general principles and protection objectives and because the regional or sub-regional treaties provide for a more specific and enhanced protection than that achieved through global treaties (criterion of the added value). Also regional agreements call for the creation of marine protected areas or the adoption of effective area-based conservation measures, in particular: the Areas Protocol to the Barcelona Convention, as regards the Specially Protected Areas of Mediterranean Importance (SPAMIs); the Convention on the Conservation of European Wildlife and Natural Habitats, as regards the Network of Areas of Special Conservation Interest (Emerald Network); the ACCOBAMS, as regards areas for cetacean conservation; and the Agreement establishing the General Fisheries Commission for the Mediterranean, as regards fisheries restricted areas. For the Adriatic and Ionian Seas, four main existing forums for sub-regional cooperation have been established, namely: additional sub-regional cooperation within the institutional framework of the Barcelona Convention and its protocols; cooperation within the Joint Commission for the Protection of the Adriatic Sea (Quadrilateral Commission), based on the 1974 Belgrade Agreement between Italy and the former Yugoslavia; cooperation within the framework of the AII; and cooperation within the framework of the EUSAIR. It is suggested that the Trilateral Commission – which, after the accession of Montenegro in 2010, should be referred to as the Quadrilateral Commission – may nowadays be regarded as one of the most important institutional frameworks for the cooperation of Adriatic States. Its potential, however, has still to be fully exploited, *inter alia,* through enhanced coordination and coordination with other regional (Mediterranean) and sub-regional (Adriatic and Ionian) cooperative frameworks, particularly the AII and the EUSAIR. Despite being two separate cooperative arrangements, the AII and the EUSAIR are nowadays complementary, as they share the same priorities with intertwined governance structure and are both involved in the implementation of the EUSAIR. It is accordingly asserted that regional cooperation, particularly that of relevance for the whole Adriatic and Ionian region and falling under one of the four priority EUSAIR pillars, should be today better undertaken within the auspices of EUSAIR, although in close cooperation and coordination with the AII and the Quadrilateral Commission. The reactivation of the latter and its enlargement to all Adriatic and Ionian coastal States should be a clear priority.

4 Marine Area-based Conservation under European Union Law[1]

Mitja Grbec

4.1. The European Union Maritime Policy and Its Goals

Noteworthy is the fact that there are more than five million people employed within marine and maritime sectors in the European Union. According to data from the European Commission (2014), approximately 200 million people live and 88 million people work in European coastal regions.[2] In 2007, after one year of consultation process, the European Commission presented its vision document, a Blue Book on an Integrated Maritime Policy for the EU (EU-IMP),[3] based on an inter-sectoral – holistic – approach to maritime activities. The Blue Book had as its central goal the creation of optimal conditions for the growth of maritime sectors and coastal regions while ensuring that the objectives of European Union environmental legislation, including those of the Marine Strategy Framework Directive (MSFD) are met.[4] The latter represents the environmental pillar of the EU-IMP and, as such, a "framework within which Member States shall take the necessary measures to achieve or maintain good environmental status in the marine environment by the year 2020 at latest".

The European Union has different competences regarding different areas or sectors included within the EU-IMP. The European Union competences in the field of protection and preservation of the marine environment are shared with member States,[5] unlike in the field of conservation and management of living resources,

1 This chapter is partially based on Grbec, *op. cit.*, Chapters 3.5 and 5.6.

2 Mance, Debelić and Vilke, Integrated Maritime Policy for the European Union as the Planning Model for Croatia, in *Journal of Maritime and Transportation Sciences (Pomorski zbornik)*, 2015, p. 29.

3 See Communication from the Commission, *Integrated Maritime Policy for the EU*, 10 October 2007, COM (2007) 575 final; Report from the Commission, *Progress of the EU's Integrated Maritime Policy*, 11 September 2012, COM (2012) 491 final; Pavliha, New European Maritime Policy for Cleaner Ocean and Seas, in Martínez Gutiérrez (ed.), *Serving the Rule of International Maritime Law: Essays in Honour of Professor David Joseph Attard*, London and New York, 2010, pp. 26–28.

4 Art. 11 of the Treaty on the Functioning of the European Union (TFEU) – previously Art. 6 of the Treaty Establishing the European Community (TEC) – provides that "environmental protection requirements must be integrated into the definition and implementation of the Union policies and activities, in particular with the view of promoting sustainable development".

5 Art. 4, para. 2, e, TFEU.

DOI: 10.4324/9781003367963-4

where the organization's competences are exclusive. Nonetheless, the external competences may be also exclusive if common European Union rules are affected.[6] Both in the case of exclusive or shared competence, the organization may decide to exercise its competences internally, by adopting the relevant legislation, or externally, by entering into binding international agreements on the subject.

The EU-IMP seeks to provide a more coherent approach to maritime issues, with increased coordination between different policy areas.[7] As such, it attempts to coordinate complex and interdependent policies related to maritime affairs and to allocate ecological economic resources in a holistic, integrated manner.[8] An important role is by necessity played by integrated coastal zone management (ICZM) and marine spatial planning (MSP). Their role is, broadly speaking, to efficiently plan cross-sectoral and cross-border management of coastal zones and, furthermore, to overview and coordinate possible uses of maritime and coastal resources.[9] The ICZM and MSP are – as explained in the continuation of this paragraph – two essential tools in the implementation of the EU-IMP both at the national, at the European Union, and at the regional or sub-regional level. Accordingly, the EU-IMP bases itself on the recognition that all issues relating to maritime affairs and exploitation of maritime resources are interlinked; therefore, maritime policies need to be developed in a coordinated – holistic – way.[10]

The EU-IMP is nowadays centered around five pillars, namely: (1) Sustainable Marine and Maritime Growth (Blue Growth); (2) Maritime Transport; (3) Energy; (4) Shipbuilding; and (5) Fisheries and Aquaculture. It is supplemented (or upgraded) by five cross-cutting policies, namely: (1) Blue Growth; (2) Marine Data and Knowledge; (3) Maritime Spatial Planning; (4) Integrated Maritime Surveillance (IMS); and, of particular importance for the purposes of this book, (5) Sea Basin Strategies (SBS) (including the EUSAIR).

The Blue Growth, as a cross-cutting policy within the EU-IMP, may be defined as a set of policy measures aiming at the elimination of institutional and administrative constraints related to marine and maritime activities.[11] It is deemed to be the marine and maritime contribution towards achieving the Europe 2020 strategy for smart, sustainable, and inclusive growth.[12] One of the main aims of the said policy is to develop (maritime) sectors that have a potential for sustainable jobs and

6 See Declaration concerning the competence of the European Community with regard to matters governed by the United Nations Convention on the Law of the Sea of 10 December 1982 and the Agreement of 28 July 1994 relating to the implementation of Part XI of the Convention, *Official Journal of the European Union* L 179 of 23 June 1998. See also Arts. 3, para. 2, and 2, para. 2, TFEU.

7 See ec.europa.eu/info/research-and-innovation/research-area/environment/oceans-and-seas/integrated-maritime-policy_en.

8 Mance et al., *op. cit.*, p. 29.

9 *Ibid.*, p. 31.

10 *Ibid.*, p. 31.

11 *Ibid.*, p. 32.

12 See ec.europa.eu/info/research-and-innovation/research-area/environment/oceans-and-seas/integrated-maritime-policy_en.

growth, including coastal tourism, alternative (ocean) energies, marine biotechnology, seabed mining, and aquaculture, all in accordance, as previously pointed out, with the main principles embodied in the MSFD.[13] The latter aims, through an ecosystem-based approach to the organization and management of marine resources, to allow development initiatives without endangering the ecosystem's sustainability and the main interests of other stakeholders present in the area.[14]

Marine Data and Knowledge, as the second cross-cutting policy within the EU-IMP, is based on the realization that comprehensive marine research, including the collection and integration of marine data, is key for the sustainable development of maritime activities. Reference should be made to the fact that marine research and generally ocean observations are challenging and expensive activities that trigger the need for an enhanced cooperation in Europe and globally. The general aim of this cross-sectoral policy is accordingly that data is shared and secured for the long term. An important breakthrough in this area was the development of the Marine Knowledge 2020 strategy[15] adopted by the Commission in 2010. The aim of the latter is to improve the use of scientific knowledge on Europe's seas and oceans through a coordinated approach to data collection and assembly. Based on that, and after extensive consultation based on a prepared Green Paper in 2014,[16] the Commission published its roadmap regarding the Marine Knowledge 2020 strategy.[17]

The third cross-cutting policy or tool within the EU-IMP is MSP. It actually represents a cornerstone – or even a *conditio sine qua non* – for the implementation of the EU-IMP. The mentioned policy tool is based on the realization that coherent planning and scientific knowledge are indispensable to support the development of strategic plans for regulation, zoning, and management and for the protection of the marine environment.[18] In fact, the increased human impact on the seas and oceans and the increased demand and competition for maritime space for different purposes, including fishing, renewable energy installations, and protection of the marine environment (ecosystem conservation), highlighted the urgent need for integrated ocean management.[19]

In order to achieve the said goals, in 2014 the Parliament and the Council adopted Directive 2014/89/EU,[20] which established a framework for MSP in the European Union. The main aim of the said Directives is to promote the sustainable

13 See Communication from the Commission to the European Parliament, the Council, the European Economic and Social Committee and the Committee of the Regions, *Innovation in the Blue Economy: Realising the Potential of Our Seas and Oceans for Jobs and Growth*, COM (2014) 254 final/2, Brussels, 13 May 2014.

14 Mance et al., *op. cit.*, p. 32.

15 COM (2010) 461 final, Brussels, 8 October 2010.

16 COM (2012) 473 final, Brussels, 29 August 2012.

17 SWD (2014) 149 final, Brussels, 22 January 2014.

18 See in that regard available at ec.europa.eu/info/research-and-innovation/research-area/environment/oceans-and-seas/integrated-maritime-policy_en.

19 European Commission, Integrated Maritime Policy of the European Union, *Fact Sheet*, available at europarl.europa.eu/factsheets/en/sheet/121/integrated-maritime-policy-of-the-european-union.

20 Directive 2014/89/EU of the European Parliament and of the Council of 23 July 2014 establishing a framework for maritime spatial planning, *Official Journal of the European Union* L 257 of 28 August 2014, pp. 135–145.

growth of maritime economies and the use of marine resources through better conflict management and greater synergy between the different maritime activities, whereby account should be taken of the land-sea interface. Based on the provisions of this Directive, MSP is a process by which the relevant Member State's authorities analyze and organize human activities in marine areas with the aim to achieve ecological, economic and social objectives.[21] Accordingly, MSP aims at reducing conflicts between sectors and creating synergies between different activities. On the other hand, while creating predictability and transparency, it also encourages development, while at the same time protecting the marine environment. The latter goal is pursued mostly through early identification of impacts and opportunities for multiple use of sea space. However, traditional uses of the sea, particularly considerations related to navigation (e.g., shipping lanes) and traditional (artisanal) fisheries, should be necessarily taken into account.

It is important to note that Directive 2014/89/EU calls for an increased cross-border cooperation which is not limited exclusively to European Union member States. Areas of cooperation in this regard may include shipping, the laying of submarine cables and pipelines, protection of the marine environment and – most importantly from the standpoint of this study – nature and species conservation sites and protected areas.[22] Art. 11 of the said Directive, titled "Cooperation among member States", provides as follows:

1. As part of the planning and management process, Member States bordering marine waters shall cooperate with the aim of ensuring that maritime spatial plans are coherent and coordinated across the marine region concerned. Such cooperation shall take into account, in particular, issues of a transnational nature.
2. The cooperation referred to in paragraph 1 shall be pursued through:
   a) existing regional institutional cooperation structures such as Regional Seas Conventions; and/or
   b) networks or structures of member States' competent authorities; and/or
   c) any other method that meets the requirements of paragraph 1, for example in the context of sea-basin strategies.

Furthermore, based on the provisions of Art. 12 of the Directive (Cooperation with third countries):

> Member States shall endeavour, where possible, to cooperate with third countries on their actions with regard to maritime spatial planning in the relevant marine regions and in accordance with international law and conventions, *such as by using existing international forums or regional institutional cooperation.*[23]

21 *Ibid.*, Art. 3, para. 2.

22 *Ibid.*, Art. 8, para. 2. See also seaplanspace.eu/msp/.

23 Emphasis added.

It should be pointed out that the said obligations are applicable in all marine waters of coastal States, including the seabed and subsoil, over which such States exercises sovereign rights or jurisdiction, including, therefore, the continental shelf and the exclusive economic zone.[24] Noteworthy is the fact that all European Union coastal States were required to prepare and formally adopt their maritime spatial plans by 31 March 2021.[25]

The fourth cross-cutting policy within the EU-IMP is Integrated Maritime Surveillance (IMS). This policy is based on the realization that a safe and secure marine environment is also a precondition for the development of marine economic activities. Accordingly, IMS aims towards providing common ways for the sharing of information and data among authorities involved in different aspects of surveillance, *inter alia,* border control, prevention of marine pollution, fisheries control, general law enforcement and defence.[26] Noteworthy is the fact that, already in 2009, the Commission set out the guiding principles towards the development of a Common Information Sharing Environment (CISE) applicable to the European Union maritime domain.[27] The latter was followed in 2010 by a roadmap for establishing CISE,[28] and subsequently in 2014 by a communication on the next steps for CISE.[29] The aim of the discussed cross-sectoral policy and, ultimately, of the CISE on the European Union level is to improve the efficiency and cost-effectiveness of maritime surveillance by enabling appropriate, lawful, secure and efficient data sharing across sectors and borders throughout the European Union.[30]

The fifth and final cross-cutting policy are Sea Basin Strategies (SBS). An SBS is, according to the European Commission, a region-tailored approach based on cooperation among countries (European Union member and non-member States) within the same sea basin, with the aim to addressing common challenges and opportunities related to the development of the maritime economy and marine environmental protection. SBSs, including the EUSAIR, are, therefore, not only forming part of the European Union *acquis* but are also forming an integral part of the EU-IMP.

With regard to the Mediterranean – and, more specifically, in the Adriatic and Ionian context (EUSAIR) – reference should be first of all made to the relevant

24 According to Art. 3, para. 4 of Directive 2014/89/EU, "marine waters" mean the waters, the seabed and subsoil as defined in Art. 3, para. 1, a, of Directive 2008/56/EC, and coastal waters as defined in Art. 2, para. 7, of Directive 2000/60/EC and their seabed and their subsoil.

25 In the case of Slovenia see Decree on Maritime Spatial Planning of Slovenia, adopted in 2021 (*Uradni List* No. 116/2021), available at dokumenti-pis.mop.gov.si/javno/veljavni/PPP2192/index.html. See also Bratina, *State of the Art of MSP Situation in Slovenia*, Presentation Delivered at the EUSAIR Workshop: What can EUSAIR do to Enable the Blue and Green Sustainable Growth in the EUSAIR: MSP in EUSAIR State of the Art, 9 November 2021, available at www.adriatic-ionian.eu/wp-content/uploads/2021/11/Item-2_Natasa-Bratina_MPS_Slovenia.pdf.

26 See in that regard ec.europa.eu/info/research-and-innovation/research-area/environment/oceans-and-seas/integrated-maritime-policy_en.

27 COM (2009) 538 final, Brussels, 15 October 2009.

28 COM (2010) 584 final, Brussels, 20 October 2010.

29 COM (2014) 451 final, Brussels, 8 July 2014.

30 *Ibid.*

Communication by the Commission and the efforts by the European Union to promote an integrated maritime policy for a better Governance of the Mediterranean.[31] Based on the process of consultation and within the framework of the EU-IMP, the European Commission adopted on 11 November 2009 a Communication *Towards an Integrated Maritime Policy for better governance in the Mediterranean*,[32] which proposed a set of actions aimed at driving coastal States towards a more coordinated and holistic approach to the management of activities impacting on the sea and oceans in the said sea. Reference should be made to the fact that, according to the 2009 Communication, one main governance weakness in the Mediterranean was deemed to be represented by the fact that

> the large proportion of marine space made up of high seas makes it difficult for coastal States to plan, organize and regulate activities that directly affect their territorial sea and coasts.[33]

The said observations were also echoed in the adopted Communication by the Commission on *A Maritime Strategy for the Adriatic and Ionian Seas*,[34] which set out the framework for the elaboration of a "coherent maritime strategy and corresponding Action Plan by the end of 2013". The Communication aimed at providing a framework for the adaptation of the EU-IMP to the needs and potential of the Adriatic and Ionian Seas and coastal areas, and reflected the already at-that-time established European Union's position that sea-basin cooperation is a milestone in the development and implementation of the EU-IMP. The said achievements were further upgraded in 2012, when the European Council requested the Commission to present the EUSAIR, which was finally adopted by a Council Decision in 2014.

Reference should be made to the fact that the main aim of the EU-IMP is to support the sustainable development of seas and oceans and in that regard to develop coordinated, coherent and transparent decision-making in relation to the European Union's sectoral policies affecting the oceans, seas, islands, coastal, and outermost regions and maritime sectors. The mentioned aim should be achieved also through SBSs or macro-regional strategies (including the EUSAIR), whilst achieving good environmental status in accordance with the MSFD Directive.

4.2. The Marine Strategy Framework Directive and Its Regional Application

It is beyond doubt that the marine environment is subject to extensive pressures and impact from human activities, both on sea and on land. The latter has resulted,

31 See Grbec, *op. cit.*, Chapter 3.5.2.2.

32 Communication from the Commission to the Council and the European Parliament, *Towards an Integrated Maritime Policy for better Governance of the Mediterranean,* 11 November 2009, COM (2009) 466 final, not published in the *Official Journal.*

33 *Ibid.*, section 3.

34 COM (2012) 713 final, Brussels, 30 November 2012.

among others, in pollution of the marine environment, seabed damage, overexploitation, biodiversity loss and ocean warming and acidification. The aim of the MSFD is to maintain marine ecosystems in a healthy, productive and resilient condition while securing a more sustainable use of marine resources for the benefit of current and future generations. Its main objectives may be summarized as the protection and preservation of the marine environment, the prevention of its deterioration and, where practicable, the restoration of the marine environment in areas where it has been adversely affected.[35] The mentioned objectives should be achieved through the application of the ecosystem-based approach to the management of human activities, which should ultimately result in a sustainable use of marine goods and services. Nonetheless, priority should be given to achieving or maintaining good environmental status in the European Union's marine environment through its protection and preservation and through prevention of subsequent deterioration.[36] The overriding goal of the MSFD is, accordingly, to promote the integration of environmental considerations into all relevant policy areas. The MSFD nowadays represents an essential part and, furthermore, the environmental pillar of the previously discussed EU-IMP.[37]

Among the main requirements of the MSFD is the obligation for member States to develop national marine strategies in order to achieve, or ideally maintain, good environmental status of its waters.[38] Marine strategies should be based on regular assessment of the marine environment, on objectives and targets, on monitoring programmes and on putting in place measures to improve the state of marine waters.[39] Noteworthy is the fact that such actions should be done in close coordination with neighbouring countries at regional or sub-regional level. The MSFD is implemented in a six-year cycle, whereby the main milestones for member States have been so far:

1. in 2021 and 2018, member States had to report on the status of their marine waters and set targets to achieve good environmental status based on the 11 descriptors (objectives) set by the MSFD, which cover the health of ecosystems and the human pressure and impact affecting them;[40]

35 MSFD, Recital 43.

36 *Ibid.*, Recital 8.

37 *Ibid.*, Recital 3.

38 According to Art. 3, para. 5, MSFD,

> Good environmental status means the environmental status of marine waters where these provide ecologically diverse and dynamic oceans and seas which are clean, healthy and productive within their intrinsic conditions, and the use of the marine environment is at a level that is sustainable, thus safeguarding the potential for uses and activities by current and future generations.

39 European Commission, *Combined Evaluation Roadmap/Inception Impact Assessment,* doc. Ares (2021)2411326, available at eur-lex.europa.eu/legal-content/EN/ALL/?uri=PI_COM:Ares(2021)2411326.

40 See Commission Decision (EU) 2017/848 of 17 May 2017 laying down criteria and methodological standards on good environmental status of marine waters and specifications and standardized methods for monitoring and assessment, and repealing Decision 2010/477/EU, C/2017/2901, *Official Journal of the European Union* L 125 of 18 May 2017, pp. 43–74.

2. In 2014, member States had to set up monitoring programmes to collect data to assess progress in order to achieve good environmental status and reaching targets;
3. In 2016, member States had to set up programmes of measures that would help them to deliver their objectives, and in 2018 they had to report on their progress in implementing the programmes.

As pointed out by a recent implementation report of the MSFD:

> The MSFD is one of the most ambitious international marine protection legal frameworks, aligning the efforts of 23 (now 22) coastal and 5 landlocked States – in coordination with non-EU countries, to apply an ecosystem-based management and to achieve good environmental status in 5.720.000 km^2 of sea surface area across four sea regions, an area one fourth larger than the EU's land territory. The Directive stretched from the coastline to the deep sea, thus protecting the full range of marine biodiversity from unicellular algae to huge cetaceans, analyzing all environmental aspects from ecosystem functions to chemical properties, and assessing the effects of all human activities, from tourism to commercial fisheries bottom trawling.[41]

One of the important goals of the MSFD has been also to translate the most important international and European Union commitments related to environmental protection of the marine environment into the European Union legal order. This is achieved through the inclusion of the most important principles of contemporary environmental law into the MSFD and, consequently, within the European Union *acquis*. The cornerstone principles governing the operation of the MSFD may be summarized as follows:

1. *The ecosystem-based approach.*[42] The MSFD refers to the ecosystems approach as the guiding principle to the management of the marine environments (recitals 8 and 44), and it expressly requires its application in marine strategies (Arts. 1 and 3).

41 Report from the Commission to the Council and the European Parliament on the implementation of the Marine Strategy Framework Directive (Directive 2008/56/EC), COM/2020/259 final, Brussels, 22 June 2020.

42

> An ecosystem-based approach is a strategy for the integrated management of land, water and living resources that promotes conservation and sustainable use in an equitable way. The goal of ecosystem-based management is to maintain an ecosystem in a healthy, productive and resilient condition so that it can improve the goods and services humans want and need. Ecosystem-based management differs from current approaches that usually focus on a single species sector, activity or concern, it considers the cumulative impacts of different sectors.
>
> (*ibid.*, p. 3)

On the ecosystem approach to coastal planning and management to ensure the sustainable development of coastal zones, see Bricelj, *International Environmental Law: Contemporary Concerns and Challenges*, Paper Presented at the First Contemporary Challenges of International Environmental Law Conference, Ljubljana, 28–29 June 2012.

2. *The integration of environmental concerns into other policies and integrated cross-sectoral management of marine waters.* The MSFD requires member States to include spatial and temporal distribution controls measures in their programmes of measures (Annex VI), including ICZM and MSP.
3. *The precautionary principle and the polluter-pays principle in the marine environment.*[43] Both principles are included in the MFSD as guiding principles for its implementation (recitals 27 and 44), and they form the basis for the programme of measures Member States shall develop for their marine waters to reach good environmental status;
4. *Knowledge-based adaptive management and public information and participation.* The MSFD requires an initial assessment (Art. 8) and the undertaking of monitoring programmes (Art. 11) with the aim to achieve the general review of the marine environment. Subsequent management measures, such as environmental targets (Art. 10) and programmes of measures (Art. 13), are based on the initial assessment. Art. 3, para. 5, embodies in this regard the concept of adaptive management, as it requires that marine strategies should be updated in a six-year cycle.[44]

A crucial principle of the MSFD is that "the diverse conditions, problems and needs of the various marine region or sub-regions making up the marine environment in the Community [European Union] require different and specific solutions".[45] Accordingly, member States are required to develop a marine strategy for their own marine waters, in accordance with a plan of action set up by the MSFD, which should in any case reflect the overall perspective of the regions or sub-regions involved.[46] "Community [European Union] waters" are, for the purposes of the MSFD, divided into four regions: (1) the Baltic Sea, (2) the North-East Atlantic Ocean, (3) the Mediterranean Sea, and (4) the Black Sea. The Mediterranean Sea is then subdivided into four sub-regions, on the basis of Article 4(2)(b), namely: (i) the Western Mediterranean Sea; (ii) the Adriatic Sea; (iii) the Ionian and Central Mediterranean Sea; and (iv) the Aegean-Levantine Sea.[47] Accordingly, the MSFD clearly identifies the Adriatic Sea as a separate management sub-region

43 Report from the Commission to the Council and the European Parliament, *Contribution of the Marine Strategy Framework Directive (2008/56/EC) to the Implementation of Existing Obligations, Commitments and Initiatives of the Member States or the EU at EU or International Level in the Sphere of Environmental Protection in Marine Waters*, COM (2012) 662 final, Brussels, 16 November 2012.

44 *Ibid.*, pp. 3–4.

45 MSFD, Recital 10.

46 *Ibid.*, Recital 11. According to Art. 5, para. 1, "Each Member State shall, in respect of each marine region or subregion concerned, develop a marine strategy for its marine waters in accordance with the plan of action set out in points (a) and (b) of paragraph 2". For a further discussion see Schlacke, Maier and Markus, Legal Implementation of Integrated Ocean Policies: The EU's Marine Strategy Framework Directive, in *International Journal of Marine and Coastal Law*, 2011, pp. 59–90.

47 Art. 3, para. 2, provides that maritime regions and sub-regions are designed for the purpose of facilitating the implementation of this Directive and are determined by taking into account *hydrological, oceanographic and biogeographic features* (emphasis added).

within the wider Mediterranean region, while the Ionian Sea forms a separate sub-region, together with the Central Mediterranean. The Adriatic and Ionian Seas are based on the said provisions – the MSFD forming two different sub-regions within the wider Mediterranean Sea region.

It should be noted, however, that the geographical scope of the MSFD is limited to waters over which member States or third States of the same region or sub-region exercise sovereignty or jurisdiction in accordance with the UNCLOS[48] – and not on the high seas. This is an important consideration which has been taken – and should be taken – into account by the present and future European Union member States, including those bordering the Adriatic and Ionian Seas, when considering their options with regard to the extension of coastal state jurisdiction beyond the limits of their territorial sea (i.e., through the proclamation of exclusive economic zones). The extension of jurisdiction by a European Union coastal State, in fact, automatically entails the extension of the competences of the European Union (including the provisions of the MSFD, as transposed into national legislation) on those waters that previously formed part of the high seas.[49]

Due to the transboundary nature of the marine environment, member States should cooperate to ensure the coordinated development of marine strategies for each marine region or sub-region.[50] The MSFD has, in this regard, also an external dimension, as it calls upon member States to make every effort to ensure a close coordination not only with all member States, but also with "concerned third countries in a particular region or sub-region" and, in this regard, "where practical and appropriate", to make use of "existing institutional structures established in marine regions or sub-regions, in particular Regional Seas Conventions [i.e., the Barcelona Convention]".[51] Regional cooperation is in this regard defined by Art. 3, para. 9, of the MSFD, as cooperation and coordination of activities between member States and, whenever possible, third countries sharing the same marine region or sub-region, for the purpose of developing and implementing marine strategies. Third countries with waters in the same region or sub-region should be accordingly invited to participate in the process of implementation of the MFSD, with the aim to facilitating the achievement of a good environmental status in the marine region or sub-region concerned.[52]

48 According to Article 3(1) "marine waters" means: (a) waters, the seabed and subsoil on the seaward side of the baseline from which the extent of territorial waters is measured extending to the outmost reach of the area where a Member State has and/or exercises jurisdictional rights, in accordance with the UNCLOS, with the exception of waters adjacent to the countries and territories mentioned in Annex II to the Treaty and the French Overseas Departments and Collectivises; and (b) coastal waters as defined by Directive 2000/60/EC, their seabed and their subsoil, *in so far as particular aspects of the environmental status of the marine environment are not already addressed through that Directive or other Community legislation* (emphasis added).

49 See Grbec, *op. cit.*, Chapter 5.6.

50 MSFD, Recital 13.

51 *Ibid.*, Recital 13 and Art. 6, para. 1.

52 *Ibid.*, Recital 20.

The concerned "third countries" in the Adriatic and Ionian are currently Albania, Bosnia and Herzegovina, and Montenegro. Obviously, a third country cannot be legally bound to cooperate with European Union member States in the implementation of the provisions of a European Union Directive. Nevertheless, the MSFD obliges European Union member States to "consider the implications of their programmes of measures on waters beyond their marine waters in order to minimise the risk of damage to, and if possible have a positive impact on, those waters".[53] This provision, read in the light of the relevant UNCLOS provisions, seems to require member States to ensure at least "that they do not cause damage or threats of damage, or transfer damage to areas in the high seas".[54]

Noteworthy is the fact that, on 16 June 2008, on the occasion of the meeting of the Trilateral Commission attended for the first time by all Adriatic States and the European Union,[55] all Adriatic States signed a Joint Statement on the Environmental Protection of the Adriatic Sea.[56] With this statement, they "declared themselves committed to endeavour to cooperate towards a common operative approach in order to achieve the goals of the Marine Strategy Directive". Slovenia went even further when, on 17 December 2009, its parliament adopted a Resolution on the Strategy for the Adriatic Sea.[57] The Resolution directly exhorts for the preparation of a marine strategy for the Adriatic in line with the MSFD and calls upon the Slovenian Government to start the necessary procedure regarding the convening of a multilateral diplomatic conference. The mentioned Resolution further expressly calls for the establishment of a (marine) protected area over the waters of the Northern Adriatic.[58] Both the 2008 (Portorož) Joint Statement and the discussed 2009 Resolution by the Slovenian parliament confirmed the commitment of Adriatic States to endeavour to cooperate in the achievement of the goals of the MSFD.

Furthermore, the Quadrilateral Commission, at the time joined also by Montenegro (2010), should have undertaken its work in four sub-commissions, one of them being the sub-commission for the unification of methods of assessment and development of indicators to assess the state of the marine environment. The latter sub-commission was, therefore, established within an existing institutional structure created within a marine sub-region (Quadrilateral Commission) with the

53 *Ibid.*, Art. 13, para. 8.

54 Schlacke et al., *op. cit.*, p. 70.

55 The extension of the Trilateral Commission to all Adriatic States was one of the goals of the Slovenian initiative named the Adriatic Sea Partnership launched at the MAP sub-regional conference on the Sustainable Development Strategy for the Adriatic in Portorož, Slovenia, on 5–6 June 2006. Montenegro became a full member of the Trilateral Commission on 25 May 2010.

56 *Skupna izjava o okoljski zaščiti Jadranskega morja* (Resolution on Strategy for Adriatic Sea), 16 June 2008, Portorož, Slovenija. At the 12th Ordinary Meeting of the Quadrilateral Commission, held in Portorož on 27–28 October 2011, the parties supported the process to establish a common frame for the definition of a Strategy for the Adriatic Sea on the basis of national strategies. Minutes, Point 1. Copy on file with the author.

57 Resolution on the Strategy for the Adriatic Sea (ReSJad), *Uradni List* No. 106/2009 of 22 December 2009.

58 *Ibid.*, Art. 7.

specific aim of coordinating activities and exchanging information regarding the implementation of the MSFD among Adriatic States.[59] Thus, it may be concluded that the implementation of the MSFD at a sub-regional level represents another important cooperative framework with regard to the environmental governance of the Adriatic Sea and Ionian Seas. The use of existing cooperative networks (i.e., the Quadrilateral Commission, the AII and the EUSAIR) in this regard should be supported and further enhanced.

It is additionally important that the MSFD recognizes that the establishment of marine protected areas, including NATURA 2000 sites designed or to be designed based on the provisions of the Habitats and Birds Directives,[60] is an important contribution and an important tool for the achievement of good environmental status. Furthermore, Art. 13, para. 4, of the MSFD provides that

> Programmes of measures established pursuant to this Article shall include spatial protection measures, contributing to coherent and representative networks of marine protected areas, adequately covering the diversity of the constituent ecosystems, such as special areas of conservation pursuant to the Habitats Directive, special protection areas pursuant to the Birds Directive, and marine protected areas as agreed by the Community or Member States concerned in the framework of international or regional agreements to which they are parties.

Accordingly, the MSFD acts as a framework, within which existing measures can be integrated and complemented with new initiatives, including those agreed at regional or sub-regional level. According to the recital of the MSFD, the establishment of such protected areas under the MSFD will be an important step towards fulfilling the commitments undertaken by the European Union at the World Summit on Sustainable Development and under the Convention on Biological Diversity (Rio de Janeiro, 1992; CBD), as approved by Council Decision 93/626/EEC, and will contribute to the creation of coherent and representative networks of such areas.[61]

Noteworthy is the fact that, with regard to the goal of setting coherent and representative networks of marine protected areas, the MSFD goes beyond the NATURA 2000 Network based on the provisions of the Birds and Habitats Directives (European Union's *acquis*), as it includes within such networks also marine protected areas as agreed by the organization or the member States concerned in the framework of international or regional agreements to which they are parties (i.e., Regional Seas Conventions). A prime example of such areas in the Mediterranean and Adriatic may be a (transboundary) SPAMI established on the basis of the Areas Protocol to the Barcelona Convention.

59 See Chapter 3 of this book.
60 See further in this chapter.
61 MSFD, Recital 7.

4.3. The Birds and Habitats Directives

The two principal conservation instruments in European Union law are the so-called Birds Directive[62] and Habitats Directive.[63] Reference should be made to the fact that, although envisaged as two different legal instruments, the directives work together and are in fact nowadays often referred to collectively as the Birds and Habitats Directives. As previously discussed, the two instruments represent one of the cornerstones of the MSFD. The adoption of the original Birds Directive in 1979 was driven by the concerns of the impact hunting was having on migratory bird populations. Although an early example, the Birds Directive has been seen as an example of successful, although rather strict, environmental legislation. As such, it has represented a stepping stone for the adoption of the Habitats Directive some 13 years after. The main achievement of the Birds Directive has been to impose a strict obligation on member States with regard the designation of sites which meet certain ecological criteria as Special Protection Areas (SPAs) and their subsequent protection.[64] The Habitats Directive expanded such protection to other endangered species and habitats and put in place a NATURA 2000 Network, which includes both SPAs under the Birds Directive and Special Areas of Conservation (SACs) established under the Habitats Directive for habitats types listed in Annex I and the habitats of species listed in Annex II of the Habitats Directive. The overall aim of the two directives is to ensure that such species and protected habitats are maintained in, or restored to, a favourable conservation status throughout their natural range within the European Union.[65]

A. The Birds Directive

The original Birds Directive adopted on 2 April 1979[66] on the conservation of wild birds had been substantially amended several times. A new directive was eventually adopted in 2009 in the interest of clarity and rationality. The main reason for its adoption lies in the fact that a large number of species of wild birds naturally occurring in the European territory of the Member States have been rapidly declining in numbers. Such decline represents a serious threat to the conservation of the environment, particularly due to the biological balance that was threatened.[67] The Birds Directive is based on the following assumptions: the species of wild birds naturally

62 Directive 2009/147/EC of the European Parliament and of the Council of 30 November 2009 on the conservation of wild birds, *Official Journal of the European Union* L 20 of 26 January 2010, pp. 7–25.

63 Council Directive 92/43/EEC of 21 May 1992 on the conservation of natural habitats and of wild fauna and flora, *Official Journal of the European Union* L 206 of 22 July 1992, pp. 7–50.

64 Amos, Assessing the Impact of the Habitats Directive: A Case Study of Europe's Plants, in *Journal of Environmental Law*, 2021, pp. 368–369.

65 European Commission, *The EU Birds and Habitats Directives: For Nature and People in Europe*, Brussels, 2014.

66 Directive 2009/147/EC, Recital 1.

67 *Ibid.*, Recital 3.

occurring in the European territory of member States are mainly migratory species; they constitute a common heritage; and effective birds protection is a typically trans-frontier environment problem, entailing common responsibilities.[68]

The measures undertaken by the Birds Directive primarily address the main factors which may affect the number of birds, including the repercussions of human activities, in particular the destruction and pollution of habitats, capture, and killing, as well as the trade resulting from such practices. The stringency of such measures should be adapted to the particular situation of the various species within the framework of a conservation policy.[69] Certain species of birds should be accordingly subject to special conservation measures concerning their habitats, in order to ensure their survival and reproduction in their area of distribution. Particular care should be taken that the introduction of any species of wild birds not naturally occurring in the European territory of member States does not cause harm to the local flora and fauna.

It is important to note, in this regard, that the scope of application of the Birds Directive is broad, as it relates to the conservation of all species of naturally occurring birds in the wild state in the European territory of the member States. As such, it covers the protection, management and control of these species and lays down rules for their exploitation. The Birds Directive applies to birds, their eggs, nests and habitats. Therefore, member States are required to preserve, maintain or re-establish a sufficient diversity and area of habitats. The preservation, maintenance and re-establishment of biotopes and habitats shall include primarily the following measures:

1. creation of protected areas (SPAs);
2. upkeep and management in accordance with the ecological needs of habitats inside and outside the protected zones;
3. re-establishment of destroyed biotopes and creation of new biotopes.[70]

The species mentioned in Annex I shall be the subject of special conservation measures concerning their habitat in order to ensure their survival and reproduction in the area of reproduction. Member States are required to classify the most suitable territories in number and size as SPAs for the conservation of these species, both in the geographical sea- and land-area covered by the Birds Directive. In such designated areas, member States shall take appropriate measures to avoid pollution or deteriorating of habitats or any disturbance affecting the birds, insofar as these would be significant.[71]

68 *Ibid.*, Recital 4.
69 *Ibid.*, Recital 6.
70 *Ibid.*, Art. 3, para. 2.
71 *Ibid.*, Art. 4, para. 2.

Member States are also required to take the requisite measures to establish a general system of protection for all species of birds covered by the Directive, prohibiting in particular:

1. deliberate killing or capture by any method;
2. deliberate destruction of, or damage to, their nests and eggs or removal of their nests;
3. taking their eggs in the wild and keeping these eggs even if empty,
4. deliberate disturbances of these birds particularly during the period of breeding and rearing, in so far as disturbances would be significant having regard to the objectives of the Directive; or
5. keeping birds of species the hunting and capture of which is prohibited.[72]

B. The Habitats Directive

The Habitats Directive significantly expanded the European Union protection regime in order to potentially include all species of flora and fauna within the territory of member States.[73] Noteworthy is the fact that the Habitats Directive implements the Convention on the Conservation of European Union Wildlife and Natural Habitats (Bern, 1979; Bern Convention) within European Union law. The interrelations between the two instruments are noteworthy, primarily due to the fact that the Bern Convention is a mixed agreement to which both the European Union and European Union member States are parties. The influence of the Bern Convention on the Habitats Directive is straightforward, particularly when it comes to its language and structure. However, on the other hand, particularly due to the mixed competences of the European Union in the field of environmental protection and due to the majority of votes that the European Union and its member States exercise within the institutional bodies of the Bern Convention, one can see that also the Habitats Directive has influenced, in turn, the development and interpretation of the Bern Convention.[74]

Of particular importance is the funding provided to the bodies of the Bern Convention by the European Union, particularly with the aim to expand habitat protection outside the European Union, particularly in Central Europe, Western Balkans, and the Caucasus.[75] The Habitats Directive and the Bern Convention are the primary legal instruments for species protection in Europe. When it comes to the protection of habitats and habitats species in the EUSAIR (through the NATURA 2000 Network), reference should be made both to the Bern Convention and the

72 *Ibid.*, Art. 5.

73 Amos, *op. cit.*, p. 369.

74 Epstein, The Habitats Directive and Bern Convention: Synergy and Dysfunction in Public International and EU Law, in *The Georgetown International Law Review*, 2014, p. 139.

75 *Ibid.*, p. 139.

Habitats Directive, particularly in the light of their links and interdependency.[76] The Habitats Directive should be assessed also from the standpoint that all the EUSAIR States, including non-European Union countries (Albania, Montenegro, North Macedonia, and Serbia), are parties to the Bern Convention.

The aim of the Habitats Directive is provided by Art. 2, para. 1: to contribute towards ensuring biodiversity through the conservation of natural habitats and of wild fauna and flora. "Natural habitats" means terrestrial or aquatic areas distinguished by geographic, abiotic and biotic features, whether entirely natural or semi-natural. However, not all types of habitats are protected by the Habitats Directive: only "natural habitats types of community [European Union] interest". These are defined as habitats which are first of all located within the territory covered by the Habitats Directive (i.e., the territory of the European Union) and which fulfil at least one of the following conditions: (1) are in danger of disappearance in their natural range; (2) have a small natural range following their regression or by reason of their intrinsically restricted area; (3) present outstanding examples of typical characteristics of one or more of the following biogeographical region (Alpine, Atlantic, Black Sea, Boreal, Continental, Macaronesian, Mediterranean, Pannonian, and Steppic). In order to be protected, such habitats shall be expressly listed in Annex I, while species of habitats should be listed in Annex II of the Habitats Directive. Some criticism towards the Habitats Directive entailed that the inclusion within the Habitats Directive is conditional on whether the previously mentioned criteria for being "of European Union interest" are met. In the case of species that would depend on whether they are rare, endangered, or endemic to Europe Annex IV includes, in this regard, a list of species of European Union interest in need of strict protection.[77] Some other species (for example, regional habitats) that are not deemed to be of community interests and, as such, are not included in one of the annexes of the Habitats Directive, are not protected under the instrument. This is, by all means, an important difference between the Habitats Directive and the Birds Directive, as the latter, on the basis of the provisions of Art. 1, covers all naturally occurring European bird species.[78]

The principal measure of the European Union conservation regime, as embodied in the Habitats Directive, is the achievement of a "favourable conservation status". This will be achieved when population dynamics data on the species concerned indicate that it is maintaining itself on a long-term basis as a viable component of its natural habitat; that the natural range of the species is neither being reduced or is likely to be reduced for the foreseeable future; and that there is – and will probably continue to be – a sufficiently large habitat to maintain its populations

76 See further in this chapter on the links between the NATURA 2000 Network and the Emerald Network of protected areas established on the basis of the Bern Convention.

77 Annex V provides a list of species of community (European Union) interests whose hunting in the wild and exploitation may be regulated with specific management measures. Annex VI lists prohibited methods and means of killing and transporting.

78 See Amos, *op. cit.*, p. 300.

on a long-term basis.[79] Favourable conservation status shall be achieved through the designation of protected area and other measures for the protection of species. In that regard, as already mentioned, SACs indicate sites of European Union importance designed by the member States through a statutory, administrative or contractual act, where the necessary conservation measures are applied for the maintenance or restoration, at a favourable conservation status, of the natural habitats and the populations of the species for which the site is designed.[80]

A paramount achievement of the Habitats Directive has been the establishment of a coherent European ecological network of SACs, under the title NATURA 2000. This network is nowadays composed of sites hosting the natural habitats types listed in Annex I and of species listed in Annex II of the Habitats Directive. The said network shall enable the natural habitat types and the species of habitats concerned to be maintained or, where appropriate, restored at a favourable conservation status in their natural range.

Furthermore, based on the provisions of the Habitats Directive, the Natura 2000 Network shall include also the SPAs classified by the member States according to the Birds Directive. Each member State should have – and actually has – already contributed to the creation of the NATURA 2000 Network in proportion to the representation within its territory to the natural habitat types and habitats species.

Noteworthy is also the fact, that, based on Art. 10 of the Habitats Directive, member States shall endeavour, where they consider it necessary, in their land-use planning and development policies and, in particular, with a view to improving the ecological coherence of the NATURA 2000 Network, to encourage the management of features of the landscape which are of major importance for the wild fauna and flora. The said provision goes further on by saying that such features are those which, by virtue of their linear and continuous structure (such as rivers with their banks or the traditional system of marking field boundaries) or their function as stepping stones (such are ponds or small woods), are essential for the migration, dispersal and genetic exchange of wild species. The latter provision is important, as it seemingly tries to avoid the conservation technique which may, as pointed out by Amos, lead to the establishment of "islands" of protected areas, creating genetically isolated populations, which may eventually undermine the viability of species.[81] This should be avoided though the maintenance and the setting up of new ecological corridors between NATURA 2000 sites and other protected areas, either on land (green corridors) or on the sea (blue corridors). Concerns have been expressed in this regard with regard to large carnivores, while, on the other hand, plants are by their very (non-movable) nature at a greater risk in an "island" approach to conservation.[82]

79 Habitats Directive, Art. 1, i.

80 *Ibid.*, Art. 1, l.

81 See Amos, *op. cit.*, p. 369.

82 *Ibid.*, p. 369. See also *Council Conclusions on a Sustainable Blue Economy: Health, Knowledge, Prosperity, Social Equity*, Brussels, 26 May 2021, para. 24, and *Communication from the Commission to the European Parliament, the Council, the European Economic and Social Committee*

Emphasis should be, furthermore, made to the fact that, while the Habitats Directive has generally broadened the protection provided by the Birds Directive due to its extension to many other habitats and species, according to some experts it has in certain aspects reduced the protection afforded by the latter. Reference should be made to the fact that the Birds Directive imposes strict obligations regarding the designation of sites which met certain ecological criteria as SPAs and their subsequent protection.[83] The only exception or derogation from this is possible in cases where there is a risk to human life or health. On the other hand, based on Art. 6 of the Habitats Directive, member States are allowed to derogate from their habitat conservation obligations also for socioeconomic purposes,[84] which is not possible under the Birds Directive, as also confirmed by various judgments of the Court of Justice of the European Union.[85] The latter rejected on many occasions attempts by member States to derogate from their conservation objectives.[86]

On the other hand, based on the provisions of Art. 6, para. 3, of the Habitats Directive, plans and projects that are not connected to the management of the site but are likely to have a significant effect thereon, either individually or in combination with other plans or projects, shall be subject to appropriate assessment of its implications for the site, in view of the site conservation objectives. However, if in spite of a negative assessment of the implications for the site and in the absence of alternative solutions, a plan or project must be, nevertheless, carried out for imperative reasons or overriding public interest, including those of a social or economic nature, the member State shall take all compensatory measures necessary to ensure that the overall coherence of the NATURA 2000 network is protected.[87]

C. The NATURA 2000 Network and the Adriatic and Ionian Seas

As mentioned, one of the main achievements of the Birds and Habitats Directives, often referred as the Nature Directives, lies in the creation of a European Union ecological network of nature conservation areas, called the NATURA 2000 Network. All member States are bound to designate NATURA 2000 sites based on the provisions of both instruments. More than 27,000 sites are nowadays included within the network, either on land or on the sea. This, in turn, makes the NATURA 2000 Network the largest coordinated network of conservation areas anywhere in the world.

---

and the Committee of the Regions on a New Approach for a Sustainable Blue Economy in the EU – Transforming the EU's Blue Economy for a Sustainable Future, COM (2021) 240 final, Brussels, 17 May 2021, chapter 2.3.

83 See furthermore Arts. 3 and 4 of the Habitats Directive.

84 See Art. 6, para. 3, of the Habitats Directive.

85 See, for example, judgment of the Court of Justice on case C-57/89, *Leybucht Dykes* (Commission of the European Communities v. Federal Republic of Germany), 28 February 1991.

86 See Amos, *op. cit.*, p. 368.

87 See Art. 6, para. 4, of the Habitats Directive.

Sites for the NATURA 2000 Network are selected on scientific grounds in order to ensure that the best areas in the European Union are protected with regard to habitats and habitats species of European Union importance, in accordance with a prescribed procedure listed in the Habitats Directive. According to Art. 4 of the latter, member States shall, as a first step, identify and propose for protection important areas with regard to species and habitats present on their territory. The European Commission then selects, with the help of the member States, the European Environment Agency and scientific experts, sites deemed to be of community importance (SCIs). Once selected, the SCIs become part of the NATURA 2000 Network. Member States have then up to six years to designate them as SACs and, importantly, introduce the necessary management measures to maintain or restore the species and habitats present (again) to a good condition. On the basis of the Birds Directive, the procedure for site selection is similar, although it differs in certain particulars. According to the Directive, sites are classified by the member States and, after evaluation, included directly into the NATURA 2000 Network.

It seems important to point out that although the Habitats Directive strongly "recommends", it does not compulsory "require" either the use of management plans as a means of setting objectives and measures within a specific protection area or the setting up of a specific body for the purpose of managing a protected area or network of areas included in the NATURA 2000 Network. This has attracted some criticism, mostly as a result of some so-called paper areas without a proper management plan and without a functioning management body. Based on the provisions of Art. 6, while for SACs member States shall establish the necessary conservation measures, they shall only involve, "if need be", appropriate management plans specifically designed for the sites or integrated into other development plans, as well as appropriate statutory, administrative or contractual measures that correspond to the ecological requirements of the natural habitat types in Annex I and of the species in Annex II present on the sites.

As regards habitat protection within the EUSAIR, reference should be made to the fact that the Habitats Directive has strongly influenced the institutional functioning of the Bern Convention. As a result, the Emerald Network is expressly based on the provisions of the Habitats Directive relating to the NATURA 2000 Network. This resulted from the fact that, when the Standing Committee of the Bern Convention adopted the Emerald Network in 1996, it based itself on the NATURA 2000 Network requirements according to the Habitats Directive. Thus, NATURA 2000 sites within European Union member States are deemed to form part also of the Emerald Network of protected areas.[88] In turn, the Emerald Network of protected areas gives to non-European Union countries within a specific region or sub-region (including within the EUSAIR) the possibility to align their conservation policy with that of the European Union's NATURA 2000 Network of protected areas.

88 See Epstein, *op. cit.*, pp. 152–153.

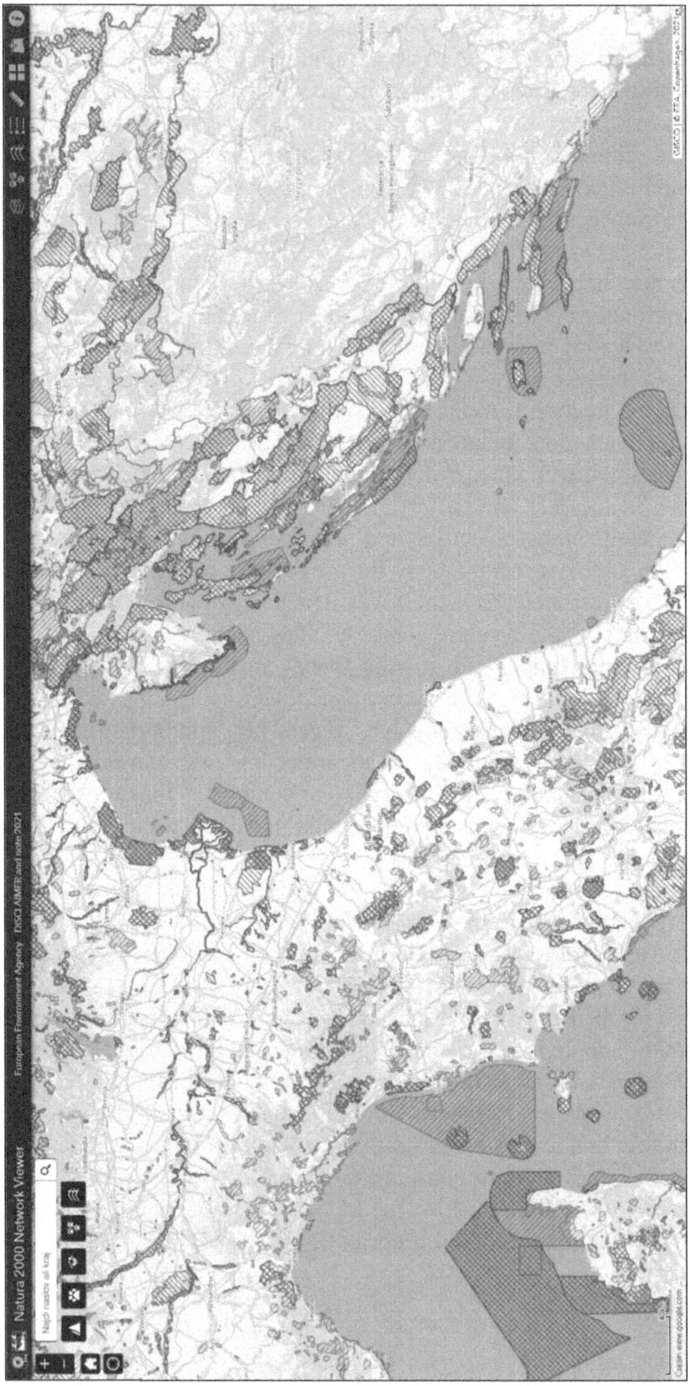

Figure 4.1 NATURA 2000 Network in the Northern and Central Adriatic

Source: Natura 2000 Network Viewer, available at natura2000.eea.europa.eu/

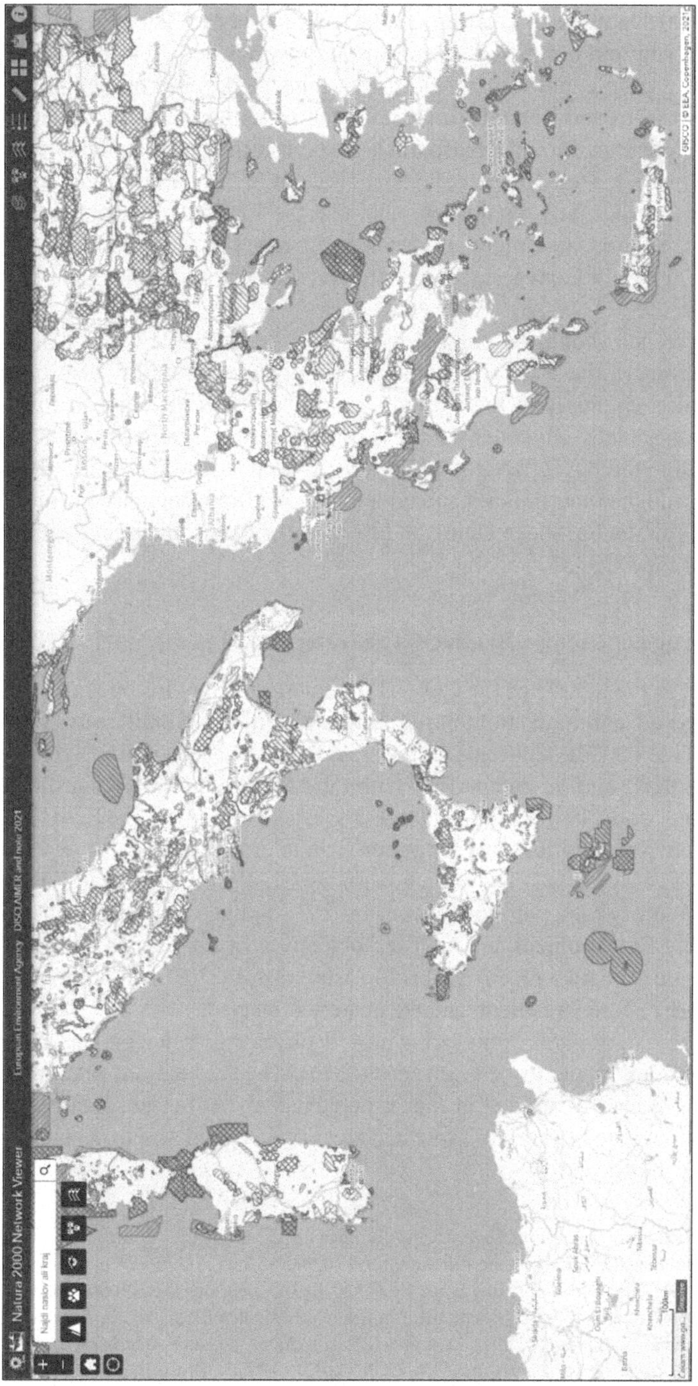

Figure 4.2 NATURA 2000 Network in the Southern Adriatic, Channel of Otranto area and Ionian Sea

Source: Natura 2000 Network Viewer, available at natura2000.eea.europa.eu/

Some general observations could be made when assessing the maps of the NATURA 2000 Network of (marine) protected sites in the Adriatic and Ionian Seas together with the Emerald Network of marine protected areas in EUSAIR's non-European Union countries. In fact, there seems to be more marine protected sites in the Northern and Central Adriatic, compared to the Southern Adriatic and Ionian Seas. Reference should be also made to the fact that there are no NATURA 2000 marine protected sites beyond the territorial sea in the Adriatic, and only one such site in the Ionian Sea. Despite the fact that the EUSAIR States that are not members of the European Union have protected many sites on land based on the provisions of the Bern Convention (Emerald Network), none of them is a marine protected area.

Again, reference should be pointed out to the fact that all EUSAIR member States are parties to the Bern Convention. This gives a possibility also to non-European Union countries in the Adriatic and Ionian Seas to establish (marine) protected areas actually equivalent to those established by European Union member States within the NATURA 2000 Network, as well as, in this regard, the possibility to coordinate their policies and undertake joint (transboundary) projects of cooperation with the European Union and its member States, including within the framework of the EUSAIR.

4.4. The European Union's Biodiversity Strategy 2030

In May 2020, in the middle of the COVID-19 emergency, the European Commission published a Communication on the European Union's Biodiversity Strategy for 2030[89] (EU-BS 2030). This replaces the previous European Union's Biodiversity Strategy for 2020[90] and, in comparison with the latter, puts forward substantially more ambitious goals. In the words of the European Commission, the EU-BS 2030 is a comprehensive, ambitious and long-term plan to protect nature and reverse the degradation of ecosystems.[91] The main goal of the EU-BS 2030 is to put European Union's biodiversity on a path to recovery by 2030 in line with the 2030 Agenda for Sustainable Development and with the objectives of the Paris Agreement on Climate Change. The final global goal is to ensure that, by 2050, all of the world's ecosystems are restored, resilient, and adequately protected.

The EU-BS 2030 is far from being just declaratory, as it contains specific actions and commitments to be realized by 2030. The said actions and commitments may be generally divided in four groups, namely: (1) establishing a larger European Union wide network of protected areas on land and at sea; (2) launching

89 Communication from the Commission to the European Parliament, the Council, the European Economic and Social Committee and the Committee of the Regions, *EU Biodiversity Strategy for 2030 – Bringing Nature Back into our Lives*, COM (2020) 380 final, Brussels, 20 May 2020.

90 Communication from the Commission to the European Parliament, the Council, the European Economic and Social Committee and the Committee of the Regions, *Our Life Insurance, our Natural Capital: an EU Biodiversity Strategy to 2020*, COM (2011) 244 final, Brussels, 3 May 2011.

91 See in that regard ec.europa.eu/environment/strategy/biodiversity-strategy-2030_en.

a European Union nature restoration plan; (3) introducing measures to enable the necessary transformative changes; (4) introducing measures to tackle the global biodiversity challenge. As emphasized by the Commission:

> To put biodiversity on the path to recovery by 2030, we need to step the protection and restoration of nature. This should be done by improving and widening our network of protected areas and by developing and ambitious EU Nature Restoration Plan.

For the purposes of this work, it is of particular interest the commitment by the European Union to establish by 2030 a larger European Union wide network of protected areas on land and at sea, although such commitment should not be seen separate from other goals and actions.

The European Commission is, in this regard, of the opinion that the current network of legally protected areas, including those under strict protection, is not sufficiently large to safeguard biodiversity and that, based on the available evidence, the Aichi Targets set under the CBD are insufficient to adequately protect and restore nature. The Commission also points out to the fact that the global Aichi Biodiversity Targets, which have been met by the European Union, although not in the Adriatic and Ionian Seas,[92] are that protected areas should cover 17 per cent on land and 10 per cent at sea, albeit scientific studies figures a necessity for a range from 30–70 percent. Furthermore, the Commission points out that global efforts are needed and that the European Union itself needs to do more and better for nature, particularly with regard to the building of a truly coherent trans-European nature network. The EU-BS 2030 sets in this regard a 2030 target, according to which at least 30 per cent of the land and 30 per cent of the sea should be protected in the European Union by that date. This is a minimum of an extra 4 per cent for land and an extra 19 per cent for protected sea in accordance with the present European Union situation. Additionally, one-third of protected areas, representing 10 per cent of European Union land and 10 per cent of European Union sea should be strictly protected, leaving therefore natural processes essentially undisturbed to respect the areas' ecological requirements. This is at least 7 per cent more on land and 9 per cent more on the sea, compared with the current situation.[93] Within this, there should be specific focus on areas of very high biodiversity value or potential.

92 Sovinc, *Analysis of Marine (Water) Protected Areas in EUSAIR and Proposals for Corrective Measures,* Final Report, EUSAIR, 2021, pp. 27–28, available at www.adriatic-ionian.eu/library/.

93 According to the Communication, 26 per cent of European Union land area is already protected, with 18 per cent as part of the NATURA 2000 Network and 8 per cent under national schemes. Eleven per cent of the European Union seas are protected, with 8 per cent as part of NATURA 2000 and 3 per cent under additional national protection. See also data provided within the COHENET contract "Achieving coherent networks of marine protected areas: analysis of the situation in the Mediterranean Sea", available at https://ec.europa.eu/environment/marine/pdf/Cohenet_Brochure.pdf.

It is important to note in this regard that member States will be responsible for designating the additional protected and strictly protected areas, either by expanding and completing the NATURA 2000 Network or under national protection schemes (marine protected areas). It is, furthermore, important to point out that all protected areas will need to have clearly defined conservation objectives and measures. The Commission, while working together with members States and the European Environmental Agency, will put forward criteria and guidance for identifying and designating additional areas, including a definition of strict protection as well as for appropriate management planning. In doing so, it will also indicate how other effective area-based conservation measures and greening of cities could contribute to the targets. Furthermore, fisheries management will need to be established in all marine protected areas, according to clearly defined conservation objectives and on the basis of the best available scientific advice.

Although the targets relate to the European Union as a whole, they could be broken down according to the European Union biogeographical regions and sea-basins or at a more local level. The Commission shares the opinion that, in order to have a truly coherent and resilient trans-European nature network, it will be important to set up "ecological corridors" to prevent ecologic isolation, allow for species migration, and maintain and enhance healthy ecosystems. In this context, investment in green and blue infrastructure and cooperation across borders among member States should be promoted and supported, including through the European Territorial Cooperation (ETC).[94] On the international level, the European Union supported the conclusion of an ambitious legally binding agreement on marine biological diversity of areas beyond national jurisdiction (so-called BBNJ negotiating process). The latter must in turn set clear global procedures for identifying, designating and effectively managing ecologically representative marine protected areas in the high seas, and, as such, it should be ratified and implemented as quickly as possible.

Furthermore, achieving good environmental status of marine ecosystems, including through strictly protected areas, must involve the restoration of carbon-rich ecosystems as well as important fish spawning and nursery areas. The EU-BS 2030 points to the fact that marine resources must be harvested sustainably and that there should be zero tolerance for illegal practices. Healthy fish stocks are the key to the long-term prosperity of fishermen and the health of our oceans and biodiversity. It is, therefore, imperative to maintain or reduce fishing mortality at

94 See, in this regard, see Communication from the Commission to the European Parliament, the Council, the European Economic and Social Committee and the Committee of the Regions, *Green Infrastructure (GI) – Enhancing Europe's Natural Capital*, COM (2013) 249 final, Brussels, 6 May 2013. See also Report from the Commission to the European Parliament, the Council, the European Economic and Social Committee and the Committee of the Regions, *Review of Progress on Implementation of the EU Green Infrastructure Strategy*, COM (2019) 236 final, Brussels, 24 May 2019. See also Bricelj (ed.), *Handbook for Recognising and Planning Green Infrastructure*, 2021, available at www.adriatic-ionian.eu/event/6th-annual-eusair-forum/handbook-for-recognising-and-planning-green-infrastructure/.

or under maximum sustainable yield level in order to achieve a healthy population age and size distribution for fish stocks. Furthermore, the bycatch of species threatened with extinction must also be eliminated or reduced to a level which allows full recovery. The full implementation of the European Union's Common Fisheries Policy, the MSFD and the Birds and Habitats Directives is, therefore, essential in order to achieve the said goals. The Commission will request member States to ensure that there is no deteriorating in conservation trends and status of all protected habitats and species by 2030.

The Commission points, furthermore, to the fact that full implementation and enforcement of European Union environmental legislation is at the heart of the EU-BS 2030. As regards the Birds and Habitats Directives, enforcement will focus on completing the NATURA 2000 Network, the effective management of all sites, species-protection provision and species and habitats that show declining trends. Furthermore, the application of an ecosystem-based management approach under European Union legislation will reduce the adverse impact of fishing, extraction and other human activities, especially on sensitive species and seabed habitats. To support this, national maritime spatial plans, which member States had to deliver in 2021, should aim at covering all sectors and activities, including area-based conservation management measures.

For the purposes of this work, of particular importance are the key European Union commitments in the field of nature protection provided by the EU-BS 2030. These may be summarized as follows:

1. legally protect a minimum of 30 per cent of the European Union's land and 30 per cent of the European Union's sea area and integrate ecological corridors, as part of the true trans-European nature network;
2. strictly protect at least one-third of the European Union's protected areas, including all remaining European Union primary and old growth forest; and
3. effectively manage all protected areas, defining clear conservation objectives and measures, and monitoring them appropriately.

Noteworthy is the fact that European Union member States will be responsible for designating the additional protected and strictly protected areas, either by expanding and completing the NATURA 2000 Network or under national protection schemes (marine protected areas), including possible (transboundary) marine protected areas established in accordance with the provisions of regional seas conventions (i.e., Specially Protected Areas of Mediterranean Importance). Fisheries management will need to be established in all marine protected areas, according to clearly defined conservation objectives and on the basis of the best available scientific advice.[95] The Commission agreed upon criteria and guidance for additional

95 Regulation 1380/2013 of the European Parliament and of the Council of 11 December 2013 on the Common Fisheries Policy, amending Council Regulations 1954/2003 and 1224/2009 and repealing Council Regulations 2371/2002 and 639/2004 and Council Decision 2004/585/EC, *Official Journal*

designations of marine protected areas with member States at the end of 2021.[96] Member States have until the end of 2023 to demonstrate significant progress in designating new protected areas and establishing integrated ecological corridors. Noteworthy is the fact that the Council of the European Union, in *Council conclusions on a sustainable blue economy: health, knowledge, prosperity, social equity* of 26 May 2021,

> Calls on Member States to use maritime spatial planning to strengthen the delivery of ecosystem goods and services and achieve ecological, economic and social objectives, as well as to minimize conflicts between different activities at sea;
>
> Acknowledges the concept of blue corridors in maritime spatial planning as a measure to improve the functional connectivity of ecological networks and to ensure sustainable fisheries and navigation in marine ecoregions.

4.5. Conclusive Summary

The EU-IMP seeks to provide a more coherent approach to maritime issues, with increased coordination between different policy areas and, as such, it attempts to coordinate complex and interdependent policies related to maritime affairs and allocate ecological economic resources in a holistic and integrated manner. An important role is by necessity played by ICZM and MSP. Their role is to efficiently plan cross-sectoral and cross-border management of coastal zones and, furthermore, to overview and coordinate possible uses of maritime and coastal resources. The overriding goal of the MSFD, as the environmental pillar of the EU-IMP, is the integration of environmental considerations into all relevant policy areas. The geographical scope of this instrument, as well as, generally speaking, of the European Union's *acquis* and coastal States legislation, is however limited to waters over which member States or third States of the same region or sub-region exercise sovereignty or jurisdiction in accordance with the UNCLOS – and not on the high seas. According to the MSFD, the establishment of marine protected areas, including NATURA 2000 Network sites designed or to be designed based on the provisions of the Habitats and Birds Directives, represents an important contribution towards the achievement of a good environmental status of the European Union waters. Measures in this regard shall include spatial protection measures, contributing to coherent and representative networks of marine protected areas, adequately covering the diversity of the constituent ecosystems, such as SACs pursuant to the Habitats Directive, SPAs pursuant to the Birds Directive, and marine protected

of the European Union L 354 of 28 December 2013, pp. 22–61. Art. 11 allows for the adoption of conservation measures in order to achieve the objectives of the MSFD and the Birds and Habitats Directives and the consequent establishment of protected areas of biological sensitivity.

96 See Commission Staff Working Document, *Criteria and Guidance for Protected Areas Designation*, SWD (2022) 23 final, Brussels, 28 January 2022.

areas as agreed by the European Union or the member States concerned in the framework of international or regional agreements to which they are parties (i.e., the Barcelona Convention).

Furthermore, with the aim to have a truly coherent and resilient trans-European nature network, it is of paramount importance to set up ecological corridors in order to prevent ecologic isolation, allow for species migration, and maintain and enhance healthy ecosystems. These goals should be pursued though the maintenance and the setting up of new ecological corridors between NATURA 2000 Network sites and other protected areas, either on land (green corridors) or at sea (blue corridors), and through their interconnection.

Noteworthy is the fact that all EUSAIR States are parties to the Bern Convention. This implies that also non-European Union countries in the Adriatic and Ionian region (i.e., Albania, Montenegro, North Macedonia, and Serbia,) are in the position to establish (marine) protected areas that are equivalent to those established by European Union member States within the NATURA 2000 Network. In this regard, it is possible to coordinate national policies and undertake joint (transboundary) projects of cooperation with the European Union and its member States, including within the framework of the EUSAIR.

5 Marine Area-based Conservation within Areas of National Sovereignty and Jurisdiction

Ilaria Tani

5.1. Legal Frameworks within Adriatic and Ionian States

Not being the focus of the present work, which aims at identifying the available means for transboundary cooperation in the field of marine spatial protection, the national legal frameworks relevant for the establishment of national marine protected areas are only briefly recalled hereafter. For each country, the analysis is limited to the main national instrument providing the legal framework for the establishment of national parks, possibly including marine protected areas, and does not include other national laws and regulations that, although relevant for the marine environment (e.g., fisheries), do not specifically provide for the establishment of spatial measures.

A. Existing National Legal Frameworks

Albania. The Protected Areas Act No. 81 of 2017[1] aims at the designation, preservation, administration, management, and sustainable use of protected areas and biological and natural resources based on the principle of sustainable development, in order to guarantee their environmental, economic, social, and cultural benefits to the entire society (Art. 1). The Ministry responsible for the protection of the environmental values – and, in particular, of protected areas – at the national level is the Ministry of Environment, Forests, and Water Administration. Currently, most marine protected sites in Albania are coastal, including transitional ecosystems such as coastal lagoons, river mouths, and deltaic systems.[2]

The Albanian law lays down the institutional framework, including both public and private entities and their tasks and responsibilities, for the conservation and sustainable management of protected areas. The latter are divided into different categories (Arts. 14–21), based on those elaborated by the International Union for the Conservation of Nature (IUCN). The same law specifies that protected areas may pursue a "national interest" or an "international interest" (Art. 6). In the second

1 Text available at extwprlegs1.fao.org/docs/pdf/alb176095.pdf.

2 European Commission, *Study on Proposals for New Marine Protected Areas in Albania, Bosnia and Herzegovina and Montenegro*, Luxembourg, 2022, p. 52.

DOI: 10.4324/9781003367963-5

case, they may belong to different networks, namely as Ramsar sites; Special Areas of Conservation; areas of the Emerald network; Biosphere Reserves; and natural heritage areas. Art. 22 specifically concerns the establishment of marine protected areas, described as "any protected portions of marine waters, including coastal areas and the seabed, together with their flora and fauna, as well as their historical, cultural and archeological features". Art. 22, para. 3, contains a list of activities that are prohibited within a marine protected area. These include, *inter alia*, the taking of marine samples and dumping. The different IUCN categories of protected areas and their respective regime or protection also apply to marine protected areas (Art. 22, para. 2). It is also envisaged that zoning measures shall be set forth in a management plan for each marine protected area, which shall specify those activities that are prohibited and those that can be undertaken only after having received the relevant authorization by the competent national authority (Art. 22, para. 4). Art. 34 regulates fishing activities in marine and coastal areas. Among the objectives of a marine protected area, remarkable is the reference made by the Albanian law to the goal of restoring ecosystems that have resulted negatively impacted by climate change (Art. 22, para. 1, let. dh).

Bosnia and Herzegovina. The Nature Protection Act of 2013[3] of the Federation of Bosnia and Herzegovina regulates the competencies of bodies that deal, *inter alia*, with the identification of habitat types and ecologically significant areas, species, and subspecies; the protection and conservation of biodiversity; the protection of marine and coastal natural values; and the establishment of a European ecological network of specially protected areas (NATURA 2000) (Art. 1). The same law describes a protected area as "a clearly defined geographical area, recognized and intended to reach nature's long-term conservation and public benefit functions, as well as cultural values, and which is governed by legal and other effective mechanisms" (Art. 8). The same provision defines "*in situ* conservation (in nature)" as the "conservation of ecological systems in natural habitats and maintenance and restoration of species capable of survival in their natural environment . . .; preservation parts of geological heritage at the place of their origin, i.e., mineral/rock deposits and fossils". Moreover, an ecological network is envisaged as "a system of interconnected or spatially close ecologically significant areas that balance biogeographical distribution significantly contributing to the preservation of natural balance and biodiversity" (Art. 8). The law of 2013 operates a distinction among different categories of protected areas: strict nature reserve (Art. 135), wilderness area (Art. 136), national park (Art. 137), nature park (Art. 138), habitat/species management area (Art. 139), protected landscape (Art. 140), and protected area with sustainable use of natural resources (Art. 141).

According to Art. 144, the establishment of protected areas, at the federal or cantonal level, can be carried out with the consent of the municipal councils in whose territory the area is protected according to the spatial plan. The relevant instrument shall contain: name and category of the protected natural value; a precise

3 Text available at extwprlegs1.fao.org/docs/pdf/bih143206.pdf.

description of the boundaries of the spatial scope of the protected area; name of the area's category; scale of the cartographic representation; and the cartographic presentation with precisely described boundaries of spatial coverage, as an integral part of the act of proclamation. The adoption of a new Nature Protection Act is ongoing in the Federation of Bosnia and Herzegovina and not yet finalized.[4]

It is to be noted that Neum-Klek Bay and Mali Ston Bay host critical habitats that have been suggested as protected sites (meeting the EBSA criteria). The surrounding area is part of NATURA 2000, in Croatian waters. Accordingly, a cross-border approach should be adopted, taking into account the ecology of the wider system, which includes Neum-Klek Bay, the Neretva Delta, and Mali Ston Bay.[5]

Croatia. The Nature Protection Act of 24 June 2013[6] recognizes protection to nature, intended as "the overall biological, landscape and geological diversity" (Art. 3). Art. 6 provides that nature protection shall be implemented, *inter alia*, through "designation of protected parts of nature" and by "establishing a system for management of nature and protected parts of nature". Art. 111 identifies nine categories of protected areas, namely: strict reserve, national park, special reserve, nature reserve (classified as of national importance) and regional park, nature monument, significant landscape, park forest, and park architecture monument (classified as of local importance). Arts. 112 and the following regulate each category of protected area. Of particular relevance to this analysis is Art. 122, which explicitly provides that "protected areas may be connected across borders with protected areas of another country".

Arts. 123 and the subsequent provisions regulate the designation of a protected area. Art. 126, in particular, establishes that the relevant designation shall indicate: the name and category of the protected area; a description of the borders of the protected area; a cartographic representation of the protected area in analogue and digital format, which constitutes an integral part of the act of designation; an indication of the scale of the cartographic representation; the special geodetic background document for entry of the legal regime into the cadastre and the land registry. The act of designation of the protected area is published in the official gazette (Art. 127) or in the official journal of the regional self-government unit and in the official gazette, depending on whether the area is of national or local importance.

4 Presentation by Mr. Josip Njavro, representative of Bosnia and Herzegovina at the Workshop organized by TSG 3 EUSAIR, *What can EUSAIR do to enable the blue and green sustainable growth in EUSAIR: MSP in EUSAIR state of the art*, held online on 9 November 2021.

5 "Transboundary collaboration in monitoring, and especially, in managing plans is required in order to establish a cross border MPA between Bosnia and Herzegovina and Croatia, taking into account the existing legislation at a national and regional scale", European Commission, *Study on Proposals op. cit.*, p. 64.

6 Text available at extwprlegs1.fao.org/docs/pdf/cro143039.pdf.

All protected areas shall be recorded in a Register of protected areas (Art. 129), which is kept by the Ministry of Environment and Energy, and all relevant data shall be public. Protected areas shall be managed by public institutions (Art. 130), which shall carry out activities of protection, maintenance and promotion of the protected area with the aim of protecting and conserving the original state of nature, ensuring the unimpeded natural processes and sustainable use of natural resources, monitoring implementation of nature protection requirements and measures in the territory they manage, and participating in collection of data for the purpose of monitoring the state of conservation of nature (Art. 131).

A specific provision refers to the funds of the operation of public institutions, which shall be ensured from State budget and budgets of local and regional self-government units, income from the use of protected areas, income from fees, and other sources established by the law and special regulations (Art. 132).

Specific provisions (Arts. 137–150) regulate the implementation of protective measures in the areas, by providing rules concerning the management plan; prohibited actions; forest protection programme; military exercises;[7] general acts on protection and conservation of a protected area; projects, actions and exploration; visiting; rights of the owners to remuneration; and care for protected areas. Further, general provisions of the Croatian law regulate access to information and public participation (Arts. 198–200), financing (Art. 204), supervision in protected areas (Arts. 206–209), and inspectional supervision (Arts. 210–225). In this regard, with particular reference to the marine and coastal environment, "authorized persons with the Coast Guard shall carry out inspectional supervision in the area of the ecological and fisheries protection zone or the exclusive economic zone of Croatia in accordance with a special regulation" (Art. 211, para. 2). Persons authorized with the Coast Guard may carry out inspectional supervision in the internal waters and territorial sea of Croatia, provided that a reasonable doubt exists with regard to violations of the Act and connected regulations and civil servants with the inspectional service of the Ministry are not present or are unable to intervene (Art. 211, para. 3). Part XIV of the Act lists the amounts of fines established for the different types of infringements.

Greece. The Law for the Management Agencies of Protected Areas in Greece (No. 4519 of 8 February 2018) regulates all issues concerning the organization and operation of protected areas management bodies. This act follows the revised national list of the NATURA 2000 Network in Greece. Presidential Decrees and management plans should gradually be adopted for all areas of the NATURA 2000

7 (1) Performance of military exercises and other activities for defence purposes which could impair the features for which it was designated as such shall be prohibited in the protected area.
(2) By way of derogation from paragraph 1 of this Article, performance of military exercises and other activities for defence purposes shall be allowed in areas in which at the moment of designation special (military) purpose was in place, in the scope and in a manner that does not endanger protected natural values.

(Art. 141)

Network. With regard to the management of fisheries and marine sites, the Greek Law of 2018 implies new responsibilities for management agencies that should be compatible with both the general fisheries legislation and the environmental legislation, especially with regard to the Habitat Directive, the MSFD, and marine spatial planning. Main challenges relate to governance, needed material, and human resources, as well as the planning and implementation of effective management measures.

Italy. The Framework Law on Protected Areas (No. 394 of 6 December 1991) sets forth the general category of protected natural areas (*aree naturali protette*), which include national parks (*parchi nazionali*), regional natural parks (*parchi naturali regionali*), and nature reserves (*riserve naturali*).[8] Both national parks and nature reserves can be composed of marine areas, while regional natural parks can only include marine areas adjoining the coast.[9] Marine specially protected areas are specifically regulated by Law No. 979 of 31 December 1982 (Provisions for the Defence of the Sea), which envisages the category of marine reserves (*riserve marine)*. Law No. 979/1982 is still applicable to all matters not explicitly regulated by Law No. 394/1991.

The definition of marine reserve, as envisaged by Art. 25 of Law No. 979/1982, is the following:

> marine nature reserves are composed of marine components, including by the waters, the seabed and the adjoining coasts, and showing remarkable interest because of their natural, geomorphological, physical and biochemical characteristics, with special regard to the coastal and marine flora and fauna, as well as the scientific, ecological, cultural, educational and economic importance.

Within marine protected areas, all activities that risk compromising the protection of the environmental characteristics and the objectives to be achieved by the protection regime are prohibited. In particular, the following activities are forbidden: hunting, collecting, and damaging fauna and flora species as well as the removal of minerals and archaeological findings; the alteration of the geophysical environment and the biochemical and hydrobiological characteristics of the water; advertising activities; the introduction of arms, explosives, and any destructive or catching equipment; navigation by motor vessels; and any kind of disposal of either liquid or solid waste. All prohibitions and any possible exceptions are specified in the regulations for each marine protected area.

8 Nature reserves can be established by either the State or the regions.

9 Other kinds of marine specially protected areas are envisaged by Decree No. 1639 of 2 October 1968, implementing the Italian framework law on fisheries. The decree provides for the creation of zones of biological protection (*zone di protezione biologica*), where fishing activities may be prohibited or restricted.

The regime of parks, including marine parks, is complex. The body in charge of the management of a national park, called the Park Institution (*Ente parco*), is entrusted with the adoption of a plan that, *inter alia*, may subdivide the area of the park on the basis of different degrees of protection, providing for the following:

- integral reserves (*riserve integrali*), where the natural environment is conserved in its integrity;
- oriented general reserves (*riserve generali orientate*), where new buildings, widening of existing constructions, and activities for the transformation of the territory are forbidden. Traditional productive uses, the implementation of strictly necessary infrastructures, interventions for the management of the natural resources performed by the Park Institution, as well as maintenance activities of the existing structures may be authorized;
- areas of protection (*aree di protezione*), where, with reference to the aims to be achieved by the establishment of the park and the general criteria fixed by the Park Institution, the agricultural-silvicultural, sheep-rearing, fishing activities, and the collecting of natural products can continue, according to the local customs and methods of biological agriculture, while the production of quality handicrafts is promoted;
- areas of economic and social promotion (*aree di promozione economica e sociale*), which make up part of the same ecosystem and are most widely modified by the impact of human processes, where all the activities aimed at the improvement of both the sociocultural life of the local populations and the enjoyment of the park by visitors are allowed, if compatible with the aims of the protection regime.

The rules applicable to marine reserves are simpler than those relating to parks. All activities for the protection, research, and promotion of a marine reserve are entrusted to the Minister of the Environment, relying on the Central Inspectorate for the Defence of the Sea. The competent harbour-master's office (*Capitaneria di Porto*) is in charge of the surveillance and management of the reserve. Proposals and advice for the appropriate management of the reserve are made by the Commission of the Reserve (*Commissione di Riserva*), appointed by the Minister of the Environment.

All Italian marine protected areas are divided into three types of zones (A, B, C), corresponding to three different levels of protection. The marine reserve established as part of the trilateral *Pelagos Sanctuary* is a special case, due to its international character.

Montenegro. The Nature Protection Act of 2016[10] represents the latest piece of Montenegrin legislation prescribing general measures for nature protection, which

10 Text available at extwprlegs1.fao.org/docs/pdf/mne178833.pdf.

include the establishment of protected areas. As a general instrument, it includes further provisions on the protection of endangered species, pollution control, environmental planning, data collection and reporting, access to information, and financing.

Slovenia. The Nature Conservation Act of 1999, as amended several times,[11] prescribes biodiversity conservation measures and a system for the protection of valuable natural features. The general goals of this law have been implemented through specific decrees. For what concerns the scope of this investigation, noteworthy are the Decree on Ecologically Important Areas of 29 April 2004 (as amended on 19 April 2013),[12] with an Annex containing the number and name of the relevant areas, which forms an integral part of the instrument; and the Decree on Special Protection Areas (NATURA 2000) of 29 April 2004 (also amended on 19 April 2013).[13]

B. Indicators for Effective National Legal Frameworks

As regards the effectiveness of the legislative instruments establishing marine protected areas, some indicators may be identified that could be used as helpful references against which to draft – and consequently measure the implementation of – national laws and regulations.[14]

a. Coordinated Implementation of International and Regional Commitments

In the Adriatic and Ionian Seas, as with any other regional sea, the regime for marine protected areas established under the domestic legislation of coastal States should fully comply with general obligations under international law and specific obligations laid down by relevant global and regional instruments.[15] While there are no contradictions between the provisions of different treaties applicable to marine protected areas, there may be differences in the standards and degree of details of texts adopted at different levels. Regional and sub-regional instruments usually ensure a stronger and more targeted protection, compared to international framework conventions. Even greater precision can be delivered within national

11 The latest amendments were effected in 2020. A consolidated version of the original act and its subsequent amendments is available at extwprlegs1.fao.org/docs/pdf/slv61725.pdf.

12 Original text of the decree available at extwprlegs1.fao.org/docs/html/slv113406.htm. The amendments of 2013 are available at extwprlegs1.fao.org/docs/html/slv130560.htm.

13 Original text of the decree available at extwprlegs1.fao.org/docs/html/slv113405.htm. The amendments of 2013 are available at extwprlegs1.fao.org/docs/html/slv130559.htm.

14 Based on *Mediterranean Countries' Needs for Legal, Policy and Institutional Reforms to Strengthen the Management of Existing Marine Protected Areas*, 27 March 2007, UNEP(DEPI)/MED WG.309/Inf.5 rev.1.

15 All the relevant instruments at the global and regional scale have been addressed elsewhere in this book (Chapters 2 and 3, respectively). For a recent assessment of the relevant regional framework, see Vezzani, *op. cit.*

instruments, which should include provisions that harmonize the approaches pursued at the global and regional scale. This can be pursued through: consultation between the various focal points for different treaties and regional organizations, in advance of international negotiations and when developing domestic implementation arrangements; the adoption or strengthening of protected areas legislation that is specifically applicable to coastal and marine protected areas and corresponds to the more specific obligations laid down by regional treaties; the prompt enactment of implementing regulations, which is necessary to actually establish marine protected areas, because modern and comprehensive framework legislation is of little use if it is not followed up by concrete implementation instruments.

b. Institutional Coordination

A critical issue is the sharing of competencies between State authorities. International instruments say nothing about how their parties should organize the distribution of powers among their respective national entities when setting up and managing marine protected areas. In fact, this would be an unwarranted invasion of the sphere of domestic jurisdiction. Each party is, therefore, free to determine whether the obligation to establish and manage marine protected areas can be better fulfilled at the national or sub-national level, or jointly through cooperation between both levels. As a consequence, competencies can overlap in a horizontal way between different authorities (e.g., Minister of the Environment, Minister of Shipping, Minister of Fisheries) or in a vertical way between national and subnational authorities (provinces, regions, autonomous communities). An efficient coordination should be ensured where local and national authorities have different functions and responsibilities. Fragmented distribution of competencies, whether at the regulatory or the management level, does not help the management of marine protected areas. Although, ideally speaking, a sharing of competencies should mean recourse to additional experience and expertise, in practice it may deteriorate into a situation of confusion and overlapping of powers, delay in the adoption of the appropriate measures, and potential disputes. For these reasons, where more than one administration is involved in a marine protected area, special measures to ensure cooperation, coordination, and accountability should be envisaged. There are many options to this purpose, ranging from integrated management committees to regular meetings between the competent authorities. The relationship between a marine protected area's managing body and other authorities also requires attention. Regulations should, therefore, support coordination between all agencies with responsibilities for activities affecting the area and establish a procedure for the resolution of any conflicts.

c. Specific Legal Provisions for Marine Protected Areas Establishment and Management

In the Adriatic and Ionian Seas, specific legislations on protected areas are in place. Nature protection acts of more general scope, however, include within the same instrument rules concerning terrestrial and marine protected areas. This approach may entail the risk to underestimate the fact that marine protected areas are fundamentally different from terrestrial protected areas, even if it is debatable whether these differences are in kind or degree. An important factor underlying these differences is the nebulous nature of boundaries in the fluid marine environment and the presence of many species that do not respect paper boundaries (highly migratory species; anadromous and catadromous species; shared and straddling fish stocks) and other natural features. These aspects have been highlighted since 1991, in the first Guidelines for the Establishment of Marine Protected Areas elaborated by the IUCN:

> In the sea, habitats are rarely precisely or critically restricted. Survival of species cannot usually be linked to a specific site. Many free swimming species have huge ranges and water currents carry the genetic materials of sedentary or territorial species over large distances, often hundreds of kilometres. The same genetic community is likely to be represented throughout a large geographic range, occurring wherever substrate and water quality are suitable. As a consequence, endemism is rare and is usually confined to species which brood or care for their young rather than have them dispersed by currents. There is no authenticated record of recent extinction of a completely marine species with planktonic larvae. The concept of critical habitats of endangered species is thus restricted in application to areas critical to marine mammals, sea turtles and sea birds and to the habitats of the occasional endemic species. Therefore, in the sea, the ecological case for protection of an area can less often be based on concepts of critical habitat of endangered species or threat of extinction but it may more probably be based on protection of critical or important habitat for commercially or recreationally important species, or for protection of a particularly good example of a habitat type with its associated genetic diversity of its communities.[16]

A special regime for marine protected areas is thus appropriate because of legal consequences that are specific to the marine environment and differentiate the latter from the terrestrial domain. Rules of international law are also fundamentally different depending on the terrestrial or marine nature of the area involved.[17] In addition, long-established rules and concessions may apply in the "public maritime

16 IUCN, *Guidelines for Establishing Marine Protected Areas*, Gland, 1991, p. 13. For a recent guidance on the establishment of protected areas, including on land, see European Commission, Commission Staff Working Document, *Criteria and Guidance for Protected Areas Designations*, SWD (2022) 23 final, 28 January 2022.

17 Several works have been devoted to the differences existing, for example, in the rules of international law concerning delimitations in the terrestrial and maritime domains. Among others, see Bardonnet, *Frontières terrestres et frontières maritimes*, in *Annuaire français de droit international*, 1989.

domain", depending on each country's legal system, even though conventional property rights cannot be exercised in marine areas.

Whatever the enabling legislation, scientific information is needed to determine the size, shape, conservation objectives, and management prescriptions for each area. Any legal instrument for the establishment of a marine protected area must clearly define the conservation and management objectives of the area concerned and delimit its boundaries, together with a zoning system and buffer zones where appropriate.

d. Adoption of Protection Measures

The Areas Protocol provides, in this regard, a useful guidance. In any event, protection measures must be selected on a case-by-case basis, taking into account the characteristics of each marine protected area and the relevant legal regime. For instance, within the territorial sea, any decision to regulate the passage of ships, if needed, must comply with the right of innocent passage provided for by international law (Art. 17 UNCLOS) and cannot permanently prohibit navigation in an extended area where main maritime routes occur.[18] In the same maritime zone, which is subject to the legal regime of territorial sovereignty, the coastal State has a margin of discretion as regards the nature of the control measures to be adopted: an activity, therefore, may be either prohibited, under certain conditions, or regulated (i.e., where the activity is authorized subject to certain general conditions or special permits). On the other hand, within the limits of its exclusive economic zone, the coastal State shall not undertake measures that may hamper the freedom of navigation of foreign vessels or contravene the primary objective of "optimum utilization" of the living resources of the zone (Art. 62 UNCLOS) (e.g., through the establishment of "no-take" zones). Moreover, national legislation (whether generic or specific to marine protected areas) must provide for use of environmental impact assessment procedures, in order to ensure that sectoral activities and programmes take account of the ecological status and conservation objectives of the area.

e. Management Planning and Zoning for Marine Protected Areas

Each marine protected area should be covered by a specific and sufficiently detailed management plan, which should always be envisaged in national legislations. Protection, planning, and management measures must be based on an adequate

18 According to Art. 25 UNCLOS:

> The coastal State may, without discrimination in form or in fact among foreign ships, suspend temporarily in specified areas of its territorial sea the innocent passage of foreign ships if such suspension is essential for the protection of its security, including weapon exercises. Such suspension shall take effect only after having been duly published.

No reference is made to the possibility to suspend the right of innocent passage for reasons related to the need of protection of the marine environment.

knowledge of the elements of the natural environment and of socioeconomic and cultural factors that characterize the area. Management plans should prescribe appropriate regulatory and management measures for different zones within the area. The plan should also include contingency measures to respond to incidents. Moreover, with a view to ensuring policy consistency, it should be specified that the regulatory provisions of zoning and management plans override any inconsistent provisions in local land-use and sectoral plans.

f. Integration of Marine Protected Areas into Coastal and Maritime Spatial Planning Policies

Also within national jurisdiction, marine protected areas should not be established in a vacuum and in isolation but as part of a logical and coherent network, which should take place at both the national and regional levels. The fluid nature of the marine environment makes it particularly important to integrate marine protected areas within a comprehensive long-term approach to planning and management of activities that affect fragile coastal and marine ecosystems. Effective solutions should consider all sectors simultaneously so that changes in policies or practices in one area are consistent with and complementary to those adopted in another. Each coastal State should adopt national strategy and programmes applying to the coastal and marine areas under its jurisdiction, including a list of areas suitable for designation and protection as coastal and marine protected areas. This can be done as part of an integrated coastal zone management process or linked to planning for large marine ecosystem management, in cooperation with neighboring countries. In all cases, consideration should be given to establishing larger mixed protected areas covering both coastal and marine components.

g. Stakeholder Involvement

Far from being a mere formality, public participation is a vital element in environmental decision-making, generally, and in matters related to marine protected areas, in particular. It enables decision-making authorities to understand how the project is perceived by local inhabitants, how it meets economic concerns, and how it is seen by non-governmental organizations in their collective pursuit of common interests. Local knowledge may be just as important as scientific knowledge in the design and management of marine protected areas. In fact, local communities often have an in-depth understanding of their ecosystems, based on generations of interaction with the resources.

Constructive working relationships with fisheries and tourism operators, local authorities, communities, scientists, nature conservation interests, and other interested parties can facilitate both the establishment and planning of marine protected areas. They are conducive to better-informed adoption of collective goals and more efficient and clear decision-making and may reduce instances of non-compliance. Relevant stakeholders should be identified and efforts made, preferably through the adoption of specific regulations, to encourage public participation in the relevant procedures.

Ecological measures are often perceived to be in competition with economic activities, even though economic development opportunities may actually depend upon the conservation of the environment, as is the case of tourism. As part of coastal and marine protected areas planning, all efforts should, therefore, be made to evaluate and enhance with the public the significance of those benefits that, while not directly quantifiable in precise monetary terms, can be achieved through protective measures.

National legislation should also include provisions on access to information. States should recognize the positive contribution that civil society active in the field of the environment can make through educational, campaigning, and monitoring activities. Where feasible, there should be close cooperation between responsible agencies and competent non-governmental organizations close to the ground, including the possibility to entrust such organizations with the management of some marine protected areas under appropriate contracts.

h. Financing Mechanisms

Inadequate or insecure funding may determine delay in the recruitment of sufficient staff, the purchase of equipment for performing basic tasks (which can be particularly costly in the case of marine areas), and the promotion of research. Appropriate funding should be granted, wherever possible, by the State or the public institutions involved to meet the needs of existing protected areas. Fundraising mechanisms involving visitors or the private sector may also be put into effect as an alternative source of financing, provided that they do not conflict with the basic objectives of the protected area. Also donors may be encouraged to support projects.

An important consideration relates to benefit-sharing. If local communities do not benefit in the medium- to long-term from the establishment of marine protected areas, it is unlikely that they will cooperate in sustained management efforts. Economic expectations should be addressed through compensation mechanisms, where necessary, and by adjusting the timeframe of expected benefits against the timeframe of any losses that may occur as a consequence of the creation of a marine protected area.

i. Monitoring, Compliance, Enforcement

Once established, marine protected areas require continuous monitoring of ecological processes, habitats, population dynamics, landscapes, and the impact of human activities. This information is essential for periodic updating of applicable regulations and management plans.

Wherever possible, incentives and non-regulatory approaches should be considered to encourage voluntary compliance and a culture of self-enforcement of rules by user groups. This is particularly important at sea, where monitoring and detection are harder than on land. Such approaches are likely to work best within a context that encourages informed public participation, education, and awareness-building.

National legislation should ensure that the management body of each marine protected area has the authority to delegate and enforce the rules and regulations it promulgates. Relevant legislation should, therefore, provide adequate powers for personnel to take enforcement action, backed by meaningful penalties. This implies that, under appropriate circumstances, coastal or marine conservation officers should have the authority to impose on-the-spot fines for minor resource and environmental offences. For more serious violations, their authority should extend to the gathering of evidence, impounding and confiscation of equipment, imposing a court summons, and, when appropriate, arrest and detention powers.

5.2. National Marine Protected Areas

The first challenge faced in the effort of assessing the number and status of national marine protected areas is the lack of an accurate inventory, which is coupled with the lack of compilation of new potential sites with the highest biodiversity value.[19] Moreover, the geographical scope of the present investigation influences the assessment of the implementation of the national legal frameworks for the establishment of marine protected areas within areas under national sovereignty and jurisdiction. In fact, among the States concerned, Albania, Bosnia and Herzegovina (although the latter only as regards a limited portion of marine waters), Croatia, Montenegro, and Slovenia rely on legal frameworks that extend and exhaust their effects within the marine areas encompassed by this work. This is due to the fact that all the maritime zones of such States fall entirely within the scope of the analysis. On the contrary, the legal frameworks in place in Greece and in Italy apply also to areas falling outside the coverage of the present investigation, as such frameworks partially extend their effects to both coastal and sea areas not included in the Adriatic and Ionian Seas: the eastern coasts and maritime zones of Greece and the western coasts and maritime zones of Italy. It derives that, in complying with the scope of the present analysis, a comprehensive overview of the actual implementation of the relevant legal frameworks and existence of national marine protected areas would only be possible for the first group of States. In any case, the lack of a complete inventory of existing national marine protected areas makes it impossible to provide reliable numbers.

Despite the efforts undertaken at various levels for the compilation of lists of marine protected areas and GIS databases, the lack of reliable inventories on existing national marine protected areas has been noted also by the competent regional bodies. Notably, the 21st Conference of the Parties to the Barcelona Convention, held in 2019, adopted Decision IG.24/6, on the *Identification and Conservation of Sites of Particular Ecological Interest in the Mediterranean, including Specially Protected Areas of Mediterranean Importance*, whereby it requested the Secretariat

19 Sovinc, *op. cit.*, p. 14.

to establish a directory of Mediterranean specially protected areas and demanded the Specially Protected Areas Regional Activity Centre (SPA/RAC) to elaborate criteria for inclusion of specially protected areas in the directory, for consideration at the 22nd Conference of the Parties.[20]

Notwithstanding the lack of comprehensive inventories, as regards the four pilot areas identified for the purpose of this work, it is noteworthy that the designation within Bosnia and Herzegovina of a national marine protected area in the Neum Bay seems imminent.[21] For a country with such a short coastline, transboundary cooperation and coordination of coastal and marine management will always be crucial, particularly with Croatia. The joint construction, around 40 years ago, of the Neum-Pelješac Peninsula wastewater system has made a significant contribution to conserving the Bay's ecosystem. If declared, the spatial measure would lead to the protection of 100 per cent of the maritime waters of Bosnia and Herzegovina.

5.3. Conclusive Summary

Existing national frameworks for the establishment of marine protected areas within areas of national sovereignty and jurisdiction include the Protected Areas Act No. 81 of 2017 of Albania; the Nature Protection Act of 2013 of the Federation of Bosnia and Herzegovina; the Nature Protection Act of 2013 of Croatia; Law No. 4519 of 2018 for the Management Agencies of Protected Areas of Greece; the Framework Law on Protected Areas No. 394 of 1991 and Law No. 972 of 1982, with subsequent amendments, of Italy; the Nature Protection Act of 2016 of Montenegro; and the Nature Conservation Act of 1999, as amended several times, of Slovenia. It may be noted that almost all the coastal States of the Adriatic and Ionian Seas have enacted recent legislation concerning the establishment, management, and monitoring of protected areas, which in all cases explicitly refer also to *marine* protected areas. Other States, such as Italy and Slovenia, have preferred to progressively update previous legislation. As regards the effectiveness of national instruments, some indicators may be identified that could be used as helpful references against which to measure both the drafting and implementation of relevant legislations, namely: the achievement under the relevant legislation of a coordinated implementation of international and regional commitments; an efficient institutional coordination; the adoption of specific legal provisions for the establishment and management of marine protected areas, as they imply differences from terrestrial protected areas; the adoption of effective protection measures; the implementation of management planning and zoning; the integration of marine protected areas into coastal and maritime spatial planning policies; the involvement

20 For the subsequent developments, see SPA/RAC/AGEM/2/2 of 20 May 2021, *Report of the Ad Hoc Group of Experts for Marine Protected Areas in the Mediterranean (AGEM)*.

21 Presentation by Mr. Josip Njavro, representative of Bosnia and Herzegovina at the Workshop organized by TSG 3 EUSAIR, *What can EUSAIR do to enable the blue and green sustainable growth in EUSAIR: MSP in EUSAIR state of the art*, held online on 9 November 2021.

of all relevant stakeholders; the provision of adequate financing mechanisms; and effective schemes and measures for monitoring, compliance and enforcement. In addition, national legislations should provide for an appropriate registering mechanism and public access to the relevant data because the first challenge faced in the effort of assessing the number and the status of national marine protected areas is the lack of an accurate inventory, which is coupled with the lack of compilation of new potential sites with the highest biodiversity value. Steps are being taken in this regard under the auspices of SPA/RAC, with a view to elaborating criteria for inclusion of specially protected areas in a Mediterranean directory.

6 Transboundary Area-based Conservation beyond the Territorial Sea within the Mediterranean Sea and the Adriatic and Ionian Seas

Ilaria Tani

6.1. The *Pelagos Sanctuary*

The *Pelagos Sanctuary for the Conservation of Marine Mammals* was established under an Agreement signed in Rome in 1999 by France, Italy, and Monaco. This agreement is the first ever concluded instrument with the specific objective of establishing a protected area for marine mammals. It entered into force on 21 February 2002 and is also believed to be the first example of a high seas marine protected area in the world.

The sanctuary extends for about 96,000 km^2 of waters located between the continental coasts of the three States parties and the islands of Corsica (France) and Sardinia (Italy). It encompasses waters having the different legal condition of maritime internal waters, territorial sea, ecological protection zone (in the case of Italy),[1] exclusive economic zone (in the case of France), and high seas.[2] Such waters are inhabited by the eight cetacean species regularly found in the Mediterranean.

The initial catalyst for the establishment of the *Pelagos Sanctuary* was the awareness that many whales were becoming accidentally entangled in the nets of tuna driftnet fishermen, leading to an international outcry from non-governmental organizations and other bodies to end such type of fishing.

Following some judicial decisions by Italian courts, Italy agreed to dismiss driftnet fishing by 1990. In the same year, the French Ministry of Merchant Marine proclaimed a triangle of waters from the tip of Corsica that was declared off limits to driftnet fishing. Tethys Research Institute, an Italian non-governmental organization with scientific purposes, proposed a *Project Pelagos* for the establishment of a marine protected area in the high seas, encompassing the most important habitat for cetaceans in the region.

At the basis of the proposal of the marine protected area, there was the recognition of its ecological richness and representativeness, its high species diversity, its intense biological activity, the presence of critical habitat for a number of diverse

1 As already remarked, Italy has proclaimed an exclusive economic zone by Law No. 91 of 14 June 2021. The zone is awaiting implementation through Presidential Decree.

2 However, should Monaco establish an exclusive economic zone, the high seas within the *Pelagos Sanctuary* would disappear.

DOI: 10.4324/9781003367963-6

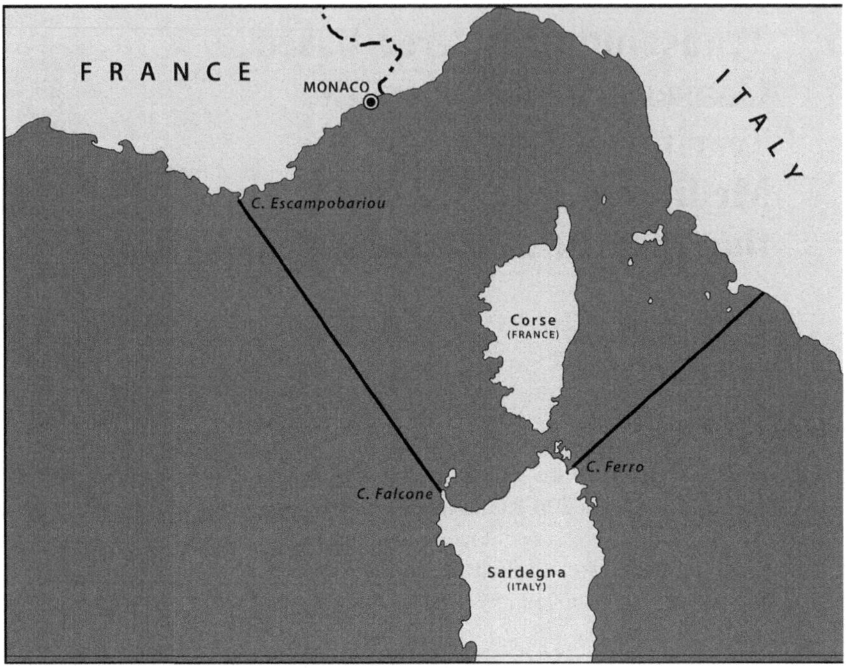

Figure 6.1 Map of the *Pelagos Sanctuary*

Source: Copyright (Routledge©2014) From *Extension of Coastal State Jurisdiction in Enclosed or Semi-Enclosed Seas: A Mediterranean and Adriatic Perspective* by Mitja Grbec. Reproduced by permission of Taylor and Francis Group, LLC, an informa business

pelagic species including cetaceans, and its opportunities for baseline research, education, and development. The proposal challenged – with success – the mainstream legal notion of the time that establishing a protected area on the high seas was impossible and generated awareness that new mechanisms were required to deal with high seas conservation.

Project Pelagos gained the support of the Rotary Clubs of Milan, Monaco, and Saint Tropez. In 1991, Prince Rainier III of Monaco granted the support of the Principality for the project and recommended that a sanctuary for cetaceans should be eventually created in the Ligurian-Corsican-Provençal basin through a trilateral agreement between France, Italy, and Monaco. In 1993, the Ministers of the Environment of the three States signed a joint declaration with the intention of setting up an institution for a Mediterranean sanctuary with a view to conserving marine mammals. At this point, however, the political will began to wane, and a number of difficulties arose. Eventually, in 1999, the idea was revitalized, and the final agreement was signed. By that time, the original catalyst for the creation of the area, the drift netting for tuna, had already been banned in the region.

The term "sanctuary" has been used following the precedent set by the National Oceanic and Atmospheric Administration (NOAA) of the United States. It reflects the fact that whales are ultimately part of a migratory population that cannot be entirely protected through the establishment of a single area but by necessarily taking into account at least a sufficient part of their life history and migratory range. In 2007, the GFCM considered that the *Pelagos Sanctuary* was "an experiment in the ecosystem approach to management".

The parties to the 1999 Agreement undertake to adopt measures to ensure a favourable state of conservation for every species of marine mammal and to protect them and their habitat from negative impacts, both direct and indirect (Art. 4). Moreover, the parties undertake to monitor the area and intensify their fight against all sources of pollution, both sea- and land-based. In particular, Art. 6, para. 2, provides for the adoption of national strategies with the aim of progressively suppressing discards of toxic components within the Sanctuary, by recognizing priority to those substances enumerated in Annex I to the Land-Based Protocol to the Barcelona Convention.

The parties prohibit in the Sanctuary any deliberate "taking" (defined as "hunting, catching, killing or harassing of marine mammals, as well as the attempting of such actions") or disturbance of mammals. Non-lethal catches may be authorized in urgent situations or for *in-situ* scientific research purposes (Art. 7a).

As regards the still crucial question of driftnet fishing, the parties undertake to comply with the relevant international and European Union regimes (Art. 7b). This is an implicit reference to European Council Regulation No. 1239/98 of 8 June 1998, which prohibited as from 1 January 2002 the keeping on board, or the use for fishing, of one or more driftnets used for the catching of the species listed in an Annex. The parties to the Agreement undertake to exchange their views, if appropriate, in order to promote, in the competent forums and after scientific evaluation, the adoption of regulations concerning the use of new fishing methods that could involve the incidental catch of marine mammals or endanger their food resources, taking into account the risk of loss or discard of fishing instruments at sea (Art. 7c).

The parties also undertake to exchange their views with the objective of regulating and, if appropriate, prohibiting high-speed offshore races in the Sanctuary (Art. 9).

The parties are bound to hold regular meetings to ensure the application of and follow up of the Agreement (Art. 12, para. 1). In this framework, they are required to encourage national and international research programmes, as well as public awareness campaigns directed at professional and other users of the sea and non-governmental organizations, relating, *inter alia*, to the prevention of collisions between vessels and marine mammals and the communication to the competent authorities of the presence of dead or distressed marine mammals (Art. 12, para. 2).

A management body of the *Pelagos Sanctuary* is, however, lacking. Prior to 2004, each party determined its own priorities and management projects at a national level. Cooperation with the other parties was informal and occurred only occasionally, in order to establish shared aims as part of the development of the management plan, which was adopted by the three parties in 2004. With the creation of a Permanent Secretariat in 2006, the parties began to routinely work together to implement the provisions of the management plan. This Secretariat takes into account also actions implemented as part of other agreements and international programmes, such as ACCOBAMS, RAMOGE, and UNEP-MAP. Moreover, in 2007, three Working Groups were established in the framework of the *Pelagos Sanctuary*, with the view to pursuing the following goals: knowledge and means of management; communication and prevention; and governance. Among the aims of the Working Groups, there are the proposal of concrete measures that meet shared objectives and respond to practical management issues for the different scenarios as well as the setting out of recommendations that include a summary of the aims, the forecast cost, financing, schedule, and evaluation criteria. In the lack of a specific management body for the area, cooperation between the parties, also through the Working Groups, remains crucial.

From the legal point of view, the most critical aspect of the Agreement is the provision on the enforcement on the high seas of the measures agreed upon by the parties. It is important not to underestimate the fact that, also in those portions of water declared as exclusive economic zones, third States enjoy a number of freedoms, including the freedom of navigation, which causes certain impacts to cetaceans, such as those deriving from collisions and underwater noise.

Art. 14 of the Agreement provides as follows:

1. Dans la partie du sanctuaire située dans les eaux placées sous sa souveraineté ou juridiction, chacun des Etats Parties au présent accord est compétent pour assurer l'application des dispositions y prévues.
2. Dans les autres parties du sanctuaire, chacun des Etats Parties est compétent pour assurer l'application des dispositions du présent accord à l'égard des navires battant son pavillon, ainsi que, dans les limites prévues par les règles de droit international, à l'égard des navires battant le pavillon d'Etats tiers.[3]

Art. 14, para. 2, of the Agreement gives the parties the right to enforce on the high seas its provisions with respect to ships flying the flag of third States "within the limits established by the rules of international law". This wording brings an element of ambiguity into the picture, as it can be interpreted in two different ways.

3

1. In the part of the Sanctuary located in the waters subject to its sovereignty or jurisdiction, any of the States Parties to the present agreement is entitled to ensure the enforcement of the provisions set forth by it.
2. In the other parts of the Sanctuary, any of the States Parties is entitled to ensure the enforcement of the provisions of the present agreement with respect to ships flying its flag, as well as, within the limits established by the rules of international law, with respect to ships flying the flag of third States.

(unofficial translation)

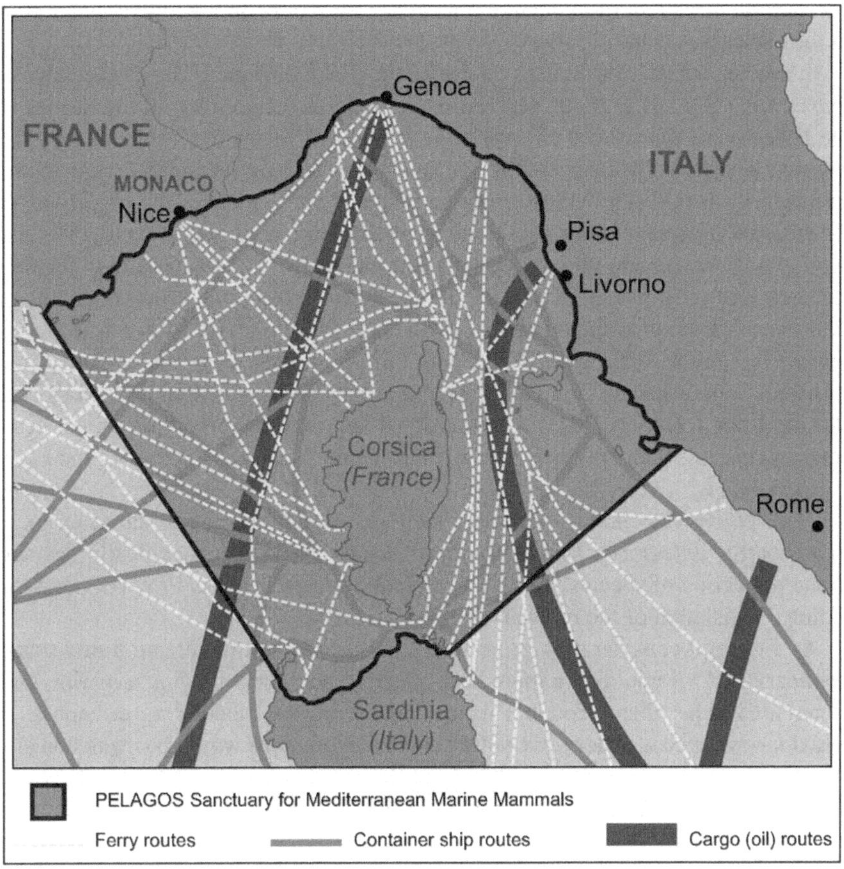

Figure 6.2 Shipping lanes within the *Pelagos Sanctuary*

Source: Agardy et al., *A Global Scientific Workshop on Spatio-Temporal Management of Noise*, Report of the Scientific Workshop, 2007, p. 18, figure 3

Under the first interpretation, the parties cannot enforce the provisions of the Agreement in respect of foreign ships, as such an action would be an encroachment upon the freedom of the high seas. The second interpretation is based on the fact that all the waters included in the Sanctuary would eventually fall within the exclusive economic zones of the three parties, if Monaco decided to establish such a zone. This seems sufficient to reach the conclusion that the parties are already entitled to enforce the rules that apply within the *Pelagos Sanctuary* in respect of all foreign ships to be found within its boundaries. This, at least, is certainly true when the clear aim of those measures is protecting and preserving the natural habitat of cetaceans (Art. 56, *b*, iii, UNCLOS specifically recognizes the relevant jurisdiction of coastal States within their exclusive economic zone). Particular attention, however, must be devoted to the navigational rights of third States, as no measure may encroach the freedom of navigation that applies not only on the high seas but also in the exclusive economic zone.

In this regard, it is of evident relevance that the inclusion of the *Pelagos Sanctuary* in the SPAMI List has secured recognition to the area by all the parties to the Barcelona Convention, enlarging the number of States that are bound by the relevant measures. Moreover, the *Pelagos Sanctuary* is recognized also in the framework of ACCOBAMS as an important area for achieving the objectives of the relevant agreement. The two Permanent Secretariats of the ACCOBAMS and the *Pelagos* Agreement have signed a Memorandum of Understanding to formalize their partnership and harmonize efforts in the protection of those species of cetaceans that are protected under ACCOBAMS and are found within the *Pelagos Sanctuary*. These sorts of initiatives may prompt the parties to undertake further measures. For instance, France has recently enacted a legislation that prohibits, starting from 1 January 2021, the intentional approach to certain species of cetaceans within less than 100 meters in all marine protected areas, including the *Pelagos Sanctuary*.[4]

The *Pelagos Sanctuary*, therefore, is an area that is subject, at the same time, to a tripartite agreement, two international legal instruments specifically devoted to the protection of species (ACCOBAMS) and habitats (Areas Protocol), and the national legislation of the relevant States.

As a general consideration, it is worth mentioning that the creation of a transboundary SPAMI could be a more cost-effective way for achieving a marine protected area rather than through a formal bilateral or multilateral agreement, as it was done in the case under review. Of course, negotiations would be needed in any case to achieve a transboundary SPAMI, as this would entail an agreement between all States concerned.[5] However, only the creation of a SPAMI would guarantee an *erga omnes partes* effect.

6.2. Transboundary Cooperation in the Strait of Bonifacio

The Strait of Bonifacio forms an international strait between Sardinia and Corsica (two Mediterranean islands belonging to Italy and France, respectively).[6] The strait enables communication between the Sea of Sardinia and the Tyrrhenian Sea.

4 *Arrêté du 3 septembre 2020 portant modification de l'arrêté du 1er juillet 2011 fixant la liste des mammifères marins protégés sur le territoire national et les modalités de leur protection* (*Journal officiel* No. 0240 of 2 October 2020). Art. 8 of the *Pelagos Sanctuary* Agreement provides that the parties regulate whale-watching for tourism. Art. 10 requires the parties to engage in mutual exchanges with the view of harmonizing as much as possible the measures adopted in this regard.

5 On the recourse to SPAMIs as a means for transboundary cooperation in the Adriatic and Ionian Seas, see Chapter 7 of this book.

6 On 28 November 1986, France and Italy signed a Convention relating to the Delimitation of the Maritime Boundaries in the Areas of the Mouths of Bonifacio, which entered into force on 15 May 1989. The delimitation line relates to the territorial seas of the two States and extends for a distance of about 40 n.m. between the two coastlines, connecting six points through five straight segments.

Its least width is 3.23 n.m., and its maximum depth is about 90 m. Navigation in the strait is very difficult due to intense and persistent winds, strong currents (3–4 knots) and the presence of several insular formations (islands, reefs, rocks, and low-tide elevations).

About 3,000 ships per year pass through the strait, navigating in an east-west direction, and ships connecting Corsica and Sardinia cross it in a north-south direction. The latter traffic is intense and growing in summer, when also many pleasure craft navigate in the area. Inside the strait, mariners are called to exercise great care to avoid the risk of collisions and ship groundings that could cause destruction or degradation of a unique, diverse, and significant ecosystem.[7]

Navigation in the Strait of Bonifacio is regulated by the regime of transit passage, as set forth in Arts. 37 to 44 UNCLOS. This regime applies to straits which are used for international navigation between one part of the high seas or an exclusive economic zone and another part of the high seas or an exclusive economic zone.[8] Under Art. 38 UNCLOS, transit passage means navigation and overflight for the purpose of continuous and expeditious transit of the strait. Unlike the regime of innocent passage through the territorial sea, the transit passage through straits extends to aircraft. Submarines are permitted to navigate in their "normal mode" (i.e., underwater), and suspension of the passage by bordering states is prohibited. In addition to merchant vessels and civil aircraft, also foreign warships and military aircraft enjoy the right of transit passage through international straits.

Although the regulatory authority of a State bordering a strait over transit passage is more limited than a coastal state's regulatory authority over innocent passage through its territorial sea, it is, nevertheless, provided by Art. 42 UNCLOS that a State bordering a strait may put into effect international standards and regulations regarding pollution and may regulate fishing activities, including the stowage of fishing gear by vessels. In addition, under Art. 41 UNCLOS, designation of sea lanes and traffic separation schemes through the strait is possible, provided that it results from the concurrent action by all States bordering the strait and is followed by formal adoption by the IMO.[9]

As the Strait of Bonifacio represents one of the most outstanding areas in the Mediterranean Sea in terms of marine biodiversity, France and Italy have long since decided to adopt in the strait a restrictive approach to navigation, insofar as ships flying their respective flags are concerned. As illustrated later, the measures adopted at the national and international level have reduced the risk of casualties in the Strait of Bonifacio. It is, however, to be regretted that the international

7 The ecological, socioeconomic and scientific attributes of the strait, as well as its vulnerability to damage by international shipping, are described in detail in Annexes 2 and 3 to Resolution MEPC.204(62).

8 The regime of passage through straits used for international navigation does not affect the legal status of the waters forming such straits, nor the exercise by the states bordering the straits of their sovereignty or jurisdiction over such waters and their space, seabed, and subsoil.

9 In the territorial sea, the coastal State may unilaterally establish sea lanes and traffic separation schemes, so long as it takes into account the recommendations of the IMO.

measures are only "recommended" by the IMO, while national measures adopted by France and Italy are mandatory only for the ships flying the flags of the two said States. Such an incongruous situation can only cast doubts on the effectiveness of the present protection regime as a whole and could be seen as an incentive for the re-flagging of French and Italian ships.

In 1979, IMO Resolution A.430(XI) endorsed the decision of France and Italy to establish a system of surveillance and information for ships passing through the strait. Navigation is possible only along a narrow 3-n.m. wide stretch and ships are asked to take a recommended route just about 1-n.m. wide. Navigation is prohibited to ships transporting oil, dangerous chemicals or other substances (listed in the Annexes to the MARPOL) and displaying a French or Italian flag. In particular, the Italian Decree of the Ministry of Merchant Marine of 26 February 1993, applicable to Italian ships only, forbids tankers carrying petroleum products or ships carrying dangerous or toxic substances to navigate the Strait of Bonifacio. Ordinance No. 1 of 15 February 1993, issued by the French Maritime Prefect for the Mediterranean, bans the transit of tankers displaying the French flag that carry hydrocarbons and other hazardous and noxious substances.[10] In the same year, the IMO adopted Resolution A.766(18) on navigation in the Strait of Bonifacio, urging ships carrying hazardous materials to avoid the seaway in question. The IMO instrument has been complemented in 1998 by circulars SN/Circ. 198 and 201, concerning routeing measures other than traffic separation schemes and mandatory ship reporting systems in the Strait of Bonifacio. The two States also established at the entrances of the strait two "precautionary areas", where ships must stop to be boarded before entering into the recommended routes of navigation[11] (see Figure 6.3).

An international agreement for the operational procedures aimed at implementing the mandatory reporting system of the ships in the Strait of Bonifacio (*Bonifacio Traffic*) was signed by France and Italy in Rome on 3 June 1999. Lastly, in order to further restrict dangerous maritime traffic through the strait, a Voluntary Agreement to Carry out a Series of Interventions Aimed at the Achievement of Higher Security Standards concerning the Maritime Transport of Dangerous Substances was signed in Rome on 1 June 2001 by the Italian Ministry of the Environment, Land and Sea, the Italian Ministry of Transportation and Navigation, Confindustria,[12] Assoporti,[13] and some environmental organizations and unions. Art. 6 of this voluntary instrument commits the signatory companies to navigate

10 For France, *Ordonnance* No. 1 of 15 February 1993 of the *Préfet maritime de la Méditerranée* of Toulon; for Italy, Decree of 26 February 1993 of the Minister of Merchant Marine.

11 For France, *Décret* No. 84/98 of 3 November 1998 of the *Préfet maritime de la Méditerranée* of Toulon, as amended by *Décret* No. 56 of 24 November 2003; for Italy, Decree of 27 November 1998 of the Minister of Merchant Marine.

12 The Italian Employers' Federation.

13 The Italian Association of Ports is an organism that brings together port authorities, other special bodies in ports, chambers of commerce of city-harbours, and the Italian Organization of Chambers of Commerce.

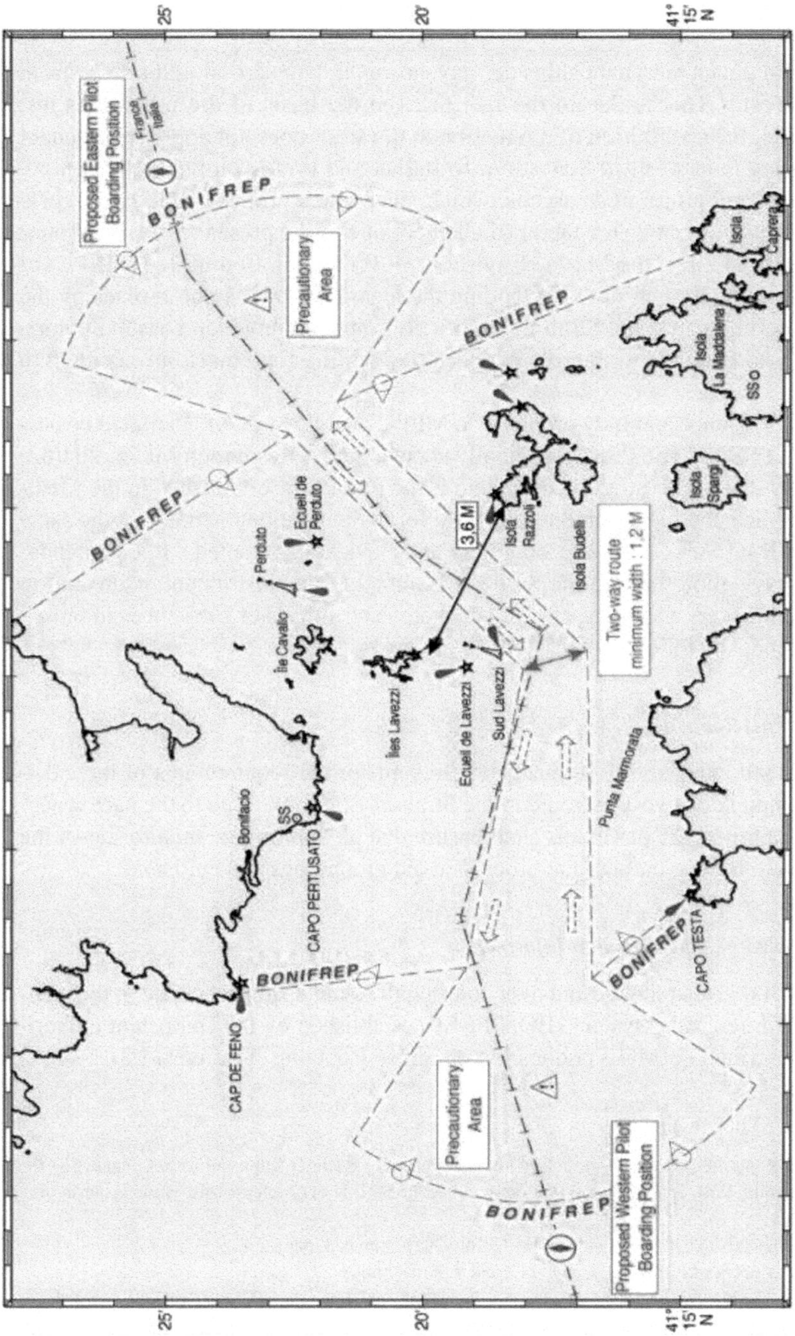

Figure 6.3 Recommended navigation through the Strait of Bonifacio

Source: Report of the IMO Maritime Safety Committee (MSC 90/28)

ships carrying dangerous substances listed in Annexes I and II to MARPOL solely based on charter party contracts that explicitly exclude the transit in the Strait of Bonifacio.

Several dozen merchant ships per day, however, keep crossing the strait from east to west.[14] This is due to the fact that, on the basis of the provisions just mentioned, the prohibition of navigation in the strait does not apply to merchant ships flying flags of third States, nor to Italian and French ships that are empty or not carrying prohibited cargoes, which, even when properly ballasted, represent an environmental risk factor of accident due to the presence of fuel in their tanks. Still, in 2011, the Marine Environment Protection Committee (MEPC) of the IMO reported that, notwithstanding the legal restrictions put in place by the two bordering states, the Strait of Bonifacio is an area in which coastal authorities are yet "confined to the role of spectator, waiting for a maritime accident to happen".[15]

In 2010, France and Italy proposed to MEPC that the Strait of Bonifacio be designated a PSSA.[16] The PSSA was finally adopted under Resolution MEPC.204(62) of 15 July 2011. The Strait of Bonifacio is the first PSSA established in the Mediterranean Sea and the second in the world for an international strait.[17] In the same year, the IMO Sub-Committee on Safety and Navigation adopted a Recommendation on navigation through the Strait of Bonifacio. This instrument, addressed to loaded oil tankers and ships carrying dangerous chemicals or substances in bulk,[18] recommends the following measures.

Use of Ships' Routeing

Vessels shall exercise full diligence and regard for the requirements of the existing recommended two-way route in the Strait of Bonifacio. Due to the narrowness of the strait, masters of vessels shall ensure that an appropriate monitoring of the ship's route is done on board in order to avoid groundings and collisions.

Ship Reporting and Navigation Information

Ships of 300 gross tonnage and over entering the strait shall participate in the mandatory ship reporting system (BONIFREP) established by the competent authorities as described in IMO's publication on Ships' Routeing (Section G I/8).

14 Traffic along the north-south direction mainly concerns passenger ships and ferries connecting the two islands. With approximately ten daily connections, it is very intense and growing during the summer.

15 Resolution MEPC.204(62), adopted on 15 July 2011, Annex 3, para. 2.4.

16 On the concept of PSSA, see Chapters 2 and 9 of this book.

17 In 2005, the IMO declared the extension of the already existing Great Barrier Reef PSSA in order to include the Torres Strait, based on a proposal by Australia and Papua New Guinea.

18 As listed in the Annex to Resolution MEPC.49(31) adopted on 4 July 1991.

Pilotage

Masters of vessels passing through the strait are recommended to avail themselves of the services of a qualified pilot.[19]

The designation of Strait of Bonifacio as a PSSA must have contributed to facilitating joint initiatives between the two bordering States, which have ultimately led to the establishment of a transboundary marine protected area, building upon the protection measures that had previously been adopted by the two States concerned.

Two marine protected areas have been established respectively by France and Italy inside the strait, which is also totally included within the area of the *Pelagos Sanctuary*. On the south-eastern side of the strait, Italy created in 1996 *La Maddalena Archipelago National Park*[20] and, on the other side, France established in 1999 the *Natural Reserve of the Strait of Bonifacio*.[21]

On the Italian part, the ecological significance of the waters of northern Sardinia is recognized by several other designations: some of them belong to a national network, such as the *Asinara National Park*,[22] the *Isola Asinara Marine Protected Area*,[23] the *Tavolara – Punta di Coda Cavallo Marine Protected Area*[24]; others are included in a network of international designation, such as the listings of NATURA 2000 sites.[25] In particular, Italy inscribed six special protection areas under the Birds Directive[26] and twelve sites of community significance under the Habitats Directive.[27] On the French part, official listings in the area in question include – besides the previously mentioned national reserve – a special protection area under the Birds Directive[28] and three sites of community importance under the Habitats Directive.[29]

The ecological significance of the Mouths of Bonifacio was further recognized at the international level in 2009, when the French protected site (*Natural Reserve*

19 Vessels should inform or confirm their estimated time of arrival (ETA) to the head office of the Bonifacio Strait pilotage service 24 hours prior to arrival. Once on Bonifacio Strait Road, vessels should confirm their ETA 2 hours prior to arrival calling Bonifacio Traffic on VHF 10.

20 Decree of the President of the Italian Republic of 17 May 1996.

21 Ministerial Decree of 23 September 1999.

22 Decree of the President of the Republic of 13 October 2002.

23 Ministerial Decree of 12 August 2002.

24 Ministerial Decree of 12 December 1997, amended by Ministerial Decree of 28 November 2001.

25 On the NATURA 2000 Network, see Chapter 4 of this book.

26 *Asinara Island*; *Piana Island – Asinara Gulf*; *Pond of Pilo, Casaraccio and Stintino Salt Marshs*; *La Maddalena Archipelago*; *North-Eastern Islands between Ceraso Cape and Pond of San Teodoro*; *Figari Cape, Cala Sabina, Punta Canigione and Figarolo Island.*

27 *North-Western Sardinian Islets and Coasts*; *Asinara Island*; *Piana Island*; *Pond of Pilo and Casaraccio*; *Pond and Juniper Forest of Platamona*; *Coghinas Mouths*; *Rossa Island – Paradiso Coast*; *Russu Mount*; *Testa Cape*; *La Maddalena Archipelago*; *Tavolara Island, Molara and Molarotto*; *Figari Cape and Figarolo Island.*

28 *Lavezzi Islands, Strait of Bonifacio.*

29 *Strait of Bonifacio, Monk Islands*; *Cerbical Islands and coastal strip*; *Pertusato/Bonifacio plateau and Lavezzi Islands.*

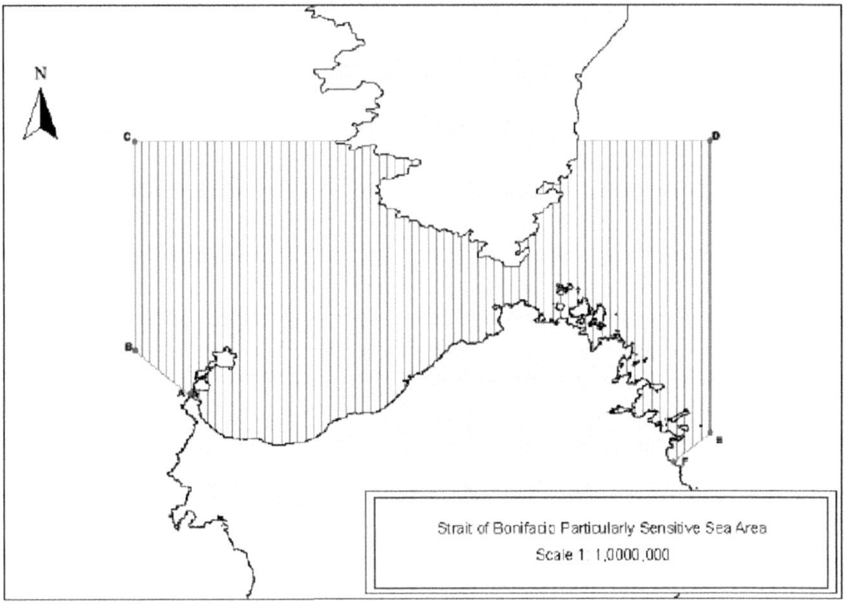

Figure 6.4 The Strait of Bonifacio PSSA

Source: Annex 22, Resolution MEPC.204(62) of 15 July 2011, *Designation of the Strait of Bonifacio as a PSSA*

of the Strait of Bonifacio) was granted the status of SPAMI.[30] Moreover, the same area is covered by the *Pelagos Sanctuary*.

Eventually, the two bordering States, thanks to diplomatic efforts which lasted more than two decades,[31] were able to make use of an innovative legal mechanism of cooperation which could be taken today by other States as an example to create transboundary marine protected areas. This example of cooperation is even more significant in view of the particular difficulties faced by the two States in question, as they border a strait used for international navigation, with all the legal implications that follow. The opportunity to move beyond unilateral legal initiatives or the simple inscription of a site in an already existing list of protected areas was offered to France and Italy in 2006, when the Parliament and the Council of the European Union adopted Regulation 1082/2006 on a European Grouping of Territorial

30 The Mouths of Bonifacio area contains 37 per cent of species of Mediterranean importance. The loggerhead sea turtle (*Caretta caretta*) may be spotted in the area. The flora includes some 15 endemic species, with one endemic to the island of Lavezzi.

31 A protocol between the two bordering States and the local authorities on the modalities for implementing the project of an international marine park in the Mouths of Bonifacio dates back to 19 January 1993.

Cooperation (EGTC).[32] In the light of the difficulties encountered by States that are members of the European Union in the field of cross-border cooperation, Regulation 1082/2006 introduced a new cooperation instrument at the European Union level as part of the reform of regional policy for the period 2007–2013.

EGTCs are legal entities that European Union member States, regional authorities, local authorities, or bodies governed by public law – as the case may be – have been encouraged to set up from 1 January 2007. The competencies of the EGTC are laid down in a binding cooperation convention established on the initiative of its members. The EGTC members also decide whether their EGTC should be a separate legal entity or whether its tasks should be delegated to one of the members. Within the bounds of its mandate, an EGTC acts on behalf of its members. EGTCs thus enjoy the legal capacity accorded to legal entities by national law.

After negotiating a text for the first EGTC to be established in the Mediterranean Sea, the two local entities concerned acted unilaterally. The Executive Board of *La Maddalena Archipelago National Park* (Italy) approved the Convention for the Establishment of the International Marine Park of the Strait of Bonifacio (*Parco Marino Internazionale delle Bocche di Bonifacio* – PMIBB) on 20 December 2010.[33] The Corsican Assembly (France), on behalf of the Corsican Environment Office, approved the same instrument on 27 January 2011.[34] The PMIBB and the EGTC statute were signed by representatives of the two States on 7 December 2012. The PMIBB was registered with the European Committee of the Regions on 11 March 2013. According to the PMIBB, the denomination of the EGTC in question, together with the related marine area under protection, is *International Marine Park of the Strait of Bonifacio*, or *Parco Marino Internazionale delle Bocche di Bonifacio* (in Italian).

As an autonomous legal entity, the EGTC is responsible, *inter alia*, for adopting the management plan for the area and for it to be periodically revised on the basis of scientific findings; proposing to the relevant authorities appropriate measures towards the strengthening of maritime safety in the Strait, also through a legal and institutional representation within the IMO; implementing joint actions of maintenance and restoration of sensitive marine and terrestrial habitats; convening an annual meeting for the assessment of all different management and protective actions within the common strategy; and examining ways to obtain regional, national, or European funding for the implementation of its projects.

32 On the EGTC instrument as a means for transboundary cooperation in the Adriatic and Ionian Seas, see Chapter 8 of this book.

33 Deliberation of the Executive Board of *La Maddalena Archipelago National Park* No. 31 of 20 December 2010.

34 *Délibération de l'Assemblée de Corse N. 11/004 du 27 janvier 2011 décidant de valider la Convention portant création du 'Parc Marin International des Bouches de Bonifacio' – Groupement Européen de coopération territoriale – 'Parcu Marinu Internaziunale di i Bocchi di Bunifaziu' (PMIBB – GECT) et ses statuts.*

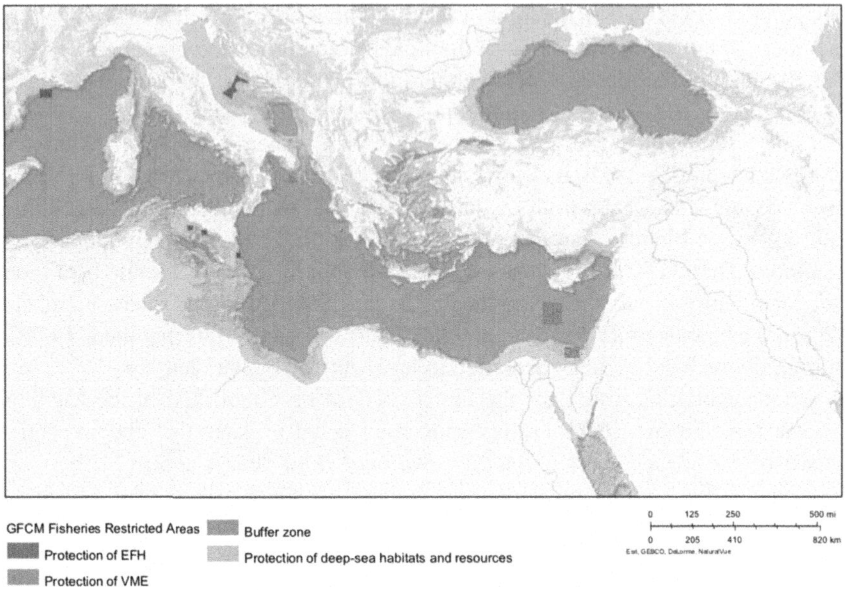

Figure 6.5 Areas of the Mediterranean and Black Seas regulated by GFCM Recommendations
Source: www.fao.org/gfcm/data/maps/fras

6.3. The GFCM Fisheries Restricted Areas

Three FRAs established within the GFCM framework are of particular relevance to the present investigation and represent opportunities for transboundary cooperation in the Adriatic and Ionian Seas. A further FRA could be soon established in the region of concern, on the basis of a recent proposal.

With a view to providing a database for all FRAs, the GFCM has recently elaborated an interactive map showing the limits of the areas and their characteristics.[35]

In addition to the identification of FRAs, representing clear examples of other effective area-based conservation tools, since 2005, the GFCM has prohibited the use of towed dredges and trawl nets at depths beyond 1,000 m. This can be considered as an example of vertical protection of a specified area, extending only to the seabed together with a selected portion of the water column. Both the South Adriatic and Ionian Seas comprise areas covered by such measure, as the depth of 1,000 m is reached in the darker parts of the map above (Figure 6.5):

A. The Lophelia Reef off Capo Santa Maria di Leuca

On the basis of, *inter alia*, Recommendation REC.CM-GFCM/29/2005/1 on the management of certain fisheries exploiting demersal and deep-water species as well

35 See available at www.fao.org/gfcm/data/maps/fras.

as the recommendation of the GFCM Scientific Advisory Committee to ban bottom trawling activities damaging the deep-water coral reefs located in international waters (referred to as Lophelia Reef off Capo Santa Maria di Leuca), since 2006, the GFCM has prohibited fishing with towed dredges and bottom trawl nets in the area bounded by lines joining the following coordinates, identified as the deep-sea FRA named *Lophelia Reef off Capo Santa Maria di Leuca* (see also Figure 6.6):

39° 27' 72" N, 18° 10' 74" E
39° 27' 80" N, 18° 26' 68" E
39° 11' 16" N, 18° 04' 28" E
39° 11' 16" N, 18° 32' 58" E

The same constitutive instrument (Recommendation REC.CM-GFCM/30/2006/3) provides that GFCM members call the attention of the appropriate authorities in order to protect the area from the impact of any other activity jeopardizing the conservation of the features that characterize these particular habitats.

The FRA in question has a permanent character and is located in GSA19, corresponding to the Western Ionian Sea, according to the division into geographical sub-areas (GSA) of the GFCM. It presently lies beyond the territorial sea of Italy but on its continental shelf. The water column above the corals located on the site is destined to become part of the exclusive economic zone of Italy as soon as the relevant law (2021) is implemented by presidential decree.

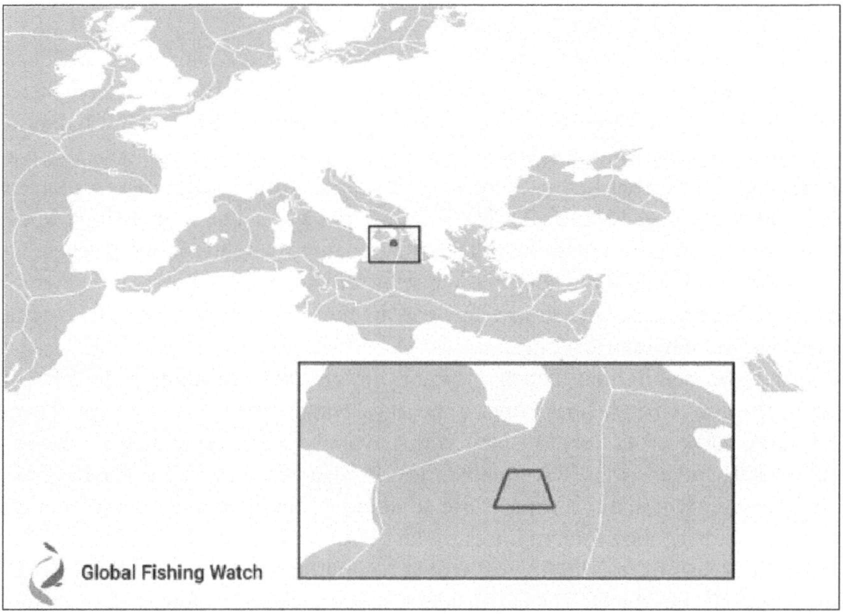

Figure 6.6 The *Lophelia Reef off Capo Santa Maria di Leuca*

Source: Global Fishing Watch (2021)

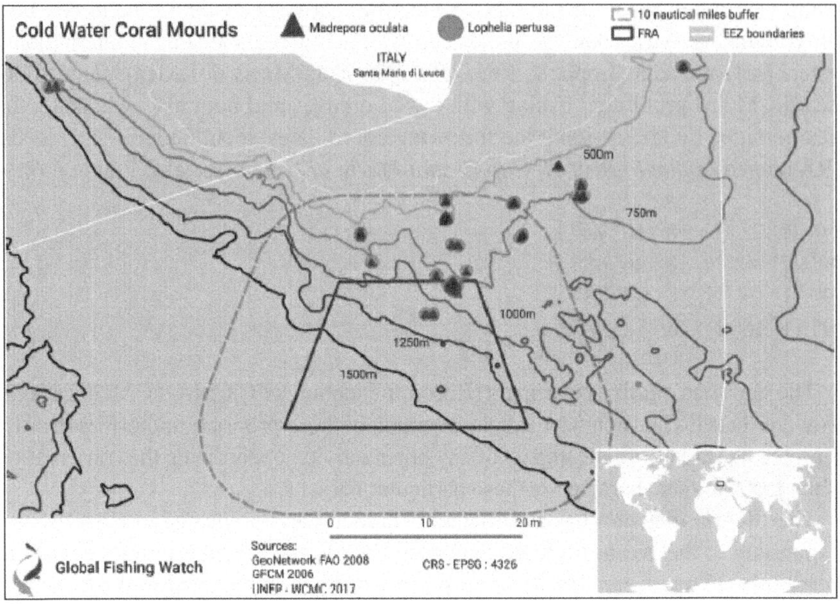

Figure 6.7 The location of cold-water coral mounds in the FRA *Lophelia Reef off Capo Santa Maria di Leuca* and its surroundings – The dots indicate the presence of *Lophelia pertusa*; the triangles indicate the presence of *Madrepora oculata*

Source: Global Fishing Watch (2021)

Depth ranges in the FRA are between 500 and 1,500 m. The reef is considered to be the largest occurrence of living white coral communities in the Mediterranean. It hosts *Lophelia pertusa* and *Madrepora oculata*, which are both listed as endangered in the Red List of Threatened Species of the International Union for the Conservation of Nature (IUCN). These two species can support high levels of biodiversity and, by releasing organic matter, contribute to the biogeochemical cycles and support both planktonic and benthic organisms. As shown in Figure 6.7, the coral mounds are concentrated between the northern border of the FRA and up to the 500-m bathymetrical line.

It is to be highlighted that the 10-n.m. buffer zone surrounding the FRA in Figure 6.7 above (dash line) is not a measure established by the GFCM: it only served the purpose of Global Fishing Watch to analyze the level of fishing activity immediately outside the FRA's boundaries. It is to be noted that trawler activity was observed within such zone, close to some of the cold-water coral mounds found just outside the northern limits of the FRA (see Figure 6.8).

On the basis of these findings, it would be appropriate for the Scientific Advisory Committee of the GFCM to consider the extension of the protective measures to at least 10 n.m. beyond the current limits of the FRA, in order to cover also those cold-water corals that remain outside the limits identified by Recommendation

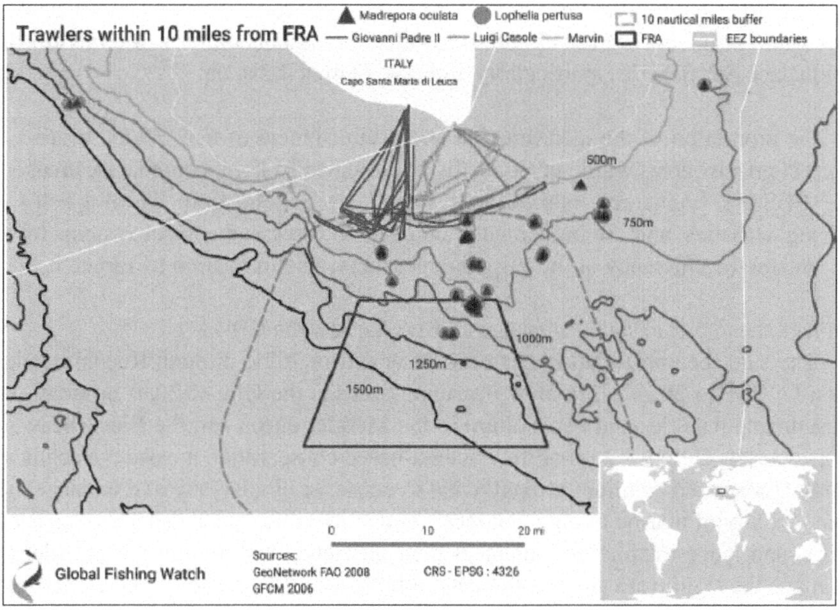

Figure 6.8 Tracks of three European Union's fleet-registered trawlers flying Italian flag that were recorded fishing within 10 n.m. of the FRA *Lophelia Reef off Capo Santa Maria di Leuca* for a total of 70 fishing hours between January 2018 and October 2020 and to depths of around 500 m

Source: Global Fishing Watch (2021)

2006/03 (particularly in the north and north-west of the FRA boundary). The same objective could be pursued through the establishment of the proposed new SPAMI off Capo Santa Maria di Leuca,[36] provided that all sites hosting biodiversity relevant to the Areas Protocol are covered.

B. The Jabuka/Pomo Pit

The *Jabuka/Pomo Pit* FRA in the Adriatic Sea was first established in 2017, through Recommendation GFCM/41/2017/3. As a basis of the measure, that instrument explicitly referred to the precautionary approach, in accordance with the Agreement for the Implementation of the Provisions of the United Nations Convention on the Law of the Sea of 10 December 1982 relating to the Conservation and Management of Straddling Fish Stocks and Highly Migratory Fish Stocks of 4 August 1995 and the Code of Conduct for Responsible Fisheries of the Food and Agriculture Organization of the United Nations.

36 As regards proposals for new SPAMIs, including in the waters off Capo Santa Maria di Leuca, see Chapter 7 of this book.

The first establishment of the FRA had followed Resolution GFCM/40/2016/2 for a mid-term strategy (2017–2020) towards the sustainability of Mediterranean and Black Sea fisheries, particularly Target 4, Output 4.2.a, on

> the promotion of the identification and establishment of new FRAs to protect priority areas within ecologically or biologically significant marine areas (EBSAs), [vulnerable marine ecosystems] VMEs, etc. from harmful fishing activities, and the implementation of monitoring and control systems to ensure the efficiency of these spatial measures, also in relation to Target 3.

In fact, the *Jabuka/Pomo Pit* is also an EBSA under the CBD.

The said recommendation has been amended in 2021, through Recommendation GFCM/44/2021/2. The new instrument recalls the GFCM 2030 Strategy for sustainable fisheries and aquaculture in the Mediterranean and the Black Seas, in particular its Output 1.3 on "Efficient area-based conservation measures, technical and nature-based solutions strengthened to conserve biodiversity and enhance the productivity of marine living resources", which identifies "new fisheries restricted areas and, once established, enhances their efficiency and monitoring in order to manage the significant adverse impacts of fisheries on vulnerable species, ecosystems and essential fish habitats".

The species that the FRA in question, since 2017, has been aiming at protecting from the impact of harmful fishing activities are the demersal fish stocks of European hake (*Merluccius merluccius*) and Norway lobster (*Nephrops norvegicus*). The first is a long-lived species, and short-term fishing closures cannot be expected to produce substantial effects; the second is a relatively long-lived species that, during the first year of its life, remains hidden in the burrows and cannot be taken by trawlers. The 2021 recommendation has enlarged the scope of protection to include reference to small pelagic stocks such as anchovy and sardine.

Scientists had initially recommended an experimental three-year closure to be reviewed on the basis of results from annual monitoring. Several area sizes were presented as possible options to protect a larger or smaller portion of the nursery grounds.

In 2002,[37] the GFCM had already recommended an increase in the mesh-size of nets or even the closure of certain areas, in order to protect demersal species. In 2016, the GFCM discussed ways to ensure the collection of the necessary data on the distribution of vulnerable marine ecosystems (VMEs), with a view to identifying priority areas. There were also extensive national efforts to monitor and ban fishing from the *Jabuka/Pomo Pit*. An area was identified (so-called *Scalata del Fondaletto*), corresponding to the northeastern slope of the *Jabuka/Pomo Pit*, where a series of temporal bans and monitoring rules were introduced for Italian fishing vessels.

37 GFCM Working Group on Demersal Species, Rome, Italy, 20–22 March 2002.

Based on the work of the MedReAct and the Adriatic Recovery Project, the Subregional Committee for the Adriatic Sea examined the proposal to establish an FRA in the *Jabuka/Pomo Pit* and agreed to present it to the Scientific Advisory Committee for its final evaluation and potential submission to the GFCM. At the Our Ocean Conference, held in Malta in October 2017, one of the commitments expressed by the European Union was to support the GFCM in establishing an FRA of at least 2,700 km^2 in the *Jabuka/Pomo Pit.*

The means through which the demersal-species and small pelagic stocks protection goal is today pursued in the area entails the protection of the corresponding VMEs and essential habitats through an innovative area-based protection tool divided into different zones.

In Zone A, any professional fishing activity with bottom-set nets, bottom trawls, set longlines, and traps has been prohibited since 2017. The 2021 recommendation has added the prohibition to fish with purse seiners and pelagic trawlers targeting anchovy or sardine.

In Zone B, since 2017, fishing activities with bottom-set trawls, set longlines, and traps have been prohibited from 1 September to 31 October each year. Fishing activities with purse seiners and pelagic trawlers targeting anchovy or sardine are prohibited in this zone all year round. Professional activities may be allowed in this zone only whether the vessel or its master is in possession of a specific authorization and that historical fishing activities are demonstrated. States – either GFCM members or cooperating non-members – are required to keep a register of the fishing vessels authorized to fish in this zone. In any case, such vessels cannot fish for more than two fishing days per week, and those using otter twin trawl gear are not entitled to fish for more than one fishing day per week.

In Zone C, these fishing activities as well as recreational fisheries are prohibited from 1 September to 31 October each year. Fishing activities with purse seiners and pelagic trawlers targeting anchovy or sardine are prohibited in this zone all year round. It is worth noting that neither the 2017 recommendation nor the 2021 one prohibit the second type of activity within Zone A and Zone B. Only professional activities may be allowed in Zone C, provided that the vessel or its master is in possession of a specific authorization and that historical fishing activities in the zone are demonstrated. Also in this case, vessels must be registered in order to be allowed in the zone. Those fishing with bottom trawls are entitled to do so only on Saturdays and Sundays, from 05:00 till 22:00 hours. Those fishing with bottom-set nets, set longlines, and traps are allowed to fish only from Monday at 05:00 till Thursday at 22:00 hours. Fishing gear on board or in use must be duly identified, numbered, and marked before starting any fishing operation or navigation within the FRA.

All catches of demersal stocks can be landed only in designated landing points: to this aim, GFCM members and cooperating non-members designate landing points in which landings of demersal stocks from the *Jabuka/Pomo Pit* FRA are authorized. The list of all landing points and the list of all authorized vessels must be communicated to the GFCM by 30 April each year. For each vessel, the information to be provided is listed in Annex 2 to the 2021 recommendation.

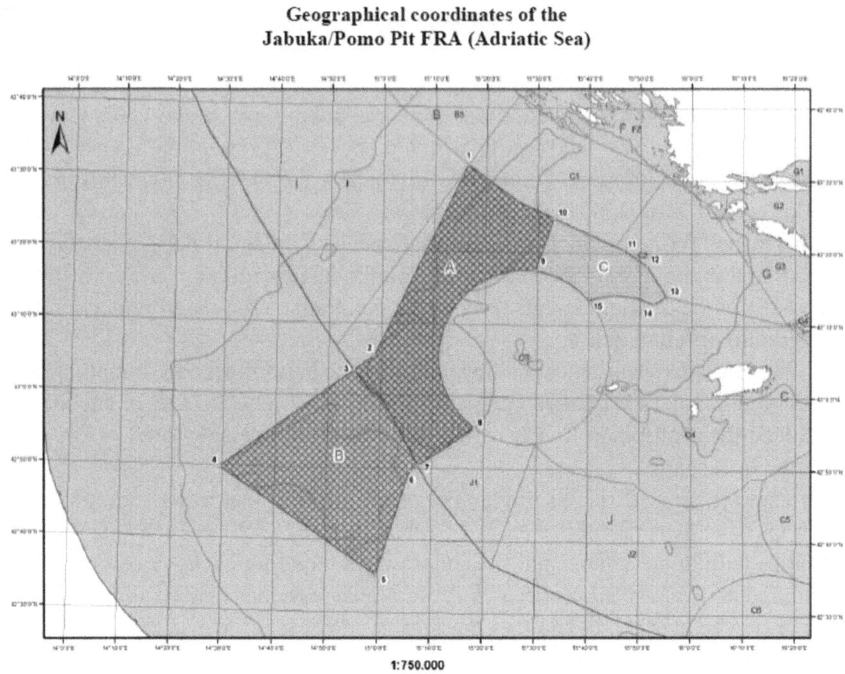

Figure 6.9 The *Jabuka/Pomo Pit* FRA and its zoning
Source: Recommendation GFCM/44/2021/2

Besides the area-based measures and time closures, the 2021 recommendation establishing the *Jabuka Pomo/Pit* FRA, as its predecessor, includes provisions addressing navigation. In particular, fishing vessels authorized to fish in Zone B or C must be equipped with vessel monitoring systems (VMS) or automated identification systems (AIS). Those vessels that are not authorized for fishing in such zones are allowed to transit through the FRA only if they follow a direct course at a constant speed of no less than 7 knots and are equipped with VMS or AIS active on board.

It is also provided that GFCM members and cooperating non-members call the attention of the relevant national and international authorities in order to protect the *Jabuka/Pomo Pit* FRA from the impact of any activity that may jeopardize the conservation of the characteristic features of the particular habitats. There is no explicit provision in the 2021 recommendation allowing States to decide to adopt stricter measures for the vessels flying their flag. However, this seems implicit in the powers of flag States.

At the time of its adoption, it was decided that the 2017 recommendation establishing the *Jabuka/Pomo Pit* FRA would produce effects until 31 December 2020. Direct information collected by the editors of this volume with the GFCM confirmed that the *Jabuka/Pomo Pit* FRA is considered one of the best examples of management for the conservation of demersal species in a transboundary area (involving Croatia and Italy). Accordingly, the 2021 recommendation confirmed the *Jabuka/Pomo Pit* FRA as a permanent FRA, together with all the associated management measures. This was decided in view of the positive contribution of such FRA to the protection of the juveniles and biomass of demersal species, according to the advice of the Scientific Advisory Committee on Fisheries. The latter, together with the Compliance Committee, is now in charge of reviewing the implementation of the 2021 recommendation on a yearly basis (in order to issue other recommendations, as appropriate).

C. The **Bari Canyon**

On the basis of a proposal elaborated in 2018 by ISMAR-CNR, the IUCN Center for Mediterranean Cooperation, University of Bari, and Coispa Bari, the GFCM at its 44th session has established an FRA in the so-called Bari Canyon, in the Southern Adriatic, through Recommendation GFCM/44/2021/3.

The *Bari Canyon* FRA is located in GSA18 – which is already identified as EBSA by the CBD,[38] together with the northern Ionian Sea – at around 20 n.m. off the city of Bari and 50 n.m. south of the *Gargano National Park*, in the Apulia Region (Figure 6.10).

In the 2018 proposal, the area was identified as: i) area of unique physical features and hydrological processes (deep-water circulation influencing the entire Mediterranean Sea); ii) a vulnerable marine ecosystem hosting numerous endangered mega- and macro-benthic organisms such as cnidarians; iii) a nursery for some deep-cartilaginous species impacted by fisheries; and iv) an area of important essential fish habitats for different commercial species such as anchovy, sardine, European hake, red mullet, and deep-rose shrimp, among others.

The *Bari Canyon* FRA is composed of two branches, almost parallel, indenting the shelf at depths of around 200 m. Depth range is between 200 and 700 m in the core area (Zone A) and between 200 and 1200 m in the buffer area (Zone B). According to the proposal, while the FRA core area would include the most valuable benthic habitats recorded in the Bari Canyon, such as the cold-water coral communities, the buffer area would extend the protection of complex and heterogeneous habitats (Figure 6.11).

The core area and the buffer area had been defined by the following coordinates in the 2018 proposal.

Core area:

41° 23’ 49” N, 17° 03’ 24” E
41° 15’ 27” N, 17° 19’ 16” E
41° 16’ 13” N, 17° 02’ 42” E
41° 23’ 03” N, 17° 19’ 49” E

38 See chm.cbd.int/database/record?documentID=204126.

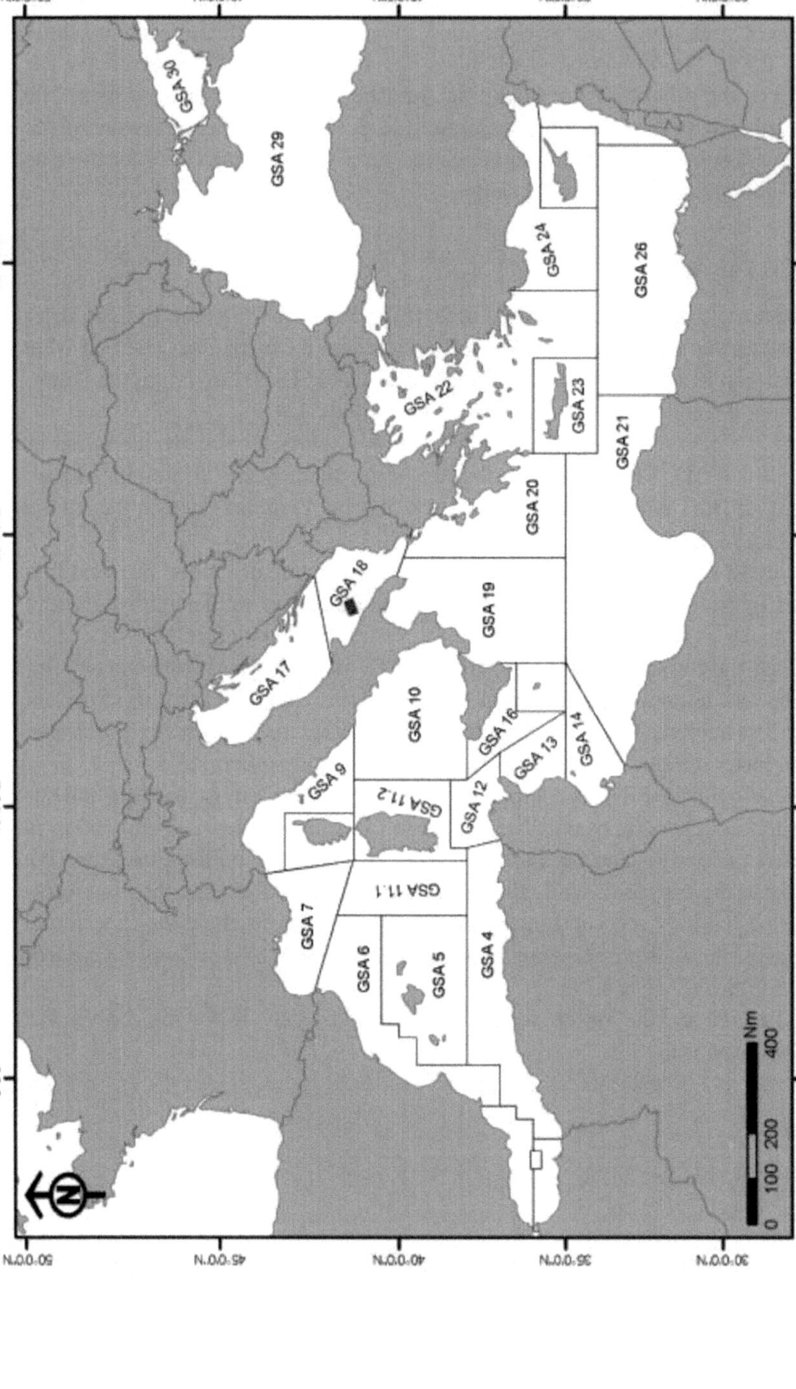

Figure 6.10 The location of the *Bari Canyon* FRA in GSA18 (Southern Adriatic)

Source: Recommendation GFCM/44/2021/3

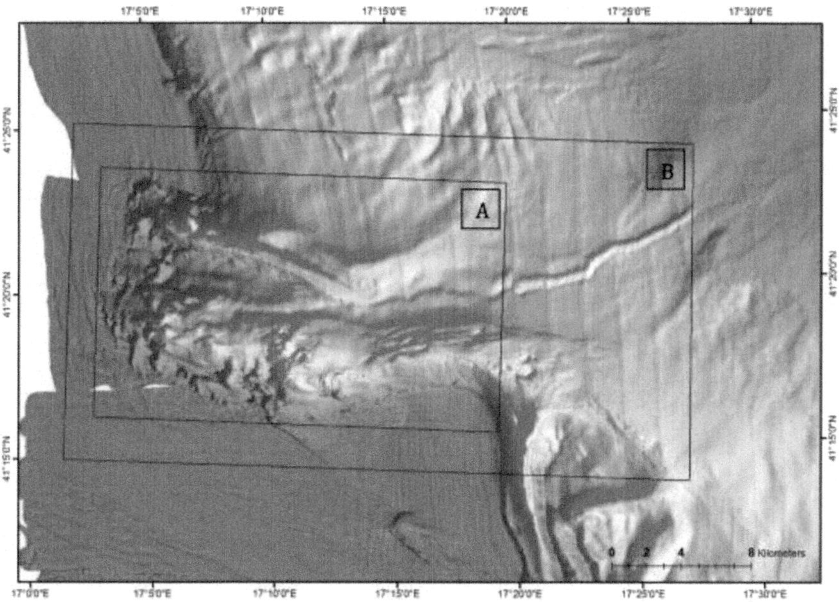

Figure 6.11 The 2018 proposed zoning of the *Bari Canyon* FRA: (A) core area; (B) buffer area

Source: Standard form for the submission of proposals for GFCM Fisheries Restricted Areas (FRAs) in the Mediterranean and the Black Sea (Bari Canyon), April 2018, p. 7

Buffer area:

41° 25' 11" N, 17° 02' 09" E
41° 24' 04" N, 17° 27' 31" E
41° 13' 50" N, 17° 27' 01" E
41° 14' 57" N, 17° 01' 26" E

The 2021 recommendation has identified five series of coordinates and has maintained the distinction between core and buffer zones, as follows (see Figure 6.12):

Zone A:

41° 23' 3" N, 17° 19' 49" E
41° 15' 27" N, 17° 19' 16" E
41° 15' 58" N, 17° 8' 12" E
41° 17' 45" N, 17° 2' 50" E
41° 23' 49" N, 17° 3' 24" E

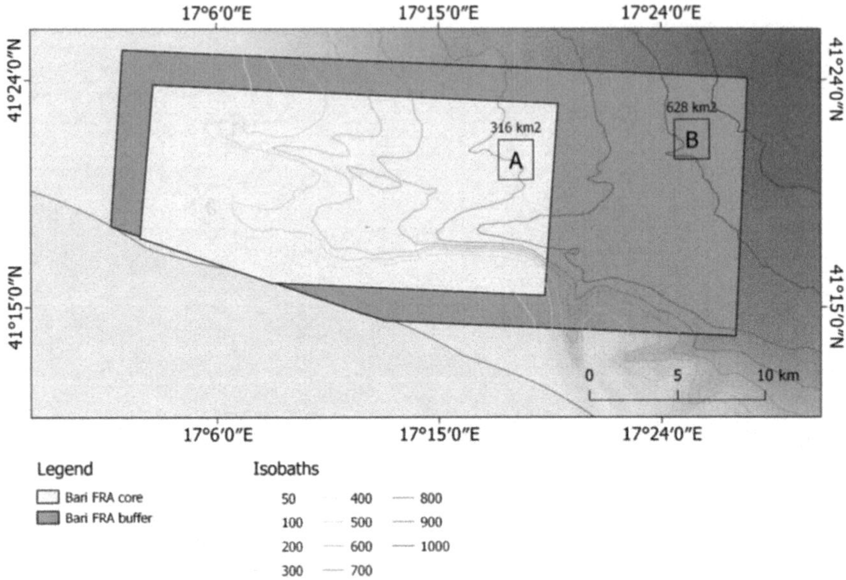

Figure 6.12 The current zoning of the *Bari Canyon* FRA: (A) core area; (B) buffer area
Source: Recommendation GFCM/44/2021/3

Zone B:

41° 24' 4" N, 17° 27' 31" E
41° 13' 50" N, 17° 27' 1" E
41° 14' 27" N, 17° 12' 48" E
41° 18' 12" N, 17° 1' 40" E
41° 25' 11" N, 17° 2' 9" E

In the core area (Zone A), the protection measures proposed in 2018 consisted of a permanent closure to any professional or recreational fishing activity. The 2021 recommendation has confirmed such prohibition. As for the buffer area (Zone B), the 2018 proposal provided that fishing activities with set longlines and traps could be allowed to vessels with a specific authorization and demonstrated historical fishing activities within the area included in the buffer zone. The proposal envisaged a permanent closure to towed nets and bottom-set nets and any recreational fishing activity. Exploratory fishing for towed nets and bottom-set nets could have been allowed to fish for a specific period of time, previous demonstration of no adverse impact on VMEs and essential fish habitats. To this aim, a dossier specifying the technical characteristics of the vessels, gear used, and proposal for the technical parameters of the campaign (e.g., length, gear) should have been provided to the competent authorities. Such technical dossier could have been used to evaluate the impact on VMEs and essential fish habitats before approval of the exploratory fishing by the competent authorities. Observers on board also should have been considered, with a view to identifying the footprint of the fishery.

The 2021 recommendation has established that fishing activities with set longlines and traps may be allowed provided that the vessel or its master are in possession of a specific authorization and historical fishing activities in the buffer zone are demonstrated. The new instrument demands GFCM member States and cooperating non-member States to establish a register of the fishing vessels authorized to fish in Zone B. It provides that GFCM member States and cooperating non-member States transmit to the GFCM Secretariat, not later than 30 April each year, a list of the authorized vessels for the forthcoming year.

The 2018 proposal suggested detailed measures to effectively enforce the protection of the FRA. In particular, monitoring, control, and surveillance measures under the umbrella of the MSFD would have included the following.

An Access Regime

The proposal suggested a closed list of authorized vessels, which should have also met a number of requirements, namely: be equipped with a VMS or AIS in correct working order as well as registration obligations, including those for the fishing gear on board. The 2021 recommendation requires that fishing vessels authorized to fish in Zone B shall be equipped with VMS or AIS in correct working order, and the fishing gear on board or in use shall be duly identified, numbered, and marked before starting any fishing operation or navigation in the FRA.

A Control Regime

The proposal suggested the designation of landing points, obligations of notice of arrival in port, and control of landings. To this end, the relevant fisheries authority should have designated landing points in which landings from captures in the FRA are authorized. The control of landings should have covered a minimum of 20 per cent of the landings. The 2021 recommendation requires that authorized fishing vessels shall only land catch of demersal stocks at the designated landing points. To this end, each GFCM member State and cooperating non-member State shall designate landing points in which the landings of demersal stocks from the *Bari Canyon* FRA is authorized. The list of such landing points must be communicated to the GFCM Secretariat by 30 April each year starting from 2022. No minimum percentage of control coverage is provided.

A Monitoring Regime

According to the 2018 proposal, in line with Recommendation MCS-GFCM/33/2009/7 and European Union Regulation 1224/2009 for fishing vessels operating or transiting in an FRA, the VMS should have given positions in the FRA every 30 minutes and communicated the entry into the FRA area with the declaration of catches on the ship's hold before the entry. The 2021 recommendation has not included such provision.

On the other hand, the new instrument provides that fishing vessels equipped with bottom-set nets, bottom trawls, set longlines, and traps without authorization shall be allowed to transit through the FRA only if they follow a direct course at a constant speed of not less than 7 knots and are equipped with VMS or AIS active on board.

A Reporting Regime

According to the 2018 proposal, the reporting provisions should have included a VME indicator of taxa capture and vulnerable species as bycatch. Measures should have included a logbook filled in for each haul and the reporting of the total catch for any commercial species obtained partially or totally in the FRA core or buffer zones. It was suggested that catches of VME indicator taxa be photographed in order to be identifiable, in addition to indicating their estimated amount in kg, and consistently recorded it in the logbook. Catches of vulnerable species as bycatch should have been reported following the GFCM Protocols for self-reporting. The 2018 proposal demanded that this information be sent to the Fisheries Management Authority and made available for port inspectors and observers on board. The GFCM Compliance Committee would, in fact, regularly review and assess the level of enforcement and compliance in the FRA and provide relevant recommendations. The GFCM Working Group on Vulnerable Marine Ecosystems would revise the management measures applied in the area and provide advise on the technical measures to decrease any adverse impact on VMEs and essential fish habitats (EFHs), as well as on the means to undertake impact assessment prior exploratory fishing. The 2021 recommendation only provides that its provisions shall apply until 31 December 2026. The Scientific Advisory Committee and the Compliance Committee shall review its implementation on a yearly basis. Based on such advice, the management measures for the *Bari Canyon* FRA shall be reviewed in 2026. In any case, it is provided that the recommendation is without prejudice to stricter measures adopted by GFCM member States and cooperating non-members for the vessels flying their flag. Moreover, GFCM member States and cooperating non-member shall call the attention of the relevant national and international authorities in order to protect the *Bari Canyon* FRA from the impacts of any activity that may jeopardize the conservation of the characteristic features of its particular habitats.

The 2018 proposal acknowledged that the spatial closures to fishing in the *Bari Canyon* FRA are likely to have a certain socioeconomic impact in the short term due to the fact that local long-liners often fish in the canyon for large specimens of valuable species (see Figure 6.13 on the localization of some relevant fishing ports). An adequate programme to mitigate these impacts, including through the involvement of stakeholders and local fishermen, should be, therefore, part of the FRA implementation strategy.

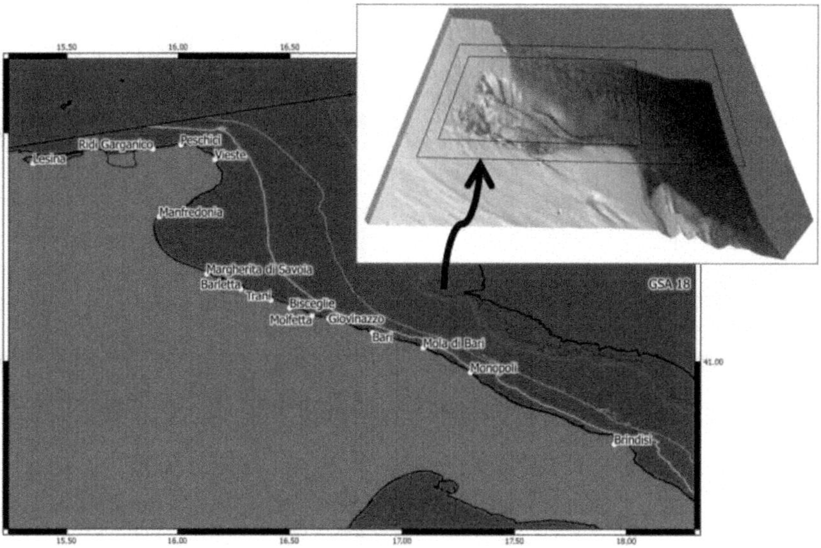

Figure 6.13 3D view of the *Bari Canyon* FRA (core and buffer areas) and the coastline with the localization of some relevant fishing ports

Source: Standard form for the submission of proposals for GFCM Fisheries Restricted Areas (FRAs) in the Mediterranean and the Black Sea (Bari Canyon), April 2018, p. 14

D. The Deep-water Essential Fish Habitats and Sensitive Habitats in the South Adriatic

Noteworthy is the proposal submitted to the GFCM by MedReAct on behalf of the Adriatic Recovery Project on 31 March 2018, with a view to protecting from the impacts of fishing the deep-water essential fish habitats and sensitive habitats in the South Adriatic. The proposed FRA is located in GSA18 (Figures 6.14 and 6.15). The area has been identified as: (1) a site of unique physical features influencing the dynamics of waters circulation and water exchange with the whole Mediterranean basin; (2) an important essential fish habitat for valuable species such as deep water shrimps (e.g., *Aristeomorpha foliacea*), deep water rose shrimp (*Parapeneus longirostris*), European hake (*Merluccius merluccius*), and blackmouth catshark (*Galeus melastomus*); (3) a key area for sea turtles, tuna, swordfish, sharks; (4) an important migratory corridor for megafauna like cetaceans; and (5) an area containing vulnerable marine ecosystems that could be significantly impacted by bottom trawling.

Fishing fleets operating in GSA18 are mainly from Albania and Italy. The Italian fleet is mainly composed of demersal trawlers.[39] The FRA proposal highlights that

39 *Standard Form for the Submission of Proposals for GFCM Fisheries Restricted Areas (FRAs) in the Mediterranean and the Black Sea*, Proposal revised by (SAC technical group/sub-regional committee), submitted by MedReAct and Adriatic Recovery Project, 31 March 2018, p. 15.

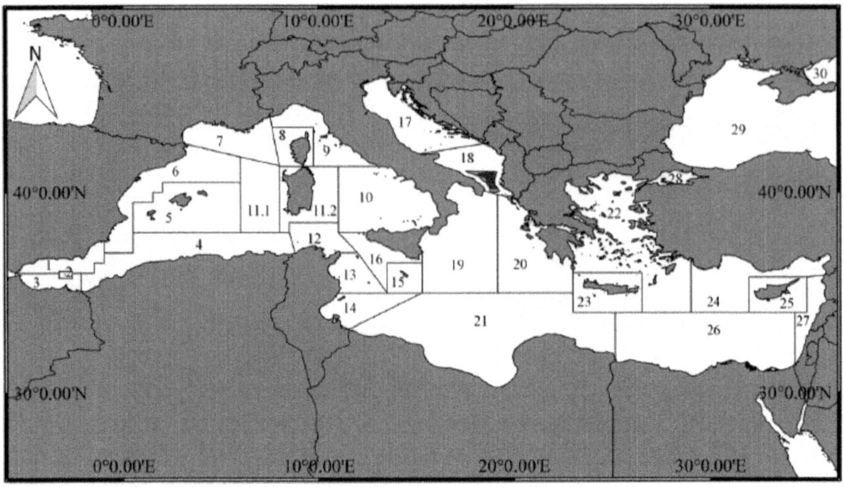

Figure 6.14 Location of the proposed FRA in GSA18 (Southern Adriatic)

Source: Standard form for the submission of proposals for GFCM Fisheries Restricted Areas (FRAs) in the Mediterranean and the Black Sea (Deep water essential fish habitats and sensitive habitats in the South Adriatic), March 2018, p. 5

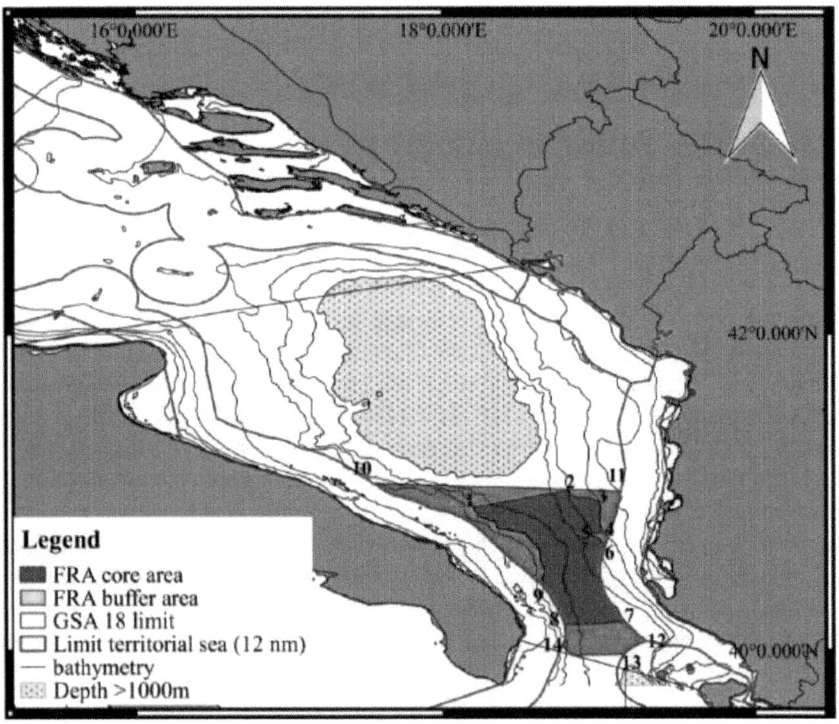

Figure 6.15 Detailed position of the proposed FRA in the Southern Adriatic

Source: Standard form for the submission of proposals for GFCM Fisheries Restricted Areas (FRAs) in the Mediterranean and the Black Sea (Deep water essential fish habitats and sensitive habitats in the South Adriatic), March 2018, p. 7

the South Adriatic Sea makes a substantial contribution to fish production. However, the steep slopes, with a maximum depth of more than 900 m, together with the presence of hard bottoms (such as deep-water corals), oil and gas extraction, military areas, and explosive sites located in the proposed FRA restrict trawling activities. According to the proposal, this circumstance would be indicative of the limited socioeconomic impact of the proposed FRA.

The proposal envisages a distinction between the core area, which covers important nursery and spawning grounds of valuable deep-water stocks and VMEs species, and a buffer zone, where other important nurseries and spawning grounds and complex and heterogeneous habitats are found. Both the core and buffer areas of the proposed FRA are inside the EBSA boundaries.

The core area covers a surface of 3,545.22 km^2 and its depth ranges between 200 m (minimum) to 968 m (maximum). The core area is delimited by the vertices having the following coordinates, using the datum WGS84:

Latitude	*Longitude*	*Vertex*
40° 54' 00" N	18° 12' 00" E	1
41° 00' 00" N	18° 48' 36" E	2
40° 55' 48" N	19° 00' 00" E	3
40° 45' 00" N	19° 01' 48" E	4
40° 44' 24" N	18° 57' 36" E	5
40° 38' 24" N	19° 02' 24" E	6
40° 10' 48" N	19° 10' 12" E	7
40° 09' 36" N	18° 46' 48" E	8
40° 24' 36" N	18° 39' 00" E	9

The buffer area covers a surface of 3,095.6 km^2 and its depth ranges between 100 m (minimum) to 900 m (maximum). It is delimited by the vertices having the following coordinates, using the same datum WGS84:

Latitude	*Longitude*	*Vertex*
41° 03' 28.8" N	17° 32' 20.4" E	10
41° 00' 13.32" N	19° 08' 23.28" E	11
40° 03' 36" N	19° 18' 10.8" E	12
39° 58' 35.4" N	19° 09' 37.68" E	13
39° 59' 45.6" N	18° 44' 52.8" E	14

Two military areas are present along the Italian side of the proposed FRA (Figure 6.16). Moreover, two explosive sites are reported inside the proposed FRA: dangerous circular area (r=5M) due to the presence of weaponry dropped from aircraft. There, navigation and fishing activities are banned for the presence of some unexploded ordnance.

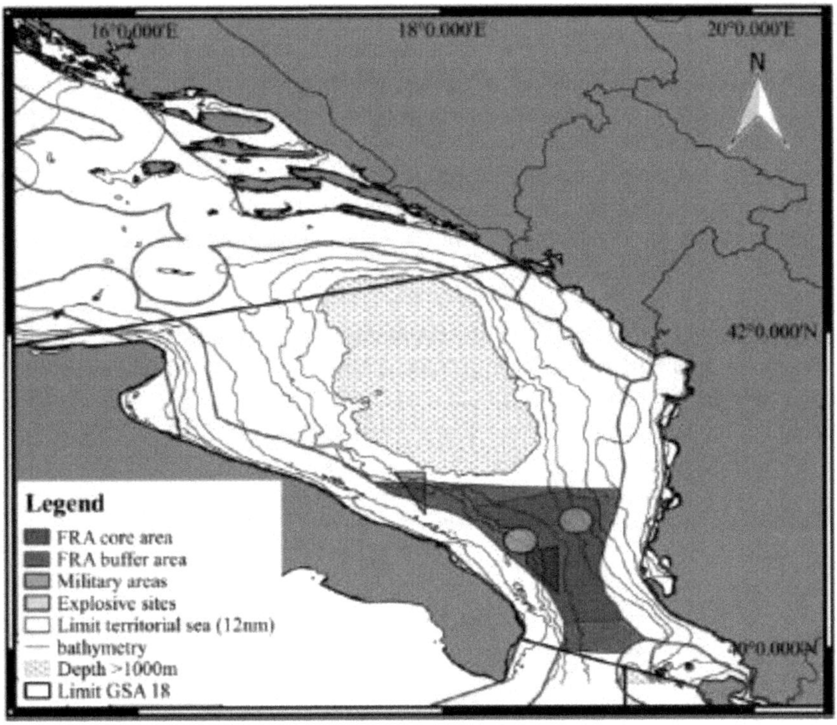

Figure 6.16 Military sites inside the proposed FRA in South Adriatic and the two explosive sites (circles representing the dangerous circular areas due to the presence on the bottom of ordnance dropped from aircraft)

Source: Standard form for the submission of proposals for GFCM Fisheries Restricted Areas (FRAs) in the Mediterranean and the Black Sea (Deep water essential fish habitats and sensitive habitats in the South Adriatic), March 2018, p. 23

From an environmental perspective, an element of concern for the deep-sea habitats of the Southern Adriatic area is the presence of the Trans Adriatic Pipeline (TAP) for the transportation of natural gas to Europe from Azerbaijan.[40] The pipeline connects with the Trans Anatolian Pipeline at the Greek-Turkish border, crossing the north of Greece, Albania, and the Adriatic Sea before coming ashore in southern Italy to connect to the Italian natural gas network. The underwater tract of the TAP starts from the city of Fier (Albania) and ends in the proximity of San Foca (Italy).

The 2018 proposal suggests specific management measures, in accordance with the relevant zoning system. In the core area, the proposal includes the permanent closure to any professional fishing activity with towed nets, bottom-set nets, and set longlines. Measures suggested in the buffer area include the subjection of any

40 See available at www.tap-ag.com/.

demersal fishing activity to a special fishing authorization, if the fishing unit can demonstrate to have carried out fishing activities in the area in the last five years. Members and cooperating non-members of the GFCM should be required to compile and transmit to the Executive Secretary of the GFCM the list of their authorized vessels. Vessels not complying with the GFCM conservation and management measures should not be authorized to fish in the FRA buffer area. In any case, the authorized vessels would be allowed to fish for a maximum of two days per week.

The proposal also suggests that GFCM member States and cooperating non-members should ensure that the area is protected from the impact of any other human activity jeopardizing the conservation of the essential fish habitats, sensitive habitats, and VMEs. The GFCM would conduct fishery independent assessments on the presence and status of such habitats and ecosystems in the area and on the effects of the conservation measures introduced with the FRA.

The 2018 proposal further highlights that the boundaries of the area and the conditions to fish therein, as referred to in the suggested management measures before, should be subject to change on the basis of the relevant advice of the GFCM Scientific Advisory Committee. Moreover, in consideration of the fact that the buffer area of the proposed FRA covers only marginally the European hake nurseries areas (a GFCM priority species for the Adriatic) and that the largest part of these nursery areas falls within the territorial waters of Italy and Albania, it would be desirable that these two States extend the proposed fishing restrictions in order to protect these important essential fish habitats in their territorial waters.

As regards the measures to effectively enforce environmental and species protection within the FRA, the proposal suggests that authorized fishing vessels should be allowed to land catches of demersal stocks only in designated ports. Fishing vessels without a special fishing authorization and equipped with towed nets, bottom-set nets, and set longlines should transit inside and through the FRA exclusively by keeping a direct course, at a constant speed exceeding 7 knots and with vessel monitoring systems (VMS) and automated identification systems (AIS) active onboard. Transit in the core area should be prohibited to any vessel carrying on board set longlines. The GFCM should define mechanisms to ensure control and enforcement of the FRA, through VMS, AIS, or remote-control systems as well as identify criteria for the regular evaluation of the status of the FRA.

Monitoring, control, and surveillance measures in the FRA could include the provision of VMS onboard and transmission of position data at regular intervals in line with Recommendation MCS-GFCM/33/2009/7 and European Union Regulation 1224/2009 for fishing vessels operating or transiting in an FRA as well as AIS onboard and transmission for fishing vessels operating or transiting in the FRA. The proposal further suggests at-sea inspections and, possibly, aerial controls by the flag States of vessels operating in the area. The GFCM Compliance Committee would regularly review and assess the level of enforcement and compliance in the FRA and provide relevant recommendations.

The proposal remarks that the socioeconomic impact of the proposed FRA should be sustainable for both Italian and Albanian fleets, considering the relatively low number of vessels currently fishing in deeper areas and the relative low fishing effort in the selected area. As a matter of fact, in the proposed FRA, the presence of explosive sites, military areas, and extraction concession already imposes several fishing and navigational restrictions.

Lately, through Resolution GFCM/44/2021/3, the GFCM noted the critical state of the European hake (*Merluccius merluccius*) due to a low biomass in the recent years and recalled the importance of protecting VMEs and EFHs as well as juvenile phases and areas of spawner aggregations in order to support the objective of reaching maximum sustainable yield by 2026 for the key Adriatic demersal stocks managed under Recommendation GFCM/43/2019/5. The GFCM further considered that its Scientific and Advisory Committee had been reiterating the importance of establishing new FRAs in the Adriatic Sea and had recommended developing a roadmap to this end.

Accordingly, the GFCM recommended that the GFCM Secretariat, with the support of relevant GFCM member States and cooperating non-members, had to launch, in 2022, a pilot project to underpin the biology and ecology of bamboo coral in the Adriatic Sea, including a quantification of the interactions between *Isidella* and bottom contact fisheries and the determination of their footprint, within the framework of the Working Group on Vulnerable Marine Ecosystems, including a session on essential fish habitats. Moreover, it recommended that the GFCM Secretariat should support, in 2023, the implementation of the roadmap towards the establishment of an FRA in the Southern Adriatic. GFCM member States and cooperating non-members should implement technical actions to advance towards complying with the requirements of Recommendation GFCM/43/2019/5 with a view to establishing additional FRAs in the Southern Adriatic, including: (1) investigating the monitoring activities needed to identify a possible FRA (fleet behaviours, impacts on sea bottom, observers on board) in the southern part of GSA18; (2) implementing an *ad hoc* socioeconomic survey covering the fleets operating in the area; (3) designing an *ad hoc* scientific survey for a better definition of VMEs to identify a possible FRA; and (4) ensuring that the key components of a future proposal include VMEs, essential fish habitats, spatial fishing fleet dynamics, and socioeconomic impacts, as provided by the national administrations.

In 2023, on the basis of the data collected, GFCM member States and cooperating non-members should jointly evaluate the possibility of establishing an FRA with the aim of protecting relevant VMEs and essential fish habitats identified, following a bottom-up approach and engaging with relevant stakeholders. The GFCM Secretariat should organize, ahead of the meeting of the Subregional Committee for the Adriatic Sea, a workshop with scientists and stakeholders to discuss the preparation of an FRA proposal, with a view to achieving these objectives. Eventually, the GFCM Scientific and Advisory Committee should evaluate the possible FRA proposal in the Southern Adriatic Sea, and the GFCM should examine such proposal at its annual session in 2023.

6.4. Conclusive Summary

A remarkable example of transboundary marine protected area beyond the territorial waters of Mediterranean coastal States is the *Pelagos Sanctuary*. The Sanctuary was established under an Agreement signed in Rome in 1999 by France, Italy, and Monaco, representing the first treaty ever concluded with the specific objective of establishing a protected area for marine mammals. The most critical aspect of the Agreement is the provision on the enforcement on the high seas of the measures agreed upon by the parties. In fact, also in those portions of water eventually declared as exclusive economic zones, third States enjoy a number of freedoms, including the freedom of navigation, which causes certain impacts to cetaceans, such as those deriving from collisions and underwater noise. The Sanctuary has been included in the SPAMI List and, accordingly, also enjoys the protection regime provided for under the Areas Protocol.

Another example of transboundary cooperation concerns the Strait of Bonifacio, an international strait regulated by the regime of transit passage under Arts. 37 to 44 UNCLOS. It is located between Sardinia and Corsica (two Mediterranean islands belonging to Italy and France, respectively). As the strait represents one of the most outstanding areas in the Mediterranean Sea in terms of marine biodiversity, France and Italy have long since decided to adopt in the strait a restrictive approach to navigation, insofar as ships flying their respective flags are concerned. To this purpose, they necessarily acted through the IMO. In 2011, the strait was also designated as a PSSA – the first established in the Mediterranean Sea and the second in the world for an international strait. Noteworthy is the initiative of two French and Italian public local entities with competencies in the field of marine environment protection, which in 2013 registered with the Committee of the Regions of the EGTC Convention establishing the *International Marine Park of the Strait of Bonifacio*. Other effective area-based conservation measures of transboundary character include FRAs established within the framework of the GFCM, two of which lie in the Adriatic and Ionian Seas, namely: the *Lophelia Reef off Capo Santa Maria di Leuca* and the *Jabuka/Pomo Pit*. Worthy of mention is the *Bari Canyon*, which does not present a transboundary character, although being located off the territorial waters of Italy in the South Adriatic Sea. A proposed transboundary FRA within the region of concern (Albania, Italy) relates to the deep-water essential fish habitats and sensitive habitats in the South Adriatic, whose establishment under the GFCM seems imminent. Since 2005, the same organization has prohibited the use of towed dredges and trawl nets at depths beyond 1,000 m in the Mediterranean and Black Seas: such other effective area-based conservation measure includes portions of the Southern Adriatic and Ionian Seas.

7 The Case for Establishing Transboundary Mediterranean SPAMIs within the Adriatic and Ionian Seas

Tullio Scovazzi

7.1. Challenges and Opportunities

As already remarked,[1] the Areas Protocol was envisaged with a view to give priority to the need to protect, preserve and manage in a sustainable and environmentally sound way areas of particular natural value in the whole Mediterranean Sea, irrespective of the present legal condition of the waters where they are located or of future changes in such legal condition. In particular, the Areas Protocol was drafted in order to be equally applicable in a scenario of waters falling either under the high seas or exclusive economic zone regime. According to Art. 9, para. 2, SPAMIs can be proposed and established:

1. in a zone already delimited, over which a State party exercises sovereignty or jurisdiction, this wording being intended to include areas of undisputed marine internal waters, territorial sea, exclusive economic zone, fishing zone, ecological protection zone or continental shelf;
2. in an area where the limits of national sovereignty or jurisdiction have not yet been defined, this wording being intended to mean areas belonging to the previously mentioned coastal zones where the boundaries between adjacent or opposite States parties have not yet been agreed upon; in this case the proposal must be made jointly by the two States parties concerned; or
3. in an area situated, partly or wholly, on the high seas; in this case the proposal must be made "by the neighbouring Parties concerned".[2]

Moreover, in order to overcome the difficulties due to different types Mediterranean coastal zones and unsettled maritime boundaries,[3] the Areas Protocol includes

1 See *supra*, Chapter 3.1.A.a.

2 There may be a margin of flexibility in the identification of the States that are "neighbouring" to a high seas area, especially in the case of geographically disadvantaged States, such as, in the Adriatic Sea, Slovenia and Bosnia and Herzegovina.

3 See Chapter 1.2 of this book.

DOI: 10.4324/9781003367963-7

two very elaborate disclaimer provisions (art. 2, paras. 2[4] and 3).[5] Apart from the legal technicalities, the idea behind them is that, on the one hand, the development of international cooperation in the field of the marine environment should not prejudice unsettled political and legal questions that have a different dimension, such as the determination of maritime boundaries; on the other hand, the existence of such legal questions should not prevent or delay the adoption of measures necessary for the preservation of the ecological balance in the Mediterranean Sea.

The message that can be drawn from the disclaimer provisions is that the establishment of a SPAMI, far from affecting in any way the position taken by any State party on pending legal and political questions, could, especially in the case of sensitive maritime boundary issues, contribute to the cooling off of the tension and to the building of a climate of progressive confidence and cooperation between the States concerned.[6]

In principle, the Areas Protocol is the ideal instrument to establish transboundary marine protected areas and to ensure their appropriate management. If such areas are intended as SPAMIs, they will be proposed by the neighbouring States concerned and will be included in the SPAMI List following a decision taken by consensus by the Meeting of the parties, which will also approve the management measures applicable to the area (Art. 9, para. 4). What is also important is that such measures have an *erga omnes partes* effect, in the sense that each party to the Areas Protocol agrees to comply with the measures applicable to the SPAMI and not to authorize nor undertake any activities that might be contrary to the objective for which the SPAMI was established (Art. 8, para. 3, b). Moreover, the parties "undertake to adopt appropriate measures, consistent with international law, to ensure that no one engages in any activities contrary to the principles or purposes" of the Areas Protocol (Art. 28, para. 2).[7]

4 "Nothing in this Protocol nor any act adopted on the basis of this Protocol shall prejudice the rights, the present and future claims or legal views of any state relating to the law of the sea, in particular, the nature and the extent of marine areas, the delimitation of marine areas between states with opposite or adjacent coasts, freedom of navigation on the high seas, the right and the modalities of passage through straits used for international navigation and the right of innocent passage in territorial seas, as well as the nature and extent of the jurisdiction of the coastal state, the flag state and the port state".

5 "No act or activity undertaken on the basis of this Protocol shall constitute grounds for claiming, contending or disputing any claim to national sovereignty or jurisdiction".

6 As it has been remarked,

> in a delicate phase of transition, characterized by the 'rush' of Mediterranean Countries towards proclaiming EEZs and by the multiplication of maritime delimitation disputes, the creation of transboundary SPAMIs may contribute to enhancing the spirit of cooperation among Mediterranean States with opposite or adjacent coasts and in certain circumstances may represent an alternative to the definition of a precise maritime boundary.
>
> (Vezzani, *op. cit.*, p. 143)

7 For example, if a third State were to authorize whaling activities inside the SPAMI *Pelagos Sanctuary*, all parties to the Areas Protocol could adopt economic sanctions against that State.

In fact, today the reality does not completely correspond to what was envisaged by the drafters of the Areas Protocol. Out of the 39 SPAMIs so far established, 37 are located inside the marine internal waters or the territorial sea of the coastal State concerned. Only two SPAMIs can be found partially or totally in waters beyond the territorial sea – namely, the *Pelagos Sanctuary for the Conservation of Marine Mammals*, jointly proposed by France, Italy and Monaco in 2001, and the *Cetacean Migration Corridor in the Mediterranean*, proposed by Spain in 2019 – and only one has a transnational character (the *Pelagos Sanctuary*). In the case of the Adriatic Sea, all the four SPAMIs so far established – namely *Miramare Marine Protected Area* (Italy, 2008), *Landscape Park Strunjan* (Slovenia, 2019), *Torre Guaceto Marine Protected Area and Natural Reserve* (Italy, 2008) and *Karaburun Sazan National Marine Park* (Albania, 2016) – are located along the coast. The same situation occurs for the two SPAMIs created in the Ionian Sea, namely *Porto Cesareo Marine Protected Area* (Italy, 2012) and *Plemmirio Marine Protected Area* (Italy, 2008).

Already in 2010, an extraordinary meeting of the focal points of the Areas Protocol, held in Istanbul within the framework of a project funded by the European Commission, discussed the question of identification of areas of conservation interest with a view to promoting the establishment of a more representative ecological network of protected areas in the Mediterranean Sea. The project identified ten "priority conservation areas lying in the open seas, including the deep sea, likely to contain sites that could be candidates for the SPAMI List".[8] Three of the areas are located in the Adriatic and Ionian Seas, namely:

Northern and Central Adriatic: This portion of the Adriatic has a high natural productivity that supports an extensive food web, including sea birds, loggerhead sea turtles and several shark species. Considering the high level of degradation of the Northwestern Adriatic Sea, establishing a protected area in this site would require significant marine restoration effort.

Santa Maria di Leuca: In addition to supporting a broad array of Mediterranean diversity, this northern extent of the Ionian has significant deep sea coral habitats.

Northeastern Ionian: The Northeastern Ionian Sea includes cetacean critical habitats and important nursery areas for several shark species.

However, concrete steps in this direction do not seem to have been taken so far by the States concerned.[9] The document on the *Post-2020 Regional Strategy for Marine and Coastal Protected Areas (MCPAs) and Other Effective Area-based*

8 See Annex III to UNEP(DEPI)/MED WG.348/5 of 4 June 2010.

9 At the Istanbul meeting, "the representative of the European Commission expressed his disappointment regarding the low commitments by the Parties for further action to protect the areas identified through the first phase of the project" (*ibid.*, para. 61).

Conservation Measures (OECMs) in the Mediterranean, presented at the Areas Protocol focal points meeting held on 23–25 June 2021, remarks that

> MPCA coverage in the Mediterranean currently stands at 8.3%, there is a clear need therefore to establish new MCPAs and to expand existing networks if the region is to advance towards meeting this ambitious post-2020 target. It is further essential that this increase in coverage coincides with a more balanced representation across countries, sub-regions and depths and includes areas beyond national jurisdiction.[10]

7.2. Potential Areas

It may be noted (Figure 7.1) that no area in the central portion of the region of concern – *i.e.*, off the coasts of Croatia, Bosnia and Herzegovina, Montenegro, Greece, and the eastern coast of Italy – has yet been included under the special protection regime of the SPAMI List.[11] It should also be noted that, while the majority of Adriatic and Ionian States have already ratified the Areas Protocol, as amended in 1995, Bosnia and Herzegovina and Greece still have to do so. The European Union ratified the Areas Protocol in 1999.

As regards the transboundary cooperation in the potential listing of new SPAMIs, the SPA/RAC has put emphasis also on actions harmonized at sub-regional level. Under the proposed approach for the elaboration of the Post-2020 SAP BIO, coordinated by SPA/RAC, and for the identification of the related priorities, the Mediterranean Sea has been divided into four sub-regions agreed by the parties to the Barcelona Convention.[12] In this division, the Adriatic Sea stands alone, while the Ionian Sea has been coupled with the wider Central Mediterranean.

As regards the potential listing of new SPAMIs, some proposals were recalled at the Mediterranean Seminar on PSSAs held in Tirana on 12 December 2019 that specifically concerned the Adriatic and Ionian Seas. Such proposals were already put forward a decade before and considered at the extraordinary meeting of the focal points for SPAs (Istanbul, 1 June 2010). In particular, such proposals identify three potential SPAMIs in the *Northeastern Ionian*, in *Santa Maria di Leuca*, and in the *Northern and Central Adriatic*.

The three new potential sites identified in the Adriatic and Ionian Seas as SPAMIs raise some remarks. The proposal concerning the *Northern and Central*

10 UNEP/MED WG 502/12 of 22 May 2021, p. 2. Notably, the sentences reproduced refer to any kind of marine protected areas and not only to SPAMIs.

11 See further in this paragraph for new potential SPAMIs in the Adriatic and Ionian Seas.

12 The sub-regions are: Western Mediterranean, Ionian and Central Mediterranean, Adriatic Sea, Aegean Sea – Levantine Sea. See *Process for the Elaboration of the Post-2020 Strategic Action Programme for the Conservation of Biodiversity and Sustainable Management of Natural Resources in the Mediterranean Region* (Post-2020 SAP BIO), Online Advisory Committee Meeting, 2 April 2020, Meeting Report, Annex V: Post-2020 SAP BIO Elaboration Guidance Document, p. 4.

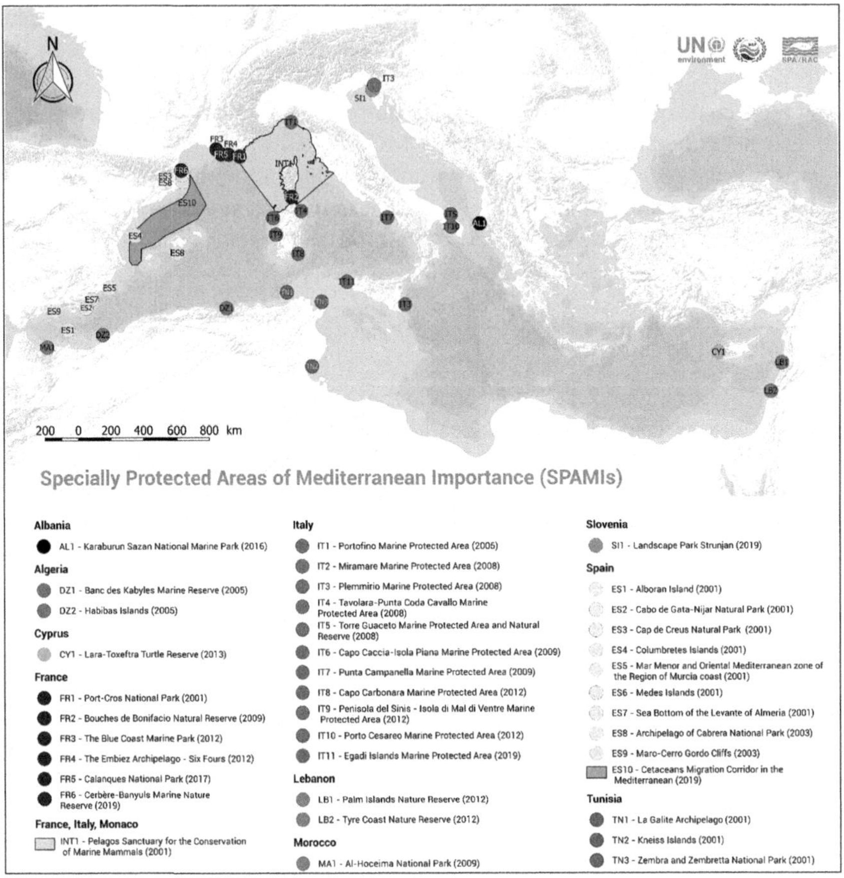

Figure 7.1 Specially Protected Areas of Mediterranean Importance (SPAMI)

Source: SPA/RAC, 2020

Adriatic could represent a further means of transboundary cooperation between the relevant coastal States.[13] This potential SPAMI would also encompass the *Jabuka/ Pomo Pit* FRA established within the GFCM framework. The proposal concerning *Santa Maria di Leuca* seems to encompass waters falling only under Italian jurisdiction, including those waters claimed by this State as internal, within the Gulf of Taranto (historic bay). The proposal concerning the *Northeastern Ionian*, encompassing a substantial portion of Greek waters, seems rather difficult to be implemented – a situation that might change, however, should Greece decide to become a party to the Areas Protocol.

13 On the recourse to new potential SPAMIs as a means of transboundary cooperation in the Adriatic and Ionian Seas, see *infra*, Chapter 8.

Recently, the establishment of a SPAMI in the South Adriatic–Ionian Strait has been put forward in a study sponsored by the European Commission.[14]

The establishment of a transboundary SPAMI is a measure that deserves careful consideration in the Northern and Central Adriatic, where the waters are bordered by Croatia, Italy and Slovenia. There are several elements that support such a measure, such as the following:

1. within the Gulf of Trieste, two small SPAMIs have already been created by Italy (*Miramare Marine Protected Area*) and Slovenia (*Landscape Park Strunjan*);[15] moreover, according to the 2021 Slovenian Maritime Spatial Plan, two new marine protected areas have been envisaged, respectively at the border with Italy (*Debeli Rtic/Punta Sottile*) and at the border with Croatia (Figure 7.2).
2. as already mentioned, the report presented to the extraordinary meeting of the focal points for the Areas Protocol held in 2010 in Istanbul listed in general the Northern and Central Adriatic among the "priority conservation areas";
3. in 2014, the Conference of the Parties to the CBD identified the Northern Adriatic as an EBSA (Decision XII/22);
4. the EUSAIR has identified the Gulf of Trieste and the Jabuka/Pomo Pit among the four pilot areas to carry out a review of the implementation of integrated coastal zone management and marine spatial planning concepts.
5. measures for the establishment of a common routeing system and traffic separation scheme and for a mandatory ship reporting system have been agreed by Croatia, Italy and Slovenia for the Northern Adriatic (Memoranda of Understanding of 19 May 2000) and measures for the establishment of a common vessel traffic service (VTS) and a common routeing system and traffic separation scheme have been agreed by Croatia and Italy for the Central Adriatic (Memoranda of Understanding of 19 May 2000);
6. in 2017, the GFCM established the *Jabuka/Pomo Pit* fisheries restricted area (Recommendation 41/2017/3);
7. in 2010, the meeting of the parties to the ACCOBAMS recommended the creation of a marine protected area in the waters along the east coast of the Cres-Lošinj archipelago (Croatia), as a zone of special importance for cetaceans.

14 European Commission, *Study on Proposals for New Marine Protected Areas in Albania, Bosnia and Herzegovina and Montenegro*, September 2021, p. 87:

> The area we propose to be considered as a sub-regional open sea area, is located in the southern Adriatic basin and the northern Ionian Sea. . . . It is characterised by steep slopes, high salinity and a maximum depth ranging from 200m to 1500m and is classified as an Ecologically and Biologically Significant Marine Area (EBSA).

15 Art. 10 of the Areas Protocol allows for changes in the delimitation or legal status of SPAMIs. In this case, Miramare Marine Protected Area and Landscape Park Strunjan could preserve their legal regime through appropriate zoning measures applicable within a bigger SPAMI.

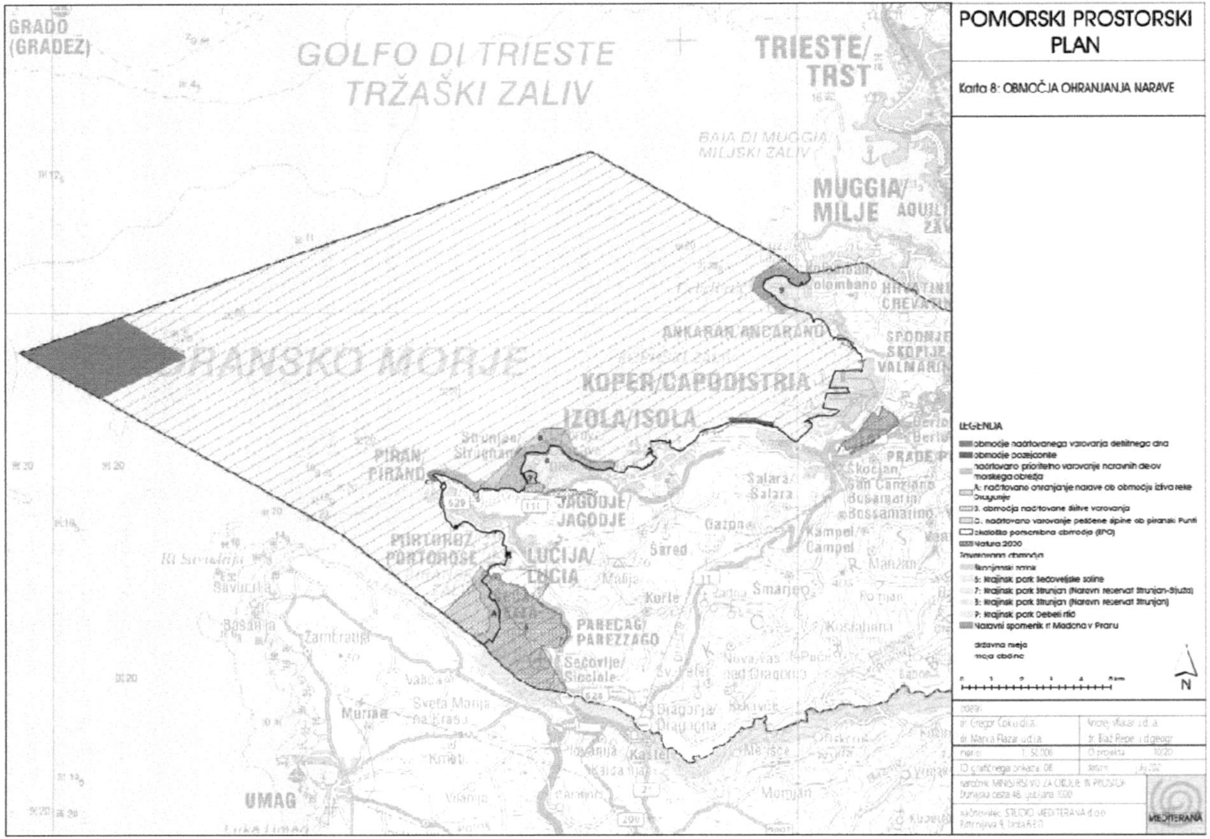

Figure 7.2 Slovenian maritime spatial planning related to nature conservation

Source: Decree on Maritime Spatial Planning, map No. 8 (*Uradni List* of the Republic of Slovenia No. 116/2021)

All these precedents could support a joint initiative by Croatia, Italy and Slovenia to establish one or two SPAMIs that would be intended to address three specific challenges:

- to build upon the existing or proposed instruments of restricted or sectoral protection, coordinating them within a larger and coherent framework of transboundary cooperation and sustainable development;
- to include marine protected areas within the framework of a broader marine spatial planning concept applying to the whole Adriatic Sea and potentially extending to the Ionian Sea;
- to integrate and balance in a sound manner economic activities (especially navigation and fishing) and environmental needs; and
- to increase confidence among the Adriatic Sea bordering States, showing that pending issues of maritime boundaries[16] are not an insurmountable obstacle against the strengthening of their environmental cooperation through the establishment of transboundary protected areas.[17]

What could deserve further elaboration, on the basis of the relevant political, legal and environmental factors, is whether one single Adriatic SPAMI should cover the whole Northern and Central Adriatic area or, instead, two self-standing SPAMIs should be established: the first in the Northern Adriatic and the second in the Central Adriatic, around the Jabuka/Pomo Pit. If appropriate, buffer zones could be attached to the two SPAMIs and ecological corridors could be envisaged to join them.

As regards other SPAMIs in the Adriatic and Ionian Seas, it has already been remarked that, given the lack of participation by Bosnia and Herzegovina and Greece to the Areas Protocol, the establishment of transboundary SPAMIs that would involve the two States is not a legally feasible option, however desirable it could be under an environmental perspective. For this reason, a possible transboundary SPAMI in the waters off Neum (Bosnia and Herzegovina and Croatia) should be disregarded for the time being. The same can be said of any possible transboundary SPAMIs in the Channel of Otranto, bordered by Albania, Greece and Italy, or in the Northern Ionian Sea, bordered by Greece and Italy. However, for the time being, different forms of cooperation, such as international parks or other effective area-based conservation measures, could be envisaged for the areas in question.

16 As already remarked in Chapter 1 of this book, the maritime boundary between Croatia and Slovenia is still disputed, according to the position taken by Croatia. See Mackelworth, Jančič, Lazar and Holcer, A Transboundary Marine Protected Area to Help Resolve the Piran Bay Border Dispute, in Mackelworth (ed.), *op. cit.*, 2016, p. 111.

17 As already remarked in Chapter 3 of this book, no action taken on the basis of the Areas Protocol can affect pending questions of delimitation of maritime boundaries.

7.3. Protection Measures and Management Authorities

The Areas Protocol is sufficiently detailed in specifying what are the objectives of specially protected areas (Art. 4), what are the protection measures that can be taken therein (Art. 6) and what is the content of the planning, management, supervision and monitoring measures (Art. 7). In the case of the proposed SPAMI or SPAMIs in the Northern and Central Adriatic, the protection measures should include navigation and, as regards the waters off Jabuka/Pomo Pit, fishing, together with other measures, as appropriate, to integrate them into broader conservation objectives.

Annex I to the Areas Protocol provides for common criteria for the choice of protected marine and coastal areas that could be included in the SPAMI List. In particular, the sites included in the SPAMI List are to be "provided with adequate legal status, protection measures and management methods and means" (para. A, e) and must fulfill at least one of six specified criteria ("uniqueness", "natural representativeness", "diversity", "naturalness", "presence of habitats that are critical to endangered, threatened or endemic species", and "cultural representativeness"). The SPAMIs must be awarded a legal status guaranteeing their effective long-term protection (para. C.1) and must have a management body,[18] a management plan,[19] and a monitoring programme[20] (paras. from D.6 to D.8). In the case of transboundary marine protected areas, the legal status, the management plan, the applicable measures and the other elements required for the proposal "will be provided by the neighbouring parties concerned" (para. C.3). A requirement that deserves special attention in the case of transboundary protected areas, which inevitably involve the authorities of more than one State, is that "the competence and responsibility with regard to administration and implementation of conservation measures . . . must be clearly defined in the texts governing the area" (para. D.4).

In the elaboration of the proposal, particular attention should be devoted to what has been described in a recent report as main barriers to effective marine and coastal protected areas management, namely:

- Lack of political will or support for marine protected areas establishment and management;

18 To be included in the SPAMI list, a protected area must have a management body, endowed with sufficient powers as well as means and human resources to prevent and/or control activities likely to be contrary to the aims of the protected area.

(para. D.6)

19 To be included in the SPAMI list an area will have to be endowed with a management plan. The main rules of this management plan are to be laid down as from the time of inclusion and implemented immediately. A detailed management plan must be presented within three years of the time of inclusion. Failure to respect this obligation entails the removal of the site from the list.

(para. D.7)

20 To be included in the SPAMI list, an area will have to be endowed with a monitoring programme. This programme should include the identification and monitoring of a certain number of significant parameters for the area in question, in order to allow the assessment of the state and evolution of the area, as well as the effectiveness of protection and management measures implemented, so that they may be adapted if need be. To this end further necessary studies are to be commissioned.

(para. D.8)

- Insufficient financing: not enough, not sustainable, heavy reliance on external fund;
- Inadequate human resources: not enough marine protected area staff, where staff are occurring, many do not have the necessary technical skills for marine protected areas management;
- Lack of sectoral and stakeholder involvement, cooperation and support: poor coherence and harmonization of policies, plans and actions;
- Insufficient knowledge: knowledge gaps for effective decision-making; (. . .)
- Lack of management plans;
- Inadequate surveillance and enforcement: unclear procedure in legislation, lack of by-laws, poor cooperation with enforcement agencies, irregular routine patrols, unclear mandates and responsibilities for enforcement;
- Insufficient monitoring and evaluation: insufficient and inadequate monitoring of management effectiveness, insufficient biodiversity and biological monitoring.[21]

A solid basis for the establishment of the proposed SPAMI or SPAMIs could be a treaty adopted by all the States geographically concerned. It would include general principles and objectives; define the limits of the area, including buffer zones if any; and set up an institutional body in charge for the adoption of more specific regulations. This course of action was followed by France, Italy and Monaco that, after having concluded a treaty for the establishment of the *Pelagos Sanctuary* (1999), submitted the area for inclusion in the SPAMI List (2001). The option of a treaty would require an extended period of time, as needed for the negotiations and the procedures of subsequent ratification according to the constitutional law of the States concerned.

However, if a treaty remains the best option, the Areas Protocol does not necessarily require a previous treaty for proposing the inclusion of a transboundary area in the SPAMI List. What is needed is the submission by the neighbouring parties of a joint proposal, with an introductory report containing information on the area's geographical location, its physical and ecological characteristics, its legal status, its management plans and the means for their implementation, and a statement justifying its Mediterranean importance (Art. 9, para. 3). It is also provided that the neighbouring parties concerned consult each other with a view to ensuring the consistency of the proposed protection and management measures as well as the means for their implementation (Art. 9, para. 3, *a*). If a treaty is not indispensable, the adoption of consistent national legislation or regulations, which implies a previous coordination at the intergovernmental level, is, thus, a specific requirement for any transboundary SPAMI proposal.

21 UNEP/MED WG.502/12 of 22 May 2021, *Post-2020 Regional Strategy for Marine and Coastal Protected Areas (MCPAs) and Other Effective Area-Based Conservation Measures (OECMs) in the Mediterranean*, para. 15.

7.4. Conclusive Summary

The establishment of a one or two transboundary SPAMIs in the Northern and Central Adriatic is supported by a number of elements, namely: a) within the Gulf of Trieste, two small SPAMIs have already been created by Italy (*Miramare Marine Protected Area*) and Slovenia (*Landscape Park Strunjan*); b) the report presented in 2010 to the extraordinary meeting of the focal points for the Specially Protected Areas Protocol listed in general the Northern and Central Adriatic among the "priority conservation areas"; c) in 2014, the Conference of the Parties to the CBD identified the Northern Adriatic as an EBSA; d) EUSAIR has identified the Gulf of Trieste and the Jabuka/Pomo among the four pilot areas to carry out a review of the implementation of integrated coastal zone management and marine spatial planning concepts; e) measures for the establishment of a common routeing system, a traffic separation scheme and a mandatory ship reporting system have been agreed by the bordering countries; f) In 2017, the GFCM established the *Jabuka/Pomo Pit* fisheries restricted area; g) In 2010, the Meeting of the Parties to the ACCOBAMS recommended the creation of a marine protected area in the waters along the east coast of the Cres-Lošinj archipelago (Croatia) as a zone of special importance for cetaceans. A joint initiative by Croatia, Italy and Slovenia to establish one or two SPAMIs in the Northern and Central Adriatic would be intended to address the following specific challenges: to build upon the existing or proposed instruments of restricted or sectoral protection, coordinating them within a larger and coherent framework of transboundary cooperation and sustainable development; to include marine protected areas with the framework of a broader marine spatial planning concept applying to the whole Adriatic Sea and potentially extending to the Ionian Sea; to integrate and balance in a sound manner economic activities (especially navigation and fishing) and environmental needs; to increase confidence among the Adriatic Sea bordering States, showing that pending issues of maritime boundaries are not an insurmountable obstacle against the strengthening of their environmental cooperation through the establishment of transboundary protected areas. A transboundary SPAMI would not be legally feasible in the Ionian Sea, as Greece is not yet a party to the Areas Protocol.

8 The Case for Pursuing Transboundary Area-based Conservation through a European Grouping of Territorial Cooperation within the Adriatic and Ionian Seas

Ilaria Tani

8.1. Legal and Operational Basis

The European Grouping of Territorial Cooperation (EGCT) is a tool consisting of an entity with legal personality under European Union law. It was introduced in 2006 with the adoption of Regulation (EC) 1082/2006 of 5 July 2006 (hereinafter: EGTC Regulation).[1] This instrument aims at improving the implementation conditions for territorial cooperation with a view to strengthening cohesion in the European Union. In doing so, it complements funding instruments for European Territorial Cooperation (ETC), known as Interreg. In particular, Art. 1 of the EGTC Regulation sets forth the following overall objective:

> to facilitate and promote, in particular, territorial cooperation, including one or more of the cross-border, transnational and interregional strands of cooperation, between its members . . . with the aim of strengthening Union economic, social and territorial cohesion.

Within this overall objective, an EGTC may formulate more specific objectives. These may definitely include transboundary cooperation between members in the field of marine environment protection, through the extension, beyond national borders, of national area-based conservation tools and other area-based effective conservation measures. In any case, the EGTC "shall act within the confines of the tasks given to it" (Art. 7, para. 1, of the EGTC Regulation).

Primarily, the tasks of an EGTC may concern the implementation of cooperation programmes, or parts thereof, or the implementation of operations supported by the European Union through the European Regional Development Fund, the European Social Fund or the Cohesion Fund.[2] However, European Union member

1 For a possible classification of transboundary governance systems in EGTCs, see Biot, Les systèmes de gouvernance des territoires transfrontaliers: la mise en œuvre du règlement européen sur le GECT (Groupements Européens de Coopération Territoriale), in *Belgeo*, 2013.

2 Member States may limit the tasks that EGTCs may carry out without financial support from the European Union (Art. 7, para. 3, of the EGTC Regulation).

DOI: 10.4324/9781003367963-8

States may limit the tasks that EGTCs may carry out without the financial support from the European Union (Art. 7 of the EGTC Regulation).

The decision to establish an EGTC is taken at the initiative of the prospective members. Entities that may become members of an EGTC include European Union member States, regional and local authorities of European Union member States, public undertakings and public bodies, and, under certain conditions, States that are not members of the European Union and their public entities. What is necessary is that the EGTC – which aims at promoting transboundary cooperation – is made up of members that are located on the territory of at least two European Union member States. In addition, the EGTC may include as members one or more third States that are "neighboring" at least one European Union member State that is a member of the same EGTC. This implies that Albania, Bosnia and Herzegovina, and Montenegro – or public bodies of these States – could become members of an EGTC in the Adriatic and Ionian region with a view to protecting the marine environment. In fact, a State that is not a member of the European Union is considered as a "neighboring State" by the EGTC Regulation when "it shares a common land border or where both the third State and the EU Member State are eligible under a joint maritime cross-border programme under the European territorial cooperation goal, or are eligible under another cross-border, sea-crossing or sea-basin cooperation programme, including where they are separated by international waters" (Art. 3a, para. 1, of the EGTC Regulation). The maritime borders between the countries concerned are included.

Each EGTC is governed by a convention (Art. 8 of the EGTC Regulation) concluded unanimously by its members, which specifies the founding elements of the entity, namely:

- the name of the EGTC and its registered office;
- the extent of the territory in which the EGTC may execute its tasks;
- the objective and the tasks of the EGTC;
- the duration of the EGTC and the conditions for its dissolution;
- the list of the EGTC members;
- the list of the EGTC organs and their respective competences;
- the applicable laws, rules, procedures and arrangements; and
- the procedures for adoption of the statutes and amendment of the convention.

Each EGTC is composed of at least an assembly, which is made up of the representatives of its members, and a director, who represents the EGTC and acts on its behalf (Art. 10 of the EGTC Regulation). Each EGTC also establishes an annual budget which shall be adopted by the assembly (Art. 11). The legal personality of the EGTC entails that the entity shall be liable for all its debts, and members shall be liable for such debts irrespective of the nature of them, each share being fixed in proportion to the member's financial contribution (Art. 12).

Among the characteristic elements of an EGTC, the possibility to create an individual legal person for activities to be carried out across national borders, including in the marine environment, is to be highlighted in the context of the present analysis. Of course, such characteristic element entails both opportunities and challenges.

8.2. Challenges and Opportunities

Starting with the challenges, some of the shortcomings of the original framework for the establishment of EGTCs came to the surface during the first years after the adoption of Regulation (EC) 1082/2006, which, accordingly, was amended by Regulation (EU) 1302/2013 of 17 December 2013. Amendments of the original EGCT Regulation have facilitated the work of EGCTs. This was ensured through more clarity and some simplifications. The main amendments included a clarification concerning the participation of third countries and overseas countries and territories; a broadening of the nature of the EGTC instrument regarding the management of cross-border public services; clarifications concerning the setting up and approval of EGTCs; a consistent structure for the EGTC founding documents; and adjustments concerning liability rules to address different member States legislations. Two very relevant amendments included the ability to incorporate a member from third (non-European Union) countries and the possibility to provide services. An aspect that could be further improved is access to funding.

It is essential to note that the EGTC limits the membership to primarily public authorities and institutions.[3] This limitation and the corresponding tasks of EGTCs characterize the legal form of this instrument. However, the EGTC Regulation does not specify such legal form, which ultimately depends on the applicable member State's law. In practice, the legal form of the EGTC will depend on the member State where the EGTC has its registered office[4] and, according to the relevant law, will be subject to public or private law. In some member States, implementing national legislation explicitly considers EGTCs as public legal entities – this being the case, among others, of Italy. In other member States, EGTCs may be considered private legal entities.

Before an EGTC may obtain a legal personality, public institutions, especially local and regional authorities, will have to go through the founding process. The roadmap towards this objective involves different steps. A first step entails a needs assessment, during which prospective EGTC members should assess whether the EGTC instrument is the most suitable option for the proposed objectives and activities. A second step involves the development of a common understanding of the respective tasks, the legal framework in force within the different member States participating in the EGTC, the identification of the location of registration of their office, as well as the means of the EGTC financing. The final step – prior to formal approval and registration – is the implementation phase, when prospective members develop the founding documents (i.e., the EGTC convention and statutes). Such documents describe the structures, the legal framework and the rules of procedure of the EGTC and are subject to the approval procedures of the corresponding national authorities. Eventually, EGTC approval and registration are finalized at the European Union level. The Committee of the Regions conducts these processes on the basis of the information provided.

3 See further in this chapter.

4 The registered office shall be located in a member State under whose law at least one of the EGTC's members is established (Art. 1, para. 5, of the EGTC Regulation).

Approval and registration procedures are not only needed when setting up an EGTC but also for certain modifications of an existing EGTC. Particularly challenging are the implications stemming from a change of membership in an EGTC; therefore, it is advisable that the differentiation of tasks and responsibilities between the EGTC members is not likely to change after the setting up of the body.

As of today, 54 authorities have been appointed within the European Union to approve and register EGTCs. Those relevant for the States bordering the Adriatic and Ionian Seas are recalled hereafter.[5] The variety of approval and registration procedures among the different States may raise difficulties. On the one hand, local and regional authorities wishing to set up an EGTC may find it challenging to contact the right authority and apply the appropriate procedures; on the other hand, authorities in charge of approving EGTC membership and registration may face difficulties in coordinating different member States.

Moreover, due to a lack of experience, some member States do not have procedures for approval and registration but simply refer back to the EGTC Regulation. Therefore, in certain cases, procedures elaborated by more experienced member States could be used as examples to be followed by less experienced prospective EGTC members, provided that the national, regional, and local legal frameworks allow for such comparison. Overall, the need to follow several steps to setting up an EGTC and the variety of approval and registration procedures show the potential complexity of processes to establish an EGTC. Such complexity often led to misconceptions of the EGTC instrument, which were partially summarized in a report edited by the Committee of the Regions.[6] Among such misconceptions, for example, there is the assumption that EGTCs must cover a continuous territory: on the contrary, the territory does not need to be continuous, as the EGTC instrument aims at transnational and interregional cooperation between member States (and neighboring countries), although the instrument is not applicable for cooperation within only one member State. This means that a network of marine protected areas falling under the jurisdiction of different States may definitely be pursued through an EGTC.

Coming to the opportunities offered by the EGTC to its members, they truly depend on the context of the EGTC and are linked to its tasks and objectives. Since the adoption of the relevant regulation in 2006, the EGTC instrument has been widely implemented, and, today, 21 member States either host an EGTC with a registered office or are members of an EGTC registered in another member State. EGTCs offer the opportunity to establish a stable, long-term commitment of their members, strengthening cooperation, including for actions of macro-regional strategies. Their legal personality, entailing legal capacity, brings advantages compared to other forms of cooperation. Among others, it offers the possibility for EGTC members to jointly hire personnel, acquire properties and manage public services. The legal personality of EGTCs also allow them to be parties to legal proceedings.

5 See further in this chapter.

6 European Committee of the Regions, *Guidebook on registering EGTCs*, 2021.

Through an EGTC, members may also build links to other programmes and funding sources, spreading the reach of territorial cooperation.

Noteworthy is that EGTCs are not necessarily connected to any financial programmes or funding source of the European Union; therefore, they are not limited to any of the European Union financial periods. By fulfilling a wide range of purposes in crucial areas (from environmental protection to transport planning, from integrated tourism to economic cooperation, etc.), the EGTC tool establishes a long-term territorial cooperation that goes beyond the project horizon. Although setting up an EGTC may take some time, running it is not an expensive solution to transboundary environmental protection. In fact, an EGTC can use the existing resources of the involved entities. Its structure allows it to act across borders for the benefit of the whole region or its members, and, in this way, it can even contribute to a more efficient use of resources. In this regard, an EGTC offers, indeed, a framework with permanent structures that facilitates the continuity of the relevant activities.[7] The joint decision-making across borders enhances participation in, and ownership of, cross-border activities: in this way, the EGTC identity-building may also contribute to combat nationalization tendencies.

More generally, EGTCs can act as strategic players that integrate different activities in a joint policy approach. Consequently, each EGTC becomes a means to deepen existing cooperation activities that may also receive further acknowledgement. The EGTC instrument may, in fact, contribute to visibility for cooperation activities, and its European nature contributes to the opportunity to promote local and regional interests at European Union level. Last but not least, with members from different member States, an EGTC may be in a favourable position when it comes to participate in tendering under European Union programmes, as its peculiar membership improves the capability to benefit as a single beneficiary in Interreg programmes.

8.3. Potential Areas and Protective Measures

Since one of the main characteristics of EGTC Regulation is its focus on public bodies, the details of rules to implement the relevant objectives in national contexts varies greatly between EU member States and implies different legal and liability regimes for EGTCs. Accordingly, when identifying potential areas to be subjected to an EGTC, a need arises also to shed light on the different approval and registration procedures applied by each member State.

In the context of this analysis, the choice has been made to focus on the potential recourse to the EGTC tool in four transboundary pilot areas within the Gulf of Trieste, the Jabuka/Pomo Pit, the Bay of Neum-Klek, and the Otranto Channel. All four areas lie within the same region and, as such, could benefit from the establishment of either one EGTC encompassing a network including of all of them or different EGTCs focusing on the specific management of each area. In any event, of

7 This benefit is closely linked to legally binding decisions due to the long-term commitment of members.

paramount necessity is the identification of the applicable EGTC approval and registration procedures in accordance with the legal framework of the relevant Adriatic and Ionian coastal States. In fact, the EGTC acquires legal personality with its registration or the publication of the founding documents (the EGTC convention and statutes) on the official gazette of the State that hosts the EGTC registered office. A final step implies that the members inform the EU member States concerned and the Committee of the Regions of the registration. Within ten working days of the registration or publication, the EGTC ensures that a request is sent to the Committee of the Regions for the publication of a notice on the Official Journal of the European Union, which announces the establishment of the EGTC.

As regards Albania, Bosnia and Herzegovina, and Montenegro, potentially acting as neighboring States, the EGTC Regulation remains the only general reference, while the legislation of Croatia, Greece, Italy, and Slovenia regulates in detail the national procedures for EGTC approval and registration. Both in the case of an EGTC encompassing a network of marine protected areas in the Adriatic and Ionian Seas and in the case of separate EGTCs focusing on the conservation of one or more areas, the relevant cooperating member States should register the office in one of the members' territory.

The possibility to resort to the EGTC instrument with a view to protecting the marine environment in a transboundary context has been already affirmed through the establishment of the PMIBB.[8] The most recent list of EGTCs, which does not include many marine features, is available through the following QR code[9]:

8 Discussed in Chapter 6 of this book.

9 The list of EGTCs, updated as of 15 July 2021, is also available at portal.cor.europa.eu/egtc/CoRActivities/Documents/Official_List_of_the_EGTCs.pdf?Web=0.

The relevant legislations concerning the approval and registration procedures for EGTCs within the Adriatic and Ionian coastal States are recalled hereafter.

Croatia. According to Croatian law,[10] the competent authority in charge of EGTC registration is the Ministry of Justice and Public Administration (*Ministarstvo pravosuđa i uprave*). It follows that, if an entity registered in Croatia intends to join an EGTC, the notice of intent to participate in the EGTC and a copy of the proposal of the EGTC convention and statutes is to be sent to this administration. Once it has received the founding documents, the Ministry consults those State administration bodies in charge of regional development and European Union funds, foreign and European affairs, as well as those bodies whose scope include tasks covered by the purpose of the EGTC in question. When it receives the results of this consultation process, the Ministry assesses the coherence of the EGTC convention and statutes with European Union regulations and Croatian law and, where necessary, formulates requests to the prospective member for modifications and amendments. The suggested modification should be considered by the prospective member and, once the founding documents have been modified accordingly, the competent Ministry proposes to the Croatian government the adoption of a decision approving participation in the EGTC and the founding convention. The government adopts the formal approval decision on the basis of the proposal approved by the Ministry of Justice and Public Administration. So far, no EGTCs have been registered in Croatia. An EGTC with the registered office in Croatia would be established as a public entity and, as such, subject to the Institutions Act (Official Gazette No. 76/93, 29/97, 47/99, 35/08 and 127/19) of Croatian law. For any subsequent modification of the EGTC, the Ministry of Justice and Public Administration would receive the notice of amendments to the convention. The same Ministry would consult the State administration bodies in charge of the consultation process mentioned previously and would eventually obtain a formal decision by the government.

Greece. According to the Greek legislation on EGTC,[11] municipalities, regions, associations and their networks, the Greek public sector, including the decentralized administrations, universities, public undertakings, bodies governed by public law, and enterprises that were assigned the task of providing services of general economic interest, in compliance with Union and national law, may participate in an EGTC. Their participation is approved by the Minister of the Interior after receipt of the agreement of the Committee referred to in Art. 4, para. 2, b, of Greek Law No. 3345/2005. The Committee includes among its members a representative of the Ministry of Economy and Development. The entity that intends to participate in an EGTC, therefore, shall notify the Committee in writing of its intention, sending copies of the proposed EGTC

10 Law No. 74/14 of 13 June 2014.

11 Law No. 4483/2017 of 28 July 2017.

founding documents. The participation of entities in EGTCs which have their registered offices abroad is approved upon agreement of the Committee and a decision is issued by the Minister of Interior within 6 months from the submission of an admissible application to the Committee together with the texts of the EGTC founding documents.[12] For EGTCs which have their registered offices in Greece, the application is to be submitted to the Committee together with the texts of the EGTC founding documents. The Minister of Interior, following an agreement of the Committee, approves the participation of the interested entities and the text of the convention.[13] Existing associations of entities, networks of cities, and other undertakings of various legal personalities seeking to fulfill purposes similar to those of an EGTC, which have their registered offices in Greece, may be transformed into an EGTC, upon decision of their administrative bodies and the approval of the Minister of Interior, following the same procedures. It is provided that the Committee keep an EGTC Register. This includes data on EGTCs having their registered offices in Greece as well as data on entities participating in an EGTC having its registered office in another member State. In particular, the EGTC Register includes the name of the EGTC and the registered office, the purposes and the duties, the statutes and convention, the personnel, the participation in national or European programmes, the projects undertaken, the implementation process of the projects undertaken, and any activity assumed by the EGTCs.

Italy. Italian law[14] provides that EGTCs registered in Italy have legal personality of public law. The EGTC acquires legal personality through its inscription in the EGTC Register, deposited with the Presidency of the Council of Ministers (General Secretariat). All entities listed in Art. 3, para. 1, of the EGTC Regulation may become members of an EGTC. In the Italian legal context, such entities include the regions and the autonomous provinces of Trento and Bolzano, as well as the local entities. The founding documents of the EGTC are approved unanimously by the members and signed in public form. It is to be noted that, without prejudice to Art. 7, paras. 1, 2, 4 and 5, of the EGTC Regulation, Italian law explicitly states that members may entrust the EGTC with, *inter alia*, the role of management Authority, the exercise of tasks of joint technical secretariat, the promotion and implementation of operations in the context of operational programmes co-financed with structural [European Union] funds and linked to the objective of "European territorial cooperation", as well as the promotion and implementation of actions of interregional cooperation within other operational programmes co-financed by [European Union] structural funds. . . . In addition to [the above tasks], the EGTC may be entrusted with the implementation of further actions of territorial cooperation, provided that

12 This deadline is interrupted if the Committee decides to request additional information.

13 The deadline provided for participation in EGTCs registered abroad is not applicable to these cases.

14 Law No. 88 of 7 July 2009.

they are coherent with the goal of strengthening economic and social cohesion, as well as in compliance with the international obligations of the State (Art. 46 of Law No. 88 of 7 July 2009).

A first phase provides that the prospective members notify their intent to establish an EGTC to the Presidency of the Council of Ministers (Department for Regional Affairs and Autonomies) together with the founding documents. The Department verifies the compliance of the transmitted documentation with the EGTC Regulation, as well as with Law No. 88 of 7 July 2009, Arts. 46, 47 and 48. After this verification of compliance, the preliminary phase formally starts and the documentation is transmitted to the competent Ministries for approval and acquisition of the relevant opinions. In case of amendments, any remarks made by the Ministries or by the relevant Department of the Presidency of the Council of Ministers must be taken into account and the documentation must be modified accordingly and shared with the foreign counterparts. Should any foreign member also propose modifications, the same Department shall be informed and proceed with verification. Once the preliminary phase has been positively concluded, the Department communicates to the prospective members the authorization to set up the EGTC. Within a maximum period of six months from the date of such authorization – after whose expiration the authorization becomes ineffective – each prospective member, or the relevant management organ if already in place, shall request the entry in the EGTC Register. For an EGTC registered in a foreign country, the EGTC is registered in the special section "EGTC Based abroad". The EGTC convention and statutes are then published on the national Official Gazette (where all modifications of the EGTC shall also be published). Within 10 days of the registration or publication, the EGTC shall send a request for registration to the European Committee of the Regions, on the basis of the model annexed to the EGTC Regulation. The European Committee of the Regions transmits this request to the relevant offices for publication in the Official Journal of the European Union. The provisions above apply also to the participation of an Italian entity in an EGTC that is already established.

Slovenia. The EGTC approval and registration process regulated by Slovenian law[15] is almost the same for an EGTC registered in Slovenia or in a foreign country. The prospective members notify their intention to the competent administration, which is identified in the Ministry of Public Administration (*Ministrstvo za javno upravo*), both in the case the members wish to establish a new EGTC and in the case they wish to adhere to an already existing EGTC. Art. 3 of Decree No. 1062 of 9 April 2015 lists the possible prospective co-founders and members of an EGTC under Slovenian law. These entities may become members of an EGTC established in Slovenia and participate in the establishment of, or join, an EGTC established in another member State. The competent administration

15 Decree No. 1062 of 9 April 2015.

shall receive the complete application, including the EGTC founding documents. Once the Ministry of Public Administration receives the application, in accordance with Art. 8 of the Slovenian decree, it prepares a proposal for the government decision referred to in Art. 7 of the same instrument. The government shall adopt the decision within 6 months of receiving the application for approval (Art. 9, para. 1). If the government does not issue a decision within such time limit, the approval shall be deemed to have been given (Art. 9, para. 3). The EGTC shall acquire legal personality with the status of public institution. The status of legal entity under public law is subject upon the entry of the EGTC in the court register (Art. 4). Once it becomes operational, the EGTC may perform tasks in the territory of Slovenia with or without a financial contribution from the European Union (Art. 5, para. 1) and its members are limitedly liable for the obligations of the public legal entity, if the latter has insured risks related to its activities under Slovenian law. The ministries in whose field tasks are determined by the EGTC convention and the government are competent to supervise the legality of the work of the EGTC bodies. The operations and rational use of public funds managed by an EGTC established in Slovenia shall be verified by the Slovenian Court of Audit (Art. 12).

Although the procedures for approval and registration of EGTCs vary among the Adriatic and Ionian coastal States, both in terms of identification of the competent administrations and the setting of time limits for the finalization of the process, it is a matter of fact that the EGTC instrument is flexible enough[16] and offers an appropriate institutional structure for territorial cooperation in the Adriatic and Ionian Seas, also with a view to pursuing, among the wide range of its possible objectives of cooperation, the goals of marine environment protection through the use of area-based management tools and other effective area-based conservation measures. In fact, once it has been set up and registered at the European Union level, the legal entity may autonomously undertake all the actions necessary to the implementation of its tasks, including the identification of the most appropriate protective measures for the areas of concern. As an autonomous legal entity, such EGTC would be in the position to identify and propose to the appropriate authorities also those measures that, although envisaged by international and regional instruments not in force for all Adriatic and Ionian coastal States (such as the Areas Protocol), are, nevertheless, deemed appropriate for the areas of concern. This is an evident advantage of the EGTC tool, as its founding convention could allow the pursue of environmental objectives that, on the basis of the international and regional instruments discussed before in this study, do not always bind all Adriatic and Ionian coastal States.

16 The benefits implied in the flexibility of EGTC legal texts was recalled by Mr. Andrej Čokert, Ministry of Public Administration of Slovenia, in his presentation on *Cross-Border Cooperation in Slovenia*, delivered at the international conference on *Cross-Border Cooperation in Europe*, held on 25 May 2018 in Dubrovnik, Croatia.

8.4. Management Authority

As specified previously, primarily public bodies may become members of an EGTC. The EGTC Regulation regulates both the number of member States and countries involved and the type of bodies permitted as members. Art. 3 specifies the EGTC membership composition as including member States or authorities at national, regional or local level; public undertakings or bodies governed by public law; and associations consisting of bodies of any of these groups. The list implicitly excludes private undertakings and bodies that are not dominated by public influence.

As of today, the EGTC instrument has been hardly used for the original intent of functioning as a management authority. Its implementation for the managing of transboundary marine protected areas in the Adriatic and Ionian Seas would, therefore, represent an example of best practice in the field of marine conservation through the use of an instrument that enhances cooperation between European Union member and non-member States, facilitates decision-making across borders, promotes jointly-developed objectives and strategies, and ensures high European visibility. The 2018 Assessment of the Application of EGTC Regulation (Final Report,), issued under the auspices of the European Commission, highlighted that the EGTC supports multi-level governance structures enhancing cross-border bottom-up approaches that allow for more intensified and higher levels of cross-border cooperation. Border regions can enhance joint planning and implementation of strategies putting their joint interests above national interests. Through the acknowledged legal entity, EGTCs obtain better visibility and improved acceptance by other public and management authorities: they are acknowledged as intermediaries that may initiate new cross-border actions and, in some cases, obtain more power in decision-making processes. EGCTs also act as a reliable and sustainable communication channel and support the harmonization of the legal framework across countries.

As an autonomous legal entity, an EGTC set up by the Adriatic and Ionian coastal States could be responsible for the management of a protected transboundary area, or network of areas, in the Adriatic and Ionian Seas and the identification of the relevant protection measures on the basis of scientific findings. Its legal personality based on public law, with tasks specified in the constitutive instruments, would ensure that the EGTC may participate through its legal and institutional representations in the most appropriate fora where marine environment protection tools are discussed and approved. For example, the PMIBB EGTC, recalled in this volume,[17] is in charge of proposing the appropriate protective measures within the Strait of Bonifacio also through a legal and institutional representation within the IMO. In addition, an EGTC would be in the position to examine ways to obtain funding for the implementation of its tasks at national, regional, or European level. The potential efficacy of a management authority of this kind can be substantively appreciated in comparison with other situations – such as in the case of the *Pelagos Sanctuary* – where the institutional settings (secretariat) and the

17 See Chapter 6 of this book.

means of management implementation (management plan) show evident limitations. The potential of having an autonomous representation within the IMO could be of utmost interest for an EGTC in charge of pursuing the objectives of environment cooperation, also through economic and social cohesion, in areas that, while hosting important biodiversity sites, are crucial for navigational purposes, such as the Gulf of Trieste and the Otranto Channel.

8.5. Conclusive Summary

The EGTC is an entity with legal personality under European Union law (EGTC Regulation 1082/2006, as amended in 2013). It aims at improving the implementation conditions for territorial cooperation with a view to strengthening cohesion in the European Union. In doing so, it complements funding instruments for ETC, known as Interreg. Each EGTC is governed by a convention concluded unanimously by its members. These may be European Union member States, regional and local authorities of European Union member States, public undertakings and public bodies under certain conditions, also belonging to States that are not members of the European Union. What is necessary is that the EGTC is made up of members that are located on the territory of at least two European Union member States. In addition, the EGTC may include one or more States that are neighboring at least one European Union member State that is a member of the same EGTC. A State that is not a member of the European Union is considered as a "neighboring State" under the EGTC Regulation when it shares a common land border or where both the third State and the EU Member State are eligible under a joint maritime cross-border programme under the European territorial cooperation goal, or are eligible under another cross-border, sea-crossing or sea-basin cooperation programme, including where they are separated by international waters (Art. 3a, para. 1). The maritime borders between the countries concerned are included. Accordingly, also Albania, Bosnia and Herzegovina, and Montenegro – or public bodies of these States – could become members of an EGTC in the Adriatic and Ionian Seas. The possibility to resort to the EGTC instrument with a view to protecting the marine environment in a transboundary context, as a possible form of territorial cooperation, has been already affirmed through the establishment of the EGTC for the *International Marine Park of the Mouths of Bonifacio*, in the Tyrrhenian Sea. As an autonomous legal entity, an EGTC set up by the Adriatic and Ionian coastal States could be responsible for the management of a protected transboundary area, or network of areas, in the Adriatic and Ionian Seas and the identification of the relevant protection measures. Its legal personality based on public law, with tasks specified in the constitutive instruments, would ensure that such management authority participate through its legal and institutional representations in the most appropriate *fora* where marine environment protection tools are discussed and approved.

9 The Case for Establishing a Particularly Sensitive Sea Area in the Adriatic and Ionian Seas[1]

Mitja Grbec

9.1. Challenges and Opportunities

As already pointed out,[2] a Particularly Sensitive Sea Area (PSSA) is defined as an area that needs special protection through action by IMO because of its significance for recognized ecological or socioeconomic or scientific reasons and which may be vulnerable to damage by international shipping activities. Reference was made to the fact that the PSSA is intended to function as "a comprehensive management tool at the international level that provides a mechanism for reviewing an area that is vulnerable to damage by international shipping and determining the most appropriate way to address that vulnerability".[3]

The legal nature of the PSSA and the diplomatic and technical process for its designation within the IMO imply important opportunities and substantial challenges. Reference should be made to the fact that the identification and designation of a PSSA and the adoption of its "associate protective measures" require consideration of three integral components: (1) the particular attributes of the proposed area; (2) the vulnerability of such an area to damage by international shipping activities; and (3) the availability of associated protective measures within the competences of the IMO to prevent, reduce or eliminate risks from such shipping activities.

Some of the most important environmental hazards associated with (international) shipping include: (1) operational discharges; (2) accidental or intentional pollution; and (3) physical damage to marine habitats or organisms.[4] As explained by the 2005 Revised Guidelines for the Identification and Designation of Particularly Sensitive Sea Areas (2005 PSSA Guidelines),[5] ships either in the course of their routine operation or due to accidents or even through willful acts of pollution

> may release a wide variety of substances either directly into the marine environment or indirectly through the atmosphere. Such release may include oil

1 This chapter is partially based on Grbec, *op. cit.*, Chapter 5.5.

2 See Chapter 2 of this book.

3 Guidance Document for Submitting PSSA Proposals to IMO (MEPC Cir/398).

4 *Ibid.*, Art. 2.1.

5 IMO, Resolution A.982(24) adopted on 1 December 2005, *Revised Guidelines for the Identification and Designation of Particularly Sensitive Sea Areas*, A 247res.982, 6 February 2006.

DOI: 10.4324/9781003367963-9

and oily mixtures, noxious liquid substances, sewage, garbage, noxious solid substances, anti-fouling systems, harmful aquatic organisms and pathogens, and even noise. In addition, ships may cause harm to marine organisms and their habitats through physical impact. These impacts may include the smothering of habitats, contamination by anti-fouling systems or other substances through grounding, and ship strikes of marine mammals.[6]

Noteworthy is the fact that associated protective measures within a PSSA are limited to actions that are to be, or have been, approved or adopted by the IMO and include the following options: (1) designation of an area as a Special Area under MARPOL Annexes I, IV or V, or a SO_x or NO_x emission control area under MARPOL Annex VI, or application of a special discharge restrictions to vessels operating in a PSSA; (2) adoption of ships' routeing and reporting systems near or in the area, under the International Convention for the Safety of Life at Sea (London, 1974, as amended; SOLAS) and in accordance with the General provisions on Ships' Routeing and the Guidelines and Criteria for Ship Reporting Systems; (3) development and adoption of other measures aimed at protecting specific sea areas against environmental damage from ships, provided they have an identified legal basis.[7]

Reference should be made to the fact that, notwithstanding the Adriatic and Ionian Seas Special Area status under Annex I of MARPOL as part of the wider Mediterranean, where all operational discharges of oily waters from ships are prohibited,[8] one of the problems in both seas is still operational pollution – in other words, illegal discharges from ships.[9] Additionally, an increasingly important problem in the Adriatic Sea is the occurrence of discharges of ballast waters, particularly from ships having their port of departure outside the Mediterranean.[10] With the expected increase of the maritime traffic in the Adriatic Sea, particularly in the

6 *Ibid.*, Art. 2.2.

7 *Ibid.*, Art. 6.1.

8 Regulations for the Prevention of Pollution by Oil. The entire Mediterranean Sea acquired the status of a Special Area based on the provisions of Annex V of MARPOL (Regulations for the Prevention of Pollution from Garbage from Ships). Furthermore, the Mediterranean Sea has been during the 79th session of MEPC in December 2022 granted, similarly to the Baltic Sea, a special area status (Sulphur Emission Control Area, SECA) under Annex VI of MARPOL (Regulations for the Prevention of Air Pollution from Ships). This decision requires ships sailing within the Mediterranean Sea to use marine fuels with less than 0.1 content of sulphur by 1 May 2025. The Mediterranean has not been granted so far a Special Area status under Annex IV of MARPOL in relation to Prevention of Pollution by Sewage from Ships.

9 It has been estimated that an annual average of 250 illegal oil spills occurred in the Adriatic in the early 2000, and there are indicators that the situation has not substantially improved since then. See Vidas, *op. cit.*, pp. 364–365.

10 The quantity of ballast waters released in 2003 in the Adriatic ports of Croatia, Italy and Slovenia amounted to 8 million tonnes, although less that 10 per cent of the mentioned quantity originated outside the Mediterranean. See also Istituto Superiore per la Protezione e la Ricerca Ambientale, *Legal and Policy Aspects Relevant for the Ships' Ballast Water Management in the Adriatic Sea Area*, Rome, 2016.

light of the actual or planned completion of new oil and particularly liquified natural gas terminals in the Adriatic ports of Omišalj, Vlore, Ploče and Trieste, which may in the future open also new export routes of (Caspian) oil and gas,[11] it would seem that maritime traffic and related quantity of discharged ballast water in the Adriatic Sea, including that originating outside the Mediterranean, may increase substantially.

A logical consolidation of the already existing measures in the field of safety of navigation and prevention of ship-source pollution could be the designation by the IMO of the entire Adriatic Sea – including potentially also a part of the Ionian Sea nearby the Channel of Otranto – as a PSSA. Such course of action has been followed by many other European Union member States, including those bordering the semi-enclosed Baltic Sea.[12] Reference should be made to the fact that the possibility of the proclamation of PSSAs in the Adriatic Sea has already been made by the 2005 Agreement on the Sub-regional Contingency Plan, by which Croatia, Italy and Slovenia agreed to cooperate in the designation of PSSAs in the area covered by the Plan. It is important to note that a PSSA may be located within or beyond the limits of the territorial sea, and as pointed out, it "offers the opportunity to enable the development of common jurisdictional and enforcement regimes for environmentally significant marine areas".[13]

At this point, it may be useful to refer again to the definition of a PSSA, which can be defined as a marine area that needs special protection through action by the IMO because of its significance for recognized "ecological or socio-economic or scientific reasons", and because it may be vulnerable to damage by international shipping activities. The three general requirements are further elaborated in the 2005 PSSA Guidelines.[14] They are not cumulative, as one criterion must be fulfilled at least. Furthermore, as provided by para. 1.5 of the 2005 PSSA Guidelines:

> Identification and designation of any PSSA and the adoption of any associated protective measures requires consideration of three integral components: the particular attributes of the proposed area, the vulnerability of such an area to damage by international shipping activities, and the availability of associated protective measures within the competences of IMO to prevent, reduce or eliminate risks from these shipping activities.

It follows that to the extent approved by the IMO, the PSSA status allows coastal States to enforce specific associated measures (within the competence of the IMO),

11 Vidas, *op. cit.*, pp. 361–363.

12 In 2004 the IMO confirmed upon a joint proposal by Belgium, France, Ireland, Portugal, Spain and the United Kingdom, the *Western European Atlantic Waters* as a PSSA (IMO Doc. MEPC 49/8/1, 11 April 2003). The same occurred in 2005 with the *Baltic Sea area* (with the exception of Russian waters) based on the joint proposal by Denmark, Estonia, Finland, Germany, Latvia, Lithuania, Poland and Sweden (IMO Doc. MEPC 51/8/1, 19 December 2003).

13 See Slim and Scovazzi, *op. cit.*, p. 36.

14 IMO Assembly Resolution A. 982(24), 1 December 2005, para. 4.

namely: compulsory reporting systems; compulsory pilotage; routeing measures; Special Area status under MARPOL; and application of discharge restrictions. Taking into account that three of the said protective measures are already in force in the Adriatic Sea (the Special Area status on the basis of Annexes I and V of MARPOL; the reporting system on the basis of SOLAS – ADRIREP; and a system of compulsory routeing measures in the Northern Adriatic coupled with proposed traffic flows in the Central and Adriatic and Channel of Otranto on the basis of COLREG), it could be asked what the added value could be of proclaiming an Adriatic PSSA. It is important to note in this regard that the proposed associated measures may have an identified legal basis also in IMO Conventions or Codes that are not in force yet or in proposed amendments to the said Conventions or Codes. An outstanding example in the past was represented by the 2004 Ballast Water Convention, between its adoption in 2004 and its entry into force in 2017.

The opportunities related to the process of identification and designation of a PSSA derive primarily from its legal nature, on which basis a PSSA may potentially represent a powerful aid in the quest for protection of a specific sensitive area from international shipping. On the other hand, challenges relate mostly to the rather complicated procedure for a PSSA designation and the endorsement of additional associated protective measures within the IMO. Noteworthy is the fact that the designation process allows the IMO to undertake a comprehensive assessment of the shipping threats to the proposed PSSA area with the aim to devise the most appropriate protective measures to address the threat.[15] However, as the (additional) associated protective measures and the PSSA itself need to be confirmed by the relevant IMO bodies, the process of a PSSA designation is not only an environmental or technical process but also a political one.

An application for a PSSA designation should be submitted by an IMO member State or more affected member States (i.e., the States bordering the PSSA area) to the IMO and include, apart from the proposed geographical extent of the PSSA, a proposal for at least one associated protective measure.[16] If there are already associated protective measures in the area, as currently the case in the Adriatic Sea (e.g., routeing measures, reporting obligations), then there is no requirement to propose additional associated protective measures, although such measures may be identified in the future. In the latter case, the application should identify the threat of damage or damage being caused to the area by international shipping activities and show how the area is already being protected from such identified vulnerability by the associated protective measures already in place.[17] Each PSSA application should accordingly consist of two parts: (1) description, significance of the area

15 Kim, Problems and Processes of Restricting Navigation in Particularly Sensitive Sea Areas, in *International Journal of Marine and Coastal Law*, 2021, p. 438.

16 2005 PSSA Guidelines, Art. 7.1.

17 *Ibid.*, Art. 7.2 and 7.3.

and vulnerability; (2) appropriate associated protective measures and IMO's competence to approve or adopt such measures.[18]

Reference should be, furthermore, made to the fact that the application needs to identify the legal basis for each proposed associated protective measure. A legal base in this regard may be: (1) any measure that is already available under an existing IMO document (whether in force or not); (2) any measure that does not exist yet but could become available through amendment of an IMO instrument or adoption of a new IMO instrument. However, the legal basis for any such measure will only be available after amendment or adoption of a new IMO instrument; (3) any measure proposed for the adoption in the territorial sea, or pursuant to Art. 211, para. 6, UNCLOS related to the exclusive economic zone,[19] where existing measures or a generally applicable measure would not adequately address the particularized needs of the proposed area. Such measures may include ships' routeing measures, reporting requirements, discharge restrictions, operational criteria and prohibited activities. They should be specifically tailored to meet the need of the area to prevent, reduce or eliminate the identified vulnerability of the area from international shipping activities.[20] The application should, furthermore, indicate the categories of ships to which the proposed associated protective measures would apply, whereby account should be taken of the relevant provisions of the UNCLOS and other pertinent documents, with particular regards to vessels entitled to sovereign immunity.[21]

Some general observations could be made in this regard. As previously stated, the PSSA may be designated either within or beyond the territorial sea, including, therefore, the exclusive economic zone and the high seas. Due to its exercise of

18 See in that regard the recent proposal submitted by France, Italy, Monaco and Spain regarding the Designation of a particular sensitive sea area in the Northwestern Mediterranean Sea to protect cetaceans from international shipping, MEPC 79/10, 9 September 2022 (pre-session public release).

19 *Ibid.*, Art. 7.5.2. Art. 211, para. 6, a, UNCLOS provides as follows:

> Where the international rules and standards referred to in paragraph 1 are inadequate to meet special circumstances and coastal States have reasonable grounds for believing that a particular, clearly defined area of their respective exclusive economic zones is an area where the adoption of special mandatory measures for the prevention of pollution from vessels is required for recognized technical reasons in relation to its oceanographical and ecological conditions, as well as its utilization or the protection of its resources and the particular character of its traffic, the coastal States, after appropriate consultations through the competent international organization with any other States concerned, may, for that area, direct a communication to that organization, submitting scientific and technical evidence in support and information on necessary reception facilities. Within 12 months after receiving such a communication, the organization shall determine whether the conditions in that area correspond to the requirements set out above. If the organization so determines, the coastal States may, for that area, adopt laws and regulations for the prevention, reduction and control of pollution from vessels implementing such international rules and standards or navigational practices as are made applicable, through the organization, for special areas. These laws and regulations shall not become applicable to foreign vessels until 15 months after the submission of the communication to the organization.

20 2005 PSSA Guidelines, Art. 7.5.2.4.

21 *Ibid.*, Art. 7.5.2.5.

sovereignty, within the territorial sea a coastal state enjoys wide rights with regard to the adoption of restrictive navigational measures (including routeing measures) and, therefore, the designation of a PSSA solely within the territorial sea would not represent, in most cases, a substantial added value.[22] On the other hand, the adoption of more stringent measures for the protection of the marine environment (including biodiversity) from international shipping activities in an exclusive economic zone, also on the basis of Art. 211, para. 6, UNCLOS, is nowadays primarily possible through the designation of a PSSA.

As already stated, a PSSA application should include a proposal for at least one additional associated protective measure. An exception is represented by the scenario – as currently the case in the Adriatic Sea – whereby some preexisting associated protective measures (i.e., routeing measures) are already in place. The first step in the process of designing an area as a PSSA is the submission of a proposal by an IMO member State or more IMO member States. Once the proposal reaches the IMO, then the MEPC considers the application and establishes an informal technical group formed by its representatives with appropriate environmental, scientific, maritime and legal expertise. The task of the informal technical group is to prepare a brief report to the MEPC, summarizing their findings and the outcome of the assessment, which should be also reflected in the MEPC final report.[23] The MEPC considers applications on a case-by-case basis, with the final aim to establish whether the application fulfils at least one of the criteria among ecological, socioeconomic or scientific attributes. After adoption by the MEPC, the particular associated protective measures are referred to the competent IMO committee, which may be, depending on the nature of the proposed associated measure(s), the Maritime Safety Committee, the Sub-Committee on Navigation, Communications and Search and Rescue or the Assembly itself.[24] The PSSA does not, in itself, provide a legal basis for the enforcement of a specific associated protective measure, as this require a separate approval process within the relevant IMO committee.[25] Eventually, the MEPC endorses a PSSA only after the proposed associated protective measures are adopted by the competent IMO committee. Due to such demanding procedure involving IMO member States, the MEPC, its informal technical group and the relevant IMO committee or the IMO Assembly itself, the procedure for the designation of a PSSA, from the time of submission of the proposal until the time of actual designation, may last more than one year.[26] Notwithstanding such challenging procedure, the IMO has so far designated 17 PSSAs, including in 2011 the Strait of Bonifacio. The latter is, for the time being, the only PSSA designed within the Mediterranean Sea.[27]

22 See Kim, *op. cit.*, p. 443.
23 2005 PSSA Guidelines, Art. 8.3.1.
24 *Ibid.*, Art. 8.3.2. See also Kim, *op. cit.*, p. 444.
25 *Ibid.*, p. 444.
26 *Ibid.*, p. 445.
27 The following PSSAS have been designated: *The Great Barrier Reef*, Australia (1990); *The Sabana-Camagüey Archipelago*, Cuba (1997); *Malpelo Island*, Colombia (2002); *The Sea around the*

The main opportunities provided by the PSSA concept include the possibility to introduce for the particular area additional associated protective measures, although limited to those having its legal basis in an adopted IMO instrument. The later may be or may not be in force. While certain associated protective measures (e.g., routing measures, reporting systems) based on legally binding IMO instruments may be introduced outside the PSSA on the basis of the endorsement by the relevant IMO committee, this is not possible for IMO documents (Conventions, Codes, Guidelines, etc.) not already in force.[28] The practical result of designing a PSSA is that the included associated protective measures are granted validity *erga omnes partes*, even if a certain IMO document has not entered into force. An additional benefit of designing a PSSA is represented by the fact that associated protective measures may differ within the area and be tailored for a specific (smaller) part of a broader PSSA.

Even in the case that the designated PSSA mirrors (only) existing measures, the sole designation of a PSSA may represent an extremely important cooperative framework for participating IMO member States and their governmental (maritime) authorities. The main advantage in this regard seems to be the internationally raised awareness about the area's vulnerability to damage by international shipping, which, in turn, may and should increase community and mariners' awareness of the sensitivity of, and risk to, navigation in the area.[29] Noteworthy is the fact that when a PSSA receives a final designation, all associated protective measures, both preexisting and new, should be identified on charts in accordance with the symbols and methods of the International Hydrographic Organization (IHO).[30]

Florida Keys, United States (2002); *The Wadden Sea*, Denmark, Germany, Netherlands (2002); *Paracas National Reserve*, Peru (2003); *Western European Waters* (2004); *Extension of the existing Great Barrier Reef PSSA to include the Torres Strait* (proposed by Australia and Papua New Guinea) (2005); *Canary Islands*, Spain (2005); *The Galapagos Archipelago*, Ecuador (2005); *The Baltic Sea area*, Denmark, Estonia, Finland, Germany, Latvia, Lithuania, Poland and Sweden (2005); *The Papahānaumokuākea Marine National Monument*, United States (2007); *The Strait of Bonifacio*, France and Italy (2011); *The Saba Bank*, in the Northeastern Caribbean area of the Kingdom of the Netherlands (2012); *Extension of Great Barrier Reef and Torres Strait to Encompass the South-West Part of the Coral Sea* (2015); *The Jomard Entrance*, Papua New Guinea (2016); *Tubbataha Reefs Natural Park, the Sulu Sea*, Philippines (2017).

28 According to IMO MSC.1/Circ.1608 of 20 August 2019, Procedure for the Submission of Documents Containing Proposals for the establishment of, or amendments to, ships' routing systems or ship reporting systems

> for proposals primarily related to matters of protection of the marine environment and wildlife, proponents should consider first a submission to the Marine Environment Protection Committee (MEPC) with a view to establish Particularly Sensitive Sea Areas (PSSAs), and/or associated protective measures, as appropriate.
>
> (Art. 3.1)

29 Kleverlaan, *Overview of IMO Instruments to Protect Sensitive Sea Areas from International Shipping* (ppt), UNEP, Adriatic Region Workshop on PSSA, held on 10–11 December 2019 in Tirana, Albania.

30 2005 Revised Guidelines, Art. 9.1.

The case of the *Wadden Sea* PSSA is particularly interesting. Before the designation of a PSSA, the Wadden Sea was already managed as a marine protected area in Germany and as a Trilateral Cooperation area with Denmark and Netherlands. Furthermore, the Wadden Sea had already – before its designation as a PSSA – the status of Special Area under Annex I and V of MARPOL. The designation of a PSSA was not accompanied by any new proposed associated protective measure.[31] On the basis of available sources, the PSSA designation of the Wadden Sea was primarily intended for international recognition of the environmental significance of the area and with the aim to internationally publicize the already existing measures and competent enforcement authorities.[32] It is suggested that such an approach may either directly or indirectly increase maritime safety and furthermore provide, as emphasized, an extremely important cooperative framework within which relevant governmental authorities could monitor the functioning of existing associated protective measures and work on proposals for their further upgrades. Due to increased awareness of the public, the designation of a PSSA may also facilitate the prevention and reporting of violations.

Another extremely important opportunity related to the designation of the PSSA is that it can be used as a supplementary measure within an already established marine protected area or, alternatively, can be proposed as a separate sectoral measure in parallel with the process of establishment of a (transboundary) marine protected area, including a SPAMI. The example of the Strait of Bonifacio, where all previous instruments – including established national marine protected areas both on the French and Italian side, a new SPAMI, a preexisting (*Pelagos Sanctuary*) SPAMI and a PSSA – coexist over roughly the same area, is a clear example in this regard.[33]

Noteworthy is the fact that out of 15 designates PSSAs, if we do not count for this purpose the two larger PSSA represented by the semi-enclosed Baltic Sea or an even larger area represented by the Western-European Waters PSSA, only one – the *Jomard Entrance* PSSA – was not previously designed as a national or international marine protected area. Nine of the 15 mentioned PSSAs were already listed as world heritage sites. Other areas were at least partially protected as wetlands of international importance.[34] Some criticism in this regard concerned the fact that the concept of PSSA has become a tool for basically reiterating rules already put in place on the basis of UNCLOS, SOLAS and MARPOL.[35]

Challenges related to the designation of a PSSA mostly refer to the technical and, at least in some instances, to a political process within a PSSA designation process within the IMO. This results from the fact that the IMO rightly tries to

31 IMO, *Identification of the Wadden Sea as Particularly Sensitive Sea Area*, IMO Resolution MEPC.101(48), 11 October 2002, IMO Doc. MEPC 48/21 (24 October 2002), Annex 5, p. 17.

32 Kim, *op. cit.*, p. 451.

33 *Ibid.*, p. 452.

34 *Ibid.*, p. 450.

35 *Ibid.*, p. 449.

balance interests related to the protection of biodiversity and marine environment with interests of international shipping. As pointed out by the 2005 PSSA Guidelines,

> Member Governments which have ships operating in the area of the designed PSSA are encouraged to bring any concerns with the associated protective measures to IMO so that any necessary adjustments are made.[36]

Also non-governmental organizations (e.g., the World Wide Fund for Nature) and other professional organizations particularly from the shipping sector (e.g., the International Chamber of Shipping; Intertanko) are allowed to present their views. The practical result of such technical and, at the same time, political process is that initial proposals for additional associated protection measures are often "watered down" during the process of a PSSA designation, both with regard the relevant number and contents. A noteworthy example, in this regard, is again represented by the *Strait of Bonifacio* PSSA, where Italy and France originally proposed, as an additional associated protective measure, a mandatory traffic separation scheme, an area to be avoided (ATBA), a VTS under the SOLAS and a mandatory pilotage system.[37] At the end of the process, the adopted additional protective measures only recommend pilotage and a two-way route.[38] It may be expected that shipping States, States with a strong interest in navigation in a particular area and shipping representative bodies (e.g., the International Chamber of Shipping) will try within the relevant IMO body to prevent any compulsory restriction on navigation, particularly if that relates to a main international shipping route.

Reference should be made to the fact that, eventually, the most important challenge is the endorsement, preparation and joint submission of a PSSA proposal to the IMO by all interested States. This is also due to the fact that a designed PSSA shall not extend to waters over which a coastal State opposing such designation exercises sovereignty or sovereign rights.[39] A proposal jointly elaborated and submitted by all interested States, as, for example, by those States bordering an enclosed or semi-enclosed sea, will have much better chances of success. The second challenge relates to the need to pass a proposal through the relevant IMO bodies and, in this regard, to convince other States, particularly those using the area for international navigation, of the environmental importance of the area and of its

36 2005 PSSA Guidelines, Art. 8.4.

37 Identification and protection of Special Areas and Particularly Sensitive Areas: Designation of the Strait of Bonifacio as a Particularly Sensitive Area, Submitted by France and Italy, IMO Doc. MEPC 61/9, 25 June 2010, Annex, p. 11.

38 Kim, *op. cit.* Designation of the Strait of Bonifacio as a Particularly Sensitive Sea Area, IMO Resolution MEPC.204(62), adopted 15 July 2011, IMO DOC MEPC 62/24/Add.1, 26 July 2011, Annex 22, p. 17.

39 See the example of Russian waters not included in a PSSA in the context of the Baltic Sea.

vulnerability to international shipping. Even in that case, third States need to be assured that, through the designation of a PSSA and adoption of associate protective measures, navigation will be regulated and made environmentally safer but not unnecessarily hindered or even prevented. Accordingly, the chances of success of a proposal are far greater if, for example, all States bordering the enclosed or semi-enclosed sea are united and submit a joint proposal with regard to the designation of the PSSA and associate protective measures. The chances of success are further enhanced, if such proposal is supported within the IMO bodies by the European Union and its member States as a united block, as, for example, the case has been during the process of adoption of the *Western European Waters* PSSA in 2004.[40]

9.2. Work Undertaken So Far

The proposal to designate an Adriatic PSSA originates from a Croatian proposal and is based on studies carried out in the period 2004–2006. In 2006, a Joint Expert Group on PSSA, comprising representatives of all Adriatic States (later replaced by the Correspondence Group), was established upon the Croatian initiative and held several meetings, including the meetings in Opatija (April 2006), Portorož (October 2006) and Zagreb (June 2007).[41] According to the prepared draft text of the proposal,[42] the associated protection measures applicable in the Adriatic PSSA would, in addition to the strengthening of the already existing measures (i.e., the potential strengthening or extension of the existing routeing measures to other parts of the Adriatic, the upgrading of the ADRIREP reporting system), include some associated protective measures having its identifiable legal basis in the 2004 Ballast Water Convention, which was not in force at that time. That would include the potential designation of the Adriatic Sea as a No-Ballast-Water Exchange Area for extra Adriatic traffic and, among others, the extension of the existing mandatory ship reporting system also on ballast waters entering the Adriatic.[43]

40 Kim, *op. cit.*, pp. 454–456.

41 See Vidas, *op. cit.*, p. 370.

42 Joint Expert Group on PSSA; *Designation of the Adriatic Sea as a Particularly Sensitive Area*, second draft (internal document, Zagreb, 28 June 2007). On file with the authors.

43 See Vidas, *op. cit.*, p. 369. Noteworthy is the fact that the contracting parties to the Barcelona Convention adopted in 2011, through the assistance of REMPEC, a *Harmonized Voluntary Arrangements for Ballast Water Management in the Mediterranean Region*. The Guidelines provided guidance and options to vessels transiting the Mediterranean with regard to ballast water management and exchange, although only on a voluntary basis. The Guidelines were applicable till the entry into force of the 2004 Ballast Water Convention in 2017. See IMO, *International Convention for the Control and Management of Ship's Ballast Water and Sediments. Communication received from the Regional Marine Pollution Emergency Response Centre for the Mediterranean Sea*, BWM.2/Circ.35, 15 August 2011, Annex 1. See in this regard also the results of the Ballast Water Management System for Adriatic Sea Protection Project (BALMAS) undertaken in the period 2013–2016 and cofinanced by the IPA Adriatic Cross-Border Cooperation Programme. More info available at www.izvrs.si/project/bewater-making-society-an-active-participant-in-water-adaptation-to-global-change-2/?lang=en.

Other associated measures proposed could have included, for example, the Special Area status on the basis of Annexes IV and VI of the MARPOL and other measures embodied in present or potential future IMO Guidelines and Codes – and this even before their entry into force.

It is accordingly regrettable that, despite an ambitious timetable for the submission of the joint proposal to the IMO (end of 2007), the work on the proposal stopped. It was encouraging, however, that authorities and stakeholders from all Adriatic States (and the European Union) participating some years later at the high-level stakeholder conference *Setting an Agenda for Smart, Sustainable and Inclusive Growth from the Adriatic and Ionian Sea*, held in Zagreb on 6 December 2012, "express[ed] readiness to continue the joint efforts towards the designation of the Adriatic Sea as a Particularly Sensitive Sea Area (PSSA), in accordance with the IMO Guidelines".[44]

It is to be hoped that the proposal will be finalized and submitted to the IMO and that the whole waters of the Adriatic Sea will be – like those of the Western European Atlantic Waters (2004) and the Baltic Sea (2005, without the Russian waters) – proclaimed as a PSSA. It is suggested, in this regard, that an Adriatic PSSA would represent a flexible tool, a potential forum and a main incentive for Adriatic States for discussing the management of the risks posed by international shipping,[45] including by operational pollution. Furthermore, as it was also emphasized by an expert, "the designation of a PSSA in the Adriatic Sea can provide a significant regional cooperative framework, in line with the European Union policy, and also highlight the awareness of the vulnerability of the Adriatic Sea environment".[46]

It seems possible to conclude that the proclamation of an Adriatic PSSA, in addition to the proclamation of one or more SPAMIs (or other kinds of marine protected areas or effective area-based management measures) over the most vulnerable Adriatic Sea areas, may substantially contribute to the protection of the Adriatic marine environment from shipping activities, including from operational pollution.[47]

9.3. Marine Areas to be Covered and Potential Associated Protective Measures

Independently of the fact that the 2006 draft proposal related to the designation of the Adriatic Sea as a PSSA was not finalized and submitted to the IMO and as a result of the existence of diverging views among Adriatic States regarding additional associated protection measures to be included (i.e., the designation of the Adriatic Sea as a "No-Ballast-Water Exchange Area" for extra Adriatic traffic), the said draft proposal may represent a sound basis either for its update and finalization

44 Conclusions of the Conference.

45 See Vidas, *op. cit.*, p. 348.

46 *Ibid.*, p. 348.

47 See discussion in Vidas and Kostelac, Ballast Water and Alien Species: Regulating Global Transfers and Regional Consequences, in Vidas and Schei (eds.), *op. cit.*, pp. 390–392.

or as a starting point for the preparation of a new PSSA proposal. Noteworthy is the fact that the draft proposal was prepared by the Joint Expert Group on PSSA, which included representatives from all Adriatic States, apart from Greece. Furthermore, the list of proposed protective measures was elaborated in close coordination with the, at that time, Trilateral Commission, which participated in the preparation of the proposal prevalently through its sub-commission on ballast water management. A lot of painstaking work was invested by different bodies and experts on the proposal. The fact that the proposal was close to its finalization makes its update, upgrade and eventual submission to the IMO a feasible option.

Based on the proposal, an Adriatic PSSA area should have embraced the entire Adriatic Sea, including the territorial seas, zones under sovereign rights or jurisdiction of coastal States and the high seas. It should have included the entire Channel of Otranto area, north from the latitude 40° 25' 00" N. Such geographical extent corresponded and still corresponds to the area of application of the existing associated protective measures in the Adriatic Sea. The proposal accordingly intended to include and, furthermore, build upon existing associated protective measures, including mandatory and proposed routeing measures and ADRIREP. Within an eventual new PSSA proposal, researches could be undertaken on whether to geographically extend the proposed PSSA further into the Ionian Sea, particularly to the area outside, but adjacent to, the Channel of Otranto.

A. Existing Associated Protective Measures

As also enumerated in the mentioned PSSA draft proposal, there are several associated protective measures adopted so far under the ambit of the IMO, applicable either specifically to the Adriatic Sea or to the Adriatic Sea as part of the wider Mediterranean Sea. These include: (1) mandatory ship reporting systems; (2) routeing systems; and (3) Special Area status under the relevant Annexes to MARPOL. The first two sets of measures are applicable specifically to the Adriatic Sea and were adopted by the IMO upon joint proposals submitted by Adriatic Sea countries: Albania, Croatia, Italy, Slovenia, Serbia and Montenegro.

The existing associated protective measures may be broadly divided into the three following groups.

a. Mandatory Ship Reporting

The Maritime Safety Committee of the IMO, at its 76th session (December 2002), adopted the mandatory ship reporting system in the Adriatic Sea (ADRIREP), which entered into force on 1 July 2003. The operational area of the mandatory ship reporting system covers the whole Adriatic Sea, north from latitude 40° 25' 00" N. Ships of the following categories are required to participate in the system: all oil tanker ships of 150 gross tonnage and above and all ships of 300 gross tonnage and above, carrying on board, as cargo, dangerous or polluting goods, in bulk or packages. The primary objective of the system is to support safe navigation and the protection of the marine environment through the exchange of information between the ship and the shore. If the ship does not submit reports and cannot be positively identified, information will be passed to the competent flag State authorities for investigation and possible prosecution, in accordance with national legislation. Information will be passed also to port State inspectors.[48]

b. Routeing

The Maritime Safety Committee of the IMO, at its 78th session (May 2004), adopted new traffic separation schemes and associated routeing measures in the Adriatic Sea, with implementation as of 1 December 2004. Accordingly, routeing system in the Adriatic Sea currently consists of the following:

- Traffic separation scheme *North Adriatic Sea – Eastern Part*;
- Traffic separation scheme *North Adriatic Sea – Western Part*;
- Precautionary area at the southern limits of the traffic separation scheme;
- Traffic separation scheme *Approaches to Gulf of Trieste*;
- Traffic separation scheme *Approaches to Gulf of Venice*;
- Traffic separation scheme in the Gulf of Trieste;
- Traffic separation scheme *Approaches to/from Koper*;
- Traffic separation scheme *Approaches to/from Monfalcone*;
- Precautionary area in the Gulf of Trieste; and
- ATBA in the *North Adriatic Sea*.

In addition, there are recommended directions of traffic flow in the Channel of Otranto and Southern and Central Adriatic Sea.[49]

c. MARPOL Special Areas

The entire Mediterranean Sea, including the Adriatic Sea, was declared as a Special Area under MARPOL Annex I (Regulations for the Prevention of Pollution by Oil; Regulation 10) and Annex V (Regulations for the Prevention of Pollution by Garbage; Regulation 5) with the aim to protecting these sensitive sea areas against the discharge of oil or oily mixtures and garbage. Subject to the provisions of Annex I, *inter alia*, any discharge into the sea of oil or oily mixtures from any oil tanker or any ship of 400 gross tonnage and above other than an oil tanker is prohibited in the Special Area. As pointed out, recent evidence indicates that this prohibition is frequently violated by ships involved in international traffic in the Adriatic Sea. Both annexes require reception facilities within Special Areas. Additionally, the Mediterranean Sea has been recently granted, similarly to the Baltic Sea, a special area status (Sulphur Emission Control Area: SECA) under Annex VI of MARPOL (Regulations for the Prevention of Air Pollution from Ships). The latter decision

48 PSSA draft proposal, on file with the author.
49 *Ibid.*

will require ships sailing within the Mediterranean Sea to use marine fuels with less than 0.1 content of sulphur as of 1 May 2025.[50]

B. New Associated Protective Measures

A first possibility would be that the designated Adriatic PSSA mirrors (only) already existing measures, similarly as the previously discussed scenario in the Wadden Sea. The advantage of such approach seems to be the internationally raised awareness about the area's vulnerability to damage by international shipping and the compulsory identification of all associated protective measures, which should be identified on charts in accordance with the symbols and methods of the IHO. The second preferred option could be the strengthening and upgrading of existing associated protective measures, coupled with eventual proposals for new associated protective measures. Such new associated protective measures could be applicable to the entire Adriatic Sea or only to part of it.[51]

Existing routeing measures could be, for example, the strengthening through the upgrade of the existing proposed traffic flows (in the central Adriatic close to the Jabuka/Pomo Pit area and within the Otranto Channel), from proposed traffic flows to compulsory traffic separation schemes. A possibility could also be the proposal for new compulsory traffic separation schemes or proposed traffic flows in other areas of the Adriatic Sea, including within the Central and Southern Adriatic. Reference was made in this regard to the Sazani Strait and the Bay of Boka Kotorska as potential areas.[52] The ADRIREP reporting system could be, in turn, upgraded with regard to the types of ships which are bound to report and with regard the information which needs to be reported, including in the field of ballast water management. Another aim of the upgrade of ADRIREP could be to help achieving harmonization and standardization of VTS in the region and to take into account advances in technology during the last two decades.

Regarding the status of the Adriatic as a Special Area under MARPOL, a further associated protective measure could be the designation of the Adriatic Sea, either alone or as part of the wider Mediterranean, as a Special Area under Annex IV of MARPOL and also a NO_x Tier III Emission Control Area (NECA) under Annex VI of MARPOL. A straightforward example in this regard is represented by the Baltic Sea PSSA, which includes among its protective measures a Special Area status based on the provisions of Annex I, IV and V, as well as a SECA (as per 19

50 Decision adopted at the 79th session of the MEPC in December 2022.

51 An interesting case from the standpoint of an eventual proposal for the designation of the Adriatic Sea a PSSA is represented by the Klek/Neum Bay. The latter represents the only exit of Bosnia and Herzegovina to the Adriatic Sea. A peculiarity is represented by the fact that the Bosnian territorial waters in front of the Klek/Neum peninsula are encircled by Croatian internal waters over which, based on the provisions of the 2005 Revised Guidelines, a PSSA cannot be designed. See Grbec, *op. cit.*, chapter 4.5.

52 Mediterranean Seminar on PSSAs, Report of the Seminar, 12 December 2019, Tirana, Albania.

May 2006) and NECA Special Areas (as per 1 January 2021) based on the relevant provisions of Annex VI to the MARPOL Convention.

It is finally argued that an important precedent with regard to the designation of an Adriatic PSSA will be represented also by the recent proposal submitted by France, Italy, Monaco and Spain regarding the Designation of a Particular Sensitive Sea Area in the Northwestern Mediterranean Sea to Protect Cetaceans from International Shipping, which was in principle adopted at the 79th session of the MEPC (December 2022) and deferred to the appropriate sub-committees for further elaboration and ultimately adoption of the proposed (recommended) associated protective measures.[53]

9.4. Conclusive Summary

The designation of a PSSA or more geographically separated PSSAs within the Adriatic and Ionian Seas may potentially represent a powerful aid in the quest for protection of a specific sensitive area from international shipping. Noteworthy is the fact that the PSSA designation process allows the IMO to undertake a comprehensive assessment of the shipping threats to the proposed PSSA area, with the aim to devise the most appropriate protective measures to address the threat. However, as the additional associated protective measures and the PSSA itself need to be confirmed by the relevant IMO bodies, the process of a PSSA designation is not only an environmental and technical process but also a political exercise. The main opportunity provided by the PSSA concept is the possibility to introduce for a particular area additional associated protective measures, although limited to those having its legal base in an adopted IMO instrument. The latter may be or may not be in force. The practical and legal result of a designed PSSA is that the included associated protective measures are granted validity *erga omnes partes*, even if a certain IMO instrument has not yet entered into force. An additional benefit of designing a PSSA is represented by the fact that associated protective measures may differ within the area and be tailored for a specific (smaller) part of a broader PSSA.

Even in the case that the designated PSSA mirrors (only) already existing measures, in the case of the Adriatic Sea that would include routeing measures (both compulsory and proposed), compulsory reporting (ADRIREP) and Special Area status under MARPOL Annexes I, V and VI. The sole designation of a PSSA may represent an extremely important cooperative framework for participating IMO member States and their governmental (maritime) authorities. The main advantage in this regard seems to be the internationally raised awareness about the area's vulnerability to damage by international shipping, which, in turn, may – and should – increase community and mariners' awareness of the sensitivity of and risk to navigation in the area. A preferred option should, however, be the strengthening and upgrading of the already existing associated protective measures through

53 See in that regard MEPC 79/10, 9 September 2022 (pre-session public release), p. 4, Section 13.

the designation of a PSSA, coupled with eventual proposals for new associated protective measures. Such new associated protective measures could be applicable to the entire Adriatic Sea, to only to part of it, or to the area adjacent to the PSSA (Ionian Sea).

Another extremely important opportunity related to the designation of the PSSA is that it can be used as a supplementary measure within an already established marine protected area. Alternatively, it can be proposed as a separate sectoral measure (other effective area-based conservation measure) in parallel with the process of establishment of a (transboundary) marine protected area, including a SPAMI. The example of the Strait of Bonifacio, where all previous instruments – including established national marine protected areas both on the French and Italian side (marine parks, NATURA 2000), a SPAMI, and a PSSA – coexist over roughly the same area, is a clear example in this regard.

Independently of the fact that the draft PSSA proposal prepared in the period 2006–2011 related to the designation of the entire Adriatic Sea as a PSSA was not eventually finalized and submitted to the IMO, the said draft proposal may represent a sound basis either for its update and finalization or as a starting point for the preparation of a new PSSA proposal.

10 The Sustainable Development of the Wider Mediterranean

Multi-stakeholder Settings, Ecosystem Approach, and Maritime Spatial Planning

Mitja Bricelj

10.1. Multi-stakeholder Settings as Transboundary Cooperation Tools

In addition to the legal perspective provided so far in this book, there are policy considerations that could shed some further light on what can be achieved for an effective protection of the wider Mediterranean Sea. Emphasis should be put on tools that, though having already been in place for some time, can be used to change the *status quo*. In fact, transformation can be achieved also through the monitoring, conservation, and sustainable use of marine and coastal resources in the form of multi-stakeholder settings with transboundary effect.

The Adriatic and Ionian macro-region is a practical example where cooperation for a healthy and reproductive ecosystem can be envisaged through the further development of multi-stakeholder cooperation. Instruments for such a cooperation encompass global conventions such as the UNCLOS (which states, in its preamble, that "the problems of ocean space are closely interrelated and need to be considered as a whole"), the CBD, and the United Nations Framework Convention on Climate Change (New York, 1992); as well as regional legal and policy instruments, including, but not limited to, the European Union environmental legislation, the Barcelona Convention, and the EUSAIR process. Specifically, though complex in its structure, the intention of the latter mechanism is rather simple. It is about establishing synergies for an integrated coastal and marine spatial planning with a view to preserving the so-called ecosystem services of the macro-region. In other words, it is about enhancing water, food, and climate security in the Adriatic and Ionian basin for the generations to come.

10.2. A Sustainable Development Strategy for the Mediterranean Region

Under the Regional Seas Program of the United Nations Environment Program (UNEP), a Mediterranean Action Plan (MAP) was established in 1975 and became the institutional framework for cooperation in addressing the common challenges posed by an increasing marine environmental degradation. A year later, the Barcelona Convention was adopted, and then amended in 1995 with a view to including

DOI: 10.4324/9781003367963-10

the key principles of sustainable development embraced by the 1992 United Nations Conference on Environment and Development through the adoption of Agenda 21.

So far, UNEP-MAP and the parties to the Barcelona Convention, including the European Union, have progressively erected a uniquely comprehensive institutional, legal, and implementation framework, integrating essential building blocks for environmental sustainability in the Mediterranean. Importantly, the Mediterranean Commission for Sustainable Development (MCSD) was established in 1995, under the auspices of the UNEP-MAP, as the multi-stakeholder advisory body of the parties to the Barcelona Convention, acting as a forum for discussion and advancement of sustainable development issues in the Mediterranean region.

Another key initiative is the Mediterranean Strategy for Sustainable Development (MSSD), which provides an integrative policy framework for all stakeholders, including MAP partners, to translate the 2030 Agenda for Sustainable Development and its Sustainable Development Goals (SDGs) at the regional, sub-regional, national, and local levels in the Mediterranean region using an ecosystem-based approach. The consultation process mobilizes Mediterranean stakeholders, including both State authorities and civil society representatives through the participation of non-governmental organizations and key experts. The first MSSD was adopted at the 14th meeting of the parties to the Barcelona Convention in Portorož (Slovenia, 2005) and remains relevant today: while the global and regional context has changed significantly, the pressures on the environment are even more pronounced. The 2005 MSSD established the marine and coastal zones as one of its seven priority fields of action. In the years since its adoption, there have been a number of sub-regional, regional, and global developments relevant to this objective. The current MSSD (2016–2025), adopted at the 19th meeting of the parties to the Barcelona Convention in Athens (Greece, 2016),[1] continues to provide a strategic policy framework, built upon a broad consultation process, underpinned by the view that investing in the environment is the best way to secure long-term sustainable jobs and socioeconomic development (such a view is conveyed in the MSSD rationale: “Investing in environmental sustainability to achieve social and economic development”).

10.3. Ecosystem Approach as Integrated Operational Approach at the Regional Level

Among the developments that continue to prove relevant to the objectives of the MSSD there has been the adoption (2008) and entry into force (2011) of the Coastal Zone Protocol to the Barcelona Convention, whereby States recognized the importance of an integrated management approach for the sustainable development of coastal zones. In addition, since 2008, the States parties to the Barcelona Convention have committed to apply the ecosystem-based approach – through the

1 UNEP(DEPI)/MED IG.22/2, *Mediterranean Strategy for Sustainable Development 2016–2025.*

so-called Ecosystem Approach Roadmap[2] – to the management of human activities, while enabling the sustainable use of marine resources and services, with the view to achieving or maintaining a good environmental status (GES) of the Mediterranean Sea and its coastal regions. Among the actions of its Strategic Direction 1.1 ("Strengthening implementation of and compliance with the Protocols of the Barcelona Convention and other regional policy instruments and initiatives supplemented by national approaches"), the MSSD 2016–2025 includes "Action 1.2. Implement the Ecosystem Approach Roadmap to achieve healthy marine ecosystems and conserve marine biodiversity".

Already the CBD recognized that biological diversity is made of plants, animals, microorganisms, and their ecosystems. In other words, biological diversity includes us as well, and our need for food security, medicines, fresh air and water, shelters, and a healthy environment. This necessitates an integrated management of the environment. The ecosystem-based approach is the strategy for such an integrated management of land, water, and living resources. It promotes their conservation and sustainable use in an equitable way. For this reason, the application of the ecosystem approach helps towards the achievement of three main objectives of the CBD: conservation, sustainable use, and fair and equitable sharing of the benefits arising out of the utilization of genetic resources.

Some key principles lying behind the concept of ecosystem approach include ecosystem's maintenance (i.e., the conservation of the ecosystem's structure and functioning); an implementing strategy that takes into account appropriate spatial and temporal scales; and an appropriate balance between the objectives of conservation and sustainable use of biological diversity. In this regard, there is a need for a shift to more flexible situations, where conservation and use are not considered theoretically but seen in the relevant context and where the relevant measures are applied in a contextualized and coherent manner. Importantly, implementing strategies should focus on the functional relationships and processes within ecosystems; management actions should be carried out at the scale appropriate for the issue being addressed, with decentralization to the lowest level; and intersectoral cooperation should be ensured.

The overall objective of the implementation of the Ecosystem Approach Roadmap is to achieve and maintain good environmental status of the Mediterranean Sea and coasts. Under the vision of *A healthy Mediterranean with marine and coastal ecosystems that are productive and biologically diverse for the benefit of present and future generations*, the parties to the Barcelona Convention adopted a list of 11 ecological objectives (EOs), addressing all key elements of the Mediterranean marine and coastal environment: (EO 1) biodiversity; (EO 2) non-indigenous species; (EO 3) harvest of commercially exploited fish and shellfish; (EO 4) marine food webs; (EO 5) eutrophication; (EO 6) sea-floor integrity; (EO 7) hydrography; (EO 8) coastal ecosystems and landscapes; (EO 9) pollution; (EO 10) marine litter;

2 UNEP(DEPI)/MED IG.21/9, Decision IG.21/3 on the Ecosystems Approach including adopting definitions of Good Environmental Status (GES) and targets.

and (EO 11) energy including underwater noise. Such EOs have been further broken down into operational objectives,[3] as well as GES definitions and associated targets.[4]

A major component of the ecosystem approach implementation is related to the monitoring and assessment of the status of the marine and coastal environment. In view of establishing a coherent region-wide framework, the parties to the Barcelona Convention adopted in 2016 the Integrated Monitoring Assessment Programme of the Mediterranean Sea and Coast and Related Assessment Criteria (IMAP).[5] The IMAP sets out all the required elements to cover in an integrated manner monitoring and assessment of biodiversity and fisheries, pollution and marine litter, and coasts and hydrography.

The IMAP implementation has further progressed with the establishment of national IMAPs, the development of a centralized data collection and management infrastructure (the so-called IMAP InfoSystem), the refinement of technical specifications on IMAP common indicators and the building of knowledge on candidate indicators, as well as the development of methodologies for an integrated assessment. A specific Roadmap is currently under implementation for the preparation of a Quality Status Report in 2023 (2023 MED QSR), as decided by the parties to the Barcelona Convention in 2019.[6] The first ever MED QSR had been delivered in 2017,[7] following a multistep comprehensive review process, complemented with inputs from numerous diverse sources, involving all relevant MAP components, parties, and key partners.

The implementation, development, and review of relevant action plans and programmes under the Ecosystem Approach Roadmap is pursued on a multilayer perspective, covering all the aspects of the legal and policy framework of the UNEP-MAP and the Barcelona Convention. Accordingly, the ecosystem approach has been raised to the programmatic level and reaffirmed as an overarching principle of the Barcelona Convention. As such, it has been integrated into the legal and policy framework of the Barcelona Convention including legally and non-legally binding instruments.

With a view to ensuring a coordinated implementation of the ecosystem approach in the Mediterranean context, a multilevel governance mechanism has been established, comprising the Ecosystem Approach Coordination Group, composed of parties representatives, and three specific correspondence groups, namely:

3 UNEP(DEPI)/MED IG.20/8, Decision IG.20/4, Implementing MAP ecosystem approach roadmap: Mediterranean Ecological and Operational Objectives, Indicators and Timetable for implementing the ecosystem approach roadmap.

4 UNEP(DEPI)/MED IG.21/9, Decision IG.21/3 on the Ecosystems Approach including adopting definitions of Good Environmental Status (GES) and targets.

5 UNEP(DEPI)/MED IG.22/28, Decision IG.22/7, Integrated Monitoring and Assessment Programme of the Mediterranean Sea and Coast and Related Assessment Criteria.

6 UNEP/MED IG.24/22, Decision IG.24/4, Assessment Studies.

7 UNEP(DEPI)/MED IG.23/23, Decision IG.23/6, 2017 Mediterranean Quality Status Report.

on GES and targets (COR GEST); on monitoring (COR MON); and on economic and social analysis (COR ESA). The three groups are composed of experts designated by the parties to the Barcelona Convention, invited experts, and respective MAP components.

The Ecosystem Approach Roadmap is also implemented through activities included in the biennial UNEP/MAP Programmes of Work. Additionally, undertakings funded by the European Union are expected to boost the implementation of the IMAP towards the delivery of the 2023 MED QSR, including the following projects:

- Towards achieving the Good Environmental Status of the Mediterranean Sea and coast through an ecologically representative and efficiently managed and monitored network of Marine Protected Areas (IMAP-MPA) 2019–2023;
- Support to Efficient Implementation of the Ecosystem Approach-based Integrated Monitoring and Assessment of the Mediterranean Sea and Coasts and to delivery of data-based 2023 Quality Status Report in synergy with the EU MSFD (EcAp MED III) 2020–2023; and
- The Marine Litter MED II Project 2020–2023.

10.4. Ecosystem Approach as Integrated Operational Approach at the Sub-regional Level

Of particular relevance to the scope of this book is the so-called GEF (Global Environment Facility) Adriatic Project (2017–2020) concerning the *Implementation of the Ecosystem Approach in the Adriatic Sea through Marine Spatial Planning*. In fact, the ecosystem approach takes into account global principles and translates them to the regional level.

The GEF Adriatic Project has been implemented by the UNEP-MAP Coordinating Unit with the Priority Actions Programme Regional Activity Centre (PAP/RAC) and the Specially Protected Areas Regional Activity Centre (SPA/RAC) in Albania and Montenegro. National coordinators have been the Ministry of Tourism and Environment with the National Agency for Protected Areas of Albania and the Ministry of Sustainable Development of Montenegro. The project built on the successful implementation of the integrated coastal zone management strategies, with the objective to restore the ecological balance of the Adriatic Sea through the implementation of the ecosystem approach and the improvement of the management capacity in the two beneficiary States through maritime spatial planning as a viable marine management tool.

On 28 June 2021, in Herceg Novi (Montenegro), the Ministry of Ecology, Spatial Planning, and Urbanism of Montenegro hosted the final conference of the GEF Adriatic Project. In this country, a national process of maritime spatial planning had been initiated with the project's support. It was recognized that the project had fostered collaboration by bringing a wide range of actors (government, academia, business, and civil society) together to address the impact of socioeconomic activities – including those related to the blue economy – on natural systems. Moreover, the GEF Adriatic project has contributed to the development of a new marine research center in Albania.[8]

More generally, it can be said that the implementation of the ecosystem approach principles at the sub-regional level also reflects the aims of the Joint Slovenian–Croatian–Italian–Montenegrin Commission for the Protection of the Waters of the Adriatic Sea and Coastal Waters against Pollution, based on the Yugoslav-Italian Agreement on the Protection of the Waters of the Adriatic Sea and Coastal Waters against Pollution of 1974. Already in 2011, at their 12th ordinary meeting (Portorož, Slovenia), the four member States decided that experts of the sub-commissions intensify their work towards a proposal of coordinating activities in implementing the ecosystem approach, the integrated coastal zone management, and the MSFD in the Adriatic Sea. The sub-commissions were also renamed accordingly, and their work had to consider the interlinkages among the three objectives. It was also considered that the sub-commission on ballast water management and contingency plans should be focusing on the upcoming entry into force of the International Convention for the Control and Management of Ships' Ballast Water and Sediments (2004; entered into force in 2017)[9]; obtain the final draft proposal of the PSSA for the Adriatic and prepare it for its submission; identify and prioritize the issues related to the implementation of the sub-regional contingency plan; and consider proposals for Special Areas under MARPOL, Annex VI, and other air-pollution-related IMO instruments.[10] The conclusions of the 2011 meeting became the starting point for the preparation of the vision that the EUSAIR is seeking to achieve.

Specifically, the EUSAIR seeks to bring together environment and sustainable development in the Adriatic and Ionian region through the identification of blue and green corridors (Figure 10.1). The ecological connectivity ensured by the corridor approach is key to ensure a general GES.

In addition, the EUSAIR has been seeking synergies between all its pillars and has been using data from all participating countries to avoid possible conflicts. The same methodology is still in use. This approach has resulted in a high consensus level in the strategy's governance, with the creation of four priority projects under the environmental pillar. The projects deal with transboundary integrated coastal zone planning and maritime spatial planning in the Adriatic and Ionic region. The EUSAIR recognizes the complexities of the region and takes them into account in its planning, together with the relevant policy developments such as the European Union Green Deal. There are also projects in progress that already integrate green infrastructure on land and river basin management with coastal and marine concerns.

With the approach described, the EUSAIR is servicing the needs of the users of the international river basins in the western Balkans and using good practices

8 On the GEF Adriatic Project, see available at www.adriatic.eco.

9 From 8 September 2017, ships must manage their ballast water so that aquatic organisms and pathogens are removed or rendered harmless before the ballast water is released into a new location. This will help preventing the spread of invasive species as well as potentially harmful pathogens.

10 Minutes of 12th meeting of the Commission for the Protection of the Waters of the Adriatic Sea and Coastal Waters against Pollution (Portorož, Slovenia, 27–28 October 2011).

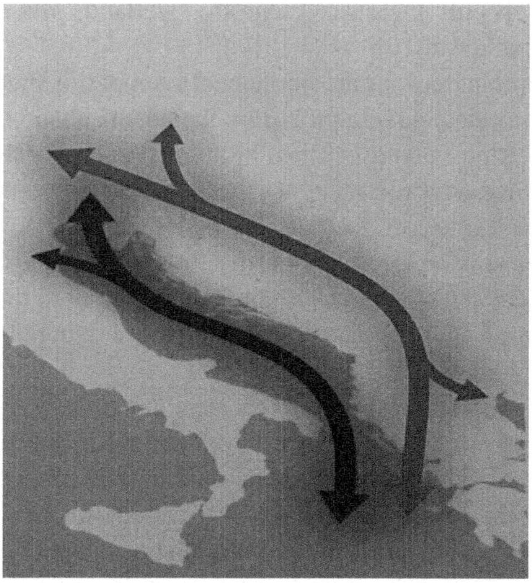

Figure 10.1 Water and land ecological corridors in the Adriatic and Ionian region

Source: Map presented at the 1st Forum of the EUSAIR, Dubrovnik, 2016

in the Adriatic and Ionian region. The approach also reveals the synergies between the macro-regional strategies (Alpine, Danube, Adriatic, and Ionian), where products are delivered through transboundary projects that involve the local communities. This provides a bottom-up approach, which benefits the users of coastal and marine resources, using solutions that respect green infrastructure and connectivity. The wish was expressed by the Slovenian presidency of EUSAIR (2020–2021) to accelerate this approach and declare new MPAs.[11]

10.5. Ecosystem Approach in the Integrated Coastal Zone Management

The scope and objectives of the Coastal Zone Protocol being already illustrated,[12] in this context it is, nevertheless, worth recalling that Art. 6 (c) of such instrument requires the parties that the ecosystem approach to coastal planning and management be applied so as to ensure the sustainable development of coastal zones. The same provision lists the ecosystem approach among the general principles of integrated coastal zone management. According to Art. 8 of the same instrument, the parties, *inter alia*, shall endeavour to ensure the sustainable use and management of coastal zones in order to preserve the coastal natural habitats, landscapes, natural resources, and ecosystems in compliance with international and regional legal instruments. Among the specific coastal ecosystems that the parties are required

11 European Union Environment Partnership Programme for Accession (EPPA) Regional Workshop on Green Infrastructure and Ecological Connectivity (24–25 June 2020, live video conference).

12 See Chapter 3 of this book.

to protect through specific measures there are "wetlands and estuaries", "marine habitats", and "dunes" (Art. 10).

Notably, an important tool for the implementation of the integrated coastal zone management is appropriate governance allowing adequate and timely participation in a transparent decision-making process by local populations and stakeholders in civil society concerned with coastal zones. Also, the parties shall take all necessary means to ensure public access to the information derived from monitoring and observation mechanisms and networks (Art. 16, para. 4). This supports the view that multi-stakeholder settings are an essential component in the roadmap towards the implementation of the ecosystem approach and integrated coastal zone management at both regional and sub-regional level.

The PAP/RAC is actively working to promote integrated coastal zone management within the system of the Barcelona Convention. In particular, it is working to closely integrate it with maritime spatial planning. The two policies are seen as one of the key tools for the implementation of the ecosystem approach. Under these circumstances, the Coastal Zone Protocol established a legal basis for considering specific sea-land interactions, which are crucial to link cross-sectoral activities, objectives, and synergies.

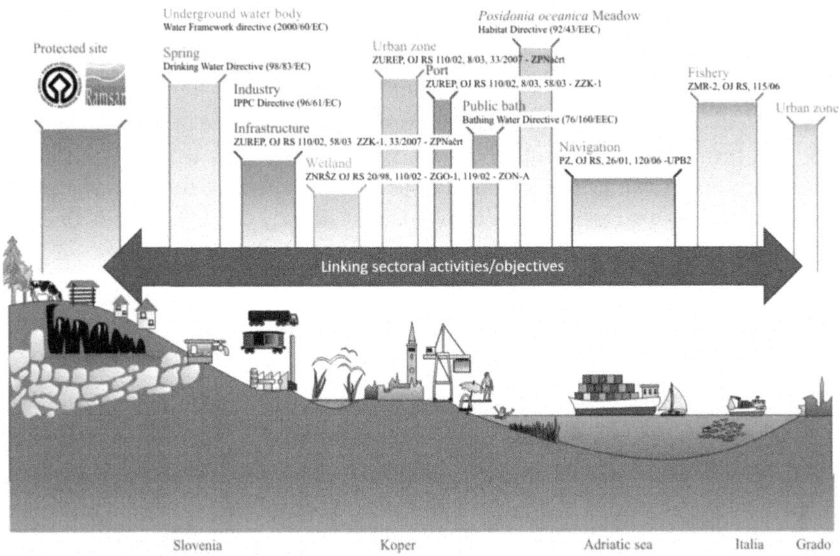

Figure 10.2 Land-sea interactions

Source: Bricelj (ed.), Handbook for Recognizing and Planning Green Infrastructure, Ljubljana, 2021[13]

13 See also Bricelj, Ecosystem Approach for Sustainable Use of Coastal and Marine Resources, in Sancin (ed.), *International Environmental Law: Contemporary Concerns and Challenges*, Ljubljana, 2012. The volume collects the papers presented at the First Contemporary Challenges of International Environmental Law Conference in Ljubljana.

In this context, an initiative funded by UNEP-MAP, namely the Coastal Area Management Program (CAMP), is oriented at the implementation of practical coastal management projects in selected Mediterranean coastal areas, applying the integrated coastal zone management as a major tool. The objectives of CAMP projects are: to facilitate at the local level the implementation of the Coastal Zone Protocol in a particular country; to develop strategies and procedures for a sustainable development in project areas; to identify and apply the relevant methodologies and tools; to contribute to the capacity-building of local, national, and regional levels; and to secure a wider use in the region of the results achieved. CAMP projects have been bringing together national and local authorities and institutions in selected coastal areas to manage coastal and marine zones in a more systematic and integrated way. The PAP/RAC assisted all countries in the Adriatic basin in preparing national CAMPs.

In order to enhance the implementation of the ecosystem approach at the transboundary level, the third pillar of the EUSAIR developed flagship projects for transnational sustainable development of the coastal and marine areas; contingency plans for accidents; measures for the protection and enhancement of natural habitats and terrestrial ecosystems; and monitoring and management of marine protected species.

The main idea of proposed projects are interventions designed to conserve, improve, and restore nature; natural functions; and processes to secure multiple ecosystem services for human society in line with the European Union technical information on Green Infrastructure.[14]

10.6. Maritime Spatial Planning and Green (and Blue) Infrastructure

Equally important, the effective implementation of an integrated coastal zone management is based on maritime spatial planning[15] as a cross-cutting policy tool enabling public authorities and stakeholders to apply a coordinated, integrated, and transboundary approach.

Maritime spatial planning supports the application of the ecosystem approach to the management of human activities. There is no doubt that healthy marine ecosystems and their multiple services, if integrated in planning decisions, can deliver substantial benefits in terms of food production, recreation, and tourism; climate change mitigation and adaptation; shoreline dynamics control; and disaster prevention. Here comes the so-called green infrastructure, which is a strategically planned network of natural and semi-natural areas with other environmental features designed and managed to deliver a wide range of ecosystem services. As regards the marine and coastal environment, such a network can improve environmental conditions and, therefore, citizens' health and quality of life, support green economy, create job opportunities, and enhance biodiversity. The NATURA 2000

14 Bricelj (ed.), *op. cit.*, Ljubljana Ljubljana, 2021.

15 Directive 2014/89/EU of the European Parliament and of the Council of 23 July 2014 establishing a framework for maritime spatial planning.

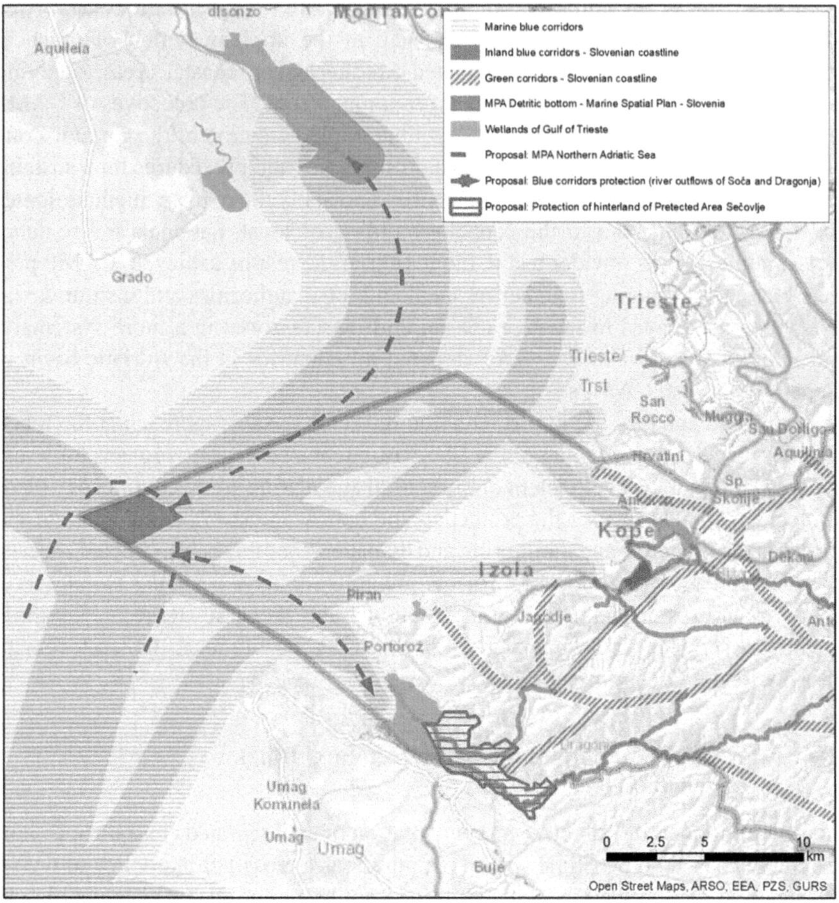

Figure 10.3 Envisaged blue and green corridors in the Gulf of Trieste.

Source: Bricelj (ed.), Handbook for Recognizing and Planning Green Infrastructure, Ljubljana, 2021.

Network, including through its coastal and marine sites, constitutes the backbone of the European Union green infrastructure.

The European Commission has developed two guidance documents to help planners, policymakers, and businesses solve socioeconomic challenges while also protecting and restoring nature.[16] Noteworthy is the fact that Slovenia has developed its maritime spatial planning in 2021[17] (Figure 10.3).

16 European Commission, Commission Staff Working Document, *Guidance on a Strategic Framework for Further Supporting the Deployment of EU-Level Green and Blue Infrastructure*, SWD (2019) 193 final, Brussels, 2019; European Commission, Commission Staff Working Document, *EU Guidance on Integrating Ecosystems and their Services into Decision-Making*, SWD (2019) 305 final, Brussels, 2019.

17 Decree on the Maritime Spatial Planning of the Republic of Slovenia, published in *Uradni List* No. 116/2021.

The ecological connectivity provided by green (and blue) infrastructure contributes to easing species' adaptation to climate change, allowing them to extend their habitat range and accommodate their migration needs through ecological corridors. Green and blue infrastructure also enhances carbon sequestration properties of environmental features in both rural and urban environments, thus mitigating the effects of climate change. These results can be further strengthened through the integration of MPAs and OECMs into maritime spatial planning within the macro-region.

10.7. Conclusive Summary

The Adriatic and Ionian macro-region is a practical example where cooperation for a healthy and reproductive ecosystem can be envisaged through the further development of multi-stakeholder cooperation. Instruments for such a cooperation encompass global conventions such as the UNCLOS (which states, in its preamble, that "the problems of ocean space are closely interrelated and need to be considered as a whole"); the CBD; and the United Nations Framework Convention on Climate Change (New York, 1992), as well as regional legal and policy instruments, including but not limited to European Union environmental legislation, the Barcelona Convention, and the EUSAIR process. Specifically, though complex in its structure, the intention of the EUSAIR is rather simple. It is about establishing synergies for an integrated coastal and marine spatial planning with a view to preserving the so-called ecosystem services of the macro-region. In other words, it is about enhancing water, food, and climate security in the Adriatic and Ionian basin for the generations to come.

Some key principles lying behind the concept of ecosystem approach include ecosystem's maintenance (i.e., the conservation of the ecosystem's structure and functioning); an implementing strategy that takes into account appropriate spatial and temporal scales; and an appropriate balance between the objectives of conservation and sustainable use of biological diversity. In this regard, there is a need for a shift to more flexible situations, where conservation and use are not considered theoretically but seen in the relevant context and where the relevant measures are applied in a contextualized and coherent manner. Importantly, implementing strategies should focus on the functional relationships and processes within ecosystems; management actions should be carried out at the scale appropriate for the issue being addressed, with decentralization to the lowest level; and intersectoral cooperation should be ensured. Maritime spatial planning supports the application of the ecosystem approach to the management of human activities.

Of extremely importance is the so-called green infrastructure, which is a strategically planned network of natural and semi-natural areas with other environmental features designed and managed to deliver a wide range of ecosystem services. The ecological connectivity provided by green (and blue) infrastructure contributes to easing species' adaptation to climate change, allowing them to extend their habitat range and accommodate their migration needs through ecological corridors. Green and blue infrastructure also enhances carbon sequestration properties of environmental features in both rural and urban environments, thus mitigating the effects of climate change. These results can be further strengthened through the integration of MPAs and OECMs into maritime spatial planning within the macro-region. There is no doubt that healthy marine ecosystems and their multiple services, if integrated in planning decisions, can deliver substantial benefits in terms of food production, recreation, and tourism; climate change mitigation and adaptation; shoreline dynamics control; and disaster prevention.

11 A Perspective From the EUSAIR Facility Point

Maritime Spatial Planning as a Cross-pillar Element of the Strategy

Iztok Škerlič

11.1. The EUSAIR Action Plan and Its Contribution to the Implementation of the Coastal Zone Protocol

The EUSAIR is described in two documents, namely: a Communication from the European Commission to the other European Union institutions and its addendum[1] and an accompanying Action Plan that complements the Communication.[2] The Action Plan can be actually considered as one of the outputs of the strategy's approach. Its declared aim is to go from "words to actions" by identifying concrete priorities for the Adriatic and Ionian macro-region. Once an action or project is selected, it should be implemented by all the countries and stakeholders concerned.

The EUSAIR Action Plan is organized in four pillars, representing four main identified areas of cooperation (so-called thematic pillars), namely: Blue Growth, Connecting the Region, Environmental Quality, and Sustainable Tourism.[3] All

1 European Commission, *Communication from the Commission to the European Parliament, the Council, the European Economic and Social Committee and the Committee of the Regions concerning the European Union Strategy for the Adriatic and Ionian Region*, COM (2014) 357 final; *Addendum to the Communication from the Commission to the European Parliament, the Council, the European Economic and Social Committee and the Committee of the Regions concerning the European Union Strategy for the Adriatic and Ionian Region,* COM (2020) 132 final, Brussels, 2 April 2020.

2 European Commission, Commission Staff Working Document, *Action Plan, Accompanying the Document: Communication from the Commission to the European Parliament, the Council, the European Economic and Social Committee and the Committee of the Regions concerning the European Union Strategy for the Adriatic and Ionian Region*, SWD (2020) 57 final, Brussels, 2 April 2020.

3 Each thematic pillar is further composed by Thematic Steering Group (TSGs) representatives from the relevant ministries of all the EUSAIR countries responsible for providing technical expertise and input. The multilevel governance is primarily reflected within the EUSAIR Governing Board (political decision-making body), which is above the thematic pillars and composed by the national coordinators of the macro-regional strategies. They are usually representatives of the ministries of foreign affairs or other high-level government representatives. In practice, however, there seems to be a slight separation between pillar coordinators and national TSGs representatives within the EUSAIR States. Pillar coordinators, therefore, appear to be fulfilling a critical and intermediate level role *vis-à-vis* the national-level TSGs and the national coordinators – a role that takes them out of the technical function attributed to the TSGs and puts them into one that is also advisory as well as strategy- and policy-oriented.

DOI: 10.4324/9781003367963-11

pillars are coordinated by two representatives, one from a European Union member State and the other from a candidate State.

Maritime spatial planning is mainly discussed within the Blue Growth and Environmental Quality pillars. It has been defined as "a practical way to organize the use of the ocean space, and the interactions among human uses (e.g., fisheries, aquaculture, shipping, tourism, renewable energy production, marine mining) and between uses and the marine environment".[4] From the said definition, it can be implied that the maritime spatial planning process in the EUSAIR is a cross-pillar topic *par excellence*.

Maritime spatial planning is primarily included within the Blue Growth pillar under the rather general topic "Maritime and marine governance and services". Reference is made there to the importance of mutual trust among EUSAIR neighboring countries, with the aim to enable them to respond jointly to the challenges related to the governance of maritime space. Reference should be, nonetheless, made to the fact that the EUSAIR builds in that regard on the experience of some already existing regional and sub-regional organizations, for example, the AII, the Trilateral (Quadrilateral) Commission, and the GFCM.[5] A notable difference between the EUSAIR and the mentioned organizations is represented by the fact that, while the AII and the GFCM were established on the basis of international law through the adoption of multilateral legal instruments, the EUSAIR is based on the *acquis* of the European Union. The argument may be accordingly put forward that European Union member States, being already members to the same organization, as well as those candidate countries waiting to access the European Union, should be even more committed – or would in fact be more committed – to cooperate within the EUSAIR, based on the *acquis*, compared to other internationally based collaborations and initiatives.

A first Action identified in the Blue Growth pillar relates to "Governance of maritime space". Joint governance is a precondition for the sustainable and transparent use of resources in a common marine space. For instance, often a joint agreement on the use of maritime space is a prerequisite for private investments and the development of sustainable blue economy in a particular area. Accordingly, attention should be paid to the implementation of the MSP Directive[6] and to the Coastal Zone Protocol to the Barcelona Convention, as emphasized also in other chapters of this book.

A second important Action refers to the "Institutional capacity to harmonize standards and regulations": in a wide range of sectors (e.g., fishery policy, maritime spatial planning, integrated coastal management), the development of common understandings and harmonized standards and regulations, as well as sharing of

4 Santos et al., Marine Spatial Planning, in Sheppard (ed.), *World Seas: An Environmental Evaluation, vol. III: Ecological Issues and Environmental Impacts*, London, 2019.

5 The mandates and functioning of these organizations and bodies are discussed in Chapter 3 of this book.

6 Directive 2014/89/EU of the European Parliament and of the Council of 23 July 2014 establishing a framework for maritime spatial planning.

best practices, is needed. This requires institutional capacity of the involved public bodies and stakeholders.

A third Action of the Blue Growth pillar concerns "Data and knowledge sharing" and has the aim to improve the evidence base for policy and decision-making in the macro-region. It is beyond doubt that both capacity-building and data-sharing can increase the efficiency and improve the quality of public services in the region, giving additional added value to transboundary cooperation. Such cooperation is needed also in those sectors that require skills and increasingly specialized professional profiles and expertise to work in the marine and maritime sectors. In this regard, the Blue Growth pillar aims at improving the levels of skills in the macro-region, including by strengthening the networks of academics and training organizations involved in the marine and maritime sectors.

The fourth and last Action described in the topic dedicated to the maritime and marine governance and services in the Blue Growth pillar of the EUSAIR Action Plan is "Citizens and business awareness and involvement". The aim here is to include citizens and businesses in the blue economy as well as in the development of blue technologies, fisheries, and aquaculture. Actors, in this regard, include not only local authorities and the civil society but also private operators and the media.

Also the Environmental Quality pillar of the EUSAIR pays attention to maritime spatial planning although from a different (environmental) perspective. In fact, one of the four Actions listed in the mentioned pillar[7] is titled "Implementing maritime spatial planning and integrated coastal zone management". The aim of the Action is ensuring coordination of different projects and initiatives with the frameworks provided by the MSP Directive and the Priority Action Plan of UNEP/MAP. The latter plays an important role in supporting the integrated coastal zone management of the Mediterranean countries and in implementing the Coastal Zone Protocol. The actors involved in this Action include national and regional authorities, research institutions, representatives of private sector, and non-governmental organizations.

In this context, the constant interaction between international law and European Union legislation is to be noted. UNEP-MAP is an antecedent to the MSP Directive, as it was established in 1975, and the two frameworks should work together in a constructive manner. In fact, within the Environmental Quality pillar, marine spatial planning is interlinked with integrated coastal zone management as an essential tool for preserving coastal and marine biodiversity. This is a necessity deriving from the fact that the increased human use of the marine and coastal space, in particular in the areas of fishing, maritime transport, tourism, and construction, has intensified pressures on coastal and marine ecosystems. An ecosystem-based approach to the coordination of activities is accordingly viewed as the best approach within the framework of both UNEP-MAP and the MSP Directive in order to ensure a sustainable use of marine resources. Both an integrated coastal zone management

7 The other three Actions being "Increasing marine knowledge", "Enhancing the network of marine protected areas", and "Enhancing best practices among managing authorities of marine protected areas".

and marine spatial planning are, therefore, important for transboundary collaboration and stakeholder cooperation across different coastal and maritime sector activities and have potential for bringing together ecosystem services and Blue Growth opportunities in a sustainable way. They are key tools for achieving a decision-making that balances sector-based interests competing for marine and coastal spaces.

From this description of the two EUSAIR pillars, it could be ascertained that several actions within the Blue Growth pillar have an interaction with the environment and, consequently, are important also from the standpoint of the Environmental Quality pillar of the EUSAIR. Especially the fisheries and aquaculture sectors can give a strong contribution to preserving marine biodiversity through mutual cooperation, data collection, scientific studies and analysis, policy planning, monitoring, control, and capacity building. In addition, the exchange of best practices among the two pillars is very important for the smooth implementation of marine spatial planning across the EUSAIR area. Both pillars pay attention to transboundary actions and joint governance – constructive initiatives that should be strongly supported by the European Commission as well as by European Union member and non-member States.

In addition to hosting critical natural habitats, Mediterranean coastal zones – particularly those bordering the Adriatic Sea – underpin crucial blue economy activities. As biologically active interfaces, where complex land-sea interactions are at play, the coasts are hotspots of climate change vulnerability. Accordingly, coastal communities need to grapple with a wide array of climate-related risks: from sea-level rise and havoc-wreaking extreme weather events to the salinization of river deltas and aquifers. In this context, the PAP/RAC of UNEP-MAP is promoting coastal plans to strengthen adaptive capacity. This is achieved by enabling robust territorial planning based on the principles of sustainable development, and by preserving the health of coastal ecosystems – thus making them more resilient to climate change. Moreover, coastal plans serve as tools for territory-based multi-stakeholder cooperation, with the aim to reduce the pressure exerted on ecosystems. This is, in turn, primarily done by identifying locally viable pathways in order to use natural resources sustainably. In doing so, developed coastal plans include the principles outlined in the Coastal Zone Protocol.

Noteworthy is also the fact that the Council conclusions of 26 May 2021[8] call on a systemic view that integrates ocean policy into Europe's new economic policy. In this regard, it has been argued that our ocean and the blue economy it supports are indispensable for achieving the transformation set out in the European Union Green Deal. Prominent examples are the contributions of oceans to energy production, the greening of transport, and sustainable food production. The contribution of a healthy ocean is, in fact, essential for a sustainable economy. The need lies in better connecting the green and the blue policies while extending the approach beyond the European Union's borders and leading the way on international ocean governance.

8 *Council Conclusions on a Sustainable Blue Economy: Health, Knowledge, Prosperity, Social Equity*, 26 May 2021. The conclusions are available in the Annex to doc. 9153/21, Outcome of proceedings.

In the mentioned Council conclusions, the need to shift the focus from the blue growth to a sustainable blue economy is being further reinforced. This fact is seen as an important point for the process of the revision of the EUSAIR Action Plan, foreseen for 2023. The conservation and sustainable use of marine biological diversity are not only commanded by international instruments, such as the CBD and the upcoming international legally binding instrument under the UNCLOS for what concerns marine areas beyond national jurisdiction, but they are seen as fundamental principles of marine and maritime economic activities also in processes such as the EUSAIR. Marine biodiversity in this context does not only represent the prerequisite for economic activities such as fisheries, biotechnologies development, and tourism. Biodiversity conservation and restoration represent *as such* an economic interest. As highlighted in the European Union's 2030 Biodiversity Strategy, expanding protection to 30 per cent of the European Union sea area and creating ecological corridors will reverse biodiversity loss, contribute to climate mitigation and resilience, and, at the same time, generate significant financial and social benefits. Investments in MPAs, in particular strictly protected areas, have shown to generate significant economic returns, in addition to multiplying the amount of fish and marine life where protection is effective.

With regard to blue and green corridors, the Izola Declaration of 11 May 2021 – *Along the Shores of the Shared Sea* – recognized green connectivity as a key objective of the Slovenian Presidency of the EUSAIR.[9] This is due to the fact that such connectivity has contributed to improving the quality of life across the Adriatic and Ionian region, and, accordingly, should become a transversal component of all pillars with the aim to contribute to Europe's green recovery and green future. In that context, the Izola Declaration recognized the EUSAIR's contribution to a sustainable blue economy in the European Union through the establishment of blue corridors.[10]

11.2. Interactions Between the Blue Economy and Environmental Quality in the EUSAIR

Noteworthy is that the interaction between the pillars of Blue Growth and Environmental Quality has been addressed by a common inter-pillar project aimed at using high quality research to strengthen dialogue and institutional capacities for effective implementation of maritime spatial planning and integrated coastal zone management in support of inclusive and sustainable growth and nature conservation in the EUSAIR.[11] The project aims to improve the ongoing process of implementation of marine spatial planning in the sea basin, including overcoming barriers for the full participation of all neighboring countries and, furthermore, to promote

9 See available at www.adriatic-ionian.eu/wp-content/uploads/2021/05/Izola-Declaration-11-May-2021.pdf.

10 Škerlič et al., *EUSAIR: Slovene Presidency 20–21: Final Report*, Izola, 2021.

11 See also Communication from the Commission to the European Parliament, the Council, the European Economic and Social Committee and the Committee of the Regions on a new approach for a sustainable blue economy in the EU Transforming the EU's Blue Economy for a Sustainable Future, COM (2021) 240 final, Brussels, 17 May 2021.

sound technically and scientifically based political decisions. The project will foster the implementation of national strategies for integrated coastal management and cross-border maritime spatial plans, and, thus, improve sea basin governance. The results of the project will also enhance administrative and institutional capacities in the area of maritime governance and services and will have a strong impact on the preservation of marine biodiversity. It has been, in fact, widely accepted that coherent planning and scientific knowledge are indispensable to support the development of strategic plans for regulation, zoning, and management and the protection of the marine environment. Noteworthy is also the fact that, with the last development of the project following the common workshop during the seventh edition of "Mediterranean Coast and Macro-Regional Strategies Week" in Izola, in September 2022, the project was expanded in order to include the topic of coastal climate change adaptation. Project outcomes are expected to improve management of fisheries and aquaculture and, hence, contribute to a more sustainable use of the natural resources linked with the sustainable growth of these sectors.

Based on the achieved results of the past European Union projects in the Adriatic-Ionian area – which includes MESMA,[12] SHAPe,[13] ADRIPLAN,[14] SUPREME,[15] MUSES,[16] PORTODIMARE,[17] CAMP,[18] ADRIAMED,[19] ECOAST[20] – and the developed tools within the past projects, the current project aims at updating existing gaps in marine and coastal knowledge; identifying conflicts and potential synergies; applying integrated coastal zone management and maritime spatial planning on different levels, including geographical and administrative; defining needs for the sustainable growth of fisheries and aquaculture; developing tools for proper site management and environmental monitoring to improve nature protection; guaranteeing coastal defense; valorizing economic activities; and planning, establishing, and properly managing (transboundary) MPAs.

The project will also take into account the national processes of implementation of the MSP Directive, which will represent a fundamental tool for capacity-building in the public sector and for a better coordination in planning activities.

12 Monitoring and Evaluation of Spatially Managed Areas (implementation period: January 2009 – January 2013).

13 Shaping an Holistic Approach to Protect the Adriatic Environment between coast and sea (implementation period: January 2011 – January 2014).

14 ADRiatic Ionian Maritime Spatial PLANning (implementation period: January 2013 – January 2015).

15 Supporting Maritime Spatial Planning in the Eastern Mediterranean (implementation period: January 2017 – December 2018).

16 Multi-Use in European Seas (implementation period: November 2016 – October 2018).

17 GeoPORtal of Tools & Data for sustainable Management of coAstal and maRine Environment (implementation period: February 2018 – January 2020).

18 Coastal Area Management Programme (CAMP Slovenia). The Final Integrated Report (2007) is available at www.rrc-kp.si/wp-content/uploads/2011/06/Camp-Final-Integrated-Report.pdf.

19 Scientific Cooperation to Support Responsible Fisheries in the Adriatic Sea. See available at www.faoadriamed.org/.

20 New methodologies for an ecosystem approach to spatial and temporal management of fisheries and aquaculture in coastal areas (implementation period: March 2016 – December 2018).

The project will, thus, focus on the development of training activities and networks. Activities specifically related to the development and application of multi-level governance mechanisms with the aim to support national and transboundary MSP in the Adriatic and Ionian Sea through a stakeholder-driven capacity-building process will include:

1. design and development, by capitalizing on PORTODIMARE results, of a decision support tool (DST) towards participatory and interactive knowledge-sharing and dialogue among sectorial, cross-sectorial, and transnational actors;
2. promotion of sectorial, cross-sectorial, and transnational dialogues to build capacity among relevant sectors of business and sector administrations or departments, to understand opportunities, challenges, barriers, and potentialities of integrated coastal management and maritime spatial planning as policy and governance instruments, with special reference to planning frameworks provided in each European Union member and non-member State involved in the project;
3. practical understanding and application of concrete case studies of the DST supporting multi-level governance and multi-level dialogue developed, aiming at the development of Action Plans focused on multi-scalar planning needs, land-sea interaction, and sectorial challenges, in order to contribute to Europe's green recovery and green future. In that context, the EUSAIR's contribution to the European Union's Sustainable Blue Economy through the establishment of blue corridors has been recognized;
4. identification of a permanent network of institutional bodies to harmonize standards and regulations for marine and maritime activities, improving the quality of public services and improving integrated governance mechanisms at a national scale, and also for international cooperation in a wide range of sectors and activities (e.g., fishery, aquaculture, maritime spatial planning, integrated coastal management, environmental impact assessment, strategic environmental assessments); and
5. analysis of specific schemes and mechanisms for transboundary planning and governance on transboundary maritime spatial planning priorities, including in the field of (transboundary) MPAs and OECMs.

11.3. The Facility Point Project as a Support Tool of the EUSAIR (Maritime) Governance Process

The Facility Point project has been funded by the Interreg ADRION V-B 2014–2020 and represents an important tool for supporting the strategy's implementation. Its budget exceeds 11.5 million euros, and the overall objective is to facilitate the coordination and implementation of the EUSAIR by enhancing the institutional capacity of public administrations and key stakeholders, as well as by assisting the progress in the implementation of joint priorities.

The project is divided into six work packages (WP). The first relates to "Management" (WP M). It is dedicated to the overall management of the project and to supporting the organization of the meetings of the governing structures of the EUSAIR and their partner organizations and bodies. WP M is coordinated by the Governmental Office for Development and European Cohesion Policy of the Republic of Slovenia, which is also the lead partner of the entire Facility Point project.

The second WP covers the necessary "Assistance to the EUSAIR Governing Board and Thematic Steering Groups (TSGs)" (WP T.1), with the aim to provide the members of the Governing Board and TSGs with administrative and operational support in their coordination and implementation of the EUSAIR Action Plan and its objectives.

The third WP is centered around "Facilitating strategic project development and financial dialogue" (WP T.2). It is coordinated by the Municipality of Izola (Slovenia). Its aim is to support the TSG members with the development of project ideas into viable strategic project proposals. This includes the pooling of funds and the coordination of the financial dialogue meetings between the EUSAIR key implementers, managing authorities of European Union structural funds, and financial institutions. During the implementation of the activities of this WP, the standardization manual for the identification of the strategic or flagship project was adopted, and the manual for the organization of the financial dialogues in each country was introduced.[21]

The main challenge and coordination tool to be established in the near future should be the Network of the EUSAIR Management Authorities. Within the framework of the European Union Strategy for the Baltic Sea Region (EUSBSR), a pilot Managing Authorities Network was set up in 2016, funded by the European Regional Development Fund (ERDF). Its main function is to explore opportunities for transnational collaboration (for ERDF-funded projects) via the Common Provisions Regulation.[22] The aim is to facilitate support from regional, country-specific, and multi-country operational programs with regard to the implementation of the EUSBSR.[23] At the same time, the coordinator acts as a contact point for project stakeholders and is responsible for internal and joint-external communication of project activities. It is ascertained that stronger collaboration through dialogues and networking offer wider opportunities for exchanging experiences, understanding the unique needs and challenges of specific projects, sharing of common practices, and identifying how to make policies and programs more effective. As such, it contributes to building cross-sector dialogue and coordination by connecting ministries and institutions and through the softening of strongly sector-driven approaches. Nonetheless, in order to be effective, this type of dialogue needs support from the

21 Internal documents of the Facility Point of the EUSAIR Project Partnership that will be published when formally approved by the partnership.

22 Regulation (EU) 2021/1060 of the European Parliament and of the Council of 24 June 2021 laying down common provisions on the European Regional Development Fund, the European Social Fund Plus, the Cohesion Fund, the Just Transition Fund and the European Maritime, Fisheries and Aquaculture Fund and financial rules for those and for the Asylum, Migration and Integration Fund, the Internal Security Fund and the Instrument for Financial Support for Border Management and Visa Policy.

23 See available at www.balticsea-region-strategy.eu/.

relevant European-level institutions (including those that work on transnational cooperation) as well as from national bodies.[24]

Apart from the activities included within the discussed WP, in conjunction with the recognized need for the setting up of a Network of Managing Authorities, reference should be made to the examples of successful European Union projects in the countries across the EUSAIR. First steps are also made with regard to the European Territorial Cooperation programs, where the plan is for EUSAIR States to jointly implement four flagship projects in cross-border areas. An outstanding example in that regard is represented by the North Adriatic Maritime Incident Response System (NAMIRS) project, which should lead towards the adoption of a holistic approach to marine pollution incident management within the North Adriatic Sea and on shore.

The NAMIRS project has been fully developed by the EUSAIR's Environmental Quality pillar and by the EUSAIR Facility Point project Partner Municipality of Izola. The project is planned to last two years, from March 2022 to February 2024, and is cofinanced by the European Commission in the framework of the European Union Civil Protection Mechanism (DG ECHO). For the first time in the history of the EUSAIR, additional funds have been obtained for the implementation of the macro-regional strategic project at the EUSAIR level, and the project can be also implemented by other Adriatic and Ionian countries. The NAMIRS project has been recognized as an outstanding achievement by the TSG3 within the framework of the embedding and financial dialogue process.

The fourth WP is titled "Building capacities for monitoring and evaluation of EUSAIR" (WP T.3). Its purpose is to provide analyses, expertise, and research studies to the EUSAIR key implementers in order to assist them with the establishment of a territorial knowledge base and with the development of a framework for monitoring and evaluation. In this regard, a very important part of the capacity-building activities has been already implemented, primarily for public administrations, but also for other stakeholders with the aim to monitor, evaluate, and revise the EUSAIR Strategy and its Action Plan.

The mentioned WP has been, in turn, coordinated by the Greek Ministry of Development and Investments, Special Service for Strategy, Planning and Evaluation. The importance of capacity-building activities has been recognized also within the mentioned Izola Declaration. The latter called upon the EUSAIR Facility Point

> to further support the smooth implementation of EUSAIR, capacity-building activities, engagement of the stakeholders, with a special emphasis on young people, communication and dialogues in order to enable further steps towards the establishment of a network of Managing Authorities.[25]

24 See OECD, *EUSAIR Synthesis Report: Multi-Level Governance and Cross-Sector Practices Supporting the European Union Strategy for the Adriatic and Ionian Region*, 2019.

25 Škerlič et al., *op. cit.*, available at www.adriatic-ionian.eu.

The fifth WP relates to "Developing and managing the EUSAIR Stakeholder platform" (WP T.4). It has been coordinated by region Marche (Italy). Through the platform, the stakeholders, project beneficiaries, and interested public have the opportunity to interact and cooperate with the EUSAIR key implementers on issues concerning the macro-region. The platform has been actively facilitating the dialogue and embedding process, particularly with regard to the European Territorial Cooperation program.

The sixth and last WP in the Facility Point project relates to "Communication" (WP C). Its purpose is to strengthen the visibility of the EUSAIR within the macro-region through a series of communication- and awareness-raising activities. The coordinator of this activity has been, again, the Government Office for Development and European Cohesion Policy of the Republic of Slovenia. This WP is recognized as crucial to the strategy. In fact, EUSAIR had little visibility within governments – particularly among experts and those working with regional development and cohesion policies at the national and subnational levels – as well as among non-government stakeholders. The European Parliament stressed the importance of transparency in adopting, monitoring, and evaluating the strategy as well as of openness and inclusiveness towards the civil society and all relevant stakeholders.[26] At the same time, it emphasized the essential role of communication and awareness-raising across all pillars for the participation of stakeholders in the decision-making process and for building public support. European Union member States should, therefore, ensure an adequate visibility of the EUSAIR goals at the national, regional, and local levels.

The project is currently entering (2023) in the last eight months of its duration; therefore, it could be foreseen whether all the targets set at the beginning of 2016 have been eventually reached. In particular, the expected achievements after the conclusion of the project are:

1. a stable operational and administrative support to the structures of the EUSAIR, in particular with regard to the Governing Board and pillars;
2. an increased knowledge base for public administration and other stakeholders about the macro-region in general, and in particular with regard to the EUSAIR, including its challenges and opportunities;
3. an increased commitment and cooperation within the macro-region; and
4. an increased awareness on the EUSAIR and recognition of its added value.

At this time, it seems already possible to affirm that all the said goals have been achieved. In fact, for the very first time in the turbulent history of the Adriatic and Ionian region, the Facility Point project has succeeded in leading the countries surrounding the Adriatic and Ionian Seas to reach agreement on a common way to go with the help of the flagship projects. As already mentioned, the flagships are

26 European Parliament, Directorate-General for Internal Policies, *New Role of Macro-regions in European Territorial Cooperation, Study: Part I*, Brussels, 2015.

specific for each pillar and were adopted at the 12th extraordinary EUSAIR Governing Board meeting in June 2020.[27]

11.4. Conclusive Summary

The EUSAIR Action Plan is one of the two fundamental documents defining the EUSAIR. The strategy is centered around four pillars, addressing four main identified topics, namely: Blue Growth, Connecting the Region, Environmental Quality, and Sustainable Tourism. Maritime spatial planning is dealt with within the first and the third pillar: as a matter of fact, the maritime spatial planning process in the EUSAIR is a cross-pillar topic *par excellence*. From the provided description of the two relevant EUSAIR pillars, it could be seen that several actions in the Blue Growth pillar have an interaction with the environment and, consequently, become of utmost importance also to the Environmental Quality pillar. In particular, the fisheries and aquaculture sectors can give a strong contribution to preserving marine biodiversity through mutual cooperation, data collection, scientific studies and analysis, policy planning, monitoring, control, and capacity building. In addition, the exchange of best practices among the two pillars is fundamental for the smooth implementation of the maritime spatial planning process in the EUSAIR. Both pillars pay specific attention to transboundary actions and joint governance and, accordingly, should be strongly supported by the European Commission, as well as by European Union member and non-member States.

In this context, the conservation and sustainable use of biodiversity are considered as foundational principles of the maritime economic activities in the EUSAIR. They are not just prerequisites for economic activities such as fisheries, biotechnologies, and tourism but also represent on their own important economic opportunities.

A crucial role in the implementation and visibility of the EUSAIR has been played by the Facility Point project, funded by the Interreg ADRION V-B 2014–2020 as a tool to support the strategy's actual operation. The overall objective of the project is to facilitate the coordination and implementation of the EUSAIR by enhancing the institutional capacity of public administrations and key stakeholders and by assisting the progress of implementation of joint priorities. The Facility Point project importantly contributed to the current situation, whereby for the very first time in their turbulent history, the countries surrounding the Adriatic and Ionian Seas have eventually reached agreement on a common way to go in the form of defining joint flagship projects for a shared marine macro-region.

27 The updated list of flagships is available at www.adriatic-ionian.eu.

12 Conclusive Remarks on an Adriatic and Ionian Seas Response to Global Challenges in the Field of Environmental Protection

Towards Coordinated Networks of Marine Protected Areas?

Mitja Grbec, Tullio Scovazzi and Ilaria Tani

12.1. Challenges and Existing Opportunities

In this conclusive chapter, a review of the current situation of environmental cooperation for the protection of the Mediterranean Sea, with a particular focus on the Adriatic and Ionian waters, is presented with a view to identifying possibilities of further developments in the area covered by the EUSAIR.

An important consideration with regard to the juridical status of the Adriatic and Ionian Seas is that once all coastal States will proclaim an exclusive economic zone – namely, Albania, Greece, Italy, and Montenegro, in addition to Croatia that has already proclaimed such a zone in 2021 – the high seas will disappear from the Adriatic and Ionian Seas. Currently, there are still substantial areas beyond the limits of national jurisdiction in the Adriatic and Ionian Seas, whereby the high seas regime is applicable. However, such areas are potential exclusive economic zones, awaiting either implementation or delimitation. It is likely that such a transitional situation will change in the future.

The present trend towards the establishment of exclusive economic zones could become an incentive towards the adoption of a coherent and coordinated Adriatic and Ionian network of marine protected areas and other effective area-based conservation measures. The UNCLOS and other treaties applicable at the world or regional level promote the establishment of marine protected areas and other effective area-based conservation measures in any kind of marine spaces, irrespective of their legal condition. There is a need to comply with the UNCLOS and customary international law and to take into account that the regime applicable in coastal areas and, in particular, the rights that are granted to coastal States vary in accordance with the legal condition of the waters where the marine protected area is established (marine internal waters, territorial sea, exclusive economic zone, continental shelf). The extension of jurisdiction by a European Union member State (e.g., Croatia) automatically entails the extension of the European Union legal order and policies on that part of the sea (in the Croatian case, on its newly proclaimed

DOI: 10.4324/9781003367963-12

exclusive economic zone). Such an order includes the EU-IMP, having the MSFD as its environmental pillar, the Birds and Habitats Directive with its NATURA 2000 Network of protected areas, and maritime spatial planning as one of the most important cross-sectoral policies. The MSFD clearly identifies the Adriatic Sea as a separate management sub-region (eco-region) within the wider Mediterranean region, while the Ionian Sea forms a separate sub-region, together with the Central Mediterranean.

Both the Adriatic and Ionian Seas qualify as juridical "enclosed or semi-enclosed seas" based on the provisions of Part IX UNCLOS. Coastal states are accordingly under a good faith obligation to establish among themselves closer means of cooperation than those applying in other seas. All States bordering the Adriatic and Ionian Seas are State parties to the UNCLOS.

With regard to the interrelation between the global, European Union, regional, sub-regional, and national legal frameworks, no significant substantive conflicts may be noticed between the provisions of the main treaties applicable in the field of marine protected areas, since all these instruments are inspired by similar general principles and protection objectives, and the regional or sub-regional treaties provide for a more specific and enhanced protection compared to that achieved through global treaties (criterion of the added value). Marine protected areas are implicitly referred to in Art. 194, para. 5, UNCLOS, which includes, among the measures for the protection and preservation of the marine environment, those necessary to protect and preserve rare or fragile ecosystems as well as the habitat of depleted, threatened, or endangered species and other forms of marine life. The establishment of marine protected areas is also envisaged, as a special measure to conserve biological diversity, by the CBD. Sectoral treaties provide for the establishment of other effective area-based conservation measures as a means to achieve their objective: this is the case of the International Convention for the Regulation of Whaling, as regards sanctuary areas; the MARPOL, as regards special areas; or the Convention for the Protection of Underwater Cultural Heritage, as regards the preservation *in situ* of this heritage.

Also regional agreements call for the creation of marine protected areas or the adoption of effective area-based conservation measures, in particular the Areas Protocol, as regards the SPAMIs; the Bern Convention, as regards the Emerald Network; the ACCOBAMS, as regards areas for cetacean conservation; and the Agreement establishing the GFCM, as regards FRAs.

For the Adriatic and Ionian Seas, four main existing forums for sub-regional cooperation have been established, namely: additional sub-regional cooperation within the institutional framework of the Barcelona Convention and its protocols; cooperation within the Quadrilateral Commission, based on the 1974 Belgrade Agreement between Italy and the former Yugoslavia; cooperation within the framework of the AII; and cooperation within the framework of the EUSAIR.

The Trilateral Commission – which is also referred to as Quadrilateral Commission after the accession of Montenegro in 2010 – may be regarded nowadays as one of the most important institutional frameworks for the cooperation of Adriatic States. Its potential, however, has still to be fully exploited, *inter alia,* through enhanced coordination and coordination with other regional (Mediterranean) and sub-regional (Adriatic and Ionian) cooperative frameworks, particularly the AII and the EUSAIR. Despite being two separate cooperative arrangements, the AII and the EUSAIR are today complementary, as they share the same priorities with intertwined governance structure and are both involved in the implementation of the EUSAIR. The argument may be put forward that regional cooperation, particularly that of relevance for the whole Adriatic and Ionian region and falling under one of the four priority EUSAIR pillars, should be nowadays better undertaken within the auspices of EUSAIR, although in close cooperation and coordination with the AII and the Quadrilateral Commission. The reactivation of the latter and its enlargement to all Adriatic and Ionian coastal States is accordingly highly advisable.

With regard to the global basis for the establishment of transboundary marine protected areas (international agreements and policy framework), all the main policy instruments approved at the international level in the last three decades, such as Agenda 21 (1992), the Plan of Implementation of the World Summit on Sustainable Development (2002), *The Future We Want* (2012), the 2030 Agenda for Sustainable Development (2015), and the recent United Nations General Assembly Annual Resolutions on Oceans and the Law of the Sea call for action towards the establishment of marine protected areas and the adoption of other effective area-based conservation measures. This action can be considered as a corollary of the customary international law obligation to protect the marine environment and as applicable to any kind of marine waters, irrespective of their legal condition (marine internal waters, territorial sea, exclusive economic zone, continental shelf, high seas, seabed beyond national jurisdiction). Rules of international law of the sea on the legal regime of different marine spaces and the activities that are carried out therein must be taken into consideration in the process for the establishment of marine protected areas and the implementation of the measures provided therein. However, it would be a mistake to think that the freedom of the high seas – as long as it will exist in the Mediterranean – is an insurmountable obstacle against the adoption of environmental measures, including the establishment of marine protected areas. Even if treaties do not apply to third parties, non-party States are bound to abide by general provisions of international law and not to undermine the reasonable measures for the protection of the environment and the sustainable development of marine resources that have been agreed upon by other States.

The general trend to protect the marine environment by establishing marine protected areas or adopting area-based conservation measures is confirmed by the practice developed within the CBD, where EBSAs have been identified and the objective to protect at least 30 per cent of sea areas has been put forward, as well as within the IMO, where PSSAs have been identified and navigation therein has been subjected to restrictions (for example, in the Mediterranean, the Strait of Bonifacio). The Annex to Decision XII/22, adopted by the Conference of the Parties to the CBD held in 2014, provides the results of seven regional workshops on the description of areas meeting the scientific criteria for EBSAs. The workshop for the Mediterranean, held in Malaga in 2014, described fifteen EBSAs, including three located in the Adriatic and Ionian Seas (Northern Adriatic, Jabuka/Pomo Pit, and South Adriatic Ionian Strait). The EBSAs criteria can provide to the interested States useful information on where marine protected areas could be established according to scientific evidence. They do not enter into the political and legal questions that are linked to creation of marine protected areas. The new concept of other effective area-based conservation measures (OECM) has been elaborated to identify measures that, while being adopted for other purposes (fishing, shipping, underwater archaeology, security, etc.), indirectly contribute to the achievement of conservation objectives.

With regard to European Union law and policies in the field of transboundary marine protected areas, the European Union Integrated Maritime Policy seeks to provide a more coherent approach to maritime issues, with increased coordination between different policy areas. As such, it attempts to coordinate complex and interdependent policies related to maritime affairs as well as to allocate ecological economic resources in a holistic and integrated manner. An important role is played by integrated coastal zone management and maritime spatial planning. Their role is to efficiently plan cross-sectoral and cross-border management of coastal zones and, furthermore, to overview and coordinate possible uses of maritime and coastal resources.

The overriding goal of the MSFD, as the environmental pillar of the European Union maritime policy, is the integration of environmental considerations into all relevant policy areas. According to the MSFD, the establishment of marine protected areas, including NATURA 2000 sites designed or to be designed based on the provisions of the Birds and Habitats Directive, is an important contribution and tool for the achievement of good environmental status. Measures in this regard shall include spatial protection measures, contributing to coherent and representative networks of marine protected areas, adequately covering the diversity of the constituent ecosystems, such as SACs pursuant to the Habitats Directive, SPAs pursuant to the Birds Directive, and marine protected areas, as agreed by the European Union or by the member States concerned in the framework of international or regional agreements to which they are parties (e.g., the Barcelona Convention). However, the geographical scope of the MSFD as well as, generally speaking, that of the European Union *acquis*, is limited to waters over which member States exercise sovereignty or jurisdiction rights in accordance with the UNCLOS and not on the high seas.

Furthermore, with the aim of having a truly coherent and resilient trans-European nature network, it is of paramount importance to set up ecological corridors in order to prevent ecological isolation, allow for species migration, and maintain and enhance healthy ecosystems. This objective should be achieved through the maintenance and the setting up of new green corridors between NATURA 2000 sites and other protected areas, either on land (green corridors) or on the sea (blue corridors), and through their interconnection.

All the EUSAIR member States are parties also to the Convention on the Conservation of European Wildlife and Natural Habitats (Bern Convention). This gives a possibility also to non-member States in the Adriatic and Ionian region (i.e.,

Albania, Montenegro, North Macedonia, Serbia) to establish protected areas that are equivalent to those established by European Union member States within the NATURA 2000 Network (Emerald network) as well as, in this regard, to coordinate their policies and undertake joint (transboundary) projects of cooperation with the European Union and its member States, including within the framework of the EUSAIR macro-region.

In the Mediterranean regional context – including the Adriatic and Ionian Seas – three protocols to the Barcelona Convention are of particular relevance for the establishment of marine protected areas, which may also be given a transboundary character. The Areas Protocol is the most appropriate tool to protect highly migratory marine species, including by the creation of "blue corridors". The instrument does not prejudice any question concerning maritime delimitations. It regulates the establishment of SPAs or SPAMIs – the latter being included in a List that ensures them an *erga omnes partes* effect. So far, 39 SPAMIs have been listed, 6 of which are located in the Adriatic and Ionian Seas, namely: *Miramare Marine Protected Area* (Italy), *Plemmirio Marine Protected Area* (Italy); *Torre Guaceto Marine Protected Area and Natural Reserve* (Italy); *Porto Cesareo Marine Protected Area* (Italy); *Karaburun Sazan National Marine Park* (Albania); and *Landscape Park Strunjan* (Slovenia). No area in the central portion of the region of concern has yet been included under the special protection regime of the SPAMI List. Three proposals identify potential SPAMIs in the Northeastern Ionian, which would encompass the Jabuka/Pomo Pit; in Santa Maria di Leuca, which would encompass waters falling only under Italian jurisdiction; and in the Northern and Central Adriatic.

The Offshore Protocol envisages "precautions" in particular for SPAs that have been identified under the Areas Protocol or established by a party. Improving participation in the Offshore Protocol by the States in the region of concern is critical, especially when considering that seabed activities are intensively carried out on the Adriatic continental shelf.

The Coastal Zone Protocol provides Mediterranean States with a legal and technical tool to ensure sustainable development throughout the shores of this regional sea. This instrument opens up to the opportunity of building transboundary integrated coastal management based on spatial planning.

Other effective area-based conservation measures, in the form of FRAs, are in place within the framework of the GFCM and aim at protecting vulnerable species and ecosystems of deep-sea habitats. In the context of the Barcelona System, noteworthy is that the MAP Programme of work for the biennium 2020–2021 included the recourse to the tool of coastal and marine protected areas among its "strategic objectives".

Existing national frameworks for the establishment of marine protected areas within areas of national sovereignty and jurisdiction include the Protected Areas Act No. 81 of 2017 of Albania; the Nature Protection Act of 2013 of the Federation of Bosnia and Herzegovina; the Nature Protection Act of 2013 of Croatia; the 2018 Law for the Management Agencies of Protected Areas of Greece; the Framework Law on Protected Areas No. 394 of 1991 and Law No. 972 of 1982, with subsequent amendments, of Italy; the Nature Protection Act of 2016 of Montenegro; and the Nature Conservation Act of 1999, as amended several times, of Slovenia. It may be noted that most coastal States of the Adriatic and Ionian Seas have enacted recent legislation concerning the establishment, management, and monitoring of protected areas, which in all cases explicitly refers also to marine protected areas. Other States, such as Italy and Slovenia, have preferred to progressively update previous legislation.

As regards the effectiveness of national instruments, some indicators may be identified that could be used as helpful references against which to measure both the drafting and implementation of relevant legislations, namely: the achievement under the relevant legislation of a coordinated implementation of international and regional commitments; an efficient institutional coordination; the adoption of specific legal provisions for the establishment and management of marine protected areas, as they imply differences from terrestrial protected areas; the adoption of effective protection measures; the implementation of management planning and zoning; the integration of marine protected areas into coastal and marine spatial planning policies; the involvement of all relevant stakeholders; the provision of adequate financing mechanisms; and effective schemes and measures for monitoring, compliance, and enforcement. In addition, national legislation should provide for an appropriate registering mechanism and public access to the relevant data, given that the first challenge faced in the effort of assessing the number and the status of national marine protected areas is the lack of an accurate inventory, which is coupled with the lack of compilation of new potential sites with the highest biodiversity value. Steps are being taken in this regard under the auspices of the SPA/RAC, with a view to elaborating criteria for inclusion of specially protected areas in a Mediterranean directory.

Examples of transboundary marine protected areas beyond the territorial waters of Mediterranean coastal States include the *Pelagos Sanctuary*, which is one of the two SPAMIs including also waters beyond the limit of the territorial sea (the other one being the *Cetacean Migration Corridor off the coasts of Spain*). The *Pelagos Sanctuary* was established under an Agreement signed in Rome in 1999 by France, Italy, and Monaco, representing the first treaty ever concluded with the specific objective of establishing a protected area for marine mammals. The Sanctuary has been included in the SPAMI List and, accordingly, also enjoys the protection regime provided for under the Areas Protocol.

Another example of transboundary cooperation concerns the Strait of Bonifacio, which is an international strait regulated by the regime of transit passage under Arts. 37 to 44 UNCLOS. It is located between Corsica and Sardinia (two Mediterranean islands belonging to France and Italy, respectively). As the strait represents one of the most outstanding areas in the Mediterranean Sea in terms of marine biodiversity, France and Italy have decided to adopt a restrictive approach to navigation therein, insofar as ships flying their respective flags are concerned. To this purpose, they necessarily acted through the IMO. In 2011, the strait was also designated as a PSSA – the first established in the Mediterranean Sea and the second in the world for an international strait. Noteworthy is the initiative of two French and Italian public local entities with competencies in the field of marine environment protection, which in 2013 registered with the Committee of the Regions of the EGTC Convention the establishment of the *International Marine Park of the Strait of Bonifacio*. Other effective area-based conservation measures of transboundary character include FRAs established within the framework of the GFCM, three of which lie in the Adriatic and Ionian Seas, namely: the *Lophelia Reef off Capo Santa Maria di Leuca*, the *Jabuka/Pomo Pit*, and *Bari Canyon*.

Among the main goals emphasized by both global and regional – Mediterranean and European Union – legal and policy documents are the effective management of all protected areas, the definition of clear conservation objectives and measures, and an appropriate monitoring. This is even more important in a transboundary context. In the European Union and the EUSAIR context, an interesting tool in this regard may be represented by the EGTC, which is an entity with legal personality under European Union law (EGTC Regulation 1082/2006, as amended in 2013). It aims at improving the implementation conditions for territorial cooperation with a view to strengthening cohesion in the European Union. In doing so, it complements funding instruments for European Territorial Cooperation (ETC), known as Interreg. Each EGTC is governed by a convention concluded by its members. These may be European Union member States, regional and local authorities of European Union member States, public undertakings and public bodies under certain conditions, also belonging to States that are not members of the European Union. What is necessary is that the EGTC is made up of members that are located on the territory of at least two European Union member States. In addition, the EGTC may include one or more States that are neighboring at least one European Union member State that is a member of the same EGTC. A State that is not a member of the European Union is considered as a "neighboring State" under the EGTC Regulation when:

> it shares a common land border or where both the third State and the EU Member State are eligible under a joint maritime cross-border programme under the European territorial cooperation goal, or are eligible under another cross-border, sea-crossing or sea-basin cooperation programme, including where they are separated by international waters.
>
> (Art. 3a, para. 1)

Accordingly, Albania, Bosnia and Herzegovina, and Montenegro – or public bodies of these States – could become members of an EGTC in the Adriatic and Ionian Seas. The possibility to resort to the EGTC instrument with a view to protecting the marine environment in a transboundary context, as a possible form of territorial cooperation, has been already affirmed through the establishment of the EGTC for the *International Marine Park of the Strait of Bonifacio*, in the Tyrrhenian Sea.

The designation of a PSSA or more PSSAs within the Adriatic and Ionian Seas may potentially represent a powerful aid in a quest for protection of a specific sensitive area from international shipping. Noteworthy is the fact that the PSSA designation process allows the IMO to undertake a comprehensive assessment of the shipping threats to the proposed PSSA area with the aim to devise the most appropriate protective measures to address the threat. However, as the additional associated protective measures and the PSSA itself need to be confirmed by the relevant IMO bodies, the process of a PSSA designation is not only an environmental and technical process but also a political exercise. The main opportunity provided by the PSSA concept is the possibility to introduce for a particular area additional associated protective measures, although limited to those having their legal base in an adopted IMO instrument. The latter may be or may not be in force. The practical and legal result of a designed PSSA is that the included associated protective measure are granted a validity *erga omnes partes*, even if a certain IMO instrument has not entered into force. An additional benefit of designing a PSSA is represented by the fact that associated protective measures may differ within, and may be tailored for, a specific (smaller) part of a broader PSSA.

Even in the case that the designated PSSA in the Adriatic Sea mirrors only already existing measures, it would include routeing measures (both compulsory and proposed), compulsory reporting (ADRIREP), and Special Area status under relevant Annexes to MARPOL. Reference should be made to the fact that the sole designation of a PSSA may represent an extremely important cooperative framework for participating member States and their governmental (maritime) authorities. The main advantage in this regard seems to be the internationally raised awareness about the area's vulnerability to damage by international shipping, which in turn may and should increase community and mariners' awareness of the sensitivity of, and risk to navigation within, the area. A preferred option should accordingly be the strengthening and upgrading of the already existing associated protective measures through the designation of a PSSA, coupled with eventual proposals for new associated protective measures. Such new associated protective measures could be applicable to the entire Adriatic Sea, to only to part of it, or even to an area adjacent to the Adriatic PSSA in the nearby Ionian Sea.

12.2. Objectives and Ways Forward

As all the EUSAIR countries are either European Union member States or aspire to join the European Union in a (not too distant) future, the key European Union commitments in the field of nature protection provided by the Biodiversity Strategy for 2030 seem to be particularly relevant. The latter may be summarized as follows:

1. legally protect a minimum of 30 per cent of the European Union's land and 30 per cent of the European Union's sea area and integrate ecological corridors, as part of the true trans-European nature network;
2. strictly protect at least a third of the European Union's protected areas, including all remaining European Union primary and old growth forest; and
3. effectively manage all protected areas, defining clear conservation objectives and measures, and monitoring them appropriately.[1]

1 See *EU Biodiversity Strategy for 2030*, COM (2020) 380 final, Brussels, 20 May 2020.

These commitments are fully in line, *mutatis mutandis*, with the Kunming-Montreal 2030 Global Targets, adopted in 2021 by the Conference of the Parties to the CBD,[2] and the Post-2020 Regional Strategy for marine and coastal protected areas and other effective area-based conservation measures in the Mediterranean, adopted in 2021 by the Meeting of the Parties to the Barcelona Convention.[3]

Based on the provisions of the Biodiversity Strategy for 2030, European Union member States are responsible for designating the additional protected and strictly protected areas, either by expanding or completing the NATURA 2000 Network or under national protection schemes (marine protected areas), including eventual (transboundary) marine protected areas established in accordance with the provisions of regional seas conventions (i.e., the Barcelona Convention). Fisheries management will need to be implemented in all marine protected areas, according to clearly defined conservation objectives and on the basis of the best available scientific advice. In 2022, the European Commission issued a staff working document on criteria and guidance for protected area designations.[4] The criteria and guidance have a non-binding character and aim to help Member States fulfil the protected areas targets of the 2030 Biodiversity Strategy.

The European Commission pointed out, in this regard, that full implementation and enforcement of European Union environmental legislation is at the heart of the 2030 Biodiversity Strategy. As regards the Birds and Habitats Directives, implementation and enforcement will focus on completing the NATURA 2000 Network, effectively managing all sites, and protecting species and habitats that show declining trends. Furthermore, the application of an ecosystem-based management approach under European Union legislation will reduce the adverse impact of fishing, extraction, and other human activities, especially on sensitive species and seabed habitats. To support this, national maritime plans, which member States had to deliver by 2021,[5] should aim at covering all sectors and activities, including other effective area-based conservation measures.

The targets put forward by the 2030 Biodiversity Strategy may be achieved by European Union member States – and specifically the EUSAIR coastal States – through the application of one or more of the following strategies, which, far from being mutually exclusive, can be seen in a cumulative way.

1. *Expanding and completing the NATURA 2000 – Emerald Network or through the establishment of marine protected areas under national protection schemes.*

2 See Chapter 2 of this book.

3 See Chapter 3 of this book.

4 See European Commission, Staff Working Document, *Criteria and Guidance for Protected Area Designations*, SWD (2022) 23 final, Brussels, 28 January 2022.

5 See Report from the Commission to the European Parliament and the Council outlining the progress made in implementing Directive 2014/89/EU establishing a framework for maritime spatial planning, COM (2022) 185 final, Brussels, 3 May 2022. The Decree on Maritime Spatial Planning of Slovenia, adopted in 2021, published in *Uradni List* No. 116/2021), could be seen as a good example of progress in this regard.

The NATURA 2000 Network could be, for example, expanded not only in the Northern and Central Adriatic, but also in the Southern Adriatic (Channel of Otranto area) as well as within the Ionian Sea. The EUSAIR coastal States that are not members of the European Union (Albania, Bosnia and Herzegovina, Montenegro) may contribute to this goal through the enlargement of the Emerald network, by establishing additional marine protected areas or through the designation of new marine protected areas under their national legislation.

In this regard, also some transboundary marine protected areas may be envisaged. Taking into account that the Croatian waters surrounding the Bosnian waters in the Klek/Neum Bay have been already protected as NATURA 2000 sites, the plans within Bosnia and Herzegovina to protect the waters in the Klek/Neum Bay, in close cooperation and coordination with neighbouring Croatia, seem to be of particular importance. Bosnia and Herzegovina can achieve the said goal either on the basis of its national legislation or, alternatively, on the basis of the Bern Convention, contributing in such a way to the enlargement of the Emerald network of (marine) protected areas. The NATURA 2000–Emerald Network of marine protected areas could be strengthened also in the Southern Adriatic, particularly in the Channel of Otranto area and surrounding Ionian Sea, through prompt action and coordination by Albania, Greece, and Italy.

2. *Establishing marine protected areas, including transboundary, in accordance with the provisions of the Barcelona Convention and its Protocols.* Reference should be made in this regard to the possibility of establishing two transboundary SPAMIs or one bigger SPAMI in the Northern and Central Adriatic (including the Jabuka/Pomo Pit area) based upon a joint proposal by Croatia, Italy, and Slovenia.[6] It would be intended to address the following specific challenges:

- to build upon the existing or proposed instruments of restricted or sectoral protection, coordinating them within a larger and coherent framework of transboundary cooperation and sustainable development;
- to include marine protected areas with the framework of a broader marine spatial planning concept applying to the whole Adriatic Sea and potentially extending to the Ionian Sea;
- to integrate and balance in a sound manner economic activities (especially navigation and fishing) and environmental needs; and
- to increase confidence among the Adriatic Sea bordering States, showing that pending issues of maritime boundaries are not an insurmountable obstacle against the strengthening of their environmental cooperation through the establishment of transboundary protected areas.

6 For the scientific basis of such a proposal, see Chapter 7 of this book.

A transboundary SPAMI would not be legally feasible for the time being in the Ionian Sea and the Strait of Otranto area, as Greece is not yet a party to the Areas Protocol, nor in the Klek/Neum Bay area, due to the fact that Bosnia and Herzegovina is not a State party to the said Protocol. The ratification of the Areas Protocol by Greece and Bosnia and Herzegovina should be accordingly encouraged.

3. *Establishing other effective area-based conservation measures applicable to parts of Adriatic and Ionian Seas.*[7] Other effective area-based conservation measures have already been established in the Adriatic (*Jabuka/Pomo Pit, Bari Canyon*) and Ionian Sea (*Lophelia Reef off Santa Maria di Leuca*) in the form of FRAs within the framework of the GFCM and are likely to be increased in the near future (roadmap to establish an FRA in the Southern Adriatic Sea).

Resort to other forms of other effective area-based conservation measures should also be considered by the States concerned. For instance, Art. 11 of Regulation (EU) 1380/2013 on the Common Fisheries Policy allows for the adoption of conservation measures necessary for compliance with obligations under Union environmental legislation and, consequently, for the establishment of protected areas of biological sensitivity, including FRAs, also under the auspices of the European Union Common Fisheries Policy.

Additionally, several proposals for marine protected areas for cetaceans have been identified within the framework of the ACCOBAMS, four of which would be located in the Adriatic and Ionian Seas.[8] However, the parties still have to achieve the objective of creating and maintaining a network of marine protected areas for cetaceans, which should coincide with those sites recognized as CCHs.

The possibility of establishing protected areas, based on the relevant provisions of the Convention on the Protection of Underwater Cultural heritage, around submarine cultural properties could be considered, as it has been done by Italy in the Tyrrhenian Sea. The same approach could be used also in other areas located within the heritage-rich Adriatic and Ionian Seas, which are important for the *in situ* preservation of underwater cultural heritage.[9]

4. *Establishing a PSSA applicable to the entire Adriatic Sea, including the whole Otranto Channel area.* An important tool which may help in the achievement of the goals put forward by the 2030 Biodiversity Strategy and other global policy instrument is represented by the designation of the entire Adriatic Sea, including the wider Otranto Channel area, as a PSSA. Noteworthy is the fact that a PSSA can be used as a supplementary measure within an already established marine

7 The European Commission envisaged that, should Member States rely on OECMs with regard the achievement of the said targets, tailored conservation objectives and measures would be necessary also for OECM's. See European Commission, Staff Working Document, *Criteria and Guidance op. cit.*, pp. 12–13.

8 See Chapter 3 of this book.

9 See Chapter 2 of this book.

protected area or other effective area-based conservation measure (e.g., FRA). Alternatively, it can be proposed as a separate sectoral measure in relation to threats posed by international shipping, in parallel with the process of establishment of a (transboundary) marine protected area, including a SPAMI. The example of the Strait of Bonifacio, where all previously mentioned instruments – national marine protected areas both on the French and Italian side, NATURA 2000 sites, international marine park comanaged by an EGTC, a SPAMI, and a PSSA – coexist over roughly the same area, is a clear example in this regard.

One of the most important challenges in the process of designing a PSSA is represented by the endorsement, preparation, and joint submission of a PSSA proposal to the IMO by all affected States. The chances of success of a proposal are far greater if all States bordering an enclosed or semi-enclosed sea (i.e., all coastal States bordering the Adriatic and Ionian Seas) are united and submit a joint proposal with regard to the designation of a certain area (e.g., the Adriatic Sea) as a PSSA, together with the relevant associate protective measures. The chances of success are further enhanced if such a proposal is supported within the IMO bodies by the European Union and its member States as a united block, for example, as the case has been during the process of adoption of the *Western European Waters* PSSA in 2004. Despite the fact that the draft PSSA proposal prepared in the period 2006–2011 relating to the designation of the entire Adriatic Sea as a PSSA was not finalized and submitted to the IMO, consideration may be given either to the updating and finalization of the former proposal or to the preparation of a new PSSA proposal.

5. *Effectively managing all protected areas, defining clear conservation objectives and measures, and monitor them appropriately.* The aim of effectively managing all protected areas, defining clear conservation objectives and measures and monitoring them appropriately could be achieved in the Adriatic and Ionian Seas also with the help of an innovative legal entity, the EGTC, in accordance with the relevant European Union legislation. As an autonomous legal entity, an EGTC set up by the Adriatic and Ionian coastal States could be responsible for the management of a protected transboundary area, or network of areas, in the Adriatic and Ionian Seas and the identification of the relevant protection measures. Its legal personality based on public law, with tasks specified in the constitutive instruments, would ensure that such management authority participate through its legal and institutional representations in the most appropriate fora where marine environment protection tools are discussed and approved.

Appropriate legal frameworks already exist. The Adriatic and Ionian States have already shown a capacity to cooperate in a fruitful manner. The present challenge is to build upon existing achievements and to progress on the way of an improved system of marine environmental protection, of which marine protected areas and other effective area-based conservation measures represent a strong component. The European Union and the EUSAIR represent important actors in this direction.

12.3. Post Scriptum

In June 2023, while this book was in printing, the Agreement under the UNCLOS on the Conservation and Sustainable Use of Marine Biological Diversity of Areas beyond National Jurisdiction (BBNJ Agreement)[10] was adopted at the United Nations.[11]

The BBNJ Agreement addresses a number of subjects – such as "marine genetic resources, including the fair and equitable sharing of benefits", "area-based management tools, including marine protected areas", "environmental impact assessment", "capacity-building and transfer of marine technology" – relevant for the protection and the sustainable use of the marine environment. *Inter alia*, it provides for an international procedure for the establishment of area-based management tools (ABMTs), including marine protected areas. Proposals for establishing ABMTs, including marine protected areas, are submitted by a single State or by several States with a management plan encompassing the proposed measures, and outlining monitoring, research and review activities.[12]

The BBNJ Agreement only applies "to areas beyond national jurisdiction".[13] It follows that, if and when the BBNJ Agreement enters into force for the Mediterranean States, it will be applicable in the Mediterranean waters that are still under the high seas regime. It will not be applicable wherever such States in the meantime establish their exclusive economic zones. Moreover, the BBNJ Agreement includes a non-prejudice provision, according to which it must be "interpreted and applied in a manner that does not undermine relevant legal instruments and frameworks and relevant global, regional, subregional and sectoral bodies and that promotes coherence and coordination with those instruments, frameworks and bodies".[14] In this regard, it already exists in the Mediterranean a legal instrument – the Protocol concerning Specially Protected Areas and Biological Diversity in the Mediterranean[15] – that allows the establishment of marine protected areas in high seas waters. Also the other instruments examined in this book and aimed at the establishment of marine protected areas and other effective area-based conservation measures will fall under the non-prejudice provision.

It should be in general remarked that there are in the BBNJ Agreement notions, such as the definitions of "area-based management tool", "marine protected area", "sustainable use" and "marine genetic resources", that could be understood as a commonly agreed conceptual basis at the international level. In particular,

> 'Area-based management tool' means a tool, including a marine protected area, for a geographically defined area through which one or several sectors

10 A reference to the relevant negotiations is made in para. 2.3.A of this book.

11 See UN Doc.A/CONF.232/2023/4 of June 2023.

12 Art. 19

13 Art. 3.

14 Art. 5, para. 2.

15 Para. 3.1.A.a.

> or activities are managed with the aim of achieving particular conservation and sustainable use objectives in accordance with this Agreement.[16]
>
> 'Marine protected area' means a geographically defined marine area that is designated and managed to achieve specific long-term biological diversity conservation objectives and may allow, where appropriate, sustainable use provided it is consistent with the conservation objectives.[17]

It appears that marine protected areas are a particular component of the broader category of ABMTs. Both are geographically defined areas. The specificity of marine protected areas is that they are established for the particular purpose of achieving long-term conservation objectives, while ABMTs are established for managing one or several sectors or activities (for example, fishing or navigation) in order to achieve both conservation and sustainable use objectives. Also the notion of other effective area-based conservation measures (OECMs), which has been developed in the context of the Convention on Biological Diversity and is frequently used in this book,[18] seems to be a particular component of the broader category of ABMTs.

16 Art. 1, para. 1.
17 Art. 1, para. 9.
18 Para. 2.3.C.e.

References

Amos, Assessing the Impact of the Habitats Directive: A Case Study of Europe's Plants, in *Journal of Environmental Law*, 2021.

Bardonnet, Frontières terrestres et frontières maritimes, in *Annuaire français de droit international*, 1989.

Bickl, EEZ in the Adriatic. Challenges and Opportunities in a Semi-enclosed Sea, in *The NCLOS Blog*, 2020.

Biot, Les systèmes de gouvernance des territoires transfrontaliers: la mise en œuvre du règlement européen sur le GECT (Groupements Européens de Coopération Territoriale), in *Belgeo*, 2013.

Bricelj, *International Environmental Law: Contemporary Concerns and Challenges*, Paper Presented at the First Contemporary Challenges of International Environmental Law Conference, Ljubljana, 28–29 June 2012.

Bricelj (ed.), *Handbook for Recognizing and Planning Green Infrastructure*, Ljubljana, 2021.

Caffio, La cooperazione marittima tra i paesi adriatici, in *Rivista Marittima*, 2021.

Cataldi (ed.), *The Mediterranean and the Law of the Sea at the Dawn of the 21st Century*, Bruxelles, 2002.

Cataldi, The Italian Law Authorizing the Creation of an Exclusive Economic Zone, in *Italian Yearbook of International Law*, 2021.

Charney and Smith (eds.), *International Maritime Boundaries*, vol. IV, The Hague, 2002.

Churchill, The European Union and the Challenges of Marine Governance: From Sectoral Response to Integrated Policy? in Vidas and Schei (eds.), *The World Ocean in Globalisation: Climate Change, Sustainable Fisheries, Biodiversity, Shipping, Regional Issues*, Leiden and Boston, 2011.

Churchill and Lowe, *The Law of the Sea*, Manchester, 1999.

Cordonnery, Hemmings and Kriwoken, Nexus and Imbroglio: CCAMLR, the Madrid Protocol and Designating Antarctic Marine Protected Areas in the Southern Ocean, in *International Journal of Marine and Coastal Law*, 2015.

Day, Dudley, Hockings, Holmes, Laffoley, Stolton, Wells and Wenzel, *Guidelines for Applying Protected Areas Management Categories to Marine Protected Areas*, 2nd ed., Gland, 2019.

Drius et al., Not Just a Sandy Beach. The Multi-Service Value of Mediterranean Coastal Dunes, in *Science of the Total Environment*, 2019.

Duan, *The International Legal Regime Relating to Marine Protected Areas in Areas Beyond National Jurisdiction: Identifying and Addressing Gaps*, Leiden, 2022.

Dudley, *Guidelines for Applying Protected Areas Management Categories*, Gland, 2008.

Epstein, The Habitats Directive and Bern Convention: Synergy and Dysfunction in Public International and EU Law, in *The Georgetown International Law Review*, 2014.

Ferri, The Legal Regime Governing Mediterranean Fisheries: The General Fisheries Commission for the Mediterranean of the FAO and the Added-Value of Article XIV Bodies, in *Italian Yearbook of International Law*, 2021.

Francalanci and Scovazzi (eds.), *The Mediterranean: Selected Maps*, Genoa, 1992.

Freestone, Laffoley, Douvere and Badman, *World Heritage in the High Seas: An Idea Whose Time Has Come*, World Heritage Reports No. 44, Paris, 2016.

Genov et al., Linking Organochlorine Contaminants with Demographic Parameters in Free-ranging Common Bottlenose Dolphins from the Northern Adriatic Sea, in *Science of the Total Environment*, 2019.

Gestri, I rapporti di vicinato marittimo tra l'Italia e gli Stati nati dalla dissoluzione della Iugoslavia, in Ronzitti (ed.), *I rapporti di vicinato dell'Italia con Croazia, Serbia-Montenegro e Slovenia*, Rome, 2005.

Grbec, Extension of Coastal State Jurisdiction in the Mediterranean: Quasi EEZs or real sui-generis zones? in Martínez Gutiérrez (ed.), *Serving the Rule of International Maritime Law: Essays in Honour of Professor David Joseph Attard*, London and New York, 2010.

Grbec, *Extension of Coastal State Jurisdiction in Enclosed and Semi-Enclosed Seas. A Mediterranean and Adriatic Perspective*, London and New York, 2014.

Juste Ruiz, *Mediterranean Cooperation and Third States*, Paper Delivered at the 11th Mediterranean Research Meeting, Florence and Montecatini Terme, 24–27 March 2010.

Juste Ruiz and Bou Franch (dir.), *Derecho del mar y sostenibilidad ambiental en el Mediterráneo*, Valencia, 2014.

Kelleher, *Guidelines for Marine Protected Areas*, Gland-Cambridge, 1999.

Kim, Problems and Processes of Restricting Navigation in Particularly Sensitive Sea Areas, in *International Journal of Marine and Coastal Law*, 2021.

Leanza, *Il regime giuridico internazionale del mare Mediterraneo*, Napoli, 2008.

Le Hardy, La protection des mammifères marins en Méditerranée – L'accord créant le sanctuaire corso-liguro-provençal, in Cataldi (ed.), *The Mediterranean and the Law of the Sea at the Dawn of the 21st Century*, Bruxelles, 2002.

Mackelworth (ed.), *Marine Transboundary Conservation and Protected Areas*, Abingdon, 2016.

Mackelworth, Jančič, Lazar and Holcer, A Transboundary Marine Protected Area to Help Resolve the Piran Bay Border Dispute, in Mackelworth (ed.), *Marine Transboundary Conservation and Protected Areas*, Abingdon, 2016.

Mance, Debelić and Vilke, Integrated Maritime Policy for the European Union as the Planning Model for Croatia, in *Journal of Maritime and Transportation Sciences* (*Pomorski zbornik*), 2015.

Notarbartolo di Sciara and Agardy, Building on the Pelagos Sanctuary for Mediterranean Marine Mammals, in Mackelworth (ed.), *Marine Transboundary Conservation and Protected Areas*, Abingdon, 2016.

Oanta, Maritime Delimitations in the Mediterranean: Current Challenges, in *Italian Yearbook of International Law*, 2021.

Pavliha, New European Maritime Policy for Cleaner Ocean and Seas, in Martínez Gutiérrez (ed.), *Serving the Rule of International Maritime Law: Essays in Honour of Professor David Joseph Attard*, London and New York, 2010.

Prieur, Le protocole de Mardid à la convention de Barcelone relatif à la gestion intégrée des zones côtières de la Méditerranée, in Juste Ruiz and Bou Franch (dir.), *Derecho del mar y sostenibilidad ambiental en el Mediterráneo*, Valencia, 2014.

Raftopoulos, The Mediterranean Response to Global Challenges: Environmental Governance and the Barcelona Convention System, in Vidas and Schei (eds.), *The World Ocean in Globalisation: Climate Change, Sustainable Fisheries, Biodiversity, Shipping, Regional Issues*, Leiden and Boston, 2011.

Raftopoulos, Sustainability Governance, Public Trust and the Conventional Protection of the Mediterranean Environment, in Juste Ruiz and Bou Franch (dir.), *Derecho del mar y sostenibilidad ambiental en el Mediterráneo*, Valencia, 2014.

Rodríguez, OSPAR Regulatory Regime for Establishing Marine Protected Areas in Areas beyond National Jurisdiction of the OSPAR Maritime Area, in Juste Ruiz and BouFranch (dir.), *Derecho del mar y sostenibilidad ambiental en el Mediterráneo*, Valencia, 2014.

Schlacke, Maier and Markus, Legal Implementation of Integrated Ocean Policies: The EU's Marine Strategy Framework Directive, in *International Journal of Marine and Coastal Law*, 2011.

Scovazzi (ed.), *Marine Specially Protected Areas – The General Aspects and the Mediterranean Regional System*, The Hague, 1999.

Scovazzi, La révision de l'Accord RAMOGE, in *Annuaire de Droit Maritime et Océanique*, 2004.

Scovazzi, Maritime Delimitations in the Mediterranean Sea, in *Cursos Euromediterraneos Bancaja de Derecho Internacional*, 2004–2005.

Scovazzi, Marine Protected Areas in the Mediterranean, in Juste Ruiz and Bou Franch (dir.), *Derecho del mar y sostenibilidad ambiental en el Mediterráneo*, Valencia, 2014.

Scovazzi, Marine Protected Areas in Waters beyond National Jurisdiction, in Ribeiro (ed.), *30 Years after the Signature of the United Nations Convention on the Law of the Sea*, Coimbra, 2014.

Scovazzi, Harlequin and the Mediterranean, in Wolfrum, Seršić and Šošić (eds.), *Contemporary Developments in International Law – Essays in Honour of Budislav Vukas*, Leiden, 2016.

Scovazzi, International Cooperation as regards Protection of the Environment and Fisheries in the Mediterranean Sea, in *Anuario de Derecho Internacional*, 2018.

Scovazzi, The Agreement on the Conservation of Cetaceans of the Black Sea, the Mediterranean Sea and the Contiguous Atlantic Area, in Mekouar and Prieur (coord.), *Droit, humanité et environnement – Mélanges en l'honneur de Stéphane Doumbé-Billé*, Bruxelles, 2020.

Scovazzi, The Protection of Underwater Cultural Heritage in the Mediterranean Sea, in *Italian Yearbook of International Law*, 2021.

Scovazzi, The Italian Exclusive Economic Zone, in *Questions of International Law*, 2022.

Scovazzi and Tani, Problems Posed by Marine Protected Areas Having a Transboundary Character, in Mackelworth (ed.), *Marine Transboundary Conservation and Protected Areas*, London, 2016.

Sersic, The Adriatic Sea: Semi-enclosed Sea in a Semi-enclosed Sea, in Cataldi (ed.), *The Mediterranean and the Law of the Sea at the Dawn of the 21st Century*, Bruxelles, 2002.

Šilc et al., Sand Dune Vegetation along the Eastern Adriatic Coast, in *Phytocoenologia*, 2016.

Škrk, Exclusive Economic Zones in Enclosed or Semi-Enclosed Sea, in Vukas (ed.), *The Legal Regime of Enclosed or Semi-Enclosed Seas: The Particular Case of the Mediterranean, in Contributions to the Study of Comparative and International Law*, Zagreb, 1988.

Slim and Scovazzi, *Study of the Current Status of Ratification, Implementation and Compliance with Maritime Agreements and Conventions Applicable to the Mediterranean Sea Basin*, 2009.

Sovinc, *Analysis of Marine (Water) Protected Areas in EUSAIR and Proposals for Corrective Measures*, Final Report, EUSAIR, 2021.

Tani, Ferrero and Pizzeghello (eds.), *Atlas of Maritime Limits and Boundaries in Central Mediterranean: Legal Texts and Illustrative Maps*, Genoa, 2020.

Treves, *Potential Exclusive Economic Zones in the Mediterranean*, Paper Delivered at the 11th Mediterranean Research Meeting, Florence and Montecatini Terme, 24–27 March 2010.

Vezzani, The Conservation of Biodiversity in the Mediterranean Sea through Marine Protected Areas: The Barcelona System Faced with the Expansion of Coastal State Jurisdiction, in *Italian Yearbook of International Law*, 2021.

Vidas, Particularly Sensitive Sea Areas: The Need for Regional Cooperation in the Adriatic Sea, in Ott (ed.), *Croatian Accession to the European Union: Institutional Challenges*, Zagreb, 2006.

Vidas and Kostelac, Ballast Water and Alien Species: Regulating Global Transfers and Regional Consequences, in Vidas and Schei (eds.), *The World Ocean in Globalisation: Climate Change, Sustainable Fisheries, Biodiversity, Shipping, Regional Issues*, Leiden and Boston, 2011.

Vidas and Schei (eds.), *The World Ocean in Globalisation: Climate Change, Sustainable Fisheries, Biodiversity, Shipping, Regional Issues*, Leiden and Boston, 2011.

Index

Note: Page numbers in *italics* indicate figures.